THE
CHRISTIAN RECORD

VOLUME 1
1843-1844

EDITED BY
BY JAMES M. MATHES

Charleston, AR

2021

The pagination of this edition matches with the pagination of the original. In other words, if you were to take a quote from this edition, it would match perfectly, and come from the same pages as in the original. The only changes made in this edition are to font size, and the correction of obvious typos.

The Christian Record (Volume 1, 1843-1844) **is published in the United States of America by:**

Cobb Publishing
www.CobbPublishing.com
CobbPublishing@gmail.com
479.747.8372

ISBN: 978-1-947622-81-4

THE

CHRISTIAN RECORD,

EDITED AND PUBLISHED

BY JAMES M. MATHES.

"Neither pray I for these alone, but for them also which shall believe on me through their word; that they all may be one; as thou Father art in me and I in thee; that they also may be one in us: that the world may believe that thou hast sent me."

John xvii. 20, 21.

VOLUME I	NUMBER I.

JULY 4, 1843.

BLOOMINGTON, INDIANA.

MARCUS L. DEAL, PR.

THE CHRISTIAN RECORD.

VOL. I.   JULY, 4, 1843.   NO. I.

PREFACE.

If an apology be required of us, by our brethren for offering to the Religious community another Periodical; let the following suffice:— We have in Indiana *alone,* more than TWENTY THOUSAND brethren and sisters, who have taken the word of God *alone,* as the rule of their faith and manners; and comparatively, very few of them read any of our Periodicals; perhaps not more than *one,* in a *hundred!* We have but one paper in the State, ("The Israelite") which, although it is ably edited by our beloved and intelligent brother FIELD; is not taken by many in "Central" or "Northern," Indiana.

In the judgment of many intelligent brethren, a work, such as we propose publishing, is much needed in "Central Indiana." 1. As a medium of communication for the brethren; and 2. To meet and refute the many misrepresentations, which the prejudiced part of community, are daily circulating; to our injury: 3. And last, though not least, to bring the whole subject of Christianity, as understood and taught by us, before the people, in this part of the State, in a plain, familiar style, so that they may be able to compare what we teach, with what the Apostles taught; "prove all things, and hold fast that which is good."

For the last eight years, I have travelled and labored, in "Central Indiana," as a public teacher of Christianity: I have to the very best of my ability, met the opposition at every point, and defended what I conceived to be the truth of the Bible, against the attacks of its opposers, I have during that period, Baptized, upon a profession of their faith in Christ, more than Two THOUSAND PERSONS; and from my intimate acquaintance with the Churches and people of Indiana, and the character of the opposition with which we have to contend; *I think* that I understand their *wants*.

We shall speak candidly and freely, upon all the great matters now interesting the Christian world. We have no party interest at stake; therefore none to advocate, or defend. We shall occasionally draw the contrast between TRUTH and ERROR; in doing which, we shall speak *earnestly,* and perhaps some may think *severely,* but we shall aim at doing justice to all; and we now say that if any of our Religious neighbors, whose systems we may examine, think we treat them unfairly; they shall be permitted to speak for themselves in our columns; while their articles are *well-written, short, and of the right sort of spirit:* but the "Christian Record," never shall be the medium of PERSONAL INVECTIVE AND PRIVATE REVENGE.

We offer the hand of friendship, to the whole Corpse Editorial: we ask no indulgence of any, that we are not willing to grant, and we hope never to violate that golden rule, "Do unto all men, as you would have, them do unto you."

We solicit communications from our dear brethren, every where: short, pithy articles, on practical subjects; and the heart-cheering intelligence of the progress of the Gospel and Kingdom of Christ, will find a place in the "Record." But we shall decline publishing, long, dry speculative articles; as we think they would be of no advantage to any one.

We shall, to the very best of our ability, answer such questions, (no matter whether proposed by Our dear brethren, or our opponents) as are scriptural, and in our judgment, calculated when answered, to do good; but we shall take the advice of Paul to his son Timothy, and "Avoid untaught questions, knowing that they do gender strife."

We are disposed to promise but little, and attempt to do more: we shall therefore only promise to do the very best that we can, to make the "CHRISTIAN RECORD" interesting and useful: In short we hope to make it worthy of its title.

We shall not *seek* controversy, nor *decline* it when fairly called out.

And now reader, we ask of you a candid tend prayerful perusal; try us by the infallible standard, the word of God, if we speak according to that, receive it, and if we do not, reject it.

And now may the God of peace, who brought back again from the dead our Lord Jesus Christ, that great Shepherd of the Sheep, direct our minds and hearts into all truth! Amen.

J. M. MATHES, ED.

CHRISTIAN UNION, NO. 1.

By the phrase "Christian Union," I do not mean a union of sects," neither do I mean a union brought about by a compromise of some of the antagonist points of our speculative theology; or such a one, as children sometimes agree upon, "Let me alone, and I will let you alone:" But as the language imports, I mean a thorough Union in Christ Jesus, of all those who love God, and obey our Lord Jesus Christ in sincerity. Such a union as was enjoyed by the first Christians, "who were of one heart, and of one soul," "their hearts being knit together in love."

In the investigation of this subject, I propose to enquire 1st, Is Christian Union desirable!

I shall first answer for myself. From my very heart I desire to see all the lovers of the Lord Jesus Christ, united together in love, upon the "one foundation" of the "Apostles and prophets, Jesus Christ himself being the chief corner stone." For this, I have prayed night and day; and for this I have labored and toiled, for the last eight years: and although I have not fully realized my desire, I am not yet discouraged; and I am determined to labor on, and continue to pray for Christian union until I am called home, or the master comes! While looking over the divisions of "Protestant Christendom," and seeing so many of my beloved brethren, who worship the same God, have the same faith and Baptism, acknowledge the same Lord, and comforted by the same holy spirit; I say, to see such torn from me, by sectarian pride, jealousy, or prejudice, so that we cannot *eat,* or co-operate together in the Masters cause, fills my eyes with weeping, and my heart with mourning, and I am now disposed to take up the lamentation of the weeping prophet, "Jeremiah." Oh that my head were waters, and my eyes a fountain of tears, that I might weep day and night, for the slain of the daughter of my people: Is there no balm in Gilead? is there no physician there? then why is not the health of the daughter of my people recovered."

But I am happy to know that I am not alone in this desire for Union; and that thousands of kindred spirits throughout the whole length and breadth of the land are striving together with me in their prayers night and day, and in their labors of love, for the same glorious object. The most intelligent, pious and humble, of all denominations, are with us, on this point, and greatly desire to see the walls of separation erased by human device, thrown down; and the followers of the Lamb, flowing together in love, converse with them *individually,* and they will perhaps all agree, that the present, is an unhappy state of things, and that if all the church, or denomination to which they belong, would agree to it, they would go for a general union of all Christians upon the BIBLE ALONE.

The pious and humble of all parties, seem fully sensible, that something is wanting, "to perfect the Saints in love," and to present Christianity in all its loveliness to the world; and that, that something is *Christian Union:* and hence we seldom hear a prayer offered up, but among other petitions, we hear the following, or something like it: "Lord hasten the happy time, when the watchman upon the walls of Zion, shall all see eye to eye." "When thy people shall all flow together in love; when there shall be no more Barbarian, Sythian, Bond or Free; but when they shall all be one in Christ our living head."

Now I take it for granted, that all who offer the above petition, really desire Christian union. We shall say nothing at this time, about the propriety of praying (or union, and refusing it at the same time; this we shall notice in its proper place.

That the different denominations really desire union, is provable, not only by their own acknowledgements, as individuals, and their prayers; but also by their actions. How often is it the case, that some two or more of the most popular denominations in a Town or neighborhood in order that they may have a higher state of spiritual enjoyment, and produce a more powerful impression upon sinners; unite together for a week, or ten days, for the purpose of holding a "protracted meeting."— They agree to preach upon no controverted subjects; but such only as they can investigate without infringing upon each others *reserved rights*. They sing, pray, exhort, preach and perhaps eat, together; the Saints are comforted, sinners are alarmed, and every thing seems to move on harmoniously. To what is the success to be attributed, to their union, most unquestionably. But alas! The meeting is no sooner over, than the trumpet, is blown. "Every man to his tent, O Israel!" Now I reason thus: if union be desirable for ten days; or during a "protracted meeting," it would certainly be much more so, could it last through all time, and be consummated, in another and happier world! All Christians look to a time, which they call "Millennium," as the consummation of all earthly bliss, because in that glorious period, there will be no division: nothing to hurt nor destroy in all the holy mountain, not a jarring note among all the followers of the lamb.

Now just the reverse of this, is the state of things we see in the Religious world; and let me ask, who that loves the Lord, and desires the happiness of mankind, does not *feel* that something is wanting to give fullness of joy! and who, with this feeling, does not sigh for the "rest that remains for the people of God," and where division shall cease for ever! The holy Apostles of the Lamb desired to see all Christians united; and hence Paul said to the Corinthians: "Now I beseech you brethren, by the name of our Lord Jesus Christ, that ye all speak the same thing, and that there be no divisions among you; but that ye be perfectly joined together in the same mind, and in the same judgment." To the Philippians he said: "Fulfill ye my joy, that ye be like minded, having the same love, being of one accord, of one mind."

Our blessed Lord desired to see all his followers united in one: hence in his intercessory prayer, John 17: 20. he said, "Neither pray I for these alone: but for all them also, who shall believe on me through their word; that they all may be one; as thou father art in me, and I in thee, that they also may be one in us; that the world may believe that thou didst send me." Again 23d verse, "I in them and thou in me, that they may be made perfect in one."

Who can read the above prayer of our Lord for union, and not feel ashamed and confounded, if he has ever, for one moment opposed the union of all Christians, or advocated division! Or, who can read it, and not rejoice, if he is engaged in the same glorious cause for which Jesus prayed!

But God our heavenly Father, desires the union of all his children — hence Paul tells us "That there is one God and Father, over all. through all, and in all." (Eph.4. 6.) And again, "that it was God's eternal purpose that in the dispensation of the fullness of times, he might gather together in one, all things in Christ, which are in heaven and which are in earth; even in him." (Eph: 1. 9. 10.)

We may, I think, safely set it down, that God the Father, our Lord Jesus Christ, the Angels, the holy Apostles of the Lamb; all the good and pious among men, desire Christian Union. While upon the other hand the Devil and his Angels, and all the enemies of God and man. stand opposed to it. We therefore call upon all our brethren of all denominations, to take a bold stand, with us, in favor of the union of all Christians, upon *"the one foundation,"* and against the powers of darkness! Let the bitterness of party spirit be forgotten, while with one heart and soul we contend for the cause of "Christian Union."

J. M. MATHES, Ed.

UNIVERSALISM, No. 1.

Universalists affirm, that God from all eternity foresaw whatever comes to pass; and that this foreknowledge is equivalent to foreordination; or at least, that it implies, that God foreordained all things what ever comes to pass. That every thing that does, ever *did, or* ever *will* come to pass, was foreordained, before time began his march! This is fully asserted by Mr. George Rogers in his "Pro and Con," of Universalism. Now if the above sentiment be correct, what follows? either, there is no such thing as sin, in the universe of God; or if there is, God is its author!

To illustrate—God foresaw from all eternity, that A., would kill B. and that foreknowledge made it absolutely necessary that A. should do the murder at the appointed time! If A. should defer the matter an hour, the purpose of God would be frustrated which is impossible. According to Universalism, then, if I understand it, A. was only the passive instrument, in the hand of God, in carrying out his eternal decree, and of course no more to be blamed, than the gun with which he shot B!

Well then, I ask, who is the author of the murder? It is true, that A. is the *immediate* author; but he is not the *prime* agent; for in perpetrating the fatal deed, he acted under the *fiat* of an immutable decree! and consequently he was so tied up in fate, that he could not do otherwise than perform the bloody deed; on the very day, and in the manner, and with the weapon which he did!!

Indeed, there are but two horns to the dilemma, and Universalism may take its choice: it must either say that A. did no wrong in killing his neighbor B. as he was only doing what God from all eternity foreordained that he should do, and consequently that there is no such thing as sin in the Universe! or, to admit the soul-chilling doctrine, that God is the *real* author of every crime that has ever been committed among men, since the first pair transgressed in the garden of delights!!

But Universalists say, that God will punish every sinner according to the demerits of his crimes, and there is no escape. Now I would ask what is the sinner to be punished for? for doing what God from all eternity foreordained that he should do, and consequently, what he could not avoid doing? for acting out the eternal purpose and will of God!!

But how, and when does God punish the sinner? Universalists say, that the punishment is all received in this life; such as war, famine, pestilence and the sword, those mighty agents of the king of terrors; and particularly conscience, which they tell us is a little hell, to the sinner!! Now I would ask, if all punishment is received in this life, why is not the punishment always proportioned to the crime? But we see that such is not the fact; for the greater sinners, very frequently suffer the less punishment, and the less sinners suffer the greater punishment! — Some men who grind the faces of the poor, oppress the hireling in his wages, and violently take away the rights of the Widow and the Orphan and "say in their hearts, there is no God," seem to get along through life without any punishment. They are seldom or never sick, while the kingdom of nature, pours its treasures at their feet; and all the circumstances surrounding them, seem favorable to their earthly enjoyment; and as to the unquenchable fires of a guilty conscience, which Universalists tell us will burn for ever, and ever, that is, during the sinner's life time; they have been long since extinguished: so; that he is not now punished either in Body or Mind! Upon the other hand, some of the very best men that ever lived, have been the most afflicted. They have been punished in body, from Infancy, to old age, sickness, and sorrow, hunger and nakedness, have been their constant lot through life!

Paul, the great Apostle to the Gentiles, for example, while he was a great sinner, persecuting the children of God, even unto strange cities suffered no punishment; not even in conscience, for he says of himself, "I have served God with a pure conscience, from my forefathers;" of course then his conscience was no hell to him! But after he reformed his life, and became a disciple of Christ; he suffered a vast amount of punishment; he was stoned, beaten with rods; and suffered all sorts of hardships, from hunger and thirst, cold and nakedness! I ask why was this so, if Universalists are correct, in saying, *"That God* will punish every man, (in this life) according to his crimes, and there is no escape"!!

J. M. MATHES.

GREENCASTLE DEBATE.

Our readers have, perhaps, all heard of the Discussion which took place, in the Town of Greencastle, Putnam county, Ind., on the 24, and 25th of May, last; between the Editor, and Mr. E Manford, a Universalist Preacher, of Terre-Haute, Editor of the "Christian Teacher."— Two Propositions were discussed: "1st, Does the New Testament teach, that all mankind will be in Christ *unconditionally,* in the Resurrection,"

"2nd —Does the New Testament teach the doctrine of the endless punishment of the wicked?"

Mr. Manford affirmed the first of these, and I the second. Mr. Manford met my expectation very well; he is certainly a gentleman, so far as I am able to judge.

There was not a jar between us during the whole time; the audience was large and attentive, and I have no doubt good will result from the discussion.

I could give a synopsis of the arguments on both sides, but will not, unless it becomes necessary. It becomes me not to express an opinion here, as to the merits of the debate; I only mean to say that I suppose, we both did the very best we could to sustain our respective propositions; and that I am perfectly satisfied with the result.

J. M. MATHES.

OUR PAPER.

Although we have succeeded beyond our expectation, in obtaining Subscribers; yet we need a great many more, to place the "Christian Record" on a firm basis. Trusting to the goodness of our cause, and the liberality of the brethren, and friends, we have ventured to launch our little vessel; and our first number is now before you. Shall it be sustained? We offer to furnish a paper of almost unparalleled cheapness considering the manner in which it is put up. The present number, is not a fair specimen of what the Record will be, as the paper is not quite so good as we intend to print the work on, in future: though it was the very best we could do at the present. Arrangements are now made for the punctual appearance of the C. Record regularly every month.

We shall send this No. to many of our friends and brethren, who have not had an opportunity to send us their names. Will they examine it, and if pleased with it, show it to their friends, and send us all the names of good responsible subscribers they can? Will all our subscribers use their influence to increase the circulation of our paper?— Much may be done in this way. Each subscriber can obtain another, I am sure, and this without any sacrifice, and with but little effort, our means of doing good in society would be doubled! Brethren, will you try? And we now say to all, that if any one will send us free of cost, 5.00 in current money, ("Indiana Scrip," will be taken,) we will send him six copies, as *he* may direct. J. M. MATHES.

THE GLORIOUS APPEARING OF THE LORD.

Perhaps there never was a time, since the Lord Jesus made his first visit to our world, when so much was said about the "second advent" of the Messiah, as there is at the present time. Every paper we read, and almost every speaker to whom we listen, has something to say on the subject. The Infidel world, and wicked professors are scoffing at the idea of the speedy return of Lord; while "Luke-warm Christians are saying, "My Lord delayeth his coming." My heart has been grieved, to hear men in high places, speak of the immediate return of the Master, as the dream of a Fanatic: and treat the subject as one, in which they had no interest!

But it is too late in the day, to stop investigation by a *sneer or scoff*. The people will think and examine; and we believe that those who desire to oppose Mr. Miller, and those who with him contend for the speedy return of the Lord, before they can succeed in a single point, must read and study the prophecies and acquaint themselves with a subject, of which at the present, many of them appear to be wholly ignorant.

But thousands of pious souls are now looking up with joyful expectation—fully believing, that "the coming of the Lord draweth nigh," and hasteneth greatly. "The Alarm," has been sounded, from the heights of the Ozark Mountain, by our excellent brother the "Layman." Its report has reached us, and we have considered its fearful import! It is indeed big with *alarm!*

The Lay-man, writes the fate of the "Gentile church," as he calls the present dispensation in lines of blood! He makes you see the son of man, coming in the clouds of heaven, clad in the ensigns of royalty, to take vengeance upon a corrupt christendom, and an ungodly world. While you contemplate the dreadful scene; he makes you listen to the crash of falling thrones and empires; the fruitless lamentations of their unhappy occupants; while you see scepters, crowns and diadems mingle with the dust forever! and with terrible sublimity, he rolls up the heavens, with the blast of the "last trump," in 1847. Our Layman, has made out a system of interpreting the prophecies, which concentrates upon the close of the present dispensation; and not upon the destruction of the material world, as has been generally supposed. He regards the burning of the world, spoken of in Scripture altogether figurative; and declares the orthodox notion of that subject unphilosophic. He thinks that the second advent of the Lord will be pre-Millennial: that the Lord will come personally, to destroy the wicked, and reward the righteous—that the "cleansing of the sanctuary," which he understands to be the purification of the church, will take place at the introduction of the Millennium. He thinks that the righteous dead, will be raised immortal when the Lord comes; the wicked will be destroyed, and the living saints, though not changed; with those young immortals, will "live, and reign with Christ," a thousand prophetic years. He appears not to be fully satisfied as to the length of Christ's glorious reign on earth: he is not sure whether the 1000 year are to be understood literally; or whether we are not to understand a day for a year, as in other prophecies, and thus extend the time to 365,000 common years!

During this glorious period, he believes that the saints will build houses, plant vineyards, eat and drink! He believes that previous to the introduction of the Millennium, the Jews will literally return to their own land, as he thinks that they hold a deed in "fee simple," for the premises, from the God of Abraham, Isaac and Jacob; and he thinks, that when they return, they will rebuild Jerusalem; and that they will then have another struggle for existence, with the combined powers of the pagan world. He makes a day stand for a year in prophetic language—understands the 70 weeks of Daniel to be weeks of years—the 42 months, to be 1260 years—the "thousand two hundred and three score days of John to be 1260 years, and to refer to the same period, the reign of the man of sin, the son of Perdition; which he understands to be the Pope of Rome. But time would fail us to speak of this "Alarming" production with more minuteness. Our good brother, has said many good things—all will agree—and that he has guessed at some, matters of vast importance in his scheme, and speculated upon others, I think no one who has examined the "Alarm," and read the prophecies, will deny.

Some other very interesting papers have fallen into our hands, in which this truly, important subject, has been ably examined; "The signs of the times," "The Midnight Cry," "The Trumpet of Alarm," "The Jubilee Trumpet," "The Israelite," and "The Carthage Evangelist," concerning, which, we cannot now speak particularly: but will notice them at a more convenient season. And while I am not disposed at this time, to express an opinion, as to the respective merits of the different theories of interpreting the prophecies relating, to the second coming of the Lord; yet I most cordially believe, that the coming of the Lord draweth nigh; and that it is one of the most important subjects, ever submitted to the consideration of mortals. It is indeed the Christians hope!

Reader, are you prepared for that grand and glorious event? If you are not, fly for refuge to the ark of safety, ere the day of vengeance shall overtake you! delay not a single moment! to-morrow it may be too late.

J. M. M.

FOR THE CHRISTIAN RECORD.
CHRISTIAN OBLIGATION'S, NO. 1.

Bro. Mathes:

Having learned that the Christian Record goes to type this week, I have concluded to write a short essay on Christian obligations, which, if it reach you in time, you may print if you think fit. The reason that I select this subject, is, because I think there is a greater lack in the observance of these things, than in any thing else; in fact, the head of this article implies every thing, in reference to the Christian; and a small part of that duty is, to teach first principles.

I suppose the community divided into two, or at most three classes, in regard to our views. The first I suppose to be, those individuals who understand our views, and oppose them, through principle or prejudice. The second, those who do not understand our views, and are consequently opposed to us. The third, and last, and by far the least, those who do understand what we teach, and at the same time, honestly opposed. In reference to the first class, there is little hope. In reference to the second, and third classes, a living example of what we profess to be, is the best possible avenue to their minds to convince them that our theory is right. These are a few of the reasons, which oblige us to "walk worthy of the vocation where with we are called." All actions spring from principle, and the good works of the Christian grow out of his obligations, I suppose the reason why so many professed Christians are so careless about their duty, as Christians, is, because they do not consider the extent of the obligations resting upon them.

"Happy is he that condemeth not himself in that thing which he alloweth," and if we preach to sinners the necessity of obeying the positive commands of the Gospel, and are not equally as strict ourselves in obedience to the "all things whatsoever I have commanded you." we stand reproached in the eyes of the world, and all wise and good men and that justly too.

Gentle reader, are you a disciple? If so, measure yourself by the teachings of the Apostles, and see if you are as strict in the observance of their example and precept, as you believe and teach the sinner must be in obedience to first principles, in order to enjoy the present salvation: if not, then, you are greatly at fault, for the authority is the same in one case, that it is in the other; both growing out of the fact, that all authority in heaven and in earth is given into the hands of the saviour.— The obligations which rest upon the Christian to walk in the good works unto which he is created in Christ, are the very strongest that heaven could offer. They are as high as heaven, whence they originated in the love of God, they are as deep as the grave, which the Lord Jesus has despoiled of its power, they are as strong as he, "who works all things after the council of his own will." They are as wise as he in whom "are laid up all the treasures of wisdom and knowledge," they are as benevolent as he who "died the just for the unjust that he might bring us to God," and as unchangeable as he who is "the same yesterday, to-day and forever." We are in the habit of dividing the commands of the Gospel into Moral and Positive: this is done for the sake of distinguishing those duties which are right in themselves from those which are right, only, by virtue of the authority which gave them; but, strictly speaking, there is no such thing, as positive obligation; it is all moral. The very same morality, which binds me to love the Lord with all my heart, binds me to obey him in every institution; and to "neglect the assembling of ourselves together, as the manner of some, is" just as much a breach of the morality of the Bible, as to "take the name of the Lord in vain." I do not say that the former is as bad as the latter; but it is a breach of the same code of morals, founded in the same principle of justice, the obligation of man to his God. I thus place a heinous crime in comparison with that which is considered comparatively small in order to show that they are both a transgression of the same law, and consequently sin, for "sin is transgression of law." Here are many individuals, who, I have no idea, ever think of committing sins when they are indifferent about going to meeting on the first day of the week. Probably their favorite preacher is not going to preach, or something of that sort, and so they succeed in making an excuse to stay at home. Is not this a lamentable fact?

We profess to take the Bible, *alone,* for our rule of faith and practice, and the world (as they have a right to do) expect more of us, than our sectarian friends, and my prayer, for one is, that they may not be disappointed.

The same remarks that I have made, in reference to going to meeting, will apply with equal force to all other duties, some of which we will, if the Lord spare us, speak of in another No.; and the danger of neglecting them is expressed in the following language: "For if the word spoken by angels was steadfast, and every transgression and disobedience received a just recompense of reward; how shall we escape, if we neglect so great salvation." Let us consider the greatness of this salvation. It cost nothing less than the blood of the son of God, and the Apostle, by way of contrast, brings it in comparison with that institution, which was dedicated by the blood of animals.

"Let us hold fast the profession of *our* faith; for he is faithful that promised: and let us consider one another, to provoke unto love and to good works: not forsaking the assembling of ourselves together, as the manner of some is; but exhorting one another; and so much the more, is ye see the day approaching. For if we sin willfully after that we have received the knowledge of the truth, there remaineth no more sacrifice for sins, but a certain fearful looking for of judgment and fiery indignation, which shall devour the adversaries. He that despised Moses' law, died without mercy under two or three witnesses of how much sorer punishment, suppose ye, shall he be thought worthy, who hath trodden under foot the son of God, and hath counted the blood of the covenant, wherewith he was sanctified, an unholy thing, and hath done despite unto the spirit of grace? Heb. 10-23-30.

The Apostle leaves us to infer what will be the punishment, from the difference between the two institutions. We will continue the contrast in our next No.

Martinsville Ia., June 18th, 1843.   T. J. EDMONDSON.

MILLERISM AND SECOND ADVENT, NO. 9.

We will now proceed to notice the expositions of our friends Miller and Saml. M. McCorkle, on the subjects contained in the 13 chapt. of the Apocalypse. But before we take hold of the tangled subject, we will state the points or positions, that appear to be necessary for them to demonstrate as true, before their Theories can be entitled to any credit—They must prove and demonstrate beyond doubt, the following propositions. First, that they have the ability and power, to arrive at a knowledge of the true meaning and import of unfulfilled scripture prophecies, before they are fulfilled. Secondly, That the book of Daniel and the Apocalypse, compose a history of the Christian church, from its earliest organization "to its destined dissolution." Thirdly, What the daily sacrifice, oblation, covenant, &c. were, and the precise time they had their accomplishment. Fourthly, That the *time, times* and an half of Daniel and John, and John's 40 and 2. months, mean precisely the same *time and* thing, 1260 literal years, instead of literal days. Fifthly, That Christ will make his second Advent at, or in a short time after the expiration of the 1260 years. If our expounders cannot tell what the daily sacrifice, oblation &c. were, how can they tell when they were accomplished? And if they cannot tell when they had their accomplishment, how can they tell when to date the commencement of the *time,* times and an half of Daniel and John, or John's 40 and 2 months, or the 1260 years? All those that have made themselves acquainted with the doctrines or prophecies of Mr. Miller and Saml. M. McCorkle, know, that they attempt to prove, that a final winding up of the present state of affairs, will take place at the expiration of the 1260 years. Miller says the 1260 years expired in 1798, and in 45 years thereafter, the judgment in 1843. The Alarmist, says the time was not out, till 1801 or 1802. This shows some difference of opinion existing between our prophets, but difference appears to be their constant and "besetting" companion. We have already shown, that if Christ was Messiah, and took away the sacrifice, oblation &c. at his crucifixion, that the 1260 years were out long since. This then, would prove too much for the Theories of our prophets, and, of course, disprove them. The sacrifice &c. are mentioned three times in Daniel, 8th, 9th, and 12th chapters. Besides the sacrifice &c. which our expounders say that Christ took away at his crucifixion, our prophets saw the necessity to cobble up, (from what Daniel says) a second sacrifice; which was to be taken away in the year 508; and 30 years after, an abomination that maketh desolate, set up. This second sacrifice, Mr. Miller calls, "The sacrifice abomination." Thirty years after this second sacrifice was taken away, our prophets date the beginning of the 1960 years. It then devolved upon them to show when, and by whom, this second sacrifice was set up, what it was, and how long it should continue; and by what power or personage, it should be taken away, or made to cease. For the purpose of explaining this matter, Miller and the Alarmist, bounce, without ceremony, upon the two beasts that John describes in Revelations 13th chapt. But we will now let our friends speak for themselves. Turn to Miller's fifth lect. 70th page. "Rev. 13th, 18th." "Here is wisdom. Let him that hath understanding count the number of the beast; for it is the number of a man; and his number is six hundred threescore and six. After taking the above text as the foundation of his Lect. Mr. Miller proceeds as follows: "This text has caused as much speculation as any text in the whole Bible; rivers of Ink have been shed to explain its meaning, brains have been addled in trying to find some great mystery which the wisdom of this world, was supposed, could only discover; and in trying to be wise above what was written, men have lost their balance, and *fell* into absurdities too ridiculous to mention." As we cannot make lengthy quotations from the documents of our friends, we will state their positions as correctly as we can, and then draw our inferences, and make our comparisons. In the first verse of the chapter, John says, "And I stood upon the sand of the sea, and saw a beast rise up out of the sea, having seven heads and ten horns, and upon his horns ten crowns, and upon his heads the name of blasphemy." In the 11th verse he says, "And I beheld another beast coming up out of the earth, and he had two horns like a lamb, and he spake as a dragon," verse 12th, "and he exerciseth all the power of the first beast before him, and causeth the earth and them which dwell therein to worship the first beast, whose deadly wound was healed."— In the above quotations, I understand John to call the beast which arose out of the sea, and described in the first verse, to be the first beast; and the one described in the 11th as coming out of the earth, to be the second beast. Mr. Miller divides his text as follows. "First, Show what wisdom this is spoken of in the text. Second, Speak of the beast numbered, and show what beast. Third, The number, and what we may understand by it." Of his first division we will take no notice, but will hear him on the second. "Second, The beast numbered in the text.— And, 1st, Let us enquire what beast it is. I answer. It is the first beast, see our context; 12th verse, "and he exerciseth all the power of the first beast before him;" that is, the beast which John saw come up out of the sea, (the Roman Government) having seven heads and ten horns &c." But we must hear Miller a little further on the subject, same page, 78. "In the 11th verse he" (John,) "gives us a discovery of the same beast in his ecclesiastical power; Pagan Rome in the first beast; and Papacy in the image beast, and it will be evident to anyone who will examine the chapter carefully, that John was not commanded to number the Image beast, for the civil power of that beast was before numbered in the 5th verse." In this last sentence as quoted from Miller, I understand him to say, that the 5th verse, gives the length of time the second, image, or papal beast was to continue. Let us read it; "and there was given unto him" (the first beast) "a mouth speaking great things and blasphemies; and power was given unto him to continue forty and two months," that is, according to Miller and the Alarmist, 1260 years.

Have we not just seen that Miller makes Paganism the first beast, and papalism the second beast, which he calls the "image beast." But of what is papalism the image! If I understand Miller, he makes it the image of Paganism. Then how can he make the 5th verse define the length of time the second or image beast should continue! That verse evidently defines the time the first beast should continue, the beast that John saw arise out of the sea. But why does Miller call Paganism the "sacrifice abomination." Examine the said 5th Lect. and there you will he told, it was because the pagans sacrificed human beings. It now devolves on Mr. Miller to tell us when paganism took its rise, and become the "sacrifice abomination," and when it was taken away, or made to cease. Then hear him speak on the last page of this same fifth Lect. After consulting Josephus and Maccabees for some historical facts and dates, he says. "Then, if this be correct, that Pagan Rome began his power in the year B. C. 158, and was to continue 666 years, when would Paganism fall in the Roman kingdom and the daily sacrifice abomination" be taken out of the way to make room for the abomination of desolation!" "I answer, Take 158 from 666 and you will have 508. Then in the year A. D. 508 Paganism ceased." We will now call the attention of the reader to Millers 7th Lect. 104th page, where he may see the premises laid down, and the final winding up of the present state of affairs. "The 70 weeks, or 490 years, will be accomplished A. D. 33. The pagan abomination will be taken away 475 years afterwards, which will be A.D. 508. The Papal abomination will be set up 80 years after A.D.538, and will continue 1260 years, A. D. 1798. After this 45 years, I shall stand in my lot; and all that come forth to this resurrection will be blessed, A. D. 1843?" We now have Miller's positions in full view upon the subjects of those beasts, he plainly tells us, that Paganism was the first beast, and that papalism, or popery, was the second. As it would extend this number to too great a length, we will defer a statement of the positions of the Alarmist, and our comment upon this, till our next. The positions of the Alarmist upon the subjects of the beasts, can be exhibited in a few words. When we commenced the review of the works of Miller and the Alarmist, we supposed we could notice five or six of their most important positions in seven or eight numbers, but to do justice to the part of subject now under consideration? will require another number.

JOHN MCCORKLE.

FROM THE CHRISTIAN JOURNAL.

OPINIOMSM—NO. 1.

An effort is now being made, against the interests of apostolic Christianity, which calls for our attention.

The pleaders for sectarianism, or at least many of them, are diligently laboring, in their general intercourse, and through the press, and in the pulpit, to cast odium upon us, on account of our latitudinarianism, as they sometimes term it, with respect to opinions. They charge us with tolerating all sorts and sizes of pestilential heresies; of consorting with idolaters; are the worshippers of a created Savior; and of allowing every species of maiming and mangling, to be perpetrated upon the Scriptures, by every species of heedless and barbarous interpretation to which either the winged fancy, or the noisome crawling propensity of any son of earth may incline him. And as this species of warfare requires no logic to sustain it; as it exactly adapts itself to the morbid and vulgar tastes of narrow-minded bigots; and as it is, to some extent, calculated to excite the fears, even of those who are disposed to be liberal and elevated in their religious sentiments, we need not wonder that this species of warfare should be vigorously, extensively, and perseveringly waged against us.

Now admitting, for the sake of argument, that the case is just as bad with us, as it is represented to be, we would ask, How much worse is our condition, than that of the "evangelical sects?" If, upon a little examination, it shall appear that their condition is worse than ours, even taking their false representation of ours to be true, then, surely our accusers ought to take shame to themselves, and get the splinter out of their own eye, before they so officiously and ostentatiously come forward, to pick the mote out of ours.

To obtain a peep, then, at the condition of those who have dubbed themselves, "evangelical sects," it must not be forgotten, that these sects, all claim to be *"branches"* of Christ's Church. According to their plan, then, we have Christ's church, under the similitude of a tree. The Methodists are one branch of this tree: the Presbyterians another; the Episcopalians another; the Baptists &c. &c.; many branches, but all of them one, and but one tree:—all inserted into the stock, or body of the tree, by some species of spiritual engrafting. On this slate of the case, we offer the following remarks:—

1. That, according to this view of the subject, the several sects, termed evangelical, constitute but one church. Now, what sort of Scripture interpreters are the members of this church? Do they all interpret by the same rules? Do they all arrive at the same results? No person will pretend it for a moment. The Bible is carried through the theological crucible of one class, and lo! out comes Methodism! through another, and out comes Presbyterianism! through another, and behold Episcopalian ism! through another and some one or another of the numerous castes of Baptistism, is the result! Again, a certain class of texts passes through the interpretation crucible, and behold, sprinkling, the same texts are subjected to the Baptist analysis, and immersion is the result. In the hands of the calvinistic interpreter, the Bible produces the *five points of Calvinism;* whilst in the hands of another class of interpreters, the FIVE POINTS of Armenius appear—the perfect antipodes of the points of Calvin. Here Congregationalism is poured forth —there the Presbyterial form—there diocesan Episcopacy! And thus this work of evangelical interpretation goes on, until such a din and clashing is produced, as perhaps transcends the confusion of old Babel itself, at the time of the confusion of tongues; and then—wonderful to

tell—these interpreters, turn upon us, and say, "Ye silly ones, why don't you work this thing evangelically, learnedly, harmoniously, as we do"!!—I am often made to think of the fox that had lost his tail!

2. If, then, this great diversity of interpretation, may be so far tolerated, in this evangelical church, of many dissimilar branches, as that the cords of the fellowship of its members shall not be severed; why may not a great diversity *of* interpretation be tolerated among us? Is this denied us, because we have not plunged into their inconsistencies? If, *par ex:* a member of the Presbyterian church, interprets the Scriptures Methodistically, he is put out *of* the Presbyterian church, and his chance, for lodgings and other accommodations, is to go and join the Methodists. He still may be a very good Christian, but not a Presbyterian Christian. He is now only a Methodist Christian: and as such, is entitled, according to the stipulations of the holy sectarian alliance, which has obtained among the evangelicals, to Presbyterian fellowship. We are more consistent. We bear, in the first instance, with all that diversity of opinion and of interpretation, in our fellow members, which we conceive to be, by any possibility, compatible with Christianity. We do not forget that *we* are fallible, that Christ received us, to his fellowship, with all the frailties of our nature, and the errors of our understanding and that "HE, who can have compassion on the ignorant, and on such as are out of the way," has commanded us so to receive one another, "as Christ received us to the glory of God." Rom. 15:7.

3. But we even fellowship *idolaters;* or, what amounts to the same thing, persons who believe that Jesus is a *created* being. Well, how is this charge made to lay against us? Why, we fellowship all who profess to believe Jesus to be the *Son of God,* and submit to immersion!— Well, is not this the apostolic order? "If thou believest with all thine heart thou mayest. And he answered and said, I believe that Jesus Christ is the Son of God?" Acts 8: 37. See also Rom. 10. 9. Mat. 16: 16. Why did not Philip ask, Do you believe, that there are three persons in the God-head? Not a word of it. If then we practice as did the inspired men, who dare blame us? Does their doctrine need to be added to, or mended by men, uninspired? On the subject of trinity, I at present neither affirm nor deny. But I say that the mode of the divine existence is a subject hard to be understood. There are clouds, and darkness round about it; but blacker clouds, and a more intense darkness, round about the greater part of what has been said of it. I have at this moment, the recollection of hearing a gentleman of considerable eminence, preach on the subject of trinity. Now, thought I, we shall have the fog blown off. He told us "that unless we believed the trinity, we could not be Christians! That there were three persons in the Godhead; not precisely persons either," said he; "but on account of the poverty of our language we can find no term that more nearly expresses our idea, than the word *persons"!* This left me flat! I reasoned thus: "Faith comes by hearing—hearing by the word of God:" and he acknowledges that there is no word that will express the thing to be believed! This is a fair sample of the greater part of all that has been said on this much vexed question, by uninspired men. They have profaned the subject; they have darkened counsel by words without knowledge!

But, is it a fact that we DO fellowship persons who believe that Christ is a *created being.* Old Father Stone does not so believe. I have heard him; with my own ears, preach against that view of the subject! Here several questions present themselves to my mind. 1. Which is more in accordance with Christianity, to fellowship a man of sterling piety and morality, who has fallen into some errors of the head, concerning the person and character of Jesus, or to fellowship a bigot, whose understanding is all orthodox, but whose heart at the same time is so bitter, as that he cannot deny himself the superlative felicity of peddling falsehoods against his religious opponents. 2d. Which is the most consistent with Christianity, to fellowship an individual, such as the one just named, or one that represents the Father as an Almighty tyrant, creating rational immortals for perdition; willing and decreeing their perdition; and bringing them into the world with a nature such as would render it as impossible for them to serve God and be saved, as it is for a stone, by the laws of its own nature, and in opposition to the law of gravitation, to ascend to the throne of God? In other words, which is the more heinous offence, to degrade the Father, or to degrade the Son? For myself, I can say, that I could as easily give to the Arian, as to the Calvinist, the right hand of fellowship. 3. Which is the more consistent, to fellowship the person who is, to some extent, in error concerning the person and character of Jesus, but, who is profoundly intelligent in respect to Christianity in general, or one who is a perfect dunce in the whole matter? but who, forsooth, makes an orthodox profession—who takes things in the *lump*—who lives by mere *sound*—who is led by a mere *gingle* of doctrines—I will illustrate my meaning. "Do you believe;" said a man to me "in the *direct* operation of the Spirit"? Very probably I do, said I, if you will tell me what you mean by the phrase direct influences, &c. I can answer you positively, the man was at a total loss: he knew not the meaning of the words. And it is so with a great multitude of very orthodox folks. Of the abstruse parts of their religious creeds, they know little or nothing. They, *in* many instances, profess to believe they know not what: and for the meritoriousness of such mutton headed profession, they are admitted into the church, as soundly orthodox.

4. Once more, and we are done for the present. Much as the Presbyterians have spoken against us for not having a human creed, they do not require their own members to subscribe to the Westminister Confession! None but Bishops, Elders, and Deacons are required to subscribe to that document. Still, however, they send it out as the faith of their church. How do they know that it contains the faith of their church?— The church has never said so: unless indeed, the Bishops, Elders, and Deacons comprise the Presbyterian Church! Do the ordinary members believe by proxy?

A. RAINES.

COLUMBUS DEBATE.

The debate at Columbus, Bartholomew County, Ia., between Mr. E. Manford Editor of the "Christian Teacher," a Universalist preacher, and our beloved brother Jacob Wright, was concluded on last Thursday evening, the 29th ult., having lasted three days. I had the pleasure of being present all the time.

Two Propositions were discussed; to wit: "1—Does the Bible teach the final holiness and happiness of all mankind?" This Mr. M. affirmed, and bro. W. denied. And "2—Does the New Testament teach the doctrine of the endless punishment of the wicked?" This bro. W. affirmed, and Mr. M. denied. The audience was large, and very attentive throughout.

Mr. Manford is a practiced debater; and I am informed that he stands at the head, of his party in this State. He is certainly a young man of very fair talents. Concerning brother Wright, I need say nothing at this time: he is well known to the brethren generally, as a successful Evangelist of the true gospel.

Mr. Manford prosecuted the debate, with a great deal of energy and zeal; indeed I am sure, that he did every thing for his cause, which talent and zeal, could do: but it is hard to kick against the goads!

Brother Wright, laid down his premises, with judgment, and argued with good effect: and sustained the truth manfully, to the entire satisfaction of the brother-hood, so far as I know. "Truth is mighty, and powerful above all things, and will prevail." EDITOR.

REV. JAMES SCOTT.—Where is the Rev. James Scott, of Morgan county, Indiana, We expected to have heard from him long since on the subject of "Paul's Baptism." This we had a right to expect. Has he forgotten the agreement? I hope not!

J. M. MATHES.

NEWS FROM THE CHURCHES.

MILL-CREEK, WASHINGTON COUNTY. IA, MAY 17TH, 1843.

My dear brother J. M. Mathes:

By the request of the Church of Christ at this place, I address you this line, for the purpose of informing you, that it is her most ardent desire that you should attend her next annual meeting, which will commence on Friday before the first Lord's day in September next.

* * * Since you left here we have added some twenty or thirty, to the congregation at Mill-Creek. We praise the name of the Lord, for the great success, his truth has had in our section recently! The spirit of enquiry is now awake. Do come brother Mathes!

In hopes of a blessed Immortality,

I am your brother in the Lord,

GEORGE K. PORTER.

(If the Lord will, I expect to be with the dear brethren and friends at Mill-Creek, at the time specified above. J. M. MATHES.

Brother Love H. Jameson, writing from Indianapolis, under date of April 25th, says: "Yesterday morning, I immersed 14 persons, and the prospect is good for many more."

Brother Richard Gosney, of Williamsburgh, Johnson county, Ia., writes under date of April 25th, and speaks of a gradual increase in the church in that Village; he speaks of good times at Edinburgh in the same county, thinks about 20 additions were recently made to the church in that place; he also reports 6 additions at a meeting recently held near Blackhawk, in Shelby county, and the prospect good for many more.

ERRATTA.—Fifth page, fifth line from bottom, where the word *erased* may occur, read (*raised*.

Tenth page fifth line from bottom, read (*thus*) *for this*.

THE CHRISTIAN RECORD.

VOL. I.   AUGUST, 1843.   NO. II.

CHRISTIAN UNION—NO. 2.

HAVING, in our first number, ascertained that God, our heavenly Father, the Lord Jesus Christ, the holy Angels, the holy Apostles of the Lamb, and all the humble and pious, of all denominations, desire Christian Union, we will now inquire, Are those denominations, called "Evangelical," united according to the prayer of the divine Savior?

Not many, I suppose, can be found, bold enough to affirm; and those who do, cannot, in my judgment, produces single proof which partakes of the nature of the proposition. I know it is sometimes said, that all the "Evangelical Sects," taken together, constitute the *Universal,* or *Catholic Church;* Or "Mystical Body of Christ:" and that each Sect, taken separately; is a branch of this Catholic church: and hence they conclude, that they are now *united* according to the prayer of the Lord! But we beg leave to differ with our friends upon this subject; and we do most devoutly hope, that we shall not be considered their enemy, "because we tell them the truth." Let us then examine the above assumption, in the fear of the Lord!

1st. Does this "Mysterious, Invisible union," contended for by some of our fellow professors, really exist among them, *as denominations?* We honestly think not. They all differ from each other, in some of their "Articles of Faith," their forms of church government, their modes of worship, and the names by which they distinguish themselves from each other. Each exists, as perfectly independent of all the rest, as though no other existed in the world. It seems to us therefore; that they are not in *union* with each other! But it may be said, that their differences are all about *mere non-essentials;* and that upon all the great *essential* matters, they perfectly agree! Well, this may be true, to some extent; but if it is, I think any one would be led to conclude, that there are but few *essentials,* in their theological systems; and that all their bitter strife and contention, is a *mighty fuss about nothing!* If indeed any union exists between the different denominations, *as such,* if is certainly a very mysterious affair; so *mysterious,* that no one can understand it; and so *Invisible,* that no one can see it!

A preacher, once conversing with me upon the subject, made the following curious remark: "When we Baptize our Infants," said the Preacher, "we do not take them into the Methodist branch of Christ's church, more than into the Baptist branch; but they are brought by baptism, into the Invisible, or Catholic church of Christ." This astonished me no little! But do the Baptist friends know that this is the arrangement? Do they know that the Pedo-Baptist Ministers are daily adding to their numbers, by baptizing their babes! They have just as good a right to *count* th em, as have the Pedo-Baptists themselves! But enough of this.

2nd. But suppose it could be proved, though it cannot, that such union really exists among the different denominations, it would not reach the case; as this is not the sort of union for which Jesus prayed. "I pray not for these alone, but for them also which shall believe on me. through their word; that they may all be one; as thou Father art in me and I in thee; that they may also be one in us: that the world may believe that thou hast sent me." (John 17: 20, 21.) Now the reader will see at a glance, that the Union here prayed for by the Lord Jesus, was not a Mysterious, Invisible union; for it was to have its influence upon the world—"That the world may believe that thou hast sent me." How is the world to be converted to Jesus, by a kind of union, which they neither *see*, nor *understand?* Such an idea is preposterous! No indeed, the union for which Jesus prayed, was a *thorough, visible union:* "As thou Father art in me, and I in thee." How complete, and glorious the union!

The above prayer of the Lord, was answered, in a very eminent degree, in the first Christians.—Were they divided off into contending sects and parties; each having a different name, Creed and mode of worship? No verily.—Read the Acts of Apostles, and you will see, "that they were of one heart and of one soul;" that "they continued steadfast in the Apostles' doctrine, in Fellowship, in breaking of bread, and in prayers;" and that they all wore the same name. Their union was *visible,* for their bitterest enemies were compelled to say of them, "Behold how these Christians love one another!" But could this be said of the different denominations now? No indeed, the Atheist, the Infidel and Skeptic, now say of them, "Behold how these *professed* followers of the Lamb, *hate* one another!"

3rd. Are the different denominations, *as such,* branches of the church of Christ? We honestly think not. Every Christian is a branch of the true vine, as Jesus taught his disciples: (John 15:) "I am the Vine, ye are the branches." Who are the branches? Why the disciples, as *individuals*. But to talk of all the "Evangelical sects," *as such,* constituting the church of Christ, is, in my judgment, to talk without reference to the facts in the case: and to talk of each denomination, *as such,* being a branch of the Church of Christ, is equally absurd.

But suppose we admit, for a single moment, the *assumption* that the different denominations, are the branches to which Jesus referred, in the above passage: (John 15:) Then Christ is the true vine, out of which, they all grow; on one side grows out the "Lutheran" branch; on the other, the "Presbyterian" branches, of the *old* and the *new* school, bearing fruit according to their name; a little farther along the Vine, grows out the cluster of "Baptist" branches, which bear fruit peculiar to themselves. —Still further along the Vine, we see a very luxuriant branch growing out of the same vine; it is called the "Methodist Episcopal" branch! "Its look is more stout than its fellows;" and from the multitude and character of its fruit, it far excels some of the older branches!

Now if all these branches, with a hundred others that we might name, grow out of the same Vine, would it not be reasonable to expect them all to bear the same kind of fruit. For example:—Suppose the Vine should be a Grape Vine; we would expect all its branches to be grape-vine branches, and that they would all bear grapes, of the same name, quality and kind. But what would be your astonishment, if upon going into your garden, where grows a beautiful grape-vine, you should see growing out of it a hundred different branches, of as many different *kinds,* each having a different *name,* and bearing fruit peculiar to itself. On one side a "gourd-vine" branch, bearing gourds; and on the other a "melon" branch, bearing melons of fine size and quality! I know that you would think it very strange! What, you would say, is it possible that a grape-vine, will produce "gourd and melon branches!" Curious grape-vine this!!

But all this, would be no more astonishing, than that all denominations, *as such,* with all their diversity of name, Creed, and mode of worship, should be branches of the same Church, or Vine! If indeed, they are all branches of the same vine, why do they not all bear the fruit, and wear the name of the Vine, out of which they grow?

The conclusion therefore, to which we must come, upon the whole premises, is, that the Union for which Jesus prayed, does not *now* exist among the different sects, as *such!*

And we are now prepared to inquire, whether "Christian Union," is practicable, and if so, how it may be brought about.

We ask our friends to *be patient,* and hear us through. In this No. we may *seem* to be a little severe; but we mean no harm at all by it: we only wish to look at the matter just as it really exists.

EDITOR.

UNIVERSALISM—NO. 2

UNIVERSALISM denies, *in effect,* the doctrine of forgiveness. It teaches that "God will punish every sinner according to his crimes, and there is no escape." Now if the sinner suffers all the punishment due his crimes, and gets to heaven, can it be said in truth that he was forgiven? I think, not. It is like this: A. owes me ten dollars, for which I hold his obligation; but he is not able to pay it; I then agree to take it in personal labor or suffering: A. labors and suffers the amount due, I then approach him, and hand him his note, and say, "Sir, I forgive you the debt."—Would it not be an insult to his suffering? It certainly would; and yet this is precisely what Universalism says of our Heavenly Father! The sinner has sinned against God; God holds claims upon him for personal holiness; but this he is not able to discharge, for he is a sinner. God refuses to forgive him in the sense of remitting the punishment; but agrees to take him to heaven after he has suffered the punishment. The punishment therefore meets, and responds to all the claims of the violated law of God, and the sinner is saved.—I ask then how was he saved? Was he forgiven. I answer he was not, for he has suffered all that justice had against him! This seems to be the doctrine of Universalism on this point! To whom then will the sinner give the glory, for salvation? Universalism would seem to teach us, that by means of our own personal sufferings, we are brought into the enjoyment of heaven; and it seems to me, that if Universalism be true, we shall owe our salvation to ourselves! It cannot be said, in any proper sense of the term, that the sinner was forgiven.

But to make this matter still more plain: Let our Political government, represent the government of Jehovah; and let the man who has offended against the majesty of our laws, represent the sinner against God. We will suppose then, if you please, that B. has been guilty of manslaughter; the law is violated, and B. is arraigned, tried and condemned to suffer the penalty of the law, which is twenty-one years confinement at hard labor in the state prison! He is dragged without mercy to the walls of his horrid confinement, and there incarcerated in this gloomy dungeon, according to all the demands of law and justice: here he remains for 21 years, for there is *no escape;* at the end of the time, an officer of the government stands at the door of the Penitentiary, and as the poor man is coming into the world again, the officer says to him, "Sir, I am authorized in the name of my government to inform you that you are pardoned!" Would not the poor sufferer say, "Sir, you have come too late; if you had come when I was first incarcerated in these dismal walls, and pronounced these sweet words, "you *are pardoned,* " I should then have gone out free from this dreadful punishment, which I have undergone here, and should have been placed under ten thousand obligations to love, respect and obey my government; but you have come too late, my sufferings here, have responded to all the claims of the law, and justice has no further demands against me; I have *paid* the debt, therefore do not insult my misfortune *now,* by telling me that I am pardoned! I am under no obligations to you, nor the government, in whose name you pronounce the pardon. You have come too late!"

The application is easy: "All have sinned;" therefore all must suffer the penalty annexed, for *there is no escape:* for Universalism says that "God will not forgive the sin in the sense of remitting the punishment." This world is the Penitentiary, where the sinner has to suffer for all his crimes. The officer, in the above illustration, may represent a Universalist Preacher, telling the dying sinner that so soon as he shall have felt the last pang of death, he will be forgiven; as he will then have paid the debt, his sufferings will then have responded to all the claims of the divine law of God, which he had violated. Could not the dying sinner say to such a preacher, at such a time, "Sir, you have come too late! If you tell me the truth, I have suffered all that was due for my crimes; therefore, do not insult me now by telling me that I am pardoned; no sir, I have *paid* the debt, and am under no obligations to you, or him in whose name you profess to speak; but if I could have been pardoned, in the sense of remitting the punishment, then I should have been placed under eternal obligations, to love, honor and obey the Lord."

I hope that nothing which I have said, will rasp the feelings of my kind Universalist friends; Move them, and have ventured to use great plainness of speech. I desire to see them converted from the influence of a system, which I honestly believe to be erroneous, and very dangerous. I therefore in all humility, would exhort them, to search the scriptures, and as none of us can have any possible interest in being in error, we should certainly divest ourselves, if we can, of prepossession, and open our hearts to receive the truth.

We shall continue the investigation of the subject of pardon, in our next, EDITOR.

ON CREEDS.

A Correspondent wishes us to say, in the "Christian Record," whether we have a *human* Creed, or Confession of Faith, or Discipline: says that a Preacher in his vicinity, has recently made the charge, and he wishes to know the truth of the matter. The following is my answer:

My Dear Sir:—

It gives me no small degree of pleasure to be permitted to answer your interrogatory; which, although it may not be "exactly scriptural," is nevertheless one of vast importance to the body of believers, called "Christians." It is of great importance to us, because we have always opposed human creeds and confessions of faith; on the ground that they stand in the way of Christian Union, and the conversion of the world; but if it can now be shown that we have adopted the very thing ourselves, for which we blame others; and that while we publicly oppose a human Creed or Discipline, we secretly hug it to our bosom, it will then follow, that we are false witnesses, hypocrites, and unworthy of the confidence of our fellow-citizens.

But you wish me to "answer definitely, yea, or nay." Well then, I say the charge is *false!* We take "the Bible, the whole Bible, and nothing but the Bible," for our confession of faith, and acknowledge no Discipline but the Law of Christ. This ground we have ever maintained; and on this ground we expect to stand, and contend against "Spiritual wickedness in "high places." I can make no apology for those who make the charge. But you say, the title of the Book alluded to is "The Christian System," written by A. Campbell. Now, although Mr. Campbell has written a book of the above title, it is not our "Confession of Faith," or "Discipline." To be such, 1st—It must have been written for that purpose. 2nd—It must have been adopted by some general association, or Conference of the Church, in which all, or at least a majority of the churches were represented; and 3rd—It must be used as authority in the church in all matters of Discipline.

Now, let us examine this "Christian System," in reference to the three particulars, above mentioned; and 1st.—Was it written by Mr. Campbell for a Confession of Faith, or a Discipline? I answer it was not; and for proof I introduce the writer himself, who, in his preface to the "Christian System," 8th page, says: "The object of this volume is to place before the community in a plain, definite, and perspicuous style, the *capital principles* which have been elicited, argued out, developed, and sustained in a controversy of *twenty-five years,* by the tongues and pens of those who rallied under the banners of the Bible alone. The principle which was inscribed upon our banners when we withdrew from the ranks of the sects, was, *"Faith in Jesus as the true Messiah, and obedience to Him as our Law-giver and King, the* ONLY TEST *of Christian character, and the* ONLY BOND *of Christian Union, communion, and co-operation, irrespective of all creeds, opinions, commandments, and traditions of men."* Again, on the 9th page, Mr. Campbell says: "Our *opposition to creeds arose from a conviction, that whether the opinions in them were true, or false, they were hostile to the union, peace, harmony, purity, and joy of Christians; and adverse to the conversion of the world, to Jesus Christ."* The above may suffice to show that Mr. Campbell was not writing a creed, and that his effort in this work, is directed against all *human* creeds and disciplines, whether their principles are *true or false;* and his great object in this vol. is to call the minds of the people back to the BIBLE ALONE.

But 2nd.—Has it ever been *adopted* by us as our creed or discipline? I most positively deny that it ever has; and I now challenge any one who holds the affirmative of the above, to produce the evidence, in a tangible form, that we may examine it.

In the 3rd, and last place, we inquire, is the Book called the "Christian System," ever appealed to, and used as authority in the church, in cases of Discipline? I answer never; we always make our appeal to the *word of God.* The Law of Christ, made known to us by the holy Apostles of the Lamb, we regard as a "perfect law of liberty," and is able to make the man of God perfect, and thoroughly furnish him to every good work. EDITOR.

HOW TO MAKE A GOOD PREACHER.

EVERY church, it is presumed; must be desirous of having a good minister, yet every one may not in their own apprehension be favored with such a blessing. Many churches often feel that their minister is not quite what they desire him to be—not quite the man for the place which he is in. Their eyes are, therefore turned away from the minister whose labors they enjoy, to some other man—or to their *beau ideal* of a minister, and they desire a change. For the benefit of such we would relate the following circumstances, which we are told are substantially matters of fact.

A young man was settled in a large and popular congregation in New England, under Very flattering circumstances. The church and people had settled him, with the belief that he was a young man of more than ordinary talents, and with the expectation of his becoming a distinguished man. After a year or two, when the novelty of the thing had worn off, the current seemed to change, and the feeling prevailed that. Mr. B____ was not; nor likely to be quite what they expected. He did not grow as they thought he would; he did not perform that amount of labor which was heeded to build up the church, and interest the congregation. Things dragged heavily. The young man felt the influence of the chill atmosphere Which thus surrounded him. His spirits sunk, his health run down, and it was whispered around in the society, and in the neighboring towns, that Mr. B—— would probably have to leave—he was not the man for the place. He was not the man of talents which they had anticipated.

While things were in this state, at a meeting of the church; when the pastor was absent, (perhaps one called to see what should be done,) Mr. O_____, an intelligent and influential member, arose and said—

"Brethren, I think we have been in fault respecting our minister. I think he is a young man of superior talents, and will one day be a distinguished man. But we have not sustained and encouraged him as we should. We have not spoken of him to others with esteem and confidence, as we should. We have been standing and looking on, expecting him to raise both himself and us to eminence. Now let us adopt a different course. Let us encourage our minister with our prayers, our sympathies, and efforts. Let us speak of him with esteem and. confidence to others, and say that we think him a man of talent, and who bids fair to be a distinguished man."

The thing was agreed upon. The leading men sat the example.— Very soon every one was speaking in the favor of Mr. B_____. His people visited him, sympathized with him, encouraged him; and people out of the society soon began to remark how Mr. B_____was rising in the estimation of his people. The young man felt the change. The cold damp chill with which he was surrounded, and which was benumbing the energies of his soul, was changed by the influence of such kindly beam, and a warm genial atmosphere came over him. His spirits rose; his health returned; his energies awoke, and he soon showed to all that he had within him the elements of a man. Several revivals have attended his labors. In the affections of the church and people he has long since firmly established himself. They delight in him as a man of talent, as well as a good man. His name has become honorably enrolled among the American authors, and he is one whom his own church and the churches of New England delight to honor. Reader, Christian, would you have a good minister? Go thou and do likewise.

Biblical Recorder.

FROM THE CHRISTIAN MESSENGER.

"Bros. Wm. Gillian, and M. W. Happy are now holding a meeting at Bethel, Morgan county, May 9, 1843. Thirteen have been immersed, and took upon them the name of Jesus. The Meeting is still progressing.

"During the months of March and April, a protracted Meeting was held in Jacksonville, which resulted in 53 additions to the congregation.

"Bros. Wm. M. Brown and J. T. Jones held a meeting in Winchester in January last, which resulted in about 143 additions."

"Bro. James Conover of Jersey Prairie, has immersed about 15 lately in his neighborhood. The work there is still going on. Praised be the name of the Lord!"

"Bro. Wm. M. Brown writes, Pittsfield, May 5th, "This is to inform you of my good health, and fine spirits, and that I am still raising my voice in the cause of humanity—the Christianity of the Bible. We had 74 additions at Perry—40 at Chambersburg, and upwards of 50 to the congregation, in this place."

We learn from the same source, that our beloved brethren J. T. Johnson and John Smith, of Ky., are doing a good work in St. Louis, had obtained 28 additions.

J. M. MATHES.

D. H. STEPHENS ON BAPTISM.

The following from D. H. STEPHENS, a Minister of the Methodist Protestant Church, we commend to the attention of our Methodist friends generally:—ED.

PLEASANT RIDGE, Indiana, July 30th, 1843.

Mr. Editor: Is it not a notorious fact that the Ministry of the Methodist Episcopal Church take strong exceptions to the stress laid on *Water Baptism,* by those whom they denominate "Campbellites." To hear them harp, as they frequently do at their public meetings, on this subject, we would not be likely to think they did in reality hold the doctrine exhibited in the following extracts, from doctrinal tracts, published by order of the General Conference of the Methodist Episcopal Church. New York, 1825.

Tract 12th, page 4th—"What are the benefits we receive by baptism? The first of these is the washing away the guilt of original sin."— "By baptism we enter into covenant favor with God, that ever lasting covenant, which he hath commanded forever. And as circumcision was the way of entering into this covenant, so baptism is now."—"By baptism we are admitted into the church, and consequently made members of Christ, its head;" page 5.

Again, same page, he teaches that by baptism we "are mystically *united* to Christ, and made *one* with him. From which spiritual, vital union with him, proceeds the influence of his grace on those that are baptized."—"By baptism we, who were "by nature children of wrath," are made the children of God. And this *regeneration* which our church, in so many places ascribes to baptism is no more than barely being admitted into the church, though commonly connected therewith "being grafted into the body of Christ's Church, we are made the children of God by adoption and Grace." By water baptism then as a mean, the water of baptism, we are *regenerated* or *born again.* In consequence of our being made children of God, we are heirs of the Kingdom of heaven. —Supposing this, as it admits us into the church here, so into Glory hereafter;" page 6.

Again, on page 7, he lays down the ground of infant baptism: "As to the ground of it: if infants are guilty of original sin, then they are proper subjects for baptism: seeing in the ordinary way they cannot be saved unless this be washed away by baptism. It has been already proved that this original stain cleaves to every child of man, and that hereby they are children of wrath, and liable to *eternal damnation.*"—"This, therefore, is our first ground infants need to be washed from original sin: therefore they are proper subjects of baptism."

These extracts, although written by John Wesley, a member of the church of England, are the doctrines of the Methodist *Episcopal* Church, from the fact that this church has endorsed them. By order of the General Conference they were first published in the discipline, and then in a standard work. *Query.*—Are not many of the Ministers and members of the M. E. Church liable to be arraigned and *expelled* for disseminating doctrine contrary to the doctrine of the church? See discipline, chap. 2, sec. 7, item 3rd, page 89. D. H. STEPHENS.

Notes on a Tour to Vincennes and Washington.

On the 10th of July ult., I left home, for the purpose of visiting Vincennes and Washington. On my way I spent one night in Bruceville, which is a very pleasant village in Knox county. Here I partook of the hospitalities of Eld. Wm. Bruce. I had the pleasure of being introduced to his *twenty-fifth* child, who is a very fine-looking lad of about 12 years! There is a very interesting congregation of Disciples, who have received many accessions the present year, through the labors of our excellent brethren B. W. Fields and J. E. Noyes. While at Bruceville, I heard of the success of brethren Fields and Noyes at Carlisle, Sullivan county. They commenced the meeting on Friday before the 3rd Lord's day in July, and continued it until sometime the week following. A powerful impression was made on the community, and 23 were added to the church.

We got to Vincennes in time to deliver a discourse at 11 o'clock; A. M., on Sunday. the 23 rd. In Vincennes the "Roman Catholic" influence is superior to any other. They compose, I suppose, about one half of the *professing* part of the inhabitants— and I was much surprised to learn that many Protestants send their children to those institutions of learning in the city, which are wholly under the control of Catholics, and the result is, as might be expected, in many instances, while they are learning the rudiments of a classical education, they learn also the elementary, principles of Catholicism, are *christened* by the Priest, and come out Catholics!

Here I found a very interesting company of Disciples, in a healthy condition, numbering 65 or 70. They have an excellent Teacher, bro. J. H. Harrison, who is a bold and zealous advocate of the truth. Out audience at first was small, but it increased to the very last; was solemn and attentive throughout. A great deal of prejudice, I think, was broken down, and a good impression made on the whole community.

The meeting continued until Friday, the 23th, during which, 23 per- sons were added to the congregation, 17 of them by immersion. Bro. Noyes was with me all the time; brethren Fields and Goodwin a part of the time. While here I became acquainted with a great number of brethren from the different neighborhoods around. Never, while my mind retains its energy, shall I forget the Disciples at Vincennes and vicinity, and the happy days we spent together during my visit. The prospect for the success of the gospel, is good in this region.

From this point, accompanied by brother J. E. Noyes, I rode to Washington, in Daviess county; bro. Fields had gone before, and bro. E. Goodwin remained in Vincennes to hold forth again, and on the next day, he joined us at Washington. Here too, we were joined by our excellent bro. M. R. Trimble. Here we found considerable excitement prevailing in the community, on the account of an expected discussion, which was to have commenced on the 28th, between Mr. Williamson Terrell of the Methodist Episcopal church, and brother Elijah Goodwin. Mr. T. had not come on, but was conducting a very spirited correspondence with the brethren at Washington, on the subject. He seems to be laboring under the impression, that he is not bound to affirm in debate, his own doctrine and practice; but that we are bound to prove a *negative!* The brethren informed me that a short time before Mr. T. came to Washington, and preached a discourse, in which he strongly inveighed against us, under the opprobrious name, "*Campbellites.*" In this discourse, Mr. Terrill charged us with having a human creed or confession of faith, &c. &c. &c also attempted to sustain, as I understood, the Methodistic doctrine of "*Faith alone,*" and "infant Sprinkling," from the sacred record! The next morning bro. J. E. Noyes and others, having heard said discourse, addressed Mr. Terrell a line, calling upon him to sustain his allegations against us, and some points of his doctrines and practices, in a public discussion, with someone of the brethren whom they would select. To this, Mr. Terrell was understood to consent. Bro. E. Goodwin of Mt. Vernon, was then written to by the brethren, who consented to meet Mr. T. on those points, in Washington, on the 26th. Eld. Miller, however, had visited Washington, and Mr. T. continued to correspond with the brethren—the object of both seemed to be, as I learned, to change the issues. Neither Elder M. nor Mr. T. can see that they are bound to affirm what they preach and practice, and their allegations against us! O no! They seem to think, that we are bound to prove that their doctrine and practice are *not* taught in the Bible, and that we are *not* guilty as charged by them in their pulpit harangues.

We believe and teach, that immersion is the Apostolic mode or action of Christian Baptism; and that penitent believers are scriptural subjects of that holy ordinances Our Methodist friends admit all we ask for, on those points; but they go farther, and believe and teach that *Pouring and Sprinkling, are equally* scriptural forms of baptism; and that infants are also scriptural subjects of the ordinance.—Who does not see, that the burden of proof rests upon them? They are bound by alt that is fair and honorable in controversy, to shoulder the responsibility, and appear in defense of their system and practice. Whether there will be a debate between Mr. T. and bro. G. or not, I am not prepared to say definitely, but I *think* that Mr. T. will never muster courage enough to meet bro. Goodwin, or any other man of equal talent, and affirm before the public, what I am informed he did in the sermon above alluded to. My friend Mr. Terrill, will not be offended with me for *thinking:* we are *personal* friends, and I esteem him an excellent man, *but think* him in error. His friends are my friends, and his brother Harrison is a beloved brother, and Teacher in the Church of Christ at Columbus, Indiana.

We had indeed a precious time at Washington—the congregation was large, solemn and attentive, and I think much good seed were sown. While I remained at the meeting some 20 persons were added to the church. I left the meeting on Tuesday, the 1st day of August, to return home. I left the other brethren on the ground, to continue the meeting, which I have not since heard from; but the prospect was very good for many accessions.

The church at Washington numbers some 200, I think—are in a very prosperous condition, and are exerting a good influence upon the whole surrounding country. This church is the "pillar and support of the truth," and is successfully "holding forth the word of life," through her gifted members, Fields and Noyes.

From Washington, in company with bro. A. Asbell, I rode to Edwardsport, in Knox county, where 1 met a good audience at candle-lighting, on the 1st August inst. I spoke to them also the next day, at 10 A. M., and then left for home. In this village, a glorious work has been effected, through the instrumentality of brethren Fields and Noyes. Within one year past, they have built up a flourishing congregation here. I found the Disciples here, warm-hearted and very zealous. They enjoy many advantages, and if they will only *live out their profession,* nothing can stop the onward march of truth in Edwardsport and vicinity. May the Lord enable them to "fight the good fight of Faith," that they may at last "lay hold on eternal life." I was truly sorry that my stay among these brethren was so very short; but other pressing engagements compelled me to return home.

I returned to the bosom of my family, on Thursday, the 3rd August inst., and found all well. Thanks to the Lord for his blessing! During my tour, I had the pleasure of seeing 43 persons added to the different congregations, where we labored. Praise the Lord.

EDITOR.

FOR THE CHRISTIAN RECORD.

CHRISTIAN OBLIGATIONS—NO. 2.

ACCORDING to a promise made in the previous No. we are to continue the contrast between the two institutions, in order to show the extent, of Christian obligation under the New; and to do this, we only have make use of the words of the Apostle Paul: "But if the ministration of death, written *and* engraven in stones, was glorious, so that the children of Israel could not steadfastly behold the face of Moses for the glory of his countenance; which glory was to be done away: how shall not the ministration of the Spirit be rather glorious? For if the ministration of condemnation *be* glory, much more doth the ministration of righteousness exceed in glory. For even that which was made glorious, had no glory in this respect, by reason of the glory that excelleth." 2 Cor. 3: 7, 10. These words of the Apostle need no comment, for they teach us plainly that the old institution has no glory, when brought in comparison with the New. This may be illustrated by the faint twinkling of a star, which loses all its glory in the bright beams of noonday; and even the faint light, which it emits through the darkness of night, is all borrowed from the Sun. So it was with those *moral* stars, which appeared in the firmament of the old world, sending forth their sparkling rays from the pens of inspired Prophets; they all borrowed their light from the sun of righteousness—for the Prophets, of this salvation "have inquired and searched diligently, who prophesied of the grace that should come unto you; searching what, or what manner of time the Spirit of Christ, which was in them, did signify, when it testified beforehand the sufferings of Christ, and the glory that should follow. Unto whom it was revealed, that not unto themselves, but unto us they did minister the things which are now reported onto you by them that have preached the Gospel unto you, with the Holy Ghost sent down from heaven; which things the angels desire to look into"—1 Pe. 1: 10, 12.

We might introduce many other passages to show the superiority of the Gospel: in fact, we could hardly go amiss for proof to this point; we shall, however, let a few suffice for the present. The New dispensation is just as much superior to the Old, "as is the man who builds *a* house greater than *the* house." "Moses was a servant in another's house:" but "Christ is Lord over his own house." The Old Institution was dedicated by the blood of animals—the New by the blood of the Lord Jesus Christ, The law was a "shadow of good things to come"—Christ is the substance.

Time would fail me to speak of the tenth part of the arguments and comparisons which the Savior, and his Apostles have made use of, to show the transcendent and unspeakable glory of this spiritual house, which is composed of the Disciples of the Lord Jesus Christ, "a holy priesthood, to offer up spiritual sacrifices, acceptable to God, by Jesus Christ." Again the

Apostle Peter says; "But ye *are* a chosen generation, a royal priesthood, a holy nation, a peculiar people; that ye should show forth the praise of him who hath called you out of darkness into his marvelous light."

My dear brethren, who may read this article, ask yourselves this important question: for what purpose am I a disciple of the Lord? The answer is ready: to "show forth the praise of him who hath called you out of darkness into his marvelous light." Did you heed the call of mercy with reference to the object the Lord had in view when he suffered, bled and died upon the Roman Cross? Remember the "Church is the pillar and ground of the truth," and God is to be glorified "in the Church by Christ Jesus throughout all ages, world without end. Amen." Eph. 3:21.

The Savior says to his Disciples: "Ye are the light of the world." "A city set on a hill cannot be hid." Again: "If thine eye be single, thy whole body shall be full of light; but if thine eye be evil, thy whole body shall be full of darkness." "If, therefore, the light that is in thee be darkness, how great is that darkness?" There is no neutral ground in this matter. Our influence is either in favor of the truth, or against it. "He that gathereth not with me," saith the Savior, "scattereth abroad."

This last quotation from the language of the Savior, is a fact of fearful import, to the lukewarm professor. Is it possible that any Disciple who reads the "Christian Record," exerts an influence against the truth! Let us see what were the feelings and views of the Apostle Paul, in regard to such, ("for many walk, of whom I have told you often, and now tell you even weeping, *that they are the* enemies of the cross of Christ: whose end *is* destruction, whose God is their appetite, and *whose* glory *is* in their shame, who mind earthly things.") Phil. 3: 18,19. Yes, if anything could make the Apostle weep, it was to see an individual dishonor that cause, for which he "suffered the loss of all things."

I do not consider it necessary to undertake to show the weakness of excuses, in themselves considered, apart from the interest we have in doing our duty; for everyone who feels no interest in going to meeting, on the first day of the week, will find some excuse to stay at home, or go on a visit, to keep away from the house of God. There must be a reason for all this, There can be but two reasons why individuals are absent from the house of God on the first day of the week. It is because they cannot or will not go. If they cannot go, the excuse is a good one. If they will not go, there must be a reason or *excuse.* I am inclined to think the reason is not so much from a willful disposition to violate the Law of God, as from a want of feeling interested in doing his commandments. The inquiry of their minds is expressed in the language of *Job's Comforters,* as they are called— "Who is the Almighty, that we should serve him, or what profit shall we have if we pray unto him?" They do not feel that they will be benefited by meeting with the Lord's people, at the Lord's house, on the Lord's day, where the Lord himself has promised to be; because if we had a proper view, *by faith,* "of the things which the Lord hath prepared for them that love him," we would be even more ingenuous, in removing every difficulty out of the way, than we now are in making excuses that will do us no good in the day of judgment.

The Savior says, "do good and lend, expecting to receive nothing," for "sinners will lend to sinners, to receive as much again." Again: "Then said he also to him that bade him: when thou makest a dinner or a supper, call not thy friends, nor thy brethren, neither thy kinsmen, nor thy rich neighbors; lest they also bid thee again, and a recompense be made thee: but when thou makest a feast, call the poor, the maimed, the lame, the blind; and thou shall be blessed; for they cannot recompense thee; for thou shalt be recompensed at the resurrection of the just" Luke 14: 12, 14. This last quotation shows us that the reward of the Christian is not in this life, as some assert.

In our next we will speak of the motive of the Christian in doing good, and the time and place of his reward.

T. J. EDMONDSON.

FICTITIOUS NAMES.

WE have serious objections to publishing any article, over a *fictitious* name; and we never will, without having in our possession the real name of the writer; and not *then*, if there should be anything *personal* in the communication. We have consented to publish the Essays of "Tychicus," on Justification: and for the information of all, we say, that "Tychicus" is a beloved brother: his name is in our possession, and whenever it becomes necessary, it shall be forthcoming.

EDITOR.

JUSTIFICATION—NO. 1.

I WISH, through the "Christian Record," to direct the attention of its readers to the subject of Justification; not because I am vain enough to think myself more capable to write upon the subject than many of my brethren, even of those who are my juniors in the Kingdom of Christ. But believing it to be the duty of all who can edify with the pen, upon any subject connected with man's salvation, to do so; I venture for the first time, to attempt a few essays upon the above named subject; and in order that I may be understood, I shall give the meaning of the term as used in the Bible, and especially in the New Testament.

First,—It means to acknowledge a thing, or person, to be just; Math. 11: 19; Luke 7: 35. "Wisdom is justified of all her children."

Secondly.—To clear from imputed guilt, to free from sin by remission or forgiveness; to absolve and acquit a sinner from the guilt and punishment of sin; Luke 18: 14, "I tell you, (said Jesus,) this man went down to his house justified *rather* than the other;" (the Pharisee and Publican;) Acts 13: 38, 39. "Be it known unto you therefore men and brethren, that through this man is preached unto you the forgiveness of sins: and by him all that believe are justified from all things from which they could not be justified by the law of Moses;" 1 Cor. 6: 11: "And such were some of you: (characters named in verse 10;) but ye are washed, but ye are sanctified, but ye are justified in the name of the Lord Jesus, and by the spirit of our God." That is, they had received forgiveness of sins; their sins had been blotted out, or remitted, and they made free from the guilt and punishment of sin.

Thirdly.—To defend and maintain one in a course of righteous conduct, 1 Kings, 8: 32; 2 Chron. 6: 23, "Then hear-thou in heaven, and do, and judge thy servants, condemning the wicked, to bring his way upon his head; and justifying the righteous, to give him according to his righteousness."

To sum the whole up in a few words, Justification means, in the New Testament, acceptation, deliverance, by forgiveness, or remission of sins, from the guilt and punishment of sin, when applied to that great change which is effected in man, when he is translated out of the kingdom of darkness, into the Kingdom of God's dear Son: so that when a person is said to be justified, (in this sense,) he is also said be forgiven, his sins blotted out, saved from his sins—has obtained remission of sins, and made free from sin, and condemnation, and has *"peace* with God through our Lord Jesus Christ."

Having, now given what we understand to be the meaning of the term Justification, as used in reference to that change which is produced in a sinner, to make him a child of God; we shall next inquire how do the scriptures, in the New Testament, teach that this is done?

There are three different views taken of this subject.

First.—That we are justified by works.

Secondly.—That we are justified by faith *only;* and

Thirdly.—That we are justified by faith and obedience.

Having thus slated the different views entertained, in relation to the manner in which we are justified, we shall take leave of the reader for the present, after requesting him to "search the scriptures" to see which of the three views is the true scriptural one; for only one of them can be right.

TYCHICUS.

TO OUR PATRONS.

WE owe you an apology for the delay of this No. We were disappointed, by the man who was to have done the printing, failing to come on. We have therefore, had to wait until we could get another workman. We hope our friends will not charge us with neglect. The first Monday in every month is our publication day, and we intend to be punctual, as we are fully aware, that punctuality is a virtue, without which, no paper can long continue in favor with its readers.

We have sent the "Record," to many who had not ordered it. Now, we say to such, examine it, and show it to your friends, and send us their names, if they are willing to become subscribers; but if you are not pleased with it, and your friends are not, why then just return it to us, without injury.

Postmasters, if requested to do so, will remit money to an Editor, or send subscribers' names. Please think of this.

We return our thanks to our brethren and friends, for their exertions in sustaining the "Christian Record." It is now doing a pretty fair business. Our subscription list has continued to increase rapidly, ever since the publication of our first No. We therefore "Thank God and lake courage."

We ask our friends to make *another effort;* each subscriber get another and the Christian Record will be out of all danger.

EDITOR.

THE "CHRISTIAN TEACHER."

There are two periodicals of the above title: one of them is edited by our excellent brother Aylett Raines of Paris, Ky. Brother Raines, when a Boy, was a Preacher of Universalism, and was one of the most influential preaches they had in the west. But when he became a Man, and had "learned the way of the Lord more perfectly," he renounced Universalism, and embraced the truth as it is in Jesus: and is now one of the most talented, and zealous advocates of the cause of Christ, in Ky. Brother Raines' "Christian Teacher" is a very spirited little work; is a monthly of 16 pages each number, and is neatly stitched and covered, with colored paper—its form is convenient for binding. The price is 50 cents per annum, *in advance*. We have already received the Nov. & Dec. (11 & 12th,) Nos. for the current year, ('43.)

The other "Christian Teacher" is edited and published by Mr. Erasmus Manford of Terre-Haute, Indiana. Mr. Manford is a zealous proclaimer of *modern Universalism;* he has tendered himself somewhat conspicuous, by his numerous debates. I am informed that he has had a debate, every *full and change* of the moon, for some months past; but I think Mr. Manford will soon find; that *all will be saved,* no matter what they *believe* or *do;* it is not worthwhile to labor so hard, to effect that, which, when effected, will benefit no one in eternity! If Uncle Jonathan Kidwell is to be believed, Mr. Manford is yet a "*Boy*," and may we not be allowed to expect, that he too, like brother Raines, when he shall have become a Man, will "put away childish things." We shall see. I suggest to these "Teachers" that they exchange. What say you to it brethren?

EDITOR.

OBITUARY.

Indianapolis, July 24th, 1843.

Dear bro. Mathes:—

I have to report to you *the death of my Father*. After, a painful illness of four months, he died, a Christian, on the evening of the 27th of June. He had been an Elder in the congregation at Liberty, Jefferson county, Ind., for 12 years, and his family, with the church, of which they are all members, have sustained an irreparable loss.

The Lord be with you.

L. H. JAMESON.

For the "Christian Record."
Veil of Peace, near Spencer, Ia.,
Aug. 11, 1843.

Rev. A. Wylie, President of Indiana University:

Dear Sir: I take the liberty to request of you an answer to the following question:

Where a word in any language has different meanings, does not the meaning change *only* when the word is applied to a different thing? Or does not the same word universally have the same meaning when applied to the same thing?

Respectfully your friend,

T. C. JOHNSON.

To answer this question so as to prevent a misunderstanding, would require a dissertation of considerable length. An answer in the affirmative would give the substantial truth: and such is the answer which I readily give. Yours &c., A. WYLIE.

APPOINTMENTS,

At Vincennes, Knox county, Ind., commencing on Friday, 4 o'clock, P. M., before the 5th Lord's day in Oct., and to continue till over Lord's day.

At Bloomington, commencing on Friday, 4 o'clock, P. M., before the 1st Lord's day in November, and to continue till over Lord's day.

At Washington, Daviess county, Ind., commencing on Friday night before the 2nd Lord's day in November, and to continue several days.

Brother Elijah Goodwin of Mt. Vernon, Ind.; bro. J. E. Noyes, and myself, expect, the Lord willing, to attend the above appointments, and we expect that Elder B. W. Fields, and perhaps others, will attend the appointments at Vincennes and Washington.

A protracted meeting will commence at Gosport, Owen county, Ind., on Friday night before the first Lord's day in Oct. Brethren Blankenship, Snoddy, Johnson, and perhaps Swinford and others, and myself expect to be in attendance. EDITOR.

EXPENSE OF CHRISTENING.

The public charge for christening the Prince of Wales was £2,500, considerably more than $10,000. Sir Robert Peel was obliged to vindicate it in Parliament against the well-deserved censures of Joseph Hume. He said that the expense was really much greater, but that Queen Victoria had paid all but this *small sum* out of her own pocket!

Banner.

PROSPECTUS OF THE CHRISTIAN RECORD.

THE CHRISTIAN RECORD is published monthly, at Bloomington., Indiana, Edited and Published by J. M. MATHES, and contains 24 octavo pages, neatly stitched and covered.

TERMS.—One dollar in advance, or on the reception of the first number. Any one obtaining five subscribers and remitting the money to us free of cost, shall have the 6th copy gratis.

All letters to be addressed, *post paid,* or *free,* to "J. M. Mathes, Bloomington, Indiana "

☞*How to make remittances.*—Postmasters are authorized by law to frank letters, addressed to Editors, containing money, if written by themselves.—Don't forget this.

☞POSTAGE on this work is 1½ cents, under 100 miles, and over 100 miles 2½, as the work contains but one sheet per number. EDITOR.

ILLUSTRATIVE ANECDOTES.

A Universalist preacher once visited a village, the citizens of which were not accustomed to hearing his kind of doctrine; and, after delivering a discourse, the object of which was to prove, that all men would be saved irrespective to the kind of life they led in the present world, he proposed to visit the place again *provided* the citizens requested it. He then paused, and waited for an invitation. No one inviting him, be repeated in louder tone, I can preach here again if the citizens desire it. No one responding, at length an aged, venerable German rose to his feet, and made the following pointed and appropriate remark:

"Vel, if dis doctrine vot you breach is drue, den we haf no use for it, for we will all be saved mit out it: but if it is a lie! den we dont vont it.—Blief we'll not have any more breaching of dis kind in dis place!! *Xenia (Ohio) Reformer.*

DISAPPEARING OF FIXED STARS.

More than thirteen stars, it is said, have disappeared within the last two centuries. One of those presented such a brilliant appearance for about sixteen months as to be visible to the naked eye at mid-day. La Place supposed it was burning up, as it has never been seen since.

ERRATA.—34th page, 2nd line from bottom, reads "baptism is 'no, more than," &c.—omit 'no.'

THE CHRISTIAN RECORD.

VOL. I.] BLOOMINGTON, IND., SEPTEMBER, 1843. [NO. III.

CHRISTIAN UNION—NO. 3.

WE NOW inquire *is Christian Union practicable? We* answer it is. Christianity is the same now that it ever was, and under its divine influence, the disciples of Christ were united, during the first age of the church. The divine Savior prayed for Christian union; and who will say that he prayed for an impossibility! No, he was always heard when he prayed, for he says himself, "I know that thou always hearest me." The intercessory prayer of Jesus, recorded John 17 chap., contains three distinct petitions: In the first petition, he embraces himself: "Father glorify thou me with thy own self, with the glory which I had with thee before the world was." We ask, was his petition answered? all admit that it was. For when Jesus had risen from the dead, and "become the first fruits of them that slept," he ascended to his Father, and was crowned *Lord of all* in the presence of all the hierarchies of heaven.

The second petition embraces the Apostles, who were to be his witnesses to all nations; these- were *the men* whom the Father had *given him.* He prayed "that they might be kept from the evil that was in the world," and also "that they might *be one*" All agree that Jesus was heard in this petition also; for none of the chosen witnesses fell into sin, except Judas, who is expressly mentioned in the prayer as *lost;* and that the Apostles were *one,* in the sense of the prayer, we suppose he one will deny—they all agreed in giving their testimony, to the great facts of Christianity. In the third petition, he prayed for "all them also who shall believe on me through their (the Apostles') word; that they all may be one, as thou father art in me, and I in thee, that they may be one in us, that the world may believe that thou hast sent me." Now as Jesus was heard in the first two petitions of this prayer, we agree be must be heard in the third also, which embraces all who believe on him through the testimony of his Apostles; and their complete union in him. We therefore conclude that union is *practicable.*

But further; the Apostle Paul exhorts the Corinthian church in the following language: "Now I beseech you, brethren, by the name of our Lord Jesus Christ, that ye all speak the same thing, and that there be no divisions among you; but that ye be perfectly joined together in the same mind, and in the same judgment," 1 Cor. 1: 10. Again, the same Apostle says, "Fulfill ye my joy, that ye be like-minded, having the same love, being of one accord, of one mind," Phil. 2: 2. Christian union is surely practicable, or the inspired Apostle would not have acted so inconsistently, as to have exhorted the Christians of his day to be united, if indeed the thing is impossible!

But perhaps the objector will say, "Christian Union was practicable in the days of the Apostles; as the Christians were not then divided into sects and parties; their preachers were few, all belonged to the same church, preached the same doctrine, and observed the same religious rites, wore the same name, and had no rival Creeds, or Confessions of Faith, to sustain; but they labored together in perfect harmony, for the edification of the church, and the salvation of the world; it is nothing but what might have been expected, says the objector, that under such influences, and with such examples before them; the Christians then, should "all speak the same thing, and have no divisions among them." But says the objector, the case is very different *now;* the professed disciples of Christ are now divided off, into contending sects and parties, each having a name of its own choice, and a particular set of opinions, or *doctrines:* which are generally embodied in a Creed, or Confession of faith; and each party has its own preachers, who are licensed to preach *only according to the doctrines of the party :* thus the preachers of the different parties, are champions of rival *doctrines,* whose livings sometimes depend upon their success, in sustaining them against all *opposing doctrines:* this opens the door for corruption and hypocrisy; and the preachers become enemies to each other; they oppose, back-bite, misrepresent and abuse each other before their respective flocks—the glories of their own name and creed, are held up to admiration, and their superiority over every rival creed and name, is extolled to the skies: while all who dare to differ from them, are condemned as heretics, and their names cast out as evil. With such examples before them, and under such influences as these, the present state of things in the religious world, is just what might be expected. I therefore think, says the objector, that union now, under all the circumstances is impracticable. To which we answer, the objector slates the truth, both as to the *ancient,* and *modern* state of things; but we think his conclusion is incorrect. The objector admits that the prayer of Jesus was answered in the primitive disciples. Their preachers had but one doctrine to preach, *"Jesus and the resurrection,"* and they were faithful to their high vocations. The burthen of their message to a dying world was "Jesus and him crucified." All who believed on Jesus through their word, were one also, for they had the *one faith,* this led them to the one *practice,* so that they were of one *heart* and of *one soul,* all spoke the *same things* and *minded the same things;* for they spake only what the holy spirit taught them, and minded only what the Lord commanded them, through his inspired Apostles.

Well, as we have the word of the Apostles, faithfully recorded in the New Testament, through which we are to believe on Jesus Christ; and as Christianity is the same *now* that it was *then,* we agree that Christian union is practicable; because we have only to believe on Jesus through the word of his Apostles, according to his prayer, and then "obey from the heart the form of doctrine, delivered to us," by the holy Apostles, and we are made *one in Christ,* we shall continue *one.* But, says the objector, this argument seems to contemplate a *complete surrender* of all our party names, Creeds, Confessions of Faith, Books of discipline, and whatever else distinguishes us from each other as churches'. Yes, it contemplates nothing less than this; and we now ask, who that loves the Lord, and desires to see sinners converted, and the joy of the saints made complete, in the gathering together of the Lambs of the fold of Christ, who have been scattered abroad, on the dry fields of speculation, during a "dark and cloudy day," in which, "darkness covered the earth, and gross darkness the minds of the people," would be unwilling to make the sacrifice?

But, says the objector, our Creed is just like the Bible, for our divines took it out of the Bible; and I see no use in giving it up! and so say all the rest!!—yet, we know they cannot all be just like the Bible, for if they were, they would all be just like each other; for the plainest reason in the world, things that are *just like the same thing,* are *just like each other.* The very fact then, that the Creeds all differ from one another, proves that they are not like the Bible; or at least that there can be but one of them like it! and who shall decide which one that is! Each party we suppose, would decide in favor of its own, and of course against all the rest! But suppose we admit for a single moment, one of the greatest absurdities in the world; that is, that all the Creeds in Christendom, are just like the Bible, and that a class of men called Divines, have taken them out of the Bible—we would then ask, who has required this at their hands? have they improved upon the diction of the spirit? If not, what have they gained by it? In the language of the old Quaker, we would say to all who say that they took their Creeds out of the Bible, "Friend if thou hast taken thy creed out of the Bible, just put it back, and 'let him that stole, steal no more,' " But perhaps the objector will say "the word of God *alone* is not sufficient to govern the church; you cannot exclude disorderly members, and keep heresy out of the church without a human creed superadded."

To which we answer, if, as all affirm that creed was taken by the Divines out of the Bible, and is just like it, how does it come to pass, that the creed possesses a power to keep heresy out of the church, and exclude disorderly members, which the word of God *alone* does not!! Who does not see, that whatever power or authority for any purpose, the Creed contains, which cannot be found in equal terms, in the Bible alone, is a *usurpation* of the prerogative of the Lord Jesus Christ, whose right it is, *alone,* to reign over his Kingdom! and if the argument has any truth in it, it proves that the creed is wrong, and ought to be "given to the moles and to the bats."

In our next, we shall consider more fully, the ground upon which all Christians may be united, and some of the things which now stand in the way.

EDITOR.

UNIVERSALISM—NO. 3.

In our second number we assert, "that universalism, in effect, denies the doctrine of forgiveness of sins." This charge at first view, may seem rather uncharitable; but that I have not misrepresented the matter, I think all will agree, who read carefully, the following quotations. In our first number we said that Universalism *made God the author of Sin;* the quotations which we are about to make, fully sustain both my charges against the system. We shall first introduce Mr. George Rogers, who is one of the most ingenuous writers, and who is every way competent to testify on this subject. Mr. Rogers, will you be kind enough to tell the company whether Universalism does represent God as being the author of sin? ROGERS—exclaims the arminian objector, "the author really seems bent on proving, that as Jehovah foreknew of the existence of sin, he must also have designed it!" Yes, such is really my purpose, and this I mean to do upon your own admitted principles," ("Pro and Con of Universalism," page 286.)

Mr. Rogers, will you please be a little more definite; I am satisfied myself, but I fear all the company are not. ROGERS.—"Having then, as I think, established the conclusion that absolute foreknowledge implies absolute foreordination, I proceed to notice the objections, which seem to be against it. I have already considered the most formidable of these, viz: that it makes God the author of sin; and I now ask how, on any ground, is this to be avoided? I assert, moreover, that it is plainly scriptural!" ("Pro and Con of Universalism," page 287.)

I suppose no one will dispute the credibility of this witness; if not, it follows with the clearness of demonstration, that Universalism is obnoxious to my charges. But I would like to know, *if God is the author of Sin,* as Universalism declares, how sins can be *forgiven,* and *who by.*

According to the system, if God pardon sin, he pardons himself! What profound nonsense! Why according to the system, when we ask God to forgive us our trespasses, we *virtually and in fact,* ask God to pardon his own sins, which he has committed through us as mere mechanics!! Who can believe it?

But we will now introduce another witness; who is worthy of being heard by all; his name is "Hosea Ballou;" he is the great Apostle of modern Universalism. Mr. Ballou, will you please state what you know about Universalists denying the existence of sin, and making God the author of what we *call* sin? BALLOU—"But perhaps the objector will say, this denies the *liberty* of the *will,* and makes God the *author of Sin.* To which I reply, desiring the reader to recollect what we have said of sin, in showing its nature; by which it is discovered, that God may be the innocent and holy cause of that, which, in a limited sense, is sin; but as it respects the meaning of God, it is intended for good." ("Treatise on the Atonement," page 36.)

Then according to the testimony of Mr. Ballou, that which we call *Sin,* is designed for good in the general plan; and consequently, just as necessary, for the glory of God, and the happiness of man, as what we call *virtue!* Therefore, *sin* is no more *sin,* for God is the *"innocent and holy cause of it!"* Now it does appear to me, that any one, not hood-winked by a pure-blind theology, must see at once, that if these witnesses have told the truth, and who will impeach their veracity? It is impossible for God to forgive sins; for the plainest reason in the world; if the system be true, there is *really* no sin to forgive!! Reader, are you astonished at this? just be patient, and we will show you still more *astounding facts,* in the system of modern-Universalism, that you may marvel!

But let us for a moment, look into the New Testament. and see if there is any thing like forgiveness there. Yes, thank God, here it is: "Thus it is written and, thus it behooved Christ to suffer. and to rise from the dead the third day, and that repentance and remission of sins, should be preached in his name among all nations, beginning at Jerusalem." (Luke 24: 46.) There the Lord commissioned his Apostles to preach "Repentance and Remission of sins," not only in Jerusalem, the *beginning point,* but also among all nations:—But did the Apostles so understand the Master? We answer they did —turn to Acts 2: 37, 38; and we hear the inquiry made, by the sin-convicted multitude, "Men and brethren what shall we do?" Do?—Why do nothing at all, says Universalism; you are *sure* of heaven; *for all will be saved!*— Besides you *can* do nothing; you are not *free,* or *moral agents,* and of course you must just *stand still,* till you are moved by superior power! But what did the Apostles answer? Peter stood up with the rest of the Apostles, and being full of the Holy Spirit, he answered and said: (38:) "Repent and be baptized every one of you, in the name of Jesus Christ for the Remission of sins, and you shall receive the gift of the holy Ghost," &c. Here we have "Remission, or forgiveness of sins," in the very first sermon that was preached under the new Commission "and they that gladly received the word, were baptized, and the same day were added to them about three thousand souls." Again, the same Apostle, in Solomon's Porch, (Acts 3: 19,) says to the rebel Jews, "Repent and be converted, that your sins may be blotted out, when the times of refreshing shall come from the presence of the Lord." "Him hath God exalted with his right hand to be a Prince and a Savior, for to give repentance to Israel, and forgiveness of sins," (Acts 5: 31.) "And why tarriest thou? arise, and be baptized, and wash away thy sins, calling on the name of the Lord," (Acts 22: 16.) We might multiply quotations of this character, to almost an indefinite extent; but the reader is ready to ask why quote so many scriptures? Surely no one will be bold enough to deny that the doctrine of pardon is taught in the Scriptures! No one supposes that Universalists themselves will not very readily admit, that forgiveness of sins, in some sense, is taught in the Bible—but then they explain it all away—and virtually, make it just as impossible for God to forgive sins, in any just and proper sense of the word, as for a stone in the valley below, to ascend, by the laws of gravitation, to the top of the highest mountain! But let me ask: does not Universalism deny the doctrine, of the *common Salvation?* I do think it does! Jesus says, "He that believes and is baptized, shall be saved; and he that believes not shall be damned, (Mark 16: 16.) — Shall be saved from what? Not from Sin, nor its consequences—for Universalism says, "that God will not pardon sin, in the sense of remitting the punishment:" then according to the system, the saved person will suffer just as much punishment, as those who are not saved! Saved from what then? Not from death, for all have to die. Not from the second death, for universalists tell us that no human being is in any danger of the second death! Not from eternal damnation, for universalism affirms, that *eternal damnation* is all endured in this life—and is the punishment we receive for our sins: therefore, we are not saved from it; as all have to suffer it, the *saved* as well as the *unsaved:* and as to eternal punishment after death, Universalism affirms, that no human being is *now, or ever was,* in any danger of that, and no individual can be saved from that, to which he was never liable! Not from the *Grave!* for Universalists admit, that all have to be in the grave for a season. Forgiveness of sins, and salvation, are words of empty sound, in the system of modern-Universalism. But as taught in the New Testament, they are the sinner's hope, and the Christian's strong consolation. Dark and gloomy must be the system that lacks this precious doctrine!

Reader, are you a Universalist? We exhort you then to weigh well our premises, and consider; and be no longer deceived by a mere gingle of words. Search the scriptures; read them in their proper connexion; with a heart open to receive the truth; and we feel confident, that when you shall have examined this subject with that attention, which the importance of the matter demands, you will abandon a system which makes "God *the author of sin;"* virtually denies the doctrine of forgiveness and the present salvation —and so far as eternal salvation is concerned, makes no difference between *virtue* and *vice;* the Christian, and the highway robber!!   EDITOR.

EXPOSITION OF JOHN *3:* 5.

MANHATTAN, Aug. 30th, 1843.

Brother Mathes: What is meant by the *birth of water and spirit,* spoken of John 3: 5th? Many persons are interested in having this matter scripturally answered. Please answer through the "Record." We would direct your attention particularly, to the birth of the spirit; *how* and *when,* does it take place?

JESSE RAPER.

REPLY.

Although Nichodemus was a Ruler of the Jews, yet, be was ignorant of the character of the Lord Jesus, and his approaching reign. He had heard of the Miracles of the Savior, though it would seem, he had witnessed none of them. To gratify his curiosity therefore, he sought an interview with the Lord by night, away from the noisy multitude, that he might have a better opportunity, of forming an acquaintance with this extraordinary personage, of whom he had heard so much. He accosted the Savior, in terms the most respectful.—"Rabbi, we know thou art a teacher come from God; for no man can do these miracles that thou doest except God be with him." The answer of Jesus, clearly indicates the Ruler's ignorance: "Verily, verily, I say unto thee, except a man be born again, he cannot see the kingdom of God." The Savior here tells Nichodemus, very plainly, that he *did not know,* what he *professed to know:* namely, "That thou art a teacher come from God:" and further, that no man, *in his situation,* could *see* or *discern,* the reign or kingdom of God. And Nichodemus shows his own ignorance of the subject, by what he says in verse 4th—"How can a man be born when he is old? can he enter the second time into his mother's womb, and be born?" He had his eye on the *natural* birth, and did not understand the meaning of the second birth. He was much astonished! But the Lord, in the 5th verse explains to the Ruler, what he had said in the 3rd, and which was so mysterious to him; "Verily, verily, I say unto thee, except a man be born of water, and of the spirit, he cannot enter into the kingdom of God." In the 6th verse Jesus corrects the mistake into which Nichodemus had fallen, that is, of confounding the *second,* with the *first* birth: "That which is born of the flesh, is flesh; and that which is born of the spirit, is spirit." Nichodemus seems to be more surprised than ever! but Jesus said, "Marvel not that I said to thee, Ye must be born again! The wind blows where it listeth, and thou hearest the sound thereof, but canst not tell whence it cometh, or whither it goeth, so is every one that is born of the spirit." Now this last passage presents some difficulty, especially in the comparison which seems to be instituted between the *wind,* and an individual who is born of the spirit. To get clear of this apparent difficulty, Commentators have run into some very wild extremes. One class of interpreters seem to understand the comparison to be made between the invisible operations of the wind upon physical nature, the *effects* of which only are seen; and the *modus operandi,* of the holy spirit, in the conversion of a sinner. But anyone may see that this view of the subject is *wrong,* who will read the text; as the comparison is evidently made between the *wind,* and *one who is born of the spirit.* Another class, transfer the whole matter to the *Resurrection,* for two reasons: 1st—Because they can see no analogy, between the spiritual birth of one who becomes the child of God, and a natural birth, and because the resurrection from the dead is called a *birth,* and is ascribed to the agency of the holy Spirit. (Rom. 8: 11.) And 2nd—Because Christians are *visible,* and we can tell whence they come, and whither they go, and differ from the wind in this particular; and because in the resurrection, our glorified bodies will be like the wind, *invisible to the mortal eyes:* they therefore conclude, that no one, except the Lord himself, *ever was,* or *ever will be* "born of the spirit," until the resurrection morn!

But these interpretations, we reject for the following reason: the word, which in the common version, is rendered *Wind,* is *Pneuma,* and occurs five times in the first eight verses of this chapter, four times it is translated *Spirit,* and once *Wind.* Now we can see no good reason for translating this word, *Spirit* four times, and *Wind* once, in the same conversation, and that without any indication of a change in the subject. That the Greek word, *Pneuma,* sometimes means *Wind,* will not be denied; but we do deny that the context requires, that it should be so rendered in this place. We are therefore clearly of the opinion that the word should be rendered *Spirit,* in this as well as in the other places, where it occurs in this discourse; then this very difficult passage would read thus: "The spirit breathes when he pleases, and you hear the report of him, but know not whence he comes, or whither he goes; so is everyone who is born of the spirit."

Then the passage is consistent with the context. Jesus performed his miracles by the power of the holy Ghost; this is signified by *"The Spirit breathes where he pleases."* Nichodemus had heard of those miracles, which is declared by the Ruler himself, and by the expression, *"and you hear the report of him."* The Ruler's ignorance of the Savior, and the character of that divine agent, *the holy Spirit,* by whose power those miracles were performed, is indicated by the declaration. *"but know not whence he comes, or whither he goes:"* and then the comparison is very plain; *"so is every one who is born of the Spirit:"* that is, every one who is born of the spirit, is to you, Nichodemus, like the spirit, by whose agency the new birth is effected; you *really* know nothing about either, and therefore you are mistaken, when you say, "We *know* that thou art a teacher *come from God."*

We now come to consider more particularly, what is meant by being "born of water and of the spirit." By being born of water, we understand Christian baptism to be intended by the Savior, as this was made by him, the initiatory rite; by which individuals were *formally* introduced into his kingdom.

In this interpretation we are not alone, for almost every Confession of Faith, and Creed, in Christendom, quote this text, to prove the necessity of water baptism. The one hundred and twenty one Divines, ten Lords, and twenty Commissioners of the Parliament of England, who framed the "Westminster Confession of Faith," under question 165th, "What is baptism?" quote John 3: 5, and Titus 3: 5, to prove that baptism is a washing with water, and a *"sign of remission of sins."* The authors and finishers of the "Methodist Discipline," make about the same use of this text, only they go a little further, and appoint that this passage shall be read to the audience, by the Minister, every time he administers the ordinance of baptism, for the purpose no doubt, of impressing upon the minds of all, the absolute necessity of observing this institution. We might also quote a host of learned and great men, both Catholic and Protestant, who have all taken the same view of this text; but a few must suffice. The great John Wesley, A. M., on this passage remarks, "5—*Except a man be born of water, and of the spirit* —Except he experience that great inward change by the spirit, and be baptized (where baptism can be had) as the Outward sign and means of it." *Wesley's Notes.* See also "Doctrinal Tracts," of the M. E. Church, under the head *"Baptism."*

Dr. Whitby, one of the brightest ornaments of the church of England, thus speaks on John 3: 5th, "That our Lord here speaks of Baptismal regenerations, *the whole Christian church* from its *earliest times* has *invariably taught."*

Dr. Timothy Dwight, President of Yale College, one of the greatest Theologians, the Presbyterian church in America, has ever produced, speaking of this text, (John 3: 5,) Vol. 4th, pp. 300 - 301, says: *"To be born again,* is precisely the same thing, as to be born of water and the spirit"—"To be born of water, is to be baptized." And the Dr. adds: "He who, understanding the nature and authority of this institution, refuses to be baptized, *will never enter into the visible nor invisible kingdom of God:*" Vol. 4th, page 302. So testifies the learned President of Yale College.

George Whitfield, writing on John 3: 5, says, "Does not this versa urge the *absolute necessity of water baptism? Yes,* when it may be had But how God will deal with persons unbaptized, *we cannot tell:*" Vol. 4, p. 355.

The above reference will show that we are perfectly orthodox, on this subject; *we* shall now inquire further, what is signified by being *"born of the spirit."* We suppose no one who believes in the divinity of the Bible, will deny the spirit's agency in the new birth. Upon this subject there is no controversy, that we know of, in the religious world; the controversy is about *how* the spirit does his work upon the heart of an unconverted person—whether it does it by an *abstract* operation, or *through and by* the word of truth, the gospel of salvation? We unhesitatingly say the latter, we understand to be clearly taught in the Bible. As in the Kingdom of Nature, so in the Kingdom of Grace, there is *the begetter,* and the thing *begotten:*—first, a *begetting,* and then a *b ringing forth.* All admit that God is the father of all Christians; therefore he is the *begetter,* and this he effects, by the *agency* of his holy spirit, and by the *instrumentality* of his word. The Apostle James sustains this conclusion, chap. 1: 18: *"Of* his own will begat he us by the word of truth." But is the spirit in the word of truth? "It is the spirit that quickeneth; the flesh profiteth nothing: the words which I speak unto you, they are spirit, and they are life;" John 6: 63. Peter, what have you to say about being *born again,* has the *word* of God any thing to do in the matter? "Born again, not of corruptible seed, but of incorruptible, by the word of God which liveth and abideth forever." 1 Pet., 1: 23." When are we *begotten* of God? Answer, when we believe with all the heart, that Jesus is the Christ, as John declares, "Whosoever believeth that Jesus is the Christ, is born of God;" or more properly, is *begotten of God.* (1 John 5: 1.) From this we see, that it is through faith in the son of God, that we are *begotten* of God, and Paul will tell us that "Faith comes by hearing, and hearing by the word of God." Rom. 10: 17. In Nature there is life before birth, and a birth is not to give life, but to enjoy that life, which the individual had previous to his birth: so, in the New birth; we must be quickened, or made alive, before we are born; and then we are born into the Kingdom of Christ, to enjoy the life which we had before birth. How then are we quickened? "It is the spirit that quickeneth." John 6: 63. In conclusion we would say, *to be born again,* is precisely the same thing, as to be "born of water and of the spirit," and whenever, therefore, an individual *is constitutionally,* born of *water,* he is at the same time *born of the spirit;* for if a man is not begotten of God, he is not *constitutionally* Baptized. Now we do not pretend to say that no one will ever be saved in heaven, but those who have been baptized; far from it, for we do most cordially believe that all infants and idiots, will be saved in heaven without baptism, Faith, Repentance, or any other act of obedience; and those who have been so circumstanced, that they have never had the opportunity to understand the nature and authority of Baptism; and who have served God, to the best of their knowledge and ability. But we are prepared to say with Dr. Dwight, "He who understanding the nature and authority of the institution, refuses to be baptized, *will never* enter into the visible, nor invisible Kingdom of God."

All of which is candidly submitted by the EDITOR.

THE GLORIOUS APPEARING OF THE LORD—NO. 2.

IN our first number we took some notice of brother S. M. MCCORKLE, of the "Alarm," and his system of interpreting unfulfilled prophecy. We also promised to speak of the "Evangelist," the "Israelite," and sundry other publications; in which this very interesting topic, has been ably examined. We now design in part, to redeem our pledge. "The Carthage Evangelist," is edited and published at Carthage, Ohio, by our beloved brother WALTER SCOTT. If brother Scott is not the *strongest,* he is certainly one among the *clearest,* and most *laving* writers of the age. It is impossible to read the effusions of Father Scott's pen, and not love the man. He calls the *first advent of* the Messiah, *The Faith,* and the *second advent,* he calls *the hope* of the gospel. For many years Father Scott labored to disabuse the public mind, in reference to the *faith* of the gospel; and in connection with other kindred publications, who first raised the standard of the *Bible alone,* in the United States; labored long, and hard, and with great success, to restore the "Ancient Gospel," and a pure speech to Zion. And now, the "Evangelist," which is in its 11th vol., is teeming with the *hope* of the gospel. The, essays of the "Evangelist," upon the *second advent,* are worthy of a candid perusal by all; and nothing but the small size of our paper, prevents us from laying them before our readers. These essays show, that the writer has drunk deep into the inspiring theme? for he writes as one who is waiting for his Lord, when he shall return to be glorified in his saints, and admired in them that love him.

If we understand the "Evangelist," he teaches a *literal personal* return of the Lord, before the Millennium; at which time, the dead in. Christ will be raised and crowned. "The sanctuary cleansed," and the wicked destroyed. Although brother Scott is less dogmatical, and more modest than Mr. Miller, we understand him to admit Elder Miller's theory of interpretation, in the main. But we will let bro. Scott speak for himself in a short extract, which we take from an essay on "the Resurrection," (Evangelist; New Series, Vol. IV, No. 10.)

"At his coming, therefore, the whole earth will be filled with glorified humanity, having a capital called the Beloved City, for both Daniel in his 7th chap , and John, Rev. 19th chap , show that this power or coming of the Lord Jesus is anterior to his Kingdom in its everlasting, mountain or millennial form, and not posterior to it. Seeing the prophetic history up to his coming is now most certainly exhausted in any view which we may choose to take of it, may we not with the greatest propriety raise the midnight cry, and shout "*Behold the Bride groom cometh!* In short, the Lord Jesus is speedily coming in his own proper person, body or flesh from heaven to raise the dead, change the living, reorganize his Kingdom, and spread it in all its grandeur around the world. Brethren let us go out to meet him; the first appearance of him will be "in the clouds." Keep your eye from this time forward on the clouds, for you know not what hour the Master cometh Eternal life, and eternal death hang upon that eventful moment, and he has said to all, "Watch."

But as we have said he agrees with Mr. Miller, in the main, his position will be better understood, when we understand what Mr. Miller's theory is. We shall then turn to "Miller's Lectures," the "Signs of the Times," the "Midnight Cry," the "Trumpet of Alarm," the "Jubilee Trumpet," &c., &c.; and ascertain if we can, what Mr. Miller, and those who with him believe in the speedy return of the Lord, believe on this important subject.

Mr. William Miller is a Regular Baptist, and so far, as we can learn, he is a humble, devoted Christian—he has studied the prophecies for some 14 years, and has now published to the world the result of his investigations: he certainly deserves a candid hearing, from all those who love the appearing of the Lord. We will here give some of Mr. Miller's calculations. We quote from the "Signs of the Times," one of Mr. Miller's organs.

"The period when Manasseh was carried to Babylon, and the ten tribes ceased to be a nation. Moses' "seven times," and Ezekiel's seven years begin. Before Christ,   677
years. The captivity begins under Jehoichim. The beginning of the forty-nine Jubilees,   607
Beginning of the 2300 days of Daniel's vision in the eighth chapter,
      concerning the Ram, He-goat and Little Horn,   457
The league formed between the Romans and the Jews. Beginning of Hosea's
      2 days or 2000 years. Hosea 6: 1, 3.   158
Birth of Christ,—In the year of the world,   4157
The Crucifixion. End of the seventy weeks, A. D.   33
Taking away (Pagan) "Daily Sacrifice-" Conversion of the "Ten Kings" to
      the Christian faith,   508
Rise of Papacy. Beginning of the 1260 years, or "time, times and a half a time."
Commencement of the civil power of the Pope, and his reign over the kings,   538
One hundred and fifty years of the fifth trumpet. Beginning of the Ottoman Empire
      by Othman, or the "five months." Rev. 9: 5—   1299
The Sixth Trumpet begins to sound. Mahomet 2d attacks the Greeks at
Constantinople, and destroys the empire,   A. D.   1453
This Trumpet was to sound 391 years and fifteen days. Rev. 9. 15—   1449
Fall of the Ottoman power. Drying up of the River Euphrates.
      Beginning of the "Seventh Trumpet,"....   1844
The war begins between Catholics and Protestants in Europe.
      210 years, or "Seven Months;" in which the kings of Europe
      were destroying the Papal power,   1583
End of the Papal power over the kings in Europe,   1699
Ten kings in the Roman world—30 years between Pagan and
      Papal Rome. Rev. 17: 12,   508 to 538
Opening of the "Little Book,"—45 years to the end. Rev. 10th chapter,   1798 to 1843"

In the above calculation, Mr. Miller reckons a day for a year, a "time," one complete revolution of our planet, or 360 years, counting a day for a year. He understands the visions of Daniel and John to refer to the same events. He thinks that all the prophetic periods, will run out in 1843: at which time he looks for the second advent of the Messiah, the "cleansing of the sanctuary," and the destruction of the world by fire. He thinks the Lord will surely come immediately after the *Autumnal Equinox,* the present year! (1843.) But here we must let the matter rest for another Moon: after which we shall speak more fully of Elder Miller's faith, and present some of our objections to it.   EDITOR.

THE OLD PATHS.

In the Religious Herald, of Aug. 31st, under the head "Revival in Adair County, Ky.," a correspondent states the following curious circumstance, to-wit:—"One other circumstance," says the writer, J. C. Portman, "I will mention for the encouragement of those who are contending for the old paths. A colored man, when he came to give a relation of his faith, remarked that he had joined a church last winter and was baptized for the remission of his sins according to the teaching of said church. He believed the doctrine, and hence was baptized' but did not obtain the desired object. "But now," said he, "I have received it in my soul, and wish to join *your* church." This circumstance excited a very considerable movement in the congregation, for the circumstance of his being baptized was known to the people."

Who are those who are "contending for the old paths?" and what "old paths" are they contending for? If bro, Portman mean, by the *old paths,* the teaching and practice of the Apostles, we are at a loss to know how the story which he relates, can encourage such as are contending for the *old paths,* since the "colored man," who, according to the story, believed what the Apostles preached, and had obeyed what the Apostles commanded such to *do* "for the remission of sins," and still he was disappointed! the promise (Acts 2: 38) failed!! Instead of encouraging, we should rather be inclined to think if the poor man actually was disappointed, it would be calculated to damp the spirits, and discourage all who are "contending for the *old paths!*" for if the promise *failed* in one instance, it might also fail in ten thousand more, and of course, we could have no assurance, that any promise would be fulfilled, when the conditions were performed!

But if bro. P. mean by *old paths,* the doctrine and practice of the Regular Baptist church, contained in the "London and Philadelphia Confession of Faith," we are still at a loss to understand him. Does not bro. P, know that there are very many things found in said confession of faith, not found in the word of God, and not believed nor practiced by half the Baptist churches? How then can these things be the *old paths?* But has it indeed come to this, that the Regular Baptist church is encouraged, to hear that the promise of the Lord has failed, in the case of an obedient penitent believer! Infidelity might rejoice, and take encouragement; but surely the Baptist church will not be encouraged by this silly story!

We remark, that if this *colored man,* believed on the Lord Jesus, with all his heart, Repented of all his sins, and trusting in the dear Redeemer, and in full faith of the promise, was "baptized for the remission of sins," he was pardoned or the promise of God failed! which is impossible!!

But if this colored man did not receive the remission of his sins, when he was baptized, then it is proved that he was not a proper subject,—he lacked faith, or some other qualification, for Baptism *alone,* without a change of heart and life, by a gospel faith and Repentance, would turn out just as bro. P. says it did in this case, "he would not obtain the desired object."

But bro P. says, the church which this man joined first, believed and taught, Baptism for the remission of sins. Well, this must be the church, then, who are contending for the *old paths;* for this is what the Apostles preached and practiced! But bro. P. says, that when this man came to give a relation of his faith, he said, "now I wish to join *your* church." What church was this, he wished to join? He had, it seems, joined the church, which was contending for the *old paths;* had got tired of it, and note he wishes to join another, which he calls *your church!* The church of Jesus Christ belongs to him: but it would seem from the language of this *colored man,* that he understood the church which he *now* wished to join, belonged to bro. Portman—for he says, *now I wish to join your church.* In the language of one of old, I would say, "Jesus I know, and Paul I know, but who are ye?" Again we ask whose church was this?

But bro. P. says, "this circumstance produced a very considerable excitement among the people." We think no wonder, that the people were excited! to hear that the promise of the Lord had failed, was enough to not only produce excitement, but overwhelm with amazement, all who believed in the faithfulness of God, and fill every heart with consternation and despair! No wonder then that the audience was *very much excited*—when they heard this poor deluded man, impeach the veracity of the eternal Jehovah!! EDITOR.

DIFFICULTY AMONG THE BAPTISTS.

A WRITER in the "Religious Herald." of the 14th inst., presents some very grave matters, for the consideration of his Baptist brethren generally, and bro. Sands, the Editor, in particular. The nature of these difficulties will be clearly seen, by the following extract, which we take from said communication:—

"When I made a profession of Religion," says the writer, "generally it was only necessary to know that a man was a Baptist *to* know his creed, but now there is such a variety of sentiments among the Baptists as renders it difficult to know what any of them believe. The effect of this, on both themselves and the unconverted, is deplorable. It produces disunion, and want of affection among themselves; and confusion and infidelity among the unconverted." "The leading point of difference among our brethren is contained in this question: Can an unregenerate man do any thing which promotes his salvation? There are other points of difference, but they are branches growing out of this trunk. The settlement of this question on the basis of truth, is very important, and therefore very desirable.'"

We beg leave to make a few suggestions to bro. John Ogilvie, the writer, and brother Sands, the Editor, in reference to the difficulty: That the above difficulty really exists, not only in the East, but also among our Western Baptist brethren, we are fully aware: and that *disunion* and *Infidelity* are the result of such contradictory teaching, is to manifest to be denied by any one. A. who is a Baptist Minister, preaches "Jesus and the resurrection," with great power, and urges the sinner to accept the offered mercy, "while it is called to day." B. who is also a Minister of the same body, follows A.; he preaches what he calls, "the doctrines of *sovereign* grace," tells the poor sinner that he can do *nothing!* that he is morally dead, and can perform no act' that will be pleasing to God! that the best prayer which he can make, has sir, enough in it to *damn a world!* He then, in conclusion, exhorts sinners to *repent* and *turn* to God! and threatens them with eternal damnation if they refuse to comply!' The last preacher not only contradicts the first, but be also contradicts himself! The poor trembling sinner, who was "almost persuaded to be a Christian," by the first preacher, while he presented the love of God to man, in the gift and death of his Son, is thrown into utter confusion by the second preacher, who not only tells him, that it is out of his power to do *any thing* to promote his salvation, but who *actually* tells him that the very act of *trying* to come to Christ is sinful! The sinner says to himself, "If I refuse, I shall be *damned* myself, and if I try to comply, I shall commit sin enough to *damn a world!* what shall I do! I am perplexed! I cannot believe in such a system of contradictions!" Both preachers quoted scripture to sustain their positions; and the sinner, supposing that the Bible contains such contradictions, rejects the whole with disdain. and becomes an Infidel.

We would humbly suggest, to all the Baptist preachers in Christendom, the propriety of returning to a *pure speech*. "If any man speak, let him speak as the oracles of God." Discard all the *foreign* terms found in your theological system, and no longer speak in words "which man's wisdom teaches, but in words which the holy Ghost teaches." When sinners say, "What shall we do to be saved?" tell them just what the holy spirit, by the mouth of the Apostles, told such: "Repent and be baptized every one of you in the name of Jesus Christ for the remission of sins, and you shall receive the gift of the holy ghost." Acts 2: 38.

But we differ in opinion about what Peter and the rest of the Apostles *meant* by the above expression. No matter for that; you all agree that Peter gave the right answer, for he spake "as the spirit gave him utterance;" then go and do likewise; and keep your opinions about Peter's *meaning* to yourselves, for you have no right at all to preach your opinions—"preach the word."

We would suggest the following rule, not only to Baptist Preachers, but all others, viz:

When you address sinners, sneak to them in the language of the Apostles to such: if they wish to know what to do to be saved, tell them just what the Apostles told such inquirers in their day, a lull account of which, you may find in the Acts of Apostles. It after Baptism, they wish to become acquainted with their duty, teach them what the Apostles taught the Christians of that age, which teaching you may find in the Epistolary part of the New Testament,

In short, let all the preachers take the Apostles as a model; imitate their example, preach as they preached, teach as they taught; and union will be restored; Infidelity will lose its strongest prop, and all the difficulties complained of and deplored, by bro Ogilvie, and thousands of such noble spirits, in the Baptist church, will be removed—a pure speech will be turned upon the people —peace and harmony pervade all the holders of Zion—Salvation will go forth as brightness—Messiah's kingdom advance in all its grandeur around the earth, and God's name be glorified in the salvation of those who now sit in the region and shadow of death. EDITOR.

PUSEYISM IN THE UNITED STATES.

It is said that four Bishops, to wit: Onderdonk of New York, Doane of New Jersey, Whittingham of Maryland, and Ives of North Carolina, and a great number of the under Clergy of the Protestant Episcopal Church, are favorable to the doctrine set forth in the "Oxford Tracts," generally called "Puseyism," from Dr. Pusey, the Master spirit of the heresy at Oxford. ' Dr. Seabury, Editor of the "Churchman," is boldly advocating Dr. Pusey and the "Oxford Tracts." The ordination of Mr. Carey, has caused considerable excitement, and some dismission among the dignitaries of the Episcopal Church. Mr. C. in conversation with his Pastor, Dr. Smith, intimated, that if he did no1 succeed in obtaining ordination at the hands of the

Bishops of his own Church, he might possibly have recourse to the Ministry of Rome! Mr. C. said, "that he could receive all the decrees of the council of Trent, the Damnatory clauses excepted. That he did not deem the differences between the Episcopal and Romish churches to be such as embraced any points of faith. That he was not prepared to pronounce the doctrine of transubstantiation absurd or impossible. That he does not object to the Romish doctrine of purgatory, as defined by the Council of Trent, and that he was not prepared to consider the church of Rome as no longer an integral, or pure branch of the Church of Christ, or to say whether she, or the Episcopal Church were the more pure. That he considered the reformation an unjustifiable act. That he could receive the Creed of Pope Pious the 4th!"

Notwithstanding this full acknowledgement of many of the leading doctrines of Popery, by Mr. Carey, he was ordained a Minister of the Protestant Episcopal Church by Bishop Onderdonk, of New York Drs. Smith and Anthon dissenting! We cannot say, with certainty, how far this Romish heresy has spread in the Episcopal Church, in this country, but it is evidently gaining strength; and it is said that a very large proportion of the English Clergy, are tainted with it. From all of which, we venture to predict, that the time is not far distant when the great decisive battle will be faught between *tradition,* and the *Word of God* alone. Every thing seems to be tending to that point. Those who contend for *tradition,* will necessarily fall back into the arms of the old Mother; just where the Puseyites are going; and those who are unwilling to go there, will be compelled to abandon *tradition,* as a rule of faith and practice; and take the *Bible alone*. These, we believe, will ere long be the great rallying points, throughout all christendom.—Minor differences will be forgotten—the line will be drawn— two great parties will be formed —the one, which will embrace Romanism, will contend for the *Bible* and *tradition,* while the other, which will reject Romanism, will contend for the *Bible alone*.

J. M. M., ED.

PRAYER.

One of the most delightful and solemn exercises, in which the Christian is called to engage, is prayer. In this delightful exercise, the Christian comes with confidence into the presence of his Father in heaven. He knows that his Father sees him—that his Father hears him, and fully believes that his divine Father will answer his prayer, when presented in the name of Jesus Christ, his great high Priest, according to the divine Will. He therefore "lifts up holy hands without wrath and doubting.? He knows that God has prepared a throne grace, to which he has invited all his children to come, and with "true hearts, and in full assurance of Faith, obtain mercy, and find grace to help in time of need."

How interesting to every Christian, is that solemn moment, when he bows in the presence of the whole earth! when he asks an audience of him who built the Universe, spread the starry skies abroad, and "upholds all things by the word of his power!" When the sable curtain of night, shuts out the light of day; when the noise of busy feet, passing up and down, attending to the busy concerns of life, is no longer heard; when the bird, in strains of sweetest melody, warbles forth the praises of him, who takes care of birds, feeding them without storehouse or barn: while ten thousand little stars bespangle the firmament on high, and in silent eloquence proclaim the power and glory of Him who made them: while the broad-faced Moon, queen of night, throws her silver mantle of reflected light upon the habitations of men. We say, in such an hour, the Christian loves to offer up his evening sacrifice of praise and thanksgiving, to him whose eyes are over the righteous, and whose ears are open to their prayers. Yes, he delights, in such an auspicious moment, to join in the universal chorus of praise, and to ask his indulgent heavenly Father, for the needed grace and strength, that he may overcome the world, and be kept from its evils, and glorify God in body and spirit. Indeed, it is just as natural for the Christian to pray, as it is for water to run down hill by the laws of gravity; and if you will show us a professed disciple of the Lord, who does not pray, we will show you one who possesses not the spirit of Christ- one-who only has a *name* to live, while he is dead to the life and power of the Christian religion!

The Christian prays not for himself alone, but his petitions embrace all men—even his enemies are not forgotten. Like his divine Redeemer, who when he hung upon the cross, prayed for those who nailed him there, saying "Father forgive them, they know not what they do!" But that professor who neglects prayer, will grow cold and indifferent to the cause of Christ.—The neglect of this duty, will certainly lead him to absent himself from the house of God, and to neglect those duties, which the disciples of the Lord, perform on the first day of the week, to wit: Fellowship, breaking of bread, the Apostles' teaching, and prayers; he also neglects to exhort his brethren to love and good works: his conversation is not in heaven, but in earth; and when such a professor does go to meeting, (for he does go sometimes, when his favorite preacher is to be there!) his heart is as cold as an iceberg; he delights not in the songs of Zion; but spends all the time that elapses, between his arrival at the meeting house, and the commencement of the sermon, in talking over his worldly concerns—the price of corn, wheat and pork! and just as soon as the sermon is ended, he is happy to resume again his favorite topic of conversation! "I speak as unto wise men, judge of what I say." J. M. M., ED.

UNIVERSALIST EXPOSITOR.

THIS is the name of a very neat publication, recently gotten up in the city of Cincinnati; Edited and published by our beloved brother A. Crihfield, Editor of the Orthodox Preacher. It is a very spirited work, and is exclusively devoted to the discussion of *modern Universalism*. We have received the first number, and have read it with interest and profit; and we most heartily commend it to the attention of the public generally. Those who wish to see the capital points, and prominent features of Universalism, promptly met, and fairly refuted, by reason, argument and scripture testimony, would do well to subscribe for the "Universalist Expositor." It is issued quarterly, neatly covered and trimmed, each number containing 48 pages, of convenient size for binding, which at the end of the year will make a handsome volume of 192 pages.

Brother C. offers the work to subscribers at 50 cents per vol , in advance; or 5 vols. for 2,00; 12 vols. for 5,00; and 30 vols. for 10 dollars. We hope the "Expositor" will receive a general circulation.

☛ Subscriptions received at this office, where a specimen of the work may be seen. J. M. M., ED.

NEWS FROM THE CHURCHES.

BROTHER J. McColough of this place, has just returned from the yearly meeting of the brethren in the Crawfordsville district, which was held at Crawfordsville on the first Lord's day in Sept. inst. He reports a glorious meeting; 25 immersions, and some other additions. The meeting was attended by Eld. B. W. Stone of Ill., and his son, B. W. Stone, jun. Dr. B. F. Hall of Ky., L. H. Jameson of Indianapolis, beside the *home* preachers, J. O'Kane, G. F. Harney, J. M. Harris, and perhaps others.

At the same time, (Sept. 1st Lord's day,) brethren T. C. Johnson and J. G. Campbell, co-operated with the Elders of the congregation at Republican, 7 miles South West of this place; the church was much revived, and 7 persons were added by Immersion.

On the 3nd Lord's day in Aug. brethren P. M. Blankenship, and G. W. Snoddy, co-operated with us at "Old Union," near Gosport; the result was 4 additions, 3 of them by Immersion, and one by letter.

The yearly meeting of the Liberty Church, was held at Liberty meeting house, Owen county, on the 1st Lord's day of this month (Sept.) bro. Samuel Swinford was the principal laborer; one. was Immersed, and several others were added.

On the 3rd Lord's day of this month,(Sept.) bro. T. C. Johnson held a meeting with the church on Raccoon Creek, Owen county; 3 persons were baptized, and the brethren much revived.

At the same time, (3rd Lord's day in Sept, inst.) the yearly meeting of the church at Martinsville was held: brethren J. G. Campbell and P. M. Blankenship were the laborers. The congregation was much refreshed, and 6 very valuable additions were made to the church, 5 of them by Immersion, and one from the Baptists. Bro. Samuel Tucker has for some years been a worthy member of the Regular Baptist church, he is a young man of unblemished character, and fine mind; and we regard him as a very valuable accession to the church at Martinsville. May the Lord grant them many more such noble spirits? The other accessions, were also, of the very first character, and standing in community; one of them, bro. John Haystings, we are informed, was a Universalist, in principle; but he nobly yielded to the force of divine truth, and bowed his neck to the "Yoke of Christ." We hope that all the Universalists in the land, will follow his example.

We are informed that our beloved bro. William Baker, held a meeting, 3 miles west of Martinsville, including the 2nd Lord's day of this inst., which resulted in 8 additions to the church in that neighborhood.

EDITOR.

We hope the brethren will not forget to send us all the information they can, respecting the spread of the Gospel, the organization if churches, the movements of the different ecclesiastic bodies, &c.

EDITOR.

PROSPECTUS OF THE CHRISTIAN RECORD.

THE CHRISTIAN RECORD is published monthly, at Bloomington, Indiana, Edited and Published by J. M. MATHES, and contains 24 octavo pages, neatly stitched and covered.

TERMS.—One dollar in advance, or on the reception of the first number. Any one obtaining five subscribers and remitting the money to us free of cost, shall have the 6th copy gratis.

All letters to be addressed, *post paid,* or *free,* to "J. M. Mathes, Bloomington, Indiana"

☛*How to make remittances.*—Postmasters are authorized by law to frank letters, addressed to Editors, containing money, if written by themselves.—Don't forget this.

☛POSTAGE on this work is 1½ cents, under 100 miles, and over 100 miles 2½, as the work contains but one sheet per number.

Errata.—47th page, 4th line from bottom, for "we agree *be,*" read "we agree *he,* " &c.

49th page, 20th line from bottom, there is an omission of a part of a senca, after "one in Christ," and before "we shall continue one." The reader will supply, "and then by walking by the same rule."

50th page, 13th line from top, for "that Creed," read "that *the* Creed."

53rd page, 9th line from bottom, for "consider" read *"conclusions."*

55th page, 4th line from bottom, for "The spirit breathes *when,*" &c., read *"where,"* &c.

56th page, 13th line from bottom, for "sppoint," read *"appoint."*

☛It is due to the Editor to state, that owing to sickness, he did not read the proof of the first form of the present number.—PRINTER.

☛Hereafter the Christian Record will be sent to subscribers in town—those living in the country, will call for their numbers, at John McCorkle's, North East corner of the public square.

We calculate to present our next number in a printed cover, and clear of typographical errors.

THE CHRISTIAN RECORD.

VOL. I.   BLOOMINGTON, IND., OCTOBER, 1843.   [NO. IV.

CHRISTIAN. UNION—NO. 4.

THE following sentence, in substance, is found inscribed upon the face of every Creed, and Confession of faith, in Protestant Christendom; to wit, "The scriptures o the Old and New Testaments contain the word of God, and are the only infallible rule of faith and practice." We shall therefore summons into court, all the Creeds and confessions of faith, as witnesses, and out of their own mouths we shall condemn them as *fallible*—for they confess their own guilt—they say "the word of God contained in the Old and New Testaments, *is the only infallible rule of faith and practice.*" If these witnesses tell the truth, they are fallible, and may be wrong, and consequently, they cannot be depended on! We shall then take the ground, that Creeds and confessions of faith are unnecessary, and stand directly in the way of Christian Union, and the conversion of the world to Jesus Christ.

That they are unnecessary may be proved, 1st, from the concessions of all parties. The old school Presbyterians, will admit that the New School party, who have gone off from them, may be Christians, though they deny some of the prominent features of the "good old Confession of faith." The old and the New School Presbyterians will both agree, that the Cumberland Presbyterian church may contain some very good Christians, though she has rejected the "Westminster Book," and set up for herself. The Methodists of all schools, will admit, that the Baptists may be good Christians, though they reject the Methodist Discipline, as heretical. The Baptists admit as much for the Methodists, who reject the *five points,* and have adopted the antagonist *five points* of Arminianism. In short, all the lovers and supporters of human creeds, admit that salvation may be enjoyed, by the honest hearted of all parties; and we are happy to know, that from the stern Calvinist, down to the most enthusiastic advocate of human Creeds, in the land—all cheerfully admit, that if an individual honestly rejects every human Creed, in Protestant Christendom, as contrary to the spirit and mind of Christ: and the very best interests of our race, we say, all admit, that if such an individual believe on the Lord Jesus Christ, with all his heart, true in him for salvation, and to the very best of his knowledge and ability obey the commands of God through life, his whole conduct being regulated by the *Bible alone,* without any human Creed superadded; he will overcome the world, and receive "an abundant entrance, into the ever lasting kingdom of our Lord Jesus Christ?' This admission, cuts the throat of every human Creed and Confession of faith in Christendom, and proves them to be unnecessary appendages. For if a man can be a Christian without being a Methodist, or acknowledging the Discipline: it follows with the clearness of demonstration, that the Methodist Discipline, which contains Methodism, is a *non-essential.*—And so of all the rest! But who will say that a man can be a Christian, who rejects the Bible? No one. And who will say, that one who believes all its heavenly truths, and obeys its divine mandates, is not a Christian? No one. "And hereby we do know that we know him, if we keep his commandments?" 1 John 2: 3. Human Creeds are unnecessary, 2d. because they contain nothing valuable, which is not found in the Bible; for their *lovers* say, they "have been taken out of the Bible, and they are just like it?" Then they are unnecessary, for we have the Bible, which all acknowledge to be the fountain from which all those little streams (Creeds) have been drawn off. Who would leave the fountain, and drink at the little stream far below? We suppose no one, who understands the superiority of the former over the latter, would be guilty of such an inconsistency; and yet, this is just what the supporters of human Creeds are doing! Again, if the Creed contains any thing which is not found in equal terms in the Bible *alone,* it is unnecessary to life and Godliness; wicked in itself, and has in it the essence of rebellion against the government of the Lord Jesus Christ! and of course ought to be abandoned at once by all the lovers of the Lord Jesus Christ. 3rd—Human Creeds are unnecessary, because the church of Jesus Christ had no such thing, until three hundred years of peace and unparalleled prosperity had rolled away. These were the golden days of the church. Then there was "one. *Lord and his name one"* On the broad basis of the word of God alone, the Disciples of the Lord stood firmly united, and the truth went forth "conquering and to conquer," until Pagan Rome was revolutionized, the throne of the Caesars was invaded, and Rome's proud Emperor, bowed to the authority of him who was born in a stable. In the beginning of the fourth century, an angry controversy arose between Arius and Alexander; to settle which the first council of Nice, was assembled; and in the year 325, the famous Nicene Creed was framed, by this august body of Bishops and Presbyters, with the Emperor Constantine at their head. This was the first human Creed over acknowledged by the Christian community; and this was the beginning of sorrows to the church of Christ. But we need pursue this matter no farther now; human Creeds are the sinful offspring of party spirit, and brought forth *under heresy's deadly nightshade.* They are therefore, not only unnecessary, but injurious to the well-being of religious society, and stand opposed to Christian Union. It must be apparent to all, that upon no one of all the Creeds, or confessions of faith, which have been made since the days of Constantine, down to the present day can all Christians ever be united. The Methodists never will consent to lay the discipline aside., and subscribe to the "39 Articles," the "Westminster Book," or the "London and Philadelphia Confession of Faith." Neither will the Baptists consent to be Methodists, nor Presbyterians.

Well then, says the honest inquirer, if all Christians cannot be united upon any one Creed; upon what foundation can they cordially unite together? We answer, *upon the word of God alone,* and upon no other.

The Bible alone, contains not Methodism, Baptistism, Presbyterianism, nor Campbellism; it just contains the word of God, which all parties acknowledge to be the truth, without any mixture of error. In uniting therefore, upon the Bible *alone,* we shall not become Methodists,

Baptists, Presbyterians nor Campbellites—but we shall simply become *"Christians,"* brethren, saints, *Disciples of Christ.*

But, says the contending brother, I object to this union, for I see that if all Christians agree to meet upon the Bible alone, and give up their Creeds, they will also lose their names by which they are distinguished, as believers in particular doctrines, lest, these party names must all be given up; indeed, if we give up our Creeds, and take the Bible alone, these party names are lost forever." They can be found no where else, but in the Creeds, (that is, authoritatively.) But why are our friends so unwilling to give up their party names? All admit that these names are non-essentials.—A man may be a Methodist, a Lutheran, a Quaker or a Baptist, and still not be a Christian; and again, a man may be a Christian, and still refuse to wear the above, or any other sectarian name.

"It will never be asked us," say our friends, "when we get to heaven, what name we wore in this world, Baptist, Methodist, or Quaker; but *'are you a Christian?'*" Well, if we acknowledge that the name is a non-essential, and will never take any one to heaven, why should we be so tenacious of them? We all admit that party names will be lost in the silent shades of the tomb; why then should we refuse to give them up now?

But says the objector, "the name is nothing." Well then, if it is *nothing,* why be so tenacious about *nothing!* But if we find that the party name, *which is nothing,* stands opposed to Christian Union, and the salvation of the world, will it not be our indispensable duty, to sacrifice this *nothing,* (party name,) upon the altar of the public good; and no longer contend about *'nothing,'* to the great injury of our own spiritual enjoyment, and the ruin of many precious souls!

J. M. M., ED.

UNIVERSALISM—NO. 4.

SOME of the most prominent leaders and teachers of modern Universalism, *deny the Divinity of Christ!!* To prove this solemn charge to the conviction of all, we shall introduce a number of witnesses, all possessing the confidence of the Universalists generally.

We shall first introduce the Rev. Hosea Ballou. Reader attend!

"We have already stated," says Mr. Ballou, "some of the absurdities contained in the opinions of most Christians respecting the Mediator; we shall now be a little more particular on the subject. We shall contend, that the Mediator is a *created dependent* being." "Treat, on Atonement," 5th ed., p. 113. Again, Mr. Ballou says: "It is plain that the *nature* of the relation of Jesus to the Father, is the nature of the relation of *every man* to the Father of our spirits!" Lect. Serm., p. 208. Hear this witness again on this point: "The reader will then ask," says Mr. B., "if we would consider the Mediator no more than equal with men? We answer, yes, were it not that our Father and his Father, our God and his God, hath anointed him above his fellows." "Treat. on Atonement," page 114.

Mr. Ballou, in the above quotations, states *three* important facts, viz; 1 —Christ is a *created* being. 2 — The *nature* of the relation, which Christ sustains to the Father, is the *nature* of the relation which *every* man sustains to him!! Therefore, there is no more Divinity in Christ than there is in any of the sons of men!! 3 —Christ is a *man,* a *mere man,* and all the difference there is between him, and any other man, is, that he was more exalted in office!! This witness may stand aside.

We shall now introduce Mr. Grosh; he says, "We believe that the nature of Jesus was strictly the *human nature only,* while on earth— that he had no *existence before his earthly existence,* except in the purpose and counsel of God—that he was the chief (or beginning) of the creation of God only by the powers and *office* with which he was gifted, and by his resurrection." "Mag. and Adv.," vol. 4, page 397.

This witness states clearly, 1: *The nature* of Jesus, was strictly *human nature only,* while on earth. 2—That he had *no existence,* before be was born of the Virgin, except in the *purpose* and *counsel* of God! And 3—That the reason why he was called *the beginning of the creation of God,* was owing to the *powers* and *office* with which he *was gifted,* and his *resurrection,* and on no other account.

The author of "Universalism, Illustrated and Defended," says,— (p. 137,) "We shall not be understood to mean that he [Christ] was God, for we have shown that he did not possess the attributes of Deity."

Mr. Williamson says, (Expos. Univ., p' 13,) "Jesus of Nazareth was a *created* and *dependent* b eing, deriving all his wonderful powers from God." "If you ask me," says he, "if he was more than a man my answer is in the language of scripture, 'He was made *in all things* like unto his brethren, but was anointed with the oil of gladness above his fellows,' and endued with power greater than any other man. He claimed no higher title than the humble one—*the son of man*—an d if he claimed no more for himself, it is a misguided disciple that claims it for him."

Surely we need introduce no further testimony to sustain our charge! Here we have seen it fully stated, by these Expounders of Universalism, that our Divine Redeemer, was a *created dependent* being! that his *nature was strictly human nature,* and that *only!* that he bears the same *relation* to the Father, that *all men* do! that he was a *man,* a *mere man,* differing from other men only in *official dignity!* &c.; that he did not possess the attributes of Deity!!!

Hold! hold! says the pious reader; I am overwhelmed with amazement'. What! my Divine Redeemer nothing but a *mere man!* possessing *none of the "attributes of Deity!!!"* Be composed, gentle reader, we have many things yet to say, upon the whole subject, to which we solicit your impartial attention.

Mr. Ballou denies that the death of Christ made an atonement for sin, and also, that the Blood of Christ has efficacy to cleanse from guilt! Let us hear him:—"Christians have for a long time, believed, that the *temporal death* of Christ made an atonement for sin, and that the *literal* blood of the man who was crucified, has efficacy to cleanse from guilt; but surely this is carnality, and carnal mindedness, if we have any knowledge of the Apostle's meaning, where he says, 'To be carnally minded is death.'" Treat, on Aton., p. 122.

Well, if the Blood of Christ has no such efficacy in it, we might ask Mr. Ballou, what he thinks *can do away sin?* Mr. B. answers, "There is nothing in heaven above, nor in the earth beneath, that can do away sin but love." Treat, on Atom, p. 123.

This we regard as virtually denying the Atonement altogether. But perhaps the reader is ready to inquire whether the Universalists generally agree with Mr. Ballou. To which we answer, so far as we know, they *all* agree with him; indeed, we know that he is a kind of oracle to inquire at, and his "Treatise on [it should read *against*] the Atonement," is a standard work among Universalists, and the 5th Ed. of it, is numbered "Vol. 3rd," in the Universalist Library; he must therefore be regarded as a fair Exponent of Modern Universalism. But here we shall let the matter rest another Moon—and in the mean-time, we ask of all, and especially of our

Universalist friends, a candid perusal of what we have written, and the quotations we have made—"prove all things and hold fast to that which is good." Most of the quotations which we have made in this No., are from works in our possession, a few however, I have taken from other works, where they have been quoted.

EDITOR.

LOST RIVER ASSOCIATION.

We have just received the "Minutes of the Eighteenth annual meeting of the Lost River Association, held at Zoar meeting house, Washington county, Indiana, on the first Saturday, Lord's day, and Monday, in September, 1843:" in which is a circular letter addressed to "the churches of which she is composed, and all other brethren connected with us:" [her.]

We have examined the Minutes and Circular, and feel disposed to address a short review, *to the* Preachers, Elders, Deacons and Members composing the *"Lost River Association."*

Dear Brethren:—When we opened the minutes *of* the 18th meeting of your association, we saw the names of some with whom we were acquainted in former years, and among the rest, the names of Jonathan Jones, and Abraham Starks, were very familiar to us: these were among the first preachers we ever listened to. We remember to have often heard it said by the Baptists twenty years ago, that "Jonathan Jones was an Arminian"—that be was *"too soft."* But it would seem that the old brother has changed his views, and is now a *predestinarian,* in the fullest sense of that term! But we do not complain of Elder Jones for *changing*—there is a proverb which speaks on this wise. *"Wise men change, but fools never do."* But you inform us in your Minutes, that "The Oxfork church has excluded Eld. Abraham Stark from your union!" Why? what evil hath he done?

You also inform us that the whole number of members in all the churches composing your association, is 420; that since your last annual meeting, you have lost nine by death, dismissed by letter 22; and excluded 61, which make 92. And during the same time, you have received by Baptism 19, restored 3, by relation 2, by letter 13, making in all 37 additions, which leaves you *minus* 55!! In about 7 years and 7 months, your "Lost River Association" will be extinct; that is, if the *falling off* should continue regular. And supposing your loss in all your churches and associations, to be in the same ratio, your whole community will be swallowed up in less than eight years!! Now brethren, you must be sensible, that something is wrong in your teaching and practice, or these things would not be so. Anciently "the Lord added to the church daily the saved;" but it seems from your published report, that he is daily taking from you, those whom you have acknowledged to be of the *chosen seed!*

The 12th item of your minutes reads thus: "Report made by the committee appointed to visit Sugar Creek church; say they went to the time and place of their worship, and the said church failed to organize to do business; therefore, said church proved incorrigible; we, in consideration thereof, drop her from our union."

Now brethren, we have but few remarks to make upon this item of your minutes—but we will ask you a question or two: 1—Where in the word of God did the "Lost River Association" get authority to send a committee to Sugar Creek church, for the purpose of attending to her internal concerns, or for any other purpose?

2—Where in the Bible did your association get authority to exclude from your union a church, because she "refused to organize to do business," at the bidding of your committee? This looks to us, very much like "Lording it over God's heritage."

We now come to the CIRCULAR, the redeeming quality of which, is its brevity. This circular is written by the "Regular Baptist association, to the churches of which she is composed," &c. Now brethren, I have searched the New Testament through, to ascertain if I could, whether the Lord Jesus Christ, his holy Apostles, or the first Christians, ever constituted any "Regular Baptist churches of Jesus Christ," or any "Regular Baptist associations," but I searched in vain! It is true, I did find where the Apostles organized churches, called "The church of God," "The Temple of God," The church of the living God, the pillar and support of the truth;" but no where could I find a "Regular Baptist Church of Jesus Christ," or a "Regular Baptist Association." We have therefore come to the conclusion, that they are modern inventions, and to be classed with the *traditions, doctrines and commandments of men!* This circular purports to be written on the subject of Wisdom, which the Association calls "one of the grand attributes of God." Prov.8: 1,2, and 3; and also 9: 1, are quoted, from which the association draws the following conclusion—"So then, dear brethren, we had no hand in the great work of redemption. No more than we had in creation. But as he is Wisdom itself, he put forth all things according to his own will, and prepared all things for the support of our natural bodies, both food and raiment, and is, and will be glorified in all the work of his hands, from first to last." Now brethren, we most heartily subscribe to the above conclusion. God is the author of Creation, and Redemption, and we had no hand in either. God has prepared all things necessary for the support of our natural lives, and he has also made ample provisions for our salvation and spiritual enjoyment. No human being has been *passed by,* in the work of Creation, and in the means of temporal enjoyment; neither has he *passed* In; any, in the economy of redemption. "Jesus has, by the grace of God, tasted death for every man." "He gave himself *a* ransom for all to be testified in due time." "God has provided all things for the support of our natural bodies, both food and raiment." This is true; but will the association affirm that we enjoy food and raiment without the use of the means?—without complying with the conditions? God has decided by the mouth of Paul, to the Thess.: "If any will not work , neither shall he eat." Now we get our food and raiment from the hand of God, but we have to use the means—we have to work: we are left perfectly free to *do* and *live, or* to *not do* and *die,* that is temporally.— Just so, as the association has well remarked, "We had no hand in the great work of redemption." No indeed brethren, it is all of God; but we are addressed by our heavenly Father as rational beings, capable of *choosing or refusing* the offered grace. No rational being is lost sight of, in the rich provisions of the gospel, "whoever will come let him come and take the water of life freely." All the human family are made precisely equal, in reference to the means of salvation.— "Now I perceive of a truth, that God is no respecter of persons," said Peter at the house of Cornelius. It now remains for us, to *use the means,* and enjoy the promised blessings; or to refuse obedience, and die without mercy. Now we have no idea, that we *merit* salvation by *doing* the commands; but we understand the obedience to God's commands, to be the conditions, upon which we enjoy the blessings which God has promised to all them who obey him. God 'addresses every human being, on this wise: "Blessed are they that do his commandments, that they may have right to the tree of life, and enter in through the gates into the city."

The next item, in your circular, that I think worth while to notice, is this: you say, that some persons have invented a kind of religion, which they can *get* and *keep* too; and in the very next sentence you say, "and if it is so easy got, so it is as easy lost"! This looks like a contradiction.

The terms, "get religion, and lose religion," are ashdodical expressions, and are no where found in the Apostolic teaching

in the last paragraph, the association says: "The church of God ever has been separate from the world, in all ages, which shows the wisdom of God, procuring to himself a peculiar people, which was chosen in Christ Jesus, before the foundation of the world," &c. Now brethren, I most cordially admit, that the church of God is separate from the world, and always has been since its organization, and that the members of this church are "a peculiar people zealous of good works;" not opposed to all works! But you speak of these peculiar people, "being chosen in Christ before the foundation of the world." Now if I knew what you mean by the "*foundation of the world,*" I would know better what to say to you. If by this phrase you mean "the foundation of the material world," which I suppose is your meaning, it presents the following difficulty to my mind: the association would then seem to say, that "God's peculiar people lived anterior to the time when 'God created the Heavens and the Earth;' and consequently before Adam's dust was fashioned to a man!" And if this be your meaning, there is not one of God's peculiar people now living on the earth, or ever has been! But if you mean that some of the present inhabitants of the earth were *et ernally justified,* and *elected,* I remark that *election,* and *justification* are both *acts,* and all acts require time—no act can be eternal! Peter says, "elect according to the foreknowledge of God." Now here it is plainly said, that the Christian's election takes place according to something which preceded it, which Peter calls *foreknowledge:* this would be impossible, if the election was eternal—the thing is absurd! But the association says that God's people "were chosen in Christ before the foundation of the world." If this be so, brethren, I would like to know how it came to pass, that Paul's kinsmen "Andronicus and Junia," who were of note among the Apostles, were in Christ before him? The association will agree, I know, that Paul was one of God's people; and he says himself, that his kinsmen were in Christ before him. (Rom. 16th, and 7.) This declaration of Paul, forever explodes the doctrine of Eternal Election, for which the association contends!

The foreknowledge of God is put forth in his revealed will; whenever therefore, we believe the gospel, repent of our sins, and "obey from the heart the form of doctrine" which was delivered to us by the holy Apostles of the Lamb, we are "Elect according to the foreknowledge of God." And with this view of the subject, we can see how Paul's kinsmen were in Christ before him. They believed and obeyed the gospel before he did. The grand mistake into which all predestinations have run upon this subject, is that of making the election of the N. Testament, refer to *persons,* and not character; whereas the Apostles tell us that "God is no respecter of persons;" but they every where teach us that God is a respecter of character. The person who obeys the commands of God, from a proper motive, forms the character that God has chosen, and such an individual is one of God's elect.

We have one other suggestion to make:—We hope that brother Moses W. Sellers and H. Cornwell, when they write the next Circular letter, will not quote scripture, so indiscriminately, as we find it in the present case.—The language of Paul to the Romans, and Isaiah blended together; this is calculated to mislead.

In conclusion, we hope no offence will be taken, as none has been intended; we hope that these brethren will re-examine all these matters, with hearts open to receive the truth, and we feel confident, if ever they should be induced to do so, they will abandon a system which makes the death of Christ foolishness, and the gospel a nullity; for why should Christ die for those who were in him from all eternity, justified!

In hope that we may all come to a better understanding of the Lord's will, I subscribe myself your friend,

JAMES M. MATHES, ED.

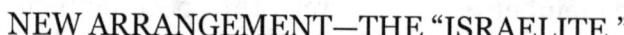

NEW ARRANGEMENT—THE "ISRAELITE."

BROTHER A. S. Tilden, the publisher of the "Israelite," has determined to suspend its further publication, and has sent us his list of subscribers, with a request that we should send them the "Christian Record," instead of the "Israelite;" this we have most cordially consented to do. Brother T. informs us, that some of the patrons of the Israelite have over-paid him, for the time they have taken it; a discount of the amount thus over-paid, will be made to such, when they make payment for the "Record." Those who are in arrears for the Israelite, will send their dues to this office, as the whole matter is transferred to this office. Brother Tilden informs us, that so far as he has had an opportunity of ascertaining the minds of the patrons of the Israelite, the above arrangement will be perfectly satisfactory. He mentioned the names of some of the most prominent brethren, in "Southern Indiana," who were favorable to the arrangement; and we do most devoutly hope, that it will be satisfactory to all. No pains shall be spared on our part, to make the "Christian Record" interesting and useful; and though we may differ a little, from our beloved brother Field, in reference to some matters connected with the coming of the Lord; still we hope to offend no one, as we do not expect to dogmatize upon this or any other subject. We expect to speak out, and enter our objections to any doctrine or practice which we believe to be wrong, in a manner too that all may understand; yet we hope never to forget that we are fallible, and as liable to be wrong as others. Indeed, we regard the difference that exists among the brethren upon the subject of the "Second Advent nigh," an honest difference of opinion, and shall treat it accordingly.

J. M. M., ED.'

THE CHRISTIAN MESSENGER.

THE *Christian Messenger* has re-commenced its periodical visits; edited by the beloved Elders B. W. Stone, and D. P. Henderson. Father Stone has long been known to the Theological world, as a good critic, a strong reasoner, and an uncompromising advocate of what he believed the Bible taught; and with all, a most loving writer. He has been an unyielding advocate of *the Bible alone,* for near half a century; and although he is now fast approaching the Jordan of death, he still wields a powerful pen. The Messenger is published at Jacksonville, Ill., at $1 in advance. J. M. M., ED.

THE QUESTION SETTLED.

IF WHERE a word in *any* language has different meanings, but universally has the same meaning, when applied to one and the same thing, and the learned will not deny it: and as the learned world agree, that the word in the original Greek which we have rendered in the common translation of the New Testament *baptize,* means *Immerse* when applied to the ordinance of

Christian Baptism: Then it follows, according to the above rule, that the word *"baptize"* invariably means *"immerse,"* when applied to that sacred ordinance. Therefore *immersion is the only scriptural mode* of Christian Baptism.

T. C. JOHNSON.

FOR THE CHRISTIAN RECORD.
CHRISTIAN OBLIGATIONS—NO. 3.

At the close of our second number we promised to say something about the reward of the Christian, and the time and place he is to receive it; but before we do this we will state a circumstance recorded in the 22nd chapter of Gen., to show the extent of a positive command, even over a moral duty, without a command. I allude to the circumstance of Abraham being required to offer up his son Isaac in sacrifice, through whom was the promise of a nation, as the sand on the sea shore for multitude, and *that seed* (Christ) in whom all nations were to be blessed. Now it was morally wrong for Abraham to kill his son, but because the Lord gave the commandment it became right, at least to make the attempt; and because he did so the Lord renewed the promise which he made to him in Ur, of the Chaldees, So, then, a positive commandment is more binding than a moral duty without a commandment.

If the above position be true, how dare any individual say any thing which Jesus Christ has commanded is a "non-essential." It would be just as easy to prove that Abraham would have been right in slaying his son without a commandment.

In the first two numbers, and thus far in the third, we have spoken, chiefly, of the obligations which rest upon the Christian to do the Lord's commandments. We will now commence where we left off in the second No., and speak of the motives connected with Christian obligations, for duty and interest always go together in the divine economy "Do good and lend expecting to receive nothing;" but if the reward is in this life, we ought not only to receive something, but even more than we bestow, for "if ye love them which love you, what reward have ye? do not even the Publicans the same? And if ye salute your brethren only, what do ye more than others? do not even the Publicans so?" Matt. 5: 46, 47. The hypocrites love to pray standing in the synagogues and in the corners of the streets, that they may be seen of men, but they have their reward; that is, the praise of men. The reward of such is in this life; but to those who, by patient continuance in well doing, seek for glory and honor, and immortality, God will award eternal life. He that receiveth a prophet, because he is a prophet, shall receive a prophet's reward. He that receiveth a righteous man, because he is a righteous man, shall receive a righteous man's reward. He that giveth a cup of cold water to a disciple of Christ, because he is such, shall in no wise lose his reward. From the quotations which we have made we see, that the motive we have in doing good is a material point.

A short time before the Saviour left his little band of followers, he addressed them in the following language: "Let not your heart be troubled, ye believe in God believe also in me. In my father's house are many mansions; if it were not so I would have told you. I go to prepare a place for you, and if I go and prepare a place for you, I will come again and receive you to myself, that where I am *there* ye may be also." John 14: 1,4. What are the motives the Saviour laid before his disciples to encourage them? He told them to believe in him— not simply to believe that he was the Messiah, but to have confidence in his promise. What did he promise them? Long life? prosperity? honor? ease? None of these things. Nothing that pertains to this life, but "In my father's house are many mansions," and "I will come again and take you to myself," &c. These are the motives the Saviour laid before his disciples to encourage them to be faithful. But he tells them that in the world they shall have tribulation—"If they have persecuted me, they will persecute you." Again: "The time shall come when he that killeth you will think that he doeth God service." Did these things discourage them? Ah no! They trusted not in an arm of flesh; but they looked for a city which hath foundations whose maker and builder is God.

The Apostle Paul, when contrasting the persecutions, tribulations, strifes, imprisonment, perils, slander, hunger, thirst, cold, and nakedness, and even death itself, all of which he had to suffer for righteousness' sake; with *that* crown of righteousness which was laid up for him in heaven; calls them light afflictions, saying, "these light afflictions shall work out for us a far more exceeding and eternal weight of glory." Again, he says to the Hebrews: "Let us go forth therefore unto him (Jesus) without the camp bearing his reproach, for here we have no continuing city, but we seek one to come." Heb. 13: 13, 14. The reason assigned by the Apostle here, why we should bear the reproach of Christ is, because "here we have no continuing city, but seek one to come," "a building of God, a house not made with hands eternal in the heavens."

Did the disciples of the Lord believe with all their hearts that he would reward them with eternal life, for serving him in this world, they would feel more interested in doing his commandments, and we have no more reason to doubt the fulfillment of his promises, than we have to doubt that he is the Son of God, for "he is not slack concerning his promise as some men count slackness."

Thus far we have labored to show that the Lord does not require us to serve him for naught. In our next, we will proceed to show in what that service consists. T. J. EDMONDSON.

PARENTAL FAULT FINDING.

It is not always necessary to find fault with and punish your children, when they do wrong. Very much may be done to reform a disobedient child, by encouraging it when it does well. Parents should ever be more careful to express their approbation of good actions, than their disapprobation of bad. Nothing can tend more to harden a child in disobedience, and render it heedless and inattentive, than a spirit of incessant fault finding, on the part of its parents: and perhaps nothing can exert a more pernicious influence both upon the parents and child. It sours the disposition of both, blunts the natural affections, and weakens the ties which bind them together, as parents and child. There are two influences which produce all human actions, one arises from *hope*, or motive, and the other from *fear*, or dread of punishment. But what parents, possessing only three grains of discernment, would not prefer to have their child influenced to perform good actions, by the hope of pleasing, and gaining their approbation; rather than by the fear of offending them, and of receiving the threatened punishment. If parents never express their gratification when their children do well, but are always censuring and finding fault with them whenever they do amiss, the children will naturally become discouraged and unhappy.— They feel that there is no use in trying to please; for whether they do well or ill, they meet with nothing but continual *fault finding*—they therefore relinquish all efforts to please, and become hardened in disobedience, and heedless of reproaches.

But Jet parents approve of the conduct of their Child whenever they can; let them show that its good behaviour makes them sincerely happy—let them reward its efforts to please, with smiles, and other expressions of their approbation and joy; and in this way they may cherish in the heart of their child some of the noblest feelings and principles of our nature.

We are commanded by the Apostle, "Not to provoke our children to wrath, least they be discouraged." This command of God, is trampled under foot, our dear children discouraged, and their present and future happiness either destroyed, or endangered by incessant *fault finding!* Again the Apostle says to Christian parents: "Bring up your children in the nurture and admonition of the Lord." This divine command imposes solemn and awful responsibilities upon us, which can only be discharged by teaching our children the great truths of the Bible, the proper dignity of their moral nature, the nature of that relation which they sustain to God their Maker, and their duty to him growing out of that relation—and the awful consequences of disobedience; praying with and for them, and continually enforcing our instructions, not by severe correction, but by an undeviating example of all that is morally, and religiously excellent; in short, by living out in their presence, all that we teach them to be; then, and not till then, will our children have confidence in our instructions, and will be led to imitate our example, and form a character, which will give them influence and respectability in time, and qualify them for a blessed immortality when time shall be no more: therefore, *do not be always finding fault.*

J. M. M., Ed.

QUESTIONS BY MOSES HALL, JR.

The following queries presented themselves to me on reading the "reflections" of the Sen'r. Editor of the Christian Messenger vol. 13th no. 4th of that work, to wit:

1st. Have not Civil and Military governments existed in some form or other ever since the days of Christ and his apostles?

2d. Did Christ or his apostles ever speak evil of or oppose such governments and teach others so do?

3d. Were those Powers spoken of in Romans 13th chapter, civil or Military or were they Ecclesiastical?

4th. Were all those in authority (1st Timothy 2d chapt.) for whom Intercessions Prayers &c. were exhorted to be made members of Christ's Kingdom?

5th. Can a Christian offer up an acceptable prayer (to God) for the success, prosperity, or continuance of any institution which he himself deems corrupt and refuses to support by his council, co-operation and choice?

6th. Is it right for Christians in these United States, to pray for the prosperity and continuance of the American Government and its institutions?

7th. Does the Constitution or laws of these United States deprive a Christian of any right, privilege or immunity his soul can desire—(unless he should desire to exercise Lordship over God's Heritage?)

8th. Is it not the duty of Christians to attend to the temporal, as well as the spiritual welfare of themselves and others?

9th. Can a man be a Christian and refuse (when in his power) to aid in promoting or sustaining the happiness of his fellow men, either temporally or spiritually?

10th. Is not the happiness of the whole human family dependent (more or less) on the civil laws or institutions by which they are governed, while in the world?

11th. Who are the most suitable characters to make and sustain such laws and institutions,— Righteous or wicked men?

12th. Would the glory of God and the happiness of man be promoted by transferring the civil and religious liberties of all Christians into the hands of infidels; into the hands of a sect, or into the hands of the Pope or the Papists?

13th. Does not the Papists or Pope stand ready to accept such a transfer?

14th. Would not such a transfer be more generous on the part of Christians, than was that of

Esau when he sold his birthright to Jacob for a morsel of meat?

15th. Is not civil and religious liberty the birthright of every American born citizen?

16th. Can this birthright be mentioned elsewhere than at the ballot box or in the councils of the nation?

17th. Are not Christians commanded to watch as well as to pray?

The above queries are submitted by one who from infancy to the present hour has held the author of the "reflections" alluded to in the highest estimation.

JUSTIFICATION—NO. 2.

Having given a definition of the term justification as used in the scriptures, and stated three different views taken of the way through which a person is justified, we shall now treat of them in their order.

First. That we are justified by works. The Jews appear to have entertained this view, for the Apostle Paul says Rom. 2, 13. "For not the hearers of the law are just before God, but the doers of the law shall be justified." This was correct enough under the former covenant; but the error was in those Jews who had embraced Christianity wishing to incorporate the law with the gospel; but the Apostle opposed this view Gal. 2, 16. "Knowing that a man is not justified by the works of the law, but by the faith of Jesus Christ, even we have believed in Jesus Christ, that we might be justified by the faith of Christ, and not by the works of the law: for by the works of the law shall no flesh be justified." There are some, however, in these latter days who teach that we are justified by works and for proof quote James 3, 21, and similar passages, and thus found a theory of justification by works. But this view is evidently wrong, because no one can be justified in the sight of God who does not please him, and the Apostle in Heb. 11, 6, says "But without faith it is impossible to please him; for he that cometh to God must believe that he is, and that he is a rewarder of them that diligently seek him." So that any thing that we might do (which is required of us in the gospel) without faith, could not be the condition of our justification. Some take this ground; that as it is said that "we must all appear before the judgment seat of Christ; that every one may receive the things *done* in his body, according to that he hath done, whether it be good or bad," the judge of all, keeps a kind of 'day book against them, and marks all their doings, and that when ever their good deeds out number their evil ones, then they are justified before God. But on the other hand, when their evil deeds exceed their righteous ones, then they are in a state of condemnation; so that the whole scheme with them is one of debt and credit. But such an idea is manifestly wrong, for it excludes the principle of forgiveness, which is abundantly taught in the scriptures, both of the old and new Testaments.

To the above we might add the view of some Roman Catholics, who contend that man possesses an inherent principle of righteousness, which acted out, results in our justification; but this view would (it seems to us) exclude the necessity of revelation, and the sacrifice of Christ the Lord; for if the principle is inherent in one, justice would say, that it was inherent in all, and consequently all would be led by that principle, and our conduct would all be right without the light of the Bible, or any of the blessings vouchsafed to us through the mediation of our Saviour.

All the above views, we conceive, stand opposed to the doctrine of Christ; for an Apostle has taught us that "by grace ye are saved, through faith; and that (grace) not of yourselves: it is the gift of God." So that grace and faith are connected in our justification. And the above theories of being justified by works are not scriptural, but mere human speculations, dangerous to believe and rely on for future happiness-sandy foundations which crumble with the touch of truth, and which if persisted in by their advocates, must prove their eternal ruin.

Secondly. That we are justified by faith *only*. This, by a popular creed, is said to be "a most wholesome doctrine, and very full of comfort."

The above view of justification has been received and adopted (probably) because it was a leading doctrine of Luther, the great Reformer, and stands opposed to Catholicism on that subject, and farther because the scriptures frequently say "We are justified by faith"—"We are justified through faith" &c; But notwithstanding Luther and the first Reformers so taught, and such phrases as the above occur in the scriptures, we think it is not strictly correct, and we should adopt the maxim of the Great Apostle of the Gentiles "Prove all things; hold fast that which is good;" from which we learn that we are not to receive any thing for truth, because it is said to be true by any man, however good or great, but that we should try what ever is taught us by men on the subject of religion, by the word of God; the only infallible criterion for us to prove such things by. We know that when persons become identified with a religious party, and receive and adopt their creed, it requires more humility and self-denial than many possess, to deny, or reject any thing taught in their adopted creed, hence if ever errors should be pointed out to them in it, they prepare to defend them, and search the scriptures, more with a view to find passages that seem to sustain their creed, than to find out the mind of Christ upon the subject; and thus instead of making "The Good Book" the rule to try the correctness of their creed, they make the creed the rule to try "the book by." This would be setting the wisdom of men above the wisdom of God! Than which nothing can be more preposterous.

Great and pious men have erred, and may err again, therefore, we should investigate and try by the "good book," every matter presented to us upon the subject of our present and future salvation. Having for many years been accustomed to receive nothing for truth upon the mere *ipsi dixit* of fallible men, and having carefully proved the above plan of justification by the gospel, we feel bound to dissent; and we offer among others, the following reasons and proofs for our opposition.

First. We are said to be "Justified freely by his (God's) grace"—"Justified by his (Christ's) blood"—"Justified by works," &c , &c. Therefore, we are not justified by *faith only,* because it is ascribed to other causes in conjunction with faith. To believe on Jesus, is said to be work: see John 6: 28, 29—"Then said they (the Jews) unto him, (Jesus,) what shall we do that we might *work* the *works* of God? Jesus said unto them, This is the *work* of God, that ye believe on him whom he hath sent." That is, this is the work which God requires of us. So that to exclude works would be to exclude faith alone if the above definition of works, given by our Saviour, be correct; and who will doubt it?

Again: A work is an act, or any kind of agency in thought, word, or deed. See Eccl. 12th chap., 14th verse. "For God shall bring every *work* into judgment with every secret thing, whether it be good or whether it be evil." Then if any act, in thought, word, or deed, is *work,* it is impossible for us to be justified by faith *only*. To obey God's commands is to act, consequently to work. Well, even to hear or give heed to what he says, is in obedience to a command; is an act. Isaiah 1: 2. "Hear, O Heavens, and give ear O Earth;" Math. 11:15. "He that hath ears to hear *let him hear.*" Math. 17: 5. "This is my beloved son, in whom I am well pleased; *hear ye him."*

Again. To believe, is to obey the Lord. I John, 3: 23; "And this is his commandment, that we should *believe* on his Son Jesus Christ." Repentance is an act of ours. Acts 2: 33; "Repent and be baptized every one of you," &c. Acts, 3, 19, "Repent and be converted that your sins may be blotted out." Acts 17. 30, "And the times of this ignorance God winked at; but now *commandeth* all men every where to *repent.*" Calling upon the name of the Lord is an act—something done by us, therefore a work. Act 2, 21. "And it shall come to pass that whosoever shall *call* on the name of the Lord shall be *saved.*"

Rom. 10, 13. "For whosoever shall call upon the name of the Lord shall be saved." To confess with our mouth the Lord Jesus is an act, something *done,* consequently a *work*. Rom. 10: 9, 10. "That if thou shalt *confess* with thy mouth the Lord Jesus, and believe in thy heart that God hath raised him from the dead, thou shalt be saved; for with the heart man believeth unto righteousness, and with the mouth *confession* is made unto salvation." To be baptized is an act, (though probably we are more passive in this act of obedience than in any we have named.) And the Saviour says, Mark 16: 16, "He that believeth and is baptized shall be saved," (pardoned.) Peter, under the infallible inspiration of the Holy Spirit, said, Acts 2: 38: "Repent and be baptized every one of you in the name of Jesus Christ for the remission of sins," &c.

Now if we are required by the Lord of all, to hear; to believe; to call upon the name of the Lord; to confess with our mouth the Lord Jesus —to be baptized in the name of the Lord Jesus, in order that our "souls may live."—That we may "be saved"—"That our sins may be blotted out"—That we may be "forgiven"—obtain "remission of sins"—Be "made free from sin"—and to obtain "salvation" from, or be "purged from our old sins;" which terms are used in the New Testament as synonymous with justification: Then justification by *faith alone* is not according to the word of God; of course is an error, and not "a wholesome doctrine," nor "very full of comfort."

October, 1843.   TYCHICUS.

MOUNT VERNON, Ind., 23rd Sept. 1843.

Bear Bro. Mathes: Below you have the minutes of our late cooperation meeting in this County, which you will see you are requested to give a place in the Ch. Record. For the information of the brethren generally, permit me to say, that we have held a yearly meeting of this kind, in this county, for the last five or six years. Some time before the meeting comes on, each Church determines by subscription or otherwise, about the amount they will give to support an Evangelist, during the following year. A statement of these amounts is taken to the co-operation meeting and added together, and an Evangelist is then appointed by the meeting, to travel and preach until the next yearly meeting, who receives the contributions thus offered by the churches, to sustain him in the work. The following minutes will show the amount promised by each church in this county. Notwithstanding we are doing but little for the cause, considering its importance, yet, fearing there are many of the churches which fail to do even this much, we have thought good to publish to the brethren what we are doing in this remote corner of the state, hoping that our "zeal may provoke many more" to GO AND DO LIKEWISE. By a reference to Mil. Bar., N. S. Vol. 3, page 355, you will see the increase of the churches in this county, during the last four years. May the good Lord bless our efforts to promote his cause, and finally save us in heaven. Amen.

ELIJAH GOODWIN.

MINUTES

Of a Co-operation Meeting of the Christian congregation in Posey County, Indiana, held at Liberty Meeting House in said County, on the 15th September, 1843.

By the request of brethren B. Carter and R. McConnel, the Elders of the church at Liberty, bro. E. Goodwin was called to the chair, and bro. John C. Welborn was appointed secretary.

The following churches were heard from by letter or otherwise:

Bone bank, whose members number			25,	and which promised	$15 00
Point, "		"	44,		21 00
Mount Vernon,	"	"	67,		40 00
Yankee Chapel,	"	"	38,		40 00
Blairsville,	"	"	25,		27 50
Mount Pleasant,	"	"	33,		35 00
Union,*	"	"	52,		
Liberty,	"	"	50,		40 00
Total number of members			334	Total amt. prom.	$218 50

*No letter from this church on account of sickness.

Bro. Elijah Goodwin, one of our Evangelists for the last year, gave a satisfactory report of his labours during the past year, of which the following is the substance:

Dearly beloved brethren: You remember that when I was appointed at our last general meeting, to travel and preach during the year which has now closed, my health was very bad, insomuch that I expressed doubts, whether I should be able to carry out the designs of that appointment. I have great reason, however, to be very thankful to our kind Heavenly Father, for the health and strength with which I have been blessed. Notwithstanding I have labored under much debility a great part of the year, I do not remember to have missed one appointment during the whole time, by reason of sickness. I have traveled, since our last co-operation meeting, about 3992 miles; about 1200 miles of which was traveled by water. I have delivered 367 public discourses on the great subject of Christianity, and have witnessed 104 additions to the good cause for which we plead. There has been no great excitement within the bounds of my labours; but the work which has been done seems to be permanent. I do believe that the churches generally, where I have preached the last year, are in better order than I have ever known them.

Morganfield, Ky., and Wonborough, Graysville, and Albion, Ill., were in my regular preaching arrangements, at each of which places there is a Christian church doing well.

Besides my regular appointments, I have visited the churches in Louisville, Ky.; New Albany, Ind., Vincennes, Washington, and St. Louis, Mo., all of which seem to be in a healthy state: indeed, brethren, you may rest assured that the cause of the BIBLE ALONE, in all matters of Religion, is gaining influence generally, and all that is wanting to gain a decided victory on the side of truth, is for all the disciples of Christ, to "walk worthy of the vocation wherewith they are called."

The meeting was informed that bro. Moses Goodwin, our other Evangelist, was lying at home very sick. No report was had from him.

It was unanimously agreed that bro. E. Goodwin "do the work of an Evangelist," for one year from this time, for the eight churches represented in this meeting, with the understanding that he will, if health permit, visit each church once a month, and that he receive the contributions promised by them. He is also to have the privilege of taking some places in Kentucky and Illinois, in his preaching arrangement.

Unanimously agreed, that we forward a MS copy of the minutes of this meeting, to bro. J. M. Mathes, requesting him to publish the same in the "Christian Record."

Unanimously agreed, that we hold another co-operation meeting in the Yankee settlement, commencing at 2 o'clock, P. M., on Friday before the 2nd Lord's day in September, 1844.

The meeting then adjourned.

E. GOODWIN, Mod. JOHN C. WELBORN, Secretary.

NEWS FROM THE CHURCHES.

VALLONIA, Ind., Sept. 28th, 1843.

Dear Brother Mathes: At our annual meeting, including the 3rd Lord's day of this month, we had an interesting time and 12 valuable additions to the congregation were obtained. The public teachers on the occasion, were Elds. John Wright, Jacob Wright, Richard Lane and T. J. EDMONDSON, J. B. BERKEY.

We have understood that some 29 persons were immersed at the annual meeting, at "Old Silver Creek," in Clark County, Ia. The meeting included the 4th Lord's day in Aug.

We have also learned that some 25 or more, were obedient to the faith, at Mill-creek, near Salem at the annual Meeting, which included the 1st. Lord's day in Sept. These meetings we expected to have at_ tended, but was prevented by sickness.

J. M. M. Ed.

Brother John Harrod of Vienna, Ind., under date of Oct. 10th, says: "I will just inform you, that I have attended three meetings in my neighborhood recently at which there were added to the church 25."

Our annual meeting at "Old Union," near Gosport, Ia., included the 1st Lord's day in this month, (Oct.) It was truly a time of joy to the disciples, 16 valuable additions were made to the church; during the meeting. The laborers were P. M. Blankinship of Martinsville, J. G. Campbell of Bloomington, T. C. Johnson of Spencer, and Samuel Swinford of Stilesville.

The next Lord's day after the meeting closed, we delivered a discourse at the same place, and another was baptized.

We met the brethren at Stilesville, at their annual meeting, including the 3rd Lord's day in this month, (Oct.) Elds. N. Waters and T. Lockhart, were also laborers at the meeting: 6 persons were baptized during the meeting.

We also co-operated with our beloved brother T. C. Johnson at Spencer for several days including the 4th, Lord's day in this month, (Oct.) the result was two immersions and several other additions to the church. J. M. M. Ed.

Owen county, Indiana, Oct.. 16tA, 1843.

MY DEAR BROTHER MATHES:—

On the evening of the 14th inst., I left home, and attended an appointment at brother John Shuler's, Morgan county, at which time I addressed the people from the parable, recorded Luke 12, 18, 19, and 1 confessed the Lord. On Lord's day, (15th inst.) I attended my appointment at sister Dow's four miles West of Martinsville, where I delivered a discourse from these words of Paul: "But now in Christ Jesus, ye who some times were afar oil, are made nigh by the blood of Christ;" Eph.2,13. At the close five persons made the good confession, who with one who had previously confessed the Lord were "buried with the Lord in Baptism." At night I spoke to the people at the same place from Heb. 5, 8, 9. At the close two young men confessed the name of Jesus, and two were reclaimed. On Monday the 16th at the house of brother Joel Bean, I addressed the people upon the subject of the *Resurrection,* from 1, Thes. 4, 14, and another young man confessed his faith in Christ, and was immersed.

My dear brother, I never saw a happier time among the brethren in all my life; while sinners were made to weep. I have no doubt but many were like Agrippa of old, "Almost persuaded to be Christians." I was truly sorry to leave them, but other pressing engagements, compelled me to return home. During my short tour, I had the pleasure of immersing 10 persons in the name of the Lord, and 3 who had been immersed were added to the congregation. These things fill my heart with joy as I pass along. Praise the Lord, for all his blessings to his children!

I am your brother in Christ.
JOHN BROWN.

☞ Rev. Williamson Terrell's communication came to hand too late, for the present No., but shall appear in our next.

☞ We owe an apology to our readers, for the many typographical errors, which appeared in our 3rd No. Sickness prevented us from reading the proof. We are now at our post.

THE CHRISTIAN RECORD.

Vol. I.]　　　　　BLOOMINGTON, IND., NOVEMBER, 1843.　　　　　[No. V.

CHRISTIAN UNION—NO. 5.

IN our last, we ascertained that the *word* of God, without any human need super-added, is the *only* ground upon which all Christians can possibly be united. But as our friends of the different denominations are Very fond of "Summaries of faith;" and seem to think the *whole* Bible too large, for a "Confession of Faith," we would offer the following, as a "summary" of the gospel, viz: "There is one body, and one spirit, even as ye are called in one hope of your calling; one Lord, one faith, one baptism, one God and Father of all, who is above all, and through all, and in you all." Paul; Eph. 4: 4, 6.

In the above summary, there are seven articles. Article I—One Body. Art. 2—One Spirit. Art. 3—One Hope. Art. 4—One Lord. Art. 5—One Faith. Art. 6—One Baptism. Art. 7—One God and Father of all.

Is this too short! Is it too long! Surely all will agree that the Apostle being guided by the unerring Spirit, has arranged it exactly right. Well then, what good reason can any professed Disciple of the Lord Jesus offer, for not being willing to lay down all uninspired creeds and confessions of faith, and for refusing to take this heaven inspired summary!

The objector will perhaps say, "We cannot unite upon the above 7 articles of faith, for we cannot agree as to the Apostle's meaning." We believe however, that if people would lay aside prejudice, and *try* to agree, the thing would not be very hard to accomplish. Let us then make an effort to agree upon the different items of this short, but comprehensive confession of faith. For this purpose, we shall examine each article, in the order in which the Apostle has set them down. And first: "There is one body." All agree, that this expression is equivalent to "There is one church." Well then, the Apostle in the first article, teaches us that Christ has but one church, body, or kingdom in the world. Upon this subject we all agree.

But as there are many churches in the world at the present time, all professing to be the church of Jesus Christ, it may be well for us to Inquire how shall we know the "one body," or church!

We answer, if a church can be found, the members of which have believed the gospel with all their heart, and have "from the heart obeyed the form of doctrine," delivered by the holy Apostles of the Lamb, all "walking by the same rule," the law of the Lord: "All minding the same things;" the commandments of God; all wearing the same name—the name of Christ. We say if such church can be found, on the face of this wide earth, it is the "One Body," or church referred to above, In other words, take up the New Testament and read the description of the church of God, and then look abroad among the churches, and if you can find any which fills the description—that is, one wearing the name, possessing "the faith once delivered to the saints," and practicing the precepts of the gospel; you may be sure, that you have found the "one body," or church. We think all will agree to this. The converse of this is equally true: if the church does not fill the description given of the church of God in the New Testament, it is not the church of God, or the "one body."

But what is this "one body" called? Methodist, Baptist, Presbyterian or Campbellite? We answer, none of the above! Just open the New Testament, and see what the church constituted on the day of Pentecost (Acts 2d chap.) was called by the Apostles. Did they call it "the Methodist church of Jesus Christ!" No. Was it called the "Baptist church of Jesus Christ!" No. Was it called the Campbellite, Quaker, Lutheran? No; none of these. By reference to the Epistolary part of the New Testament, and the "Acts of Apostles," this matter may be determined. "Paul, called to be an Apostle of Jesus Christ through the will of God, and Sosthenes our brother, unto the church of God which is at Corinth," &c. (1 Cor. 1: 1, 2.) Here the Apostle calls the "one body," "The church of God." Again: "Paul, an Apostle of Jesus Christ by the will of God, and Timothy our brother, unto the church of God which is at Corinth, with all the saints which are in all Achaia." (2 Cor. 1:].) "And all the brethren which are with me, unto the churches of Galatia." (Gal. 1: 2.) "Paul, an Apostle of Jesus Christ by the will of God, to the saints which are at Ephesus, and to the faithful in Christ Jesus." (Eph. 1: 1.) "Paul, and Timotheus, the, servants of Jesus Christ, to all the saints in Christ Jesus which are at Philippi, with the bishops and deacons." (Phil. 1: 1.) "But if I tarry long, that thou mayest know how thou oughtest to behave thyself in the house of God, which is the church of the living God, the pillar and ground of the truth." (4 Tim. 3: 15.)

We now see from these quotations from the Epistles, that the Apostles did not address the "one body," as Methodists, Baptists, Presbyterians of the Old, or New school, Quakers or Campbellites—but simply, "The church of God." "The church of the living God." "The saints and faithful in Christ Jesus," tec., &c.

Now let us turn to the Acts of Apostles; and here we have the followers of the Lord called *Disciples, children, brethren, saints, faithful,* and such like appellations; and at the 11th chap, and 26th verse, we have these remarkable words: "And the disciples were called Christians first in Antioch." They were not called Methodists, Baptists, Presbyterians, Newlights, nor Campbellites: but they were called *Christians.*— Again, "Then Agrippa said unto Paul, almost thou persuadest me to be a Christian." Acts 26: 28. If Paul had been a Methodist, would not the king have said, "almost you persuade me to be a Methodist!" He certainly would; and the very fact therefore that he uses the term *Christian,* proves that Paul wore the name, and that Agrippa knew *that to* be the name, worn and acknowledged by the followers of the despised Jesus.

But the import of the name *Christian,* and its vast importance, will be the subject of a future number. We have now perused the subject far enough for our present purpose. We have ascertained what the *One Body* was called in the primitive days of Christianity, and consequently, what it should be called now.

Art. 2. "There is one Spirit." All will agree, that this is the Holy Spirit—the *Spirit of Christ.* This one spirit dwells in the one body: for Paul says, "if you have not the spirit of Christ, you are none of his." That the holy spirit dwells in the heart of every Christian, all Christians will agree. "Because you are sons, God hath sent forth the spirit of his son into your heart, crying Abba Father," This *one spirit* bears witness with our spirit, that we are accepted with God. "The spirit itself beareth witness with our spirit, that we are the children of God. Rom. 8. 16. All Christians agree, that the spirit of God is the agent in the conversion of a sinner to God: about this there is no controversy—we only differ about *how* the spirit does the work. We teach that the spirit is the *agent,* and the word of God is the *instrument:* while some of our friends teach an abstract influence; that is, that the spirit *alone* regenerates the sinner without any instrumentality. But as to the FACT, we all agree.

We all agree that this one spirit, whose gracious influences are enjoyed by all Christians NOW, will finally be the mighty agent, in the resurrection of our bodies, from the cold grave. "But if the spirit of him that raised up Jesus from the dead dwell in you, he that raised up Christ from the dead shall also quicken your mortal bodies by his spirit that dwelleth in you." Rom. 8: 11.

The other articles of this "Summary," we shall examine in our next.

J. M. M., ED.

UNIVERSALISM—NO. 5.

Do UNIVERSALISTS believe in public prayer? This is a question often asked, but seldom satisfactorily answered. Some Universalists have been heard to pray, while others have opposed it. Mr. Rogers, a distinguished Universalist preacher, and writer, in his *tale* of "Alice Sherwood," "showing the influence of certain religious doctrines on individual and social life," gives us the following dialogue, which he puts into the mouths of Miss 'Alice,' and the 'Old Squire,' who, it seems, was a staunch Orthodox Universalist; viz: Alice is made to say, "I intimated to the old gentleman my surprise at his utterance of these pious sentiments—in as much," said I, "as I have concluded with confidence that there is no religion amongst you—you certainly never pray, and"—"Pardon me," interrupted he, "how came you by the *certain* knowledge that we never pray?" "I infer it," was my answer, "from the fact that I never either saw or heard you so engaged." "Not the most logical inference in the world my fair friend," he rejoined, "since many things are constantly transpiring around you which you neither see nor hear. Moreover, the religion of Christ courts not the eye nor the ear of man—it is modest, and is content with being visible *in its ejects*. To see or hear us pray, therefore, would be to detect us in a flagrant violation of the gospel command," &c. ("Pro and Con," pp. 11 and 12.)

Now we wish the reader to remember this, that "to see or hear a Universalist pray, is to detect him in a flagrant violation of the command of God."

Let it be remembered too, that Mr. Rogers, has given us this "tale" for the purpose of showing us the influence of Universalism, on the people of the East: for he locates his scenes, in the "Pennsylvania Valley?"

Some Universalist Preachers boast of the *moral tendency* of their principles in the East: but if Mr. Rogers is a veritable witness, Eastern Universalists so far from engaging in public prayer, regard it as a transgression of the law of God, and satisfactory evidence of self-righteousness and hypocrisy! We need not offer an argument, nor add a single text of scripture, to prove that "public prayer" is an institution of divine appointment, as well as "secret prayer." We just offer the whole Bible as proof, and promise to give chapter and verse if it is called in question.

Does Universalism admit the doctrine of man's *free* or *moral agency?* We think it does not admit it! For if God has determined to *save all men, unconditionally,* it is more than nonsense to talk about *moral agency!* No man has power to *hinder* his reconciliation to God. Paul himself was not more certain of "an eternal weight of glory," after all his obedience to God, and his toil and labor in his master's cause, than was the tyrant Nero? by whose bloody sentence, it is generally supposed, Paul suffered a cruel death! The notion therefore of *choosing* and *refusing* eternal life, is all a dream! For if Universalism be true, (God forgive the supposition!) there is no choice to make! The greatest cut-throat in the land is as sure of a happy end, as the most humble and pious Christian!

Hosea Ballou, in his "Treat, on Atonement," pp 117, 118, contends, chat as *all* power in heaven and in earth was given to Christ, man has no power; and that therefore, "The whole system of law in moral nature, must be subservient to the designs of the Redeemer;" and that as he holds in his hands the power of moral government, "it certainly must be at his option, whether man shall be reconciled to God or not." Mr. B., on page 118, denies that *man has the* power of *moral* government! (or free agency.) He says, "if they have, the great work of reconciliation might be performed by them," &c. Again, same page, Mr. Ballou says: "And we think it will not be deemed admissible, that we have power to hinder this work, of reconciliation, as that would in effect, deny the truth of all power being given to Christ." But farther on this point: "The method," says Mr. B., "by which we are brought to love any object, whatever, is, by seeing, or thinking we see, floral beauty in the object; and our love is always in proportion to apparent good qualities of the object seen." ('Treat, *on* At p. 121.) From this passage, and the whole connection in which it stands, we understand the following to be his argument, to wit: "Man has no independent will. He always *acts* as he is *acted upon* by objects which he *sees,* or *thinks he sees!* His will as not consulted, when an object is presented, in which he sees, or thinks he sees, something lovely; *he is compelled to love it!* And again, when an object is presented to him, in which he *thinks* he sees *moral deformity,* he is not able to exercise *moral agency,* but *he is compelled to hate it!* Our reconciliation to God, is, therefore, not of our own choosing—for we are *compelled!* Our enmity to God, is not a matter in which there is any exercise of moral agency—for we are *compelled to hate God,* from the false light in which his character has been presented to our minds!

We never think of attaching either *praise or blame* to a man for doing that, which he could not avoid—which he was *compelled* to do. It is only in those actions which are *voluntary,* that we see any thing to praise or blame. But Universalism denies that human actions are voluntary, and thus removes the ancient land marks between virtue and vice! This we think all must see: but to make the matter more plain if possible, we shall introduce a figure, which we once used in arguing this point, with an intelligent Universalist, and he admitted that it was a fair representation of Universalism, in reference to *moral agency*— it is this:

Man is like a "Clock," whose complicated machinery is all put in order, except the weights, by the cunning workman. The clock is set up, but it moves not, for it is not able to perform a *voluntary* action—it therefore stands still. Yet we do not *blame* the clock, for it cannot do otherwise than *stand still.* But we will suppose that the man who made it, hangs on the weights and gives momentum to the pendulum—the clock runs, but its action is not voluntary, it is *compelled* by a power not its own—it does well, but we do not think of praising it, as though it had performed a moral action. If too much weight is attached to it, it runs too fast; yet we do not *blame* the clock, for we know it acts from necessity; but we would blame the maker of it, for he was intelligent, and of course knew what would be the effect of so much weight!

Just so, according to Universalism, God has made man and placed him upon the great theatre of action. Motive is, to human action, what the weights and pendulum are to the action of the clock. The motives are withheld, and as man possesses no moral agency, *stands still.* Well, he is not to be blamed, for not acting, for he has no power to act! But his maker presents the motives —"he *sees,* or *thinks* he sees," something lovely in sin, and he is *compelled* to love it, and act accordingly! He is not blameworthy, according to the system, for his actions are not voluntary! Again his Maker presents other objects, and man sees, or thinks he sees, something more lovely than he had discovered in the former objects, he is therefore *compelled* to love the latter, more than the former objects, and his actions are produced accordingly; he now practices what we call virtue; but he deserves no praise, for he is acting like the clock, from *necessity,* and not from the exercise of moral agency!

We think now, that it must be apparent to all the unprejudiced, that if the system be true, there is no morality in human action—that *virtue* and *vice,* are two names for the same thing!

That we are not accountable beings—that neither the good, nor the bad actions which we perform, are the result of the exercise of moral agency; but the effect of *dire* necessity! If we love God, it is because we are *compelled* to do so, and have no *power to resist!* and if we love the wicked one, and practice sin, it is, according to the system, because we are compelled to do so, by the power of motive; and because we have *no power to resist!!*

But to show the absurdity of the hypothesis, let it be supposed, that a mart stands midway, between two objects, different in every respect, and calling on him to perform very different actions—the one *good,* the other *bad.* And let it be supposed, that the man "sees, or thinks he sees," an equal amount of loveliness in each—he exercises no moral agency—that is, he cannot make a choice between the two; he acts always from the strongest motive—but in this case the motives are precisely equal—the one draws this way, and the other that! How would the man act? Why he would not act at all, if the system be true, for each motive would neutralize the other!

Or, take another example; it is like this: B. is invited to a feast; he "sees or thinks he sees something lovely" in it, and he goes—he is *obliged to go,* for he has no power to *resist!* But when he arrives on the ground, he finds himself seated in an arm-chair, midway between two tables, which are groaning under the richest viands, prepared for the occasion: he is very hungry, and on these tables he "sees or thinks he sees" an equal amount of every thing which is calculated to gratify the taste, and allay the pangs of hunger. But he remains in the chair. The motive is very strong on the one hand; but it is no less so on the other! All the drawing which he feels from the table on the one hand, is neutralized by a similar draw from the other table!

Now if a man, placed in this situation, could go to either table and eat, it would prove that his action was *voluntary*—that he was a *moral agent,* and consequently, that Universalism is wrong.

We heard of a Philosopher once, who tried the experiment, by placing a Jack between two large hay-stacks, just ten feet from each. There was an equal amount of hay in each. "Now," says the Philosopher, "I shall determine, whether the strongest motives invariably influence to action; for in this instance, the motives are precisely equal; if therefore the Jack can go to either hay-stack, and eat, it will prove the doctrine to be false." Whether the Philosopher reasoned justly or not, we shall not now inquire; you can all see the principle which it is designed to illustrate.

But perhaps the reader is ready to enquire, *"Does the Bible teach* that man is a moral agent?" We answer that the scriptures of the Old and New Testaments abundantly teach the doctrine of man's moral agency, and his ability to *choose* or *refuse* the offered grace.— And we wish the reader to remember, that just so far as the scriptures prove man's moral agency, so far they disprove Universalism.

A few examples must suffice: "And the spirit and the bride say, come. And let him that heareth say come. And let him that is a thirst come. And whoever will, let him take the water of life freely." (Rev. 22: 17.) "Now then we are ambassadors for Christ, as though God did beseech you by us; we pray you in Christ's stead, be ye reconciled to God." (2 Cor. 5: 20.) If the sinner has no power to do any thing towards becoming *reconciled to God;* and if *"he has no power to hinder it,"* as Mr. Ballou affirms, why was it, that the Apostles besought sinners to "become reconciled to God?" The very language proves that Paul thought, that sinners had power to obey God, and also to resist the influence of grace. The Prophet of the Lord said to the people, on a certain occasion, "Choose you this day whom you will serve," &c. Again we offer the whole Bible in testimony—for the doctrine of man's moral agency, and accountability are taught, in almost every chapter, and nothing to contradict it. Search and see— and if you find the doctrine there, you may be sure that Universalism is wrong.   J. M. M., Ed.

BAPTISM OF THE THREE THOUSAND.

"Then they that gladly received his word were baptized; and the same day there were added unto them about three thousand." Acts ii. 41.

The supposition is, that they were baptized "the same-day" that they "received the word." How were they baptized? I answer, not by immersion.

1. There was no river or stream in or near Jerusalem in which they could be immersed. The Jordan was many miles off. The brook Kidron "has generally but little water and often none, (Robinson's Calmet, Kidron,) and Pentecost was at the driest season of the year. The brooks from Shiloh were mere rivulets. There was no possibility then of immersion in a stream at the time and place of the baptism of the three thousand.

2. The public baths could not be obtained for the baptism of the Gentiles who constituted a part of the three thousand. "Parthians, Medes, Elamites," &c., were in company. The Jews would as soon have suffered swine to be washed in their baths as these Gentiles.

3. The twelve Apostles could not have immersed "about three thousand" at that time.

Some say, "they had help. The disciples assisted." But it appears probable, that the twelve apostles alone were the officiating ministers at the day of Pentecost. Acts ii. 14. "But Peter, standing up with the eleven," &c. Again, 37, v. "Now when they heard this, they were pricked in their heart, and said unto Peter and to the rest of the Apostles, (i. e. the eleven,) &c.

Peter began to preach at nine o'clock in the morning. Besides his sermon— "With many other words did he testify and exhort," v. 40. Then there must have been, at least, a slight examination of each candidate, we will suppose is short as Philip's examination of the Eunuch, and the Confession of the latter We cannot suppose that all this could have taken less than three hours, including the sermon. We will allow the baptism to have continued from noon till 8, P. M., eight hours, or 480 minutes. The 3,000 divided amongst the 12 apostles, gave 250 to each. Then each apostle had about 250 to baptize in 480 minutes, that is 1 in 1 minute and a fraction. Now as this would have been an interesting miracle, we think it would have been mentioned if it had happened.

4. Decency and propriety forbid the supposition that the 3,000 were immersed.

It is not to be supposed that the converts were all males. Were they immersed without clothing? Is any one willing to assert it, or to suppose it? But the idea of their being immersed in their clothing, and walking home, dripping wet, to change their dresses, or of there being suitable accommodations at hand for this purpose, requires more than the "faith of miracles" to be believed. The idea of those strangers having, all of them, baptismal dresses, or borrowing them, or of being baptized naked, may seem easy to those who require men to believe such things in order to be admitted to the Lord's table—but to them only.

REMARKS ON THE ABOVE.

GREAT and good men, sometimes say very weak things, especially when they have a had cause to manage. Of this we have a striking illustration in the above article, from the pen of Mr. Hill, Editor of the *Protestant and Herald,* a large weekly paper, printed at Frankfort, Ky., and the principal organ of Presbyterianism in the West. Mr. Hill has fallen far below his usual strength, in the above article; but we attribute his failure in this instance, entirely to the weakness of his cause.

Mr. Hill thinks that the 3000 could not have been immersed; 1st; because "Jordan was too far *off* Kidron had but little water, perhaps none—and Pentecost was at the driest season of the year. The brooks from Shiloh were mere rivulets." According to this, there was no chance for their immersion, in a running stream. Mr. Hill surely has forgotten, that "Jordan overflowed all its banks in *harvest time;*" and we cannot suppose that Jordan would be so much effected, and Kidron, and the other streams in the neighborhood remain perfectly dry. Pentecost was a noted feast of the Jews, and was observed in the close of the harvest, and on the 50th day, after the second, of the feast of unleavened bread. There is therefore a strong probability, that "the brook Kidron" had much water in it, at the day of Pentecost. As to Shiloh, it is supposed to have been the same as Gihon, and to have had its rise on the West of the city. It had two pools, one Siloam, near the South East of the Temple, and the other Shiloh, somewhere to the Westward. Wood, in his "Dictionary of the Bible." thus speaks of Shiloh: "I am apt to think, the water which came from the fountains near the same place for ordinary, ran partly through the city eastward, and partly down the South side of it, and met near the pool of Siloam."

From the above facts, there is no good reason to doubt, but that the Waters of Shiloh, were amply sufficient for the immersion of the 3000.

Mr. Hill's second argument is, that "a part of the 3000 were Gentiles; and the Jews would not suffer their public baths to be used in the immersion of Gentiles!!"

If Mr. H. had been Mayor of the City of Jerusalem at the time, he could not have spoken with more positiveness, as to the use of the public baths, than he has in this article. But is it true, that any part of the 3000 were Gentiles! We answer, it is not true! Luke says, "And there were dwelling in Jerusalem Jew, devout men, out of every Nation under heaven." Acts 2:5. Now Luke says that they were JEWS. They were all citizens of Jerusalem at that time, though they had come from 'every nation under heaven? Many of them no doubt, were Gentiles by birth, but had been proselyted to the Jews' religion, and *were* cordially admitted to the Jewish worship, and of course they were no longer Gentiles. But if some of the Gentiles were baptized on the day of Pentecost, why was it that Peter never found out that 'God was no respecter of persons,' until he went down to the house of Cornelius! Acts 10: 34. And why was it, let me ask, that 'The Apostles and brethren who were in Judea,' were so excited when they heard of Peter's visit to the Centurion's house, if, as Mr. Hill says, a part of the Three Thousand were Gentiles! And if Mr. H. is correct, why was it, that the brethren in Judea had never found out that 'God had granted repentance unto life to the Gentiles,' (Acts 11: 18,) until they heard Peter rehearse the whole matter from the beginning, of his adventure to the house of Cornelius, the Gentile, and prove his statements, by the five Jewish brethren who accompanied him from Joppa on the occasion? But there is no use in multiplying testimony; there were no Gentiles among them—they were all Jews, and citizens of Jerusalem at the time, and of course had aright to use the public baths, of which there were many in the city.

The third argument is, that the 'twelve Apostles could not have immersed' so many, in so short a time! Mr. Hill allows them 8 hours to baptize about 3000: which, divided among the 12 Apostles, would 250 to each, to baptize in 8 hours, or 480 minutes, which would have been one candidate, in a fraction less than *two minutes!* Time plenty Mr. Hill, You have not had so much experience, in this thing of going down into the water, we suppose, as a Presbyterian Clergyman (Rev. Mr. Shields,) who lives not 100 miles from Bloomington, or you would not think it a MIRACLE, for a man to baptize a candidate in a little less than *two minutes!* Why sir, about a year ago, the Clergyman above alluded to, took some 10 or 12 of his flock down to a small river, and 'buried them with their Lord in baptism.' And it Was supposed by those who saw it, that it was performed much sooner, than if he had converted *Jordan into a bowl,* and *sprinkled* them, according to the usual practice of his church! The odds then, sir, is against you, so far as time is concerned!

Well, Mr. Hill, let us hear your fourth, and strongest argument.— "4.—Decency and propriety forbid the supposition that the 3000 were immersed.". Alarming indeed! Mr. Hill seems to be smitten with a kind of *decent* hydrophobia! At the very thought of an individual being immersed, all his *decent* feelings are called into action, and he stands horror stricken it the very idea! You admit, that circumcision was publicly practiced among the Jews, and that it was of divine authority too. Which think you, Mr. Hill, was the most *decent* act, circumcision, or immersion? But perhaps Mr. H. will say, either might do in those rude and barbarous times; but in this age of civilization, refinement, and 'DECENCY,' such a thing as immersion is neither *decent* nor *proper!*

Jesus reproved certain characters, in the days of his humiliation, who 'made void the law of God, by their traditions,' and I fear, that we are guilty of the very same thing, when ever we begin to reason against God's commands, upon the grounds of *decency* and *propriety*. Why my dear sir, any thing is *decent* and *proper,* which God commands! The very fact that he has commanded it, makes it so. The question then should never be, *is it decent!* but it should always be, *has God commanded it? If* he has, then we know that it is both *decent* and *proper,* for us to obey.

But Mr. Hill thinks, that so many 'strangers' as were baptized on that occasion, could not have had 'all of them baptismal dresses,' and he supposes, that they could not have borrowed them, as they were strangers in the city!

Now this is mere subterfuge! 'Strangers,' indeed! There is no evidence that there was *one stranger,* in the common sense of that term, among the converts! but on the contrary, Luke affirms, that they dwelt in Jerusalem! (Acts 2s 5.) When immersed therefore, they could immediately repair to their own homes, for the purpose of changing their clothes. But Mr. Hill's *decency* is again shocked at the idea of them 'walking home dripping wet.' Well, that would be monstrous! But perhaps those simple ones, in their anxiety to obey God, never thought of the *indecency* of 'walking home dripping wet!' If Mr. H. had been there, be would no doubt have given them a lecture on *decency, and* warned them of the disgrace that they would bring on themselves by so doing!

We have made the above remarks, without any unkind feeling toward Mr. Hill, and as we have re-published his article in the Record, will he let his readers see our 'Remarks?'

J. M. M., Ed.

WRATH AND BITTERNESS.

It would seem that certain Boys, from the East, UNIVERSALIST PREACHERS, have made an attack upon their Elder brother, Jonathan Kidwell. They charge him with Infidelity, in denying the Pentateuch, or five books of Moses.

"Uncle Jonathan," in his paper, under the head "ERASMUS MANFORD," uses up the little Bishop in real *Universal style!* He admits, however, that he does not believe, that the Pentateuch constitutes any part of the word of God; and he defends himself in part, against the unprovoked assault of these Boys, by debating that Erasmus Manford is guilty of the same thing! He states, that at a certain meeting of Universalists, at Perryville, Ind. Mr. E. Manford was called upon to lay his hand upon his breast, and say if he "believed all that was in the Pentateuch," and Mr. K. says, that Erasmus Manford acknowledged, that "he did not believe it all." This Uncle Jonathan challenges the *little bishop* to deny in the "Teacher."

The difference then, between these Universalist teachers, appears to be about this: that is, if the above statement of J. Kidwell be correct; Erasmus Manford believes a part of the Pentateuch to be the word of God, and a part of it he does not believe at all; while Uncle Jonathan maintains, that it is not the word of God; and as a whole, denies the authenticity of the five books *of* Moses, which give us the history of man's creation, and of the world for the first two thousand years, and more. Uncle Jonathan says, and we think, with some propriety, that "if E. Manford has a right to *disbelieve a part* of the Pentateuch, *he* has an equal right to *disbelieve the whole of it.*

But the way Uncle Jonathan avenges himself upon these Boys, is quite a curiosity! He pours out several vials of his hottest displeasure, in gall and bitterness upon the head of the "little bishop" of Terre Haute, as he calls the Editor of the Teacher, and tells him to "stand aside, and not meddle with men's business." He cautions him also, against *self-conceit* and *vanity,* least like a certain *little creature,* in a certain fable, in attempting to s*well* beyond his natural size, serious consequences might follow!

We have no disposition however, to interfere; we only feel disposed to advise our readers of what is going on among the leaders of the Universalist party; and the hard treatment our friend Manford has received from his old brother Jonathan.

We would however, say a word to the belligerents: Gentlemen you need not be so *wrathy;* for according to your own systems, your *belief,* or *disbelief* in the Bible, has no more to do with your eternal salvation, than your belief or disbelief in the "Persian Tales," or the story of "Sinbad the Sailor!"

And as you boast of the *moral tendency* of Universalism, you ought at least to be decorous in your treatment of each other: and bear with the infirmities of your brethren, as men professing Universalism.   J. M. M., Ed.

"PRESSLY'S LECTURES" REVIEWED—NO. 1.

"Lectures on the nature, subjects and mode of Christian baptism. By John T. Pressly, D. D., Pittsburgh: printed by A. Jaynes, Franklin Head," Third Street, 1841."

We have just finished the reading of a very neat little book, of the above title, containing 123 pages. The Author is a minister of the "Associate Reformed Church;" and at the time these Lectures were delivered he was Pastor of the first "Associate Reformed Church Allegheny." The four Lectures, of which this book is composed, seem to have been, at first, delivered orally, for the edification of the people of his charge, and afterwards published at their request. After a careful perusal of these lectures, we are prepared to say, that the Doctor is a strong and elegant writer: he seems disposed to avoid as far as possible, the *dead* languages, on the one hand, and the technicalities of the schools, on the other; the whole being designed for the plain common sense reader. The Dr.'s language is also free from those bitter personalities, and acrimonious innuendoes so common among controversial writers. It is true, he occasionally throws a *Javelin* of this kind at the Baptists; but the Dr. seems at once disposed to heal the wound which he has indicted, by the use of the "milk and honey of soft words. In short, we believe the Dr. has done as much to sustain the cause of *Infant Baptism,* as any man of the 19th century has done, or can do.

Yet, we think, Dr. Pressly has failed to make out his case; and it will be our aim, in the several Nos. of this Review, to show wherein he has failed: and to ascertain if possible, where the truth lies, upon the several subjects of which the Dr. treats in these lectures; and we ask of all, and especially of our Associate Reformed friends, a candid, and unprejudiced investigation of what we have to say: "Prove all things, hold fast to that which is good."

The first lecture is devoted to the nature of christian baptism. The Dr. sets out by quoting the great Commission, as recorded by Matt. 28: 19. He then makes some very pointed and excellent remarks against the "traditions of men," But we will let the Dr. speak for himself. "In every period of the church," says the Dr. "the pride of the depraved heart has displayed itself, in attempting to improve the institutions of heaven, by incorporating with them something of human contrivance." * * * "In every religious service in which we engage, our first inquiry, therefore, should be, what is the divine appointment! For if, regardless of the authority of God, we come before him, in the observance of rites of mere human institution, we expose ourselves to the merited rebuke, "Who hath required this at your hands?" To all this, we most heartily subscribe. The Dr. next attempts to ascertain, "some of the important doctrines which are taught in baptism:" and the first DOCTRINE which the Dr. sees *in* baptism, is "the doctrine of a *trinity of persons in the unity of the Godhead."* We once heard a Preacher of Tunker Baptist order, offer as an argument in favor of *trine Immersion*, that it was a "standing witness of the truth of the doctrine of the trinity of persons in the unity of the Godhead." One argument we think, is worth just as much us the other: but upon this point, We have no dispute with the learned Dr.

The second doctrine, which the Dr. supposes to be taught in Baptism is, "the doctrine of human depravity." If by this expression, the Dr. means OUR NEED OF SPIRITUAL CLEANSING, by the blood of Christ, which appears to be his meaning, we have no controversy with him.

The third doctrine which Dr. P says is taught in Baptism is, "Expiation by the blood of Jesus." To prove this, the Dr. argues thus: on page 14th, "By the appointment of baptism with water, then, we have presented to our view, in a significant figure, that most interesting truth, that there is a forgiveness with God. Here we see with our eyes the evidence of the fact, that a fountain has been opened for sin and for uncleanness, and that God has graciously made ample provision for the removal of our guilt. And hence in the scriptures, the reception of baptism is urged by the consideration, that in it there is an exhibition of the blessing of remission of sin. "Repent," said Peter, on the day of Pentecost, to the assembled multitude, who, under the power of conviction, inquired, "What must we do?" "Repent and be baptized, every one of you, in the name of the Lord Jesus, for the remission of sins." And when Saul of Tarsus obtained a proper sight of his sin, and was brought a humble suppliant, to the feet of Jesus, Ananias is directed to say to him, "Arise and be baptized, *and wash away thy* sins."

Who that loves God and venerates his authority, does not love to read the above paragraph? We greatly rejoice to hear men in 'high places,' express themselves thus independently, against the vain traditions of men, and in favor of the Authority of the Holy Saviour. Yes "what is the divine appointment?" Important inquiry! In connecting baptism with remission of sins, the learned Dr. expresses himself in harmony with the teaching of the Apostles of Jesus Christ; and who dare say that he is wrong! Our only fear for the Dr. is, that by a certain class of religionists, he will be considered a "Campbellite," (to use a vulgar phrase,) so far as the *design* of baptism is concerned!

The fourth doctrine which the Dr. discovers to be taught in baptism is, *"Regeneration by the holy spirit."* Under this head the Dr. very properly remarks: that "This change is a moral renovation of our nature, so through that, he who is the subject of it is a new *creature."* Several passages of scripture are quoted to sustain this position, and among the rest the language of Christ to Nichodemus. This may show that the Dr. understands the expression, "be born of water," to refer to baptism. We perfectly agree with the Dr. on this point. He says, "And in the ordinance of baptism, we are taught that this is peculiarly the work of the holy spirit." (That is, to quicken.) "Hence our Lord declares," continues the Dr., "Except a man be born of water and of the spirit, he cannot enter into the kingdom of God." And the Dr. adds, "Here a distinction is drawn betwixt the external right of baptism, and the internal change of which it is significant. To be born of water is, to receive the outward sign of baptism; to be born of the spirit, is to experience that change of heart which is effected by the agency of the Holy Spirit, the nature and necessity of which are represented by baptism with water."

Some of the *special pleaders,* for the traditions of the fathers, anxious to distinguish themselves as *opposers* of what they are pleased to term "Campbellism," have actually gone so far, as to deny that water baptism is so much as *alluded* to, in the conversation of Christ with Nichodemus, John 3: 5,! and also that water baptism is intended (Titus 3: 5.) by the phrase "washing of regeneration!" Let such men stand rebuked, in the presence of Dr. Pressly, Dr. Dwight, John Wesley and others. Hear Dr. *P on* Titus 3: 5. page 16; In the expression, the washing of regeneration, there seems manifestly to be an allusion to the application of water baptism."

We cannot notice the first division, of the Dr.'s first Lecture, more minutely. He takes up the second division of his first general head, on page 17, which is to show "The nature of the profession which is made in the reception of baptism."

We are so much pleased with most of what the Dr. says under this head, that we are disposed simply to give our readers a general out line.

"1st. A public profession of our faith," &c. "2nd. In the reception of baptism, we profess our subjection to the authority of God and our dedication to his service." "3rd. In baptism, we profess that we are under obligations to die unto sin, and to live unto God."

To prove this last position, the Dr. quotes Rom. 6th, 6, 4: "Know ye not," says the Apostle, "that so many of us as were baptized into Jesus Christ, were baptized into his death?" In showing the agreement between this text and the proposition, the Dr' remarks: "As he died for sin, so, in Baptism, we declare that we are dead to sin," &c. Dr. P. then is with us, in applying this text, to water baptism. As to the *burial,* spoken of there, the Dr. says nothing in this place, and our remarks on that point will be reserved for the proper place.

J. M. M., ED.

For the Christian Record

Mr. Editor—A friend has been kind enough to hand me your "Record" of Aug. last, in which, I find, you have done me the unexpected *honor* of introducing my name to your readers, in your "notes on a tour to Vincennes and Washington," I should not, however, have troubled you with this communication, had not your one *sided* "notes" have done me great injustice, and been calculated to make an erroneous impression on the minds of your readers; and as you have, without "my advice and consent," made so free a use of my name in your periodical, I ask it as a matter of justice that you allow me the privilege of correcting your statements about me, through the same medium.

You say, upon your arrival at Washington, "Here we found considerable excitement prevailing in the community, on account of an expected discussion which was to have commenced on the 26th between Mr. Williamson Terrell of the Methodist Episcopal church, and bro. E. Goodwin. Mr. T. had not come on," &c. Now sir, the only conclusion to which any one, unacquainted with the facts, would be likely to come, upon reading the above paragraph would be, that I had agreed to meet Mr. Goodwin on that day, and had failed; when in truth no such agreement was ever made.

The letter of Mr. Noyes and others, to me, proposing the 26th of July, was dated the 26th of June, and was not received by me until the 29th; I had heard nothing from them since I had received their first little, brief, indefinite note, dated the 15th of may some six or seven weeks before. I supposed they had dropped the matter and had made my arrangements accordingly But when I received their letter of the 23th of June, I seized the earliest opportunity to inform them that I could not attend to the discussion before the 3rd day of Oct. In their reply, dated the

10th of July, they "presume Mr. Goodwin can make it convenient to meet me at the time I had proposed," and promised to inform him to that effect. This sir, was *sixteen days* before the time of your visit. Who was it then that got up the "excitement" and "expectation" of a discussion at that time? I did not. I knew nothing of it; neither did my friends. Was it not sir, some of your "excellent" brethren of that neighborhood, for the purpose of making the *impression,* and enabling *Elder Mathis* to "*think*" that "Mr. Terrell would never muster up courage to meet bro Goodwin"? And sir as you appear to have had access to the correspondence, *you* must have been acquainted with these facts: Why then, as you chose to *Lug* my name into your paper, did you suppress them, and give the influence of your pen, your paper and your word, to an impression so different from the facts of the case?

You further say, "The brethren informed me that a short time before, Mr. T. came to Washington and preached a discourse in which he strongly inveighed against us, under the opprobrious name "Campbellite." In this discourse Mr. Terrell charged us with having a human creed or confession of faith &c. &c. &c. He also attempted, as I understood, to sustain the Methodistic doctrine of *"faith alone"* and "Infant sprinkling" from the sacred record!" You further say, "next morning bro. Noyes and others—addressed Mr. Terrell a line calling on him to sustain his allegations against us, and some points in his doctrine and practices" &c. I am sorry sir, that "the brethren" in giving you the above information, in some things came short of the truth, and in ethers transcended it. In the first place, I preached *two* discourses to which your brethren, Noyes and others, chose to object. One, at 11 o'clock on the sabbath, on the doctrine of *Justification by faith,* in which I undertook to show that *immersion in water* was not essential to pardon, as taught by Mr. Campbell in his "Christian System" from which I made numerous quotations. My other discourse was at night, on the subject of the *direct witness* of the Holy Spirit to our pardon, which I contrasted with the evidence of pardon from *immersion* as taught in different places in Mr. Campbell's book. Well sir, *it is true* that the gentlemen whom you mention, "addressed me a line next morning" just as I was mounting my horse for home, in company with some Ladies, who were already on theirs. *It is true also* that in that "line" they inquired if I would "sustain my allegations against Campbellites" or "Campbellism" in my two discourses the day and evening before. But sir, *it is not true* that there was any thing in that "line" calling on me to sustain any part of my own "doctrines and practices." If there be any thing of the kind in that "*line*" it has been inserted there since it was in my hands. It is possible, however, that such may be the case, for, owing to the circumstances under which I was placed, when I received it, I was under the necessity of writing my reply, with my pencil, on the blank leaf of the same sheet, and sending the whole back again, and though I have, several times politely requested them to return it to me, they have not seen fit to do so; and it may be that their reasons for refusing, are to be found in some such interpolations as the one you allude to.

It is not true that "I charged you with having a human creed," But *it is true* that I slated, that either Mr. Campbell had told a falsehood in the title page of his "Christian System" or *that* book contained "the Christian System as taught in the current reformation," which I considered equivalent to a confession of faith.

It is not true that "the object of both Elder Miller and Mr. Terrell was to change the issues." But *it is true* that Messrs. Noyes & Co. did try to change the issue from the ground assumed in their first letter to me, and that occupied by me in my two discourses to which they objected.

It is not true that "neither Elder Miller or Mr. Terrell could see that they were bound to affirm what they preached and practiced and their allegations against us," (you.) But *it is true* that out of the five propositions submitted by me that I took the affirmatives of three, and the two given to Mr. Goodwin, were, (if I am correctly informed) *substantially,* the two propositions affirmed by *Elder James M. Mathes* at Martinsville, in his debate with Mr. Scott!

I have another reason for *thinking*, (you see sir, I am disposed to exercise that *faculty* as well as yourself,) the course pursued by you and your Washington brethren, as too *unfair* for those who arrogate to themselves, with so much self complacency, the appellation *"Christian,"* and who denounce all who differ from their *peculiar* views as *"Sectarians."* About the first of August, (very near the time of your visit) I was in the neighborhood of Washington, when I proposed to my correspondents that, for the purpose of preventing misrepresentations on either side, we furnish corrected copies of the correspondence, and have it published in the Washington Newspaper. But to this proposition they did not agree. I suppose they thought so *fair* a course would not subserve the interests of the *"reformation"* as much as the *ex parte* notice that Elder Mathes had taken of the matter in his "notes on his tour."

I *then* proposed to publish the correspondence to *prevent* misrepresentations, but I now propose to Elder Mathes, for the purpose of *correcting* misrepresentations, to publish the correspondence in his paper. What say you sir?

I can assure my *"friend"* Mathes that I have no objections to his *"thinking"* when and what he pleases only I desire, that hereafter, when he *thinks* about me and chooses to publish his *thoughts* he should have them more in accordance with *truth* and the *facts* of the case, and governed more by that charity that *thinketh* no evil than the *thoughts* which have placed me under the necessity of writing this article.

In conclusion, permit me to say, that the sentiments you express, of personal friendship for me, of *my* excellency as a man, and the condition of error you conceive me to be in, are fully and heartily reciprocated toward Elder Mathes by

Sir, Your obedient Servt.

Bedford Ia. Oct. 6th 1843   W. TERRELL

STRICTURES UPON MR. TERRELL'S COMMUNICATION.

If, in the pages of the Christian Record, our good friend W. Terrell has been unfairly represented, we are willing to atone for it, by permitting him to speak for himself to our readers. This, we think justice demands, and if we know ourselves, we are willing to "do unto all men, as we would have them do to us," under similar circumstances. Mr. Terrell's communication is very well written, but I am sorry to say, that the spirit which he manifests, is not exactly what it ought to be! He seems to be full of bitterness against the *present Reformation*, and all those who are contending for a return to primitive Christianity. This we exceedingly regret.

Our friend seems to think that we did him great injustice in our "Notes on a tour to Vincennes and Washington." which were published in the 2nd No. of the Record; and strongly insinuates that we knew at the time, that a considerable portion of what we said about him was false! And this is the man, who recommends us to act under the influence of that charity that thinketh no evil! We said, in our *Notes*, that the people of Washington expected a discussion, on the 26th July, between Mr. T. and bro. E. Goodwin, and that Mr. T. had not come on, &c. Our friend complains of this, and positively denies having made any such agreement! Now we did not say that he had; we only said, that the people expected a discussion at that time: our impression however, was, that he had agreed to meet a Christian Preacher at that time in Washington, leaving it with the brethren to select the man. This *impression we* received from the conversation of the brethren, and from the first two letters of the correspondence, which was read: and although we had access to the whole correspondence, yet our other duties were so arduous, while we remained there, that we did not read more than the first letter of bro. J. E. Noyes and others, to Mr. T., his reply, and perhaps a part of the second letter of the brethren to Mr. T.

When we received Mr. Terrell's communication, we were much astonished, that he should call in question the truth of what we had said about the matter; we therefore sent to Washington and obtained the correspondence; and we have now carefully read the whole of it. We have also compared what we said in our Notes, with all the facts in the case, and permit us to say, that our *present* impression is, that we did our friend T. no injustice.

To prove that there was an agreement, on the part of Mr. T. to discuss, with a Christian Preacher at that time, we here publish the first letter of J. E. Noyes and others to Mr. T. and his answer of the same date, which he says, was written after the LADIES were on their horses!

Washington, Ind., May 15th, 1843.

———

Revd. Mr. TERRELL: Sir—The undersigned, members of the Christian Church, (which you are pleased to call Campbellites, are anxious to know whether you are willing to meet a preacher of the Christian church, at this place, at any time between the 1st of June and the 1st of August next, and make good your assertions in your yesterday's and last night's discourses, so far as they have any bearing upon that church. You cannot object, because you have made the attack. You must have confidence in the truth of what you have stated, or you would not have made them. Your brethren must have confidence in your abilities, or they would not permit you to hazard your reputation; and what you stated once, you certainly are willing to reiterate by the side of another intelligent Gentleman, who will have an opportunity to respond. Your immediate answer to the above, addressed to Elder John E. Noyes, at Davis' corner, is most earnestly requested.

We have the honor to be yours, with high considerations,

John E. Noyes,   W. C. Elliott,
John Brayfield,   Alfred Davis.

Washington, May 15th, 1843.

Gentlemen: Your note was handed me just as I was about to mount my horse for home. I have only to say, that I am ready at any time to make good my statements, in regard to "Campbellism." But as you have not, in your note, designated what statement you object to, and as my statements were quoted *verbatim* from Campbell's 'Christian System,' I am at a loss to know what is meant in your proposition. If you should be pleased to make any further communication with me on this subject, I desire you would be more explicit, and designate what statements about Campbellism to which you object. Respectfully your obt. Servt.

W. TERRELL.

In the above letter of the brethren to Mr. T. they ask him "if he is willing to meet a Preacher of the Christian Church at this place, [Washington,] at any time between the 1st of June and the 1st of August next," (last.) And in Mr. T.'s reply above, he answers, "I have only to say that I am ready at any time, to make good my statements," &c. Now the most prejudiced of Mr. T.'s admirers, we suppose, can see, that this was an *agreement* on the part of Mr. T., to meet a Preacher of the Christian Church in Washington, for the purpose of discussing every thing said by him in his two discourses complained of, so far as they had any bearing upon the Christian Church, which he was pleased to call *Campbellite:* and that he *agreed* to be ready at *any time,* within the range of the proposition: thus leaving it entirely with the brethren to say *when,* and *who.*

Well, they, in the exercise of the discretionary power which Mr. T. had given them, selected bro. E. Goodwin, as the man, and the 26th of July, as the time. Of this arrangement, they notified Mr. T. by letter, dated "26th June," a little more than a month after they had first addressed him on the subject. As the 26th July was within the range of the proposition and agreement, we can see no justifiable ground upon which Mr. T. could decline it. The only apology which he *can* have, is the one which he urges, to wit: "that too much time elapsed, between their *first* and *second* letters to him;" and this we *think* a very weak excuse for *backing out,* (pardon the expression,) since bro. Goodwin, the man of their choice, lived some 75 or 80 miles distant, and five weeks seems to have been absolutely necessary to enable them to confer with him on the subject: especially when it is remembered that he was absent from home at the time, and could not answer them until he returned home. Then for Mr. T. to deny, as he has done positively, in his communication, that any such *agreement* existed, is, to say the least of it, very inconsistent; and if we are not greatly mistaken, the unprejudiced part of community will *think,* that the real secret of the failure, was either a lack of confidence in those statements, be had *agreed* to defend; or a lack of courage to sustain his arm in such a contest!

Mr. T. also denies, having had any agency in getting up the excitement at Washington, and the expectation of a debate at that time; and *insinuates* that the brethren had done it *for effect!*

But we say Mr. T. had agency in the matter. He came to Washington, and "without our *advice and consent, lugged* us" into the pulpit under the opprobrious name, *Campbellites,* and made many and grievous charges against us: this, our friend will not deny. It was known to the public, that bro. Noyes and others excepted to Mr. T.'s preaching, and that they had called on him for redress, asking him to make good his assertions, by the side of a Christian Preacher, who should have the liberty of responding. It was also known that Mr. T. had answered them favorably, telling them that he was "ready at any time" to do so. This left it with the brethren to say *when* the discussion should take place. And when the public were informed that the brethren had chosen the 26th July, and had notified Mr. T. to that effect, they were considerably excited, fully expecting that they would have the satisfaction of hearing Messrs. T. & G. discuss, side by side, all those matters, whereof we had been accused by Mr. Terrell. But when Mr. T. declined the honor of attempting to sustain himself at that time; and told the brethren that it would not suit his convenience, to go to Washington for that purpose, until a more convenient season, the people felt much disappointed in their expectation; and it was but natural that they should talk a good deal about it, some *accusing,* and others *excusing.* This was the state of matters when we went to Washington in July last. We say, therefore, that our friend had *agency,* in getting up the *excitement and expectation!*

Friend Terrell says, *"It is not true,* that I charged you with having a human creed." Well, well! how we have all been deceived! Let the inhabitants of Indiana remember this! Mr. Terrell did not *charge us with having a human creed!* But Mr. Terrell says, *"It is true* that I stated, that either Mr. Campbell had told a falsehood in the title page of his "Christian System," or *that* book contained the Christian system as taught in the current reformation." Wonderful indeed! Eagle-eyed critic! What amazing discovery may we not expect him to make next! We should not at all be astonished if he were soon to discover, that either the General Conference had told a falsehood in the title page of their "Doctrinal Tracts," or *that* book contains the doctrinal tracts of the M. E. Church!

Then our friend's wonderful flourish, about the Creed, amounts to this, when he explains himself, to wit: either Mr. C. has told a falsehood, or the Christian System contains the Christian system, &c.!! O shame! where now is thy blush! That the "Christian System," contains the views of Mr. Campbell and others, upon some important matters, no intelligent man will deny; but we do deny that *that* book is our *Creed or Confession of faith;* and we feel confident that no intelligent man who is morally honest, will affirm that it is! But we exonerate Mr. T. from the charge of having said so, upon *his own* testimony. Let it stand so. Still, we know that the brethren at Washington, are not the only persons who have so understood Mr. Terrell! On more occasions than one, he has been understood to charge us with having a *human creed;* (mistake, of course;) so much so, that some of the SMALL ONES, waxing very bold, have reiterated the charge, and pledged themselves for the proof! We hope however, to hear no more of it after this. And we hope too that hereafter when Mr. Terrell, *without our advice and consent, lugs us into the pulpit,* he will be more on his guard, and endeavor to make correct impressions upon his audience.

Friend Terrell says, "*It is not true* that neither Elder Miller nor Mr. Terrell could see that they were bound to affirm what they preached and practiced, and their allegations against us.' Well, this was our impression; but we are happy to learn, that both Mr. T. and his Elder can see, that they are bound by all that is fair and honorable in controversy, to shoulder the responsibility and affirm in debate, what they preach and practice, as well as their allegations against us. We hope to hear no more quibbling.

Again, Mr. T. says, that be *thinks* our course too *unfair,* for those who arrogate to themselves with so much self-complacency, the appellation "*Christian.*" If our course has been *unfair,* we exceedingly regret it: but our friend has not proven it to be so. As to the appellation *Christian,* we have only to say, we arrogate nothing to ourselves in this matter as a dutiful bride, we desire to have the honor of wearing the name of our Husband. But if our good friend Mr. T, and others, desire to wear the unscriptural appellation *Methodist;* though we may think it very *arrogant,* we hope never to envy them!

Our friend also denies, that the brethren in their first letter to him, of May 15th, called upon him to "sustain any part of his own doctrine and practice."

The reader will please read again, the brethren's letter above, which is their first to him, and will see, that they call on him to *make good* his assertions in his two discourses, so far as they had any bearing upon the Christian Church, which he had called *Campbellite*. In Mr. Terrell's communication to us, above, he says that his first discourse "was on the subject of Justification by faith:" and his second and last, was on the subject of "the *direct witness of the Spirit to our pardon.*"

The Methodist Discipline says, 9th Article, "That we are justified by faith only, is a wholesome doctrine and very full of comfort." The doctrine of his own Discipline, was what our friend Terrell preached. Well, this part of *his own* doctrine had a bearing upon the Christian Church, for she maintains, that *obedience,* as well as *faith,* is essential to our justification. Mr. T.'s second discourse, in which be attempted to prove the *direct and immediate* witness of the Holy Spirit to our pardon, had a bearing upon the Christian Church, which, although she most cordially believes in the *witness of the Holy Spirit* to our pardon; yet, she does not believe the metaphysical abstractions of Mr. Williamson Terrell upon this subject.

We were informed by the brethren, and we presume Mr. T. will not deny it, that in his said discourses, he attempted to prove that Infants were proper subjects of Christian baptism, and that sprinkling and pouring were scriptural *modes* of administering the ordinance. This also had a bearing upon the Christian Church, for she neither believes nor practices, the one, nor the other. Then Mr. Terrell was certainly called upon, to sustain the above *parts of his own doctrine and practice;* as well as his allegations against us, as a body of professed Christians.

Mr. T. also complains of us for *thinking,* that he would never muster courage enough to meet brother G., or any other man of equal talent, in debate. Well, we still *think* that he will not, on a fair issue.

He also requests as to publish the whole correspondence between him and the Washington brethren: We have now published the first two letters, which are the most important documents in the correspondence; and for several reasons we shall, at least for the *present,* decline publishing the balance. 1st: Because there is too much of it, for the size of our paper; and 2nd: because we do not wish to encumber the Record with so much uninteresting matter; for we cannot suppose that the *one hundredth* reader of the Record, would feel interested in reading it. What do our readers generally, care whether Mr. T. *agreed* to debate or not! or whether he delivered *one* or *two* discourses in Washington! We suppose, that a majority of our readers would much prefer to see a notice of the discussion; that the time was set, the propositions agreed on, and the preliminaries all settled. We know that our good friend cannot accuse us, justly, of unfairness in this matter, as we have published his own vindication of himself, and the first two letters of the correspondence, out of which all that follow have grown.

As to what our friend says, about the brethren refusing to have the correspondence published in the Washington Newspaper; and their refusal to give him a copy of their first letter to him, we have nothing to say at present, as we know nothing about it.

We have now noticed every thing which we deem of any importance in friend Terrell's communication, and as we *think,* fully sustained what we said in our "Notes," &c. We are now perfectly willing to let the whole matter go to the public; and that they shall judge between us.

In conclusion we would say, that if Mr. Terrell, or Elder Miller, will meet brother E. Goodwin, or some other man of equal talent, in Washington. at a suitable time, and in a proper manner, discuss the issues, embraced in Mr. T.'s two discourses in Washington, and the brethren's first letter to him, we shall no longer *think* as we have *thought.*

J. M. M., Ed.

A SHORT DISCOURSE ON ISAIAH 1: 6.

From the sole of the foot even unto the head there is no soundness in it; but wounds, find bruises, and putrefying sores.

We are inclined to the opinion that there is no passage in the holy volume, which has been tortured and misapplied more than the one which we have placed at the head of this discourse. The doctrine which it is supposed to teach, and which it is introduced into many creeds and sermons to prove, is, that this text has reference to all men that have lived since the fall of man, that now lives, or that ever will live, until the close of the Gospel dispensation. 2—That the disease here spoken of is moral and not physical. 3—That all men are thus diseased from head to foot, and that they ere therefore, totally depraved in all the faculties of soul and body. 4—That this depravity is hereditary; that every child that is born brings this to tally diseased moral constitution into the world with it, so that it never can have either will or power to do any thing acceptable in the sight of God, until it is first regenerated by the spirit of God and healed of this malady.

Now we do most religiously believe this to be a wrong application of this passage of scripture. We have many objections to the doctrine of hereditary total depravity; but we do not design investigating that subject now, but our purpose is only to show, 1st: that this text has no reference to that doctrine. 2: To endeavor to ascertain the true meaning of the text.

All our arguments against this application of the text shall be drawn from the chapter in which it stands. 1: In the 13th verse, the Lord says "come now and let us reason together." But the doctrine supposed to be taught in the text says man cannot reason on the subject of salvation because of this disease. Then the text is wrongly applied, or the Lord required an impossibility, which we are not prepared to admit.

2: In verses 16, 17, the Lord commands the very persons named in the text, saying, "wash you, make you clean, put away the evil of your doing from before my face, cease to do evil and learn to do well."— But the doctrine says man cannot put away the evil of his doings; he cannot cease to do evil: he cannot learn to do well, and if he even knew what well doing is, he could not perform it by reason of this moral disease. Then if the doctrine be true, the good Lord has required all these impossibilities of his creature man!!

3: The persons spoken of in this text, are said to have gone away backward; (see verse 4;) but if they came into the world with this totally depraved character, how could they have gone backward? Could they have gone further into depravity, than total depravity itself? Impossible. 4: It is said in the same verse, of these persons, that they are *"children that are corrupting."* Now I ask, in the name of common sense, how total corruption could corrupt itself? 5: But, finally, in the first verse, it is said that this is "the vision of Isaiah the son of Amos which he saw concerning Judah and Jerusalem in the days of Uzziah, Joatham, Ahaz, and Hezekiah kings of Judah." Thus it is plain that the text had reference to Judah and Jerusalem, in the days of these four kings, and that it is contrary to the design of the inspiring spirit of JEHOVAH, to apply it to any child of man now living on the face of this broad earth.

I now proceed to inquire for the literal meaning of the text. In the 5th verse, the Lord inquires: "Why should you be stricken any more you revolt more and more." Now if we can only determine what is meant by their being stricken, every thing in the text is perfectly plain and easy. To illustrate this, I will suppose a father who has a disobedient son. He has taught his son his will, but he disobeys. He chastises him, but he still rebels. He continues to lay many stripes upon him, until he is bruised from head to foot, and is almost ready to faint of, the wounds, and yet he manifests a rebellious disposition. The father, as if almost ready to give him over to his own way, says, son I have nourished and brought you up, and you have rebelled against me. Why should you be stricken any more? you will revolt more and more. Why, your whole head is sick, your whole heart is faint; from the sole of your foot even to your head there is no soundness in it; there is not a sound place to lay the reed upon. Come now and let us reason on the subject. Put away the evil of your doings from before my face. The reader will now please turn to the chapter, and as he reads, make the application, and by so doing he will see as clear as cloudless noonday, that the text has reference to the judgments and calamities which the Lord had brought up in Judah and Jerusalem for their sins, and not to any disposition to sin which they brought into the world with them. That this view of the subject is correct, is plain from verse 7, where it is said, "Your country is desolate. Your cities are burnt with fire; your land strangers devour it in your presence, and it is desolate as overthrown by strangers."

CONCLUSIONS.

From all the facts now before us, we come to the following conclusions: 1; Man is a rational, moral agent, possessed with volition of will. 2: That God has given us, in the "HOLY BIBLE." the rules by which he would have us conduct ourselves in this world. 3: That if we rebel! against the commandments of God and continue disobedient, the disapprobation of the eternal I AM, will rest upon us in time, and in awful eternity, 4: But that we forsake the evil of our ways, and hearken to the commandments of the Lord to do them, we shall enjoy the smiles of the great Jehovah in life, in death, and during the never-ending ages of eternity.

APPLICATION.

Reader, have you bowed your neck to the yoke of Christ. O then be careful to depart from all iniquity; shun the very appearance of evil, and walk worthy the vocation wherewith you are called, and heaven will be your eternal home. But if you have not commenced a life of obedience to the commands of the Lord, O, think before you farther go. Remember your accountability to

God; put away the evil of your doings; cease to do evil: learn to do well: confess the name of Christ, before men: be planted in the likeness of his death, and arise to walk in newness of life, and thus take upon you the holy profession of Christianity, and then be faithful in the discharge of all the obligations of the Gospel, and your reward in heaven will be incorruptible, undefiled, and shall never fade away. Amen.

ELIJAH GOODWIN.

JUSTIFICATION—NO. 3.

We shall now proceed to give a concise view of the plan of justification as presented in the gospel. And in order that the inquisitive reader may have the object clearly before his mind, we shall first notice the moral condition of man in his fallen state. We shall here let the great Apostle of the Gentiles (in his epistle to the church at Rome, 1st chapter, and latter part) draw the picture under the direction of the Holy Spirit. He says, that as they did not like to retain God in their knowledge, God gave them over to a reprobate mind, to do these things which are not convenient: being filled with all unrighteousness, fornication, wickedness, covetousness, maliciousness; full of envy, murder, debate, deceit, malignity, whisperers, backbiters, haters of God, despiteful, proud, boasters, inventors of evil things, disobedient *to parents,* without understanding, bargain breakers., without mutual affection, implacable, unmerciful." Again, (in the same epistle, 3rd chapter. 12th and 16th verses inclusive,) he says: "They are all gone out of the way; they are together become unprofitable: there is none that doeth good, no not one. Their throat is an open sepulcher; with their tongues they have used deceit; the poison of asps is under their lips; whose mouth is full of bitterness and cursing. Their feet are swift to shed blood. Destruction and misery are in their ways: and the way of peace they have not known. There is no fear of God before their eyes." Again, Rom. 5: 6: "For when we were yet without strength, in due time Christ died for the ungodly."

Such, dear reader, is the picture presented to us by inspiration, of the moral condition of fallen man! A condition the most degraded, corrupt, depraved and helpless! brought about by disobedience to a positive law, which disobedience introduced sin, and placed us under its power—subjected us to all its degrading, enervating, and soul-destroying influences. Thus, at enmity with God, opposed to all good, made liable to death temporal, and to everlasting destruction from the presence of the Lord and the glory of his power." (2 Thess. 1:9) In this sad, helpless, and hopeless condition, where can he look for help? His guilty conscience forbids his looking to God, for against him he has rebelled and become his enemy! Does he turn his wishful eye to his fellow man? Behold he is alike ruined and helpless! Does he seek relief from those angels who once "dwelt on high;" but kept not their first estate, and left their own habitation? He beholds them "reserved in everlasting chains under darkness, unto the Judgment of the great day." (Jude, 6th verse.) A hope springs up within his bosom. There are those angels who sinned not, but kept their first estate; may I not get aid of them? No, they, although perfectly happy, are not *mighty* and able to save.

Thus, the fallen rebel, man, has looked through the vast universe *for* help, but none is found! When hopeless, and in despair he gives up all for lost. He turns his wishful eye to Heaven, and thus breaks forth:

Farewell happy fields where joy forever dwells.

Then as he sinks beneath his load of guilt, conscious of his coming fate—his just doom, he turns his eyes towards the place of his final destruction, and as he approaches it exclaims.

"Hail horrors! hail,
Infernal world! and thou profoundest Hell,
Receive thy new possessor!"

Thus excluded from all good, and exposed to pain, death and hell man truly is an object of pity. But, although God is just, yet we are taught that he is Love.

THE CHRISTIAN RECORD.

Under the above head, Mr. Manford, Editor of the "Teacher," speaking of our paper, says: "We think it is composed of part of the latter, (Christianity,) and all of the former system, (Campbellism,) as we may hereafter show."

We should be pleased to see friend Manford enter upon the task. Mr. Manford further says: "It is however a pretty good paper of the kind, and we think that all who believe in going to glory by water ought to take it. We will cheerfully forward subscriptions to the Editor."

We thank friend Manford for his kindness, and we will cheerfully reciprocate. We agree with Mr. Manford, that "all who believe in going to glory by water, ought to take the 'Christian Record.'" Because, were they to take it, and read it attentively, they would find out their mistake. They would learn that *water alone,* would take no one to glory! But they might also learn, that Baptism is a divine institution, and should be submitted to by all who would be disciples of Christ.

They might also learn, that "they who obey not the gospel, shall he punished with everlasting destruction, from the presence of the Lord and from the glory of his power," Universalism to the contrary notwithstanding. We therefore say to all, take the 'Christian Record.'

EDITOR.

"Tychicus" is in type, but a part of the 3rd No. is unavoidably crowded out. It shall appear in our next. We hope this will satisfy the writer.

THE CHRISTIAN RECORD.

VOL. I.] BLOOMINGTON, IND., DECEMBER, 1843. [No. VI.

CHRISTIAN UNION—NO. 6.

IN our last we presented our readers with a *summary* of the gospel, composed of seven articles, which may be found Eph. 4: 1-6. In the examination of the several items of our *summary*, we progressed through the first two articles, to wit: "There is one body, and one spirit?' the five remaining articles, we now propose briefly to discuss in the present number.

Article 3rd. "One hope."—By the one hope, we understand the Apostle to refer to the rich inheritance, which is incorruptible, undefiled and unfading, which is reserved in heaven for all the faithful children of God, connected with the glorious appearing of the "Great God and our Saviour Jesus Christ," and the resurrection of all the saints. Peter says, (1 Pet; 1: 13,) "Wherefore gird up the loins of your mind, be sober, and hope to the end for the grace that is to be brought unto you at the revelation of Jesus Christ." Again, Titus 2: 13, Paul says, 'Looking for that blessed hope, and (even) the glorious appearing of the great God and our Saviour Jesus Christ." In Heb. 11: 1, Paul defines faith to be "The sure confidence of things *hoped* for." Paul in his eloquent speech before king Agrippa, Acts 26th chap., connects the resurrection with the "hope of the promise made by God unto the fathers," for which hope, he said, he was accused by the Jews. In one place the Apostle defines hope to be the "Anchor of the soul, sure and steadfast;" and in another, he makes the Christian warrior's *Helmet* to consist of the *hope of salvation,* (or the resurrection.)

From the above, and many similar passages of scripture, it is evident that the *one hope* looks forward to the resurrection, and the bright scenes of Immortality which are to follow the glorious appearing of the Lord: and relies with implicit confidence on the promises of God.— Hope is composed *of desire* and *expectation*. We *desire* to be happy, and God has promised to make us so, if we love him and keep his commandments. Our hearts are therefore filled with strong consolation, while we obey his will. And we are thus enabled to rejoice with joy unspeakable and full of glory, in anticipation of what we shall hereafter be. The sorrows and difficulties of time cannot dismay us, while our bosom swells with the mighty hope, of being one day delivered from the bondage of corruption, and of being made partakers of the joys of Immortality. The storms may howl over the boisterous Ocean of human life; but with our anchor hope securely fixed to that within the Vail, our little bark shall out ride the storm, and at last be safely moored in the haven of eternal rest. The enemies of Christianity may marshal themselves under the Prince of Darkness, and annoy us by day and by night; but if we have on our head the Christian soldier's helmet—the *hope* of salvation—we shall not be terrified; but under the Captain of our salvation we shall overcome every foe, and finally triumph through the blood of the Lamb. And finally when Death, with his icy fingers, begins to feel about our hearts, if we have this one hope in lively exercise we shall meet, the grim monster without dread—calmly resigning the joys of Earth to those who relish nothing better, and without a sigh, we shall bid farewell to all below, and pass through the "dark valley and shadow of death," comforted by the rod and staff of Jehovah; where in the presence of God and the Lamb, hope itself shall be turned into fullness of joy.

Art. 4th. "One Lord."—On this art. we suppose there will be no difficulty in agreeing, if we will all consent to lay aside the vain jargon of Scholastic Divinity, and always speak of the *one Lord* in Bible language. Paul says, "But to us there is but one God, the Father, of whom are all things, and we in him; and one Lord Jesus Christ, by whom are all things, and we by him." 1 Cor. *8:* 6. This one Lord is the Son of the Living God. Peter said, "Thou art the Christ, the Son of the living God," Matt. 16: 16. He is called the "Image of the invisible God, the first born of every creature;" Col. 1: 15. Creation is ascribed to him.—"For by *him were* all things created, that are in heaven and that are in earth, visible and invisible, whether they be thrones, or dominions, or principalities, or powers: all things were created by him and for him; and he is before all things, and by him all things consist;" Col. 1: 16, 17. All fullness is said to dwell in him—"For it pleased the Father that in him should all fullness dwell," Col. 1: 18. Again, "For in him dwelleth the fullness of the Godhead bodily." Col. 2: 9. Christ is called God--"But unto the Son *he saith,* thy throne, O God, is forever and ever." Heb. 1:8.

But we need not multiply quotations: all Christians agree that Jesus Christ is the one Lord, and that "to us, there is but one Lord!" As Lord over his own house, or kingdom, he rules and governs it. Now whenever we admit that Jesus Christ is the one Lord, we virtually deny all *human* authority in the church of God. No man therefore, or set of men, has any right to make rules or laws for the government of God's church! To legislate in the house of God, would therefore be to usurp the throne of the one Lord, and to become lords over God's heritage, a thing forbidden by the holy Spirit. Who would be willing to be found lording it over God's heritage, "when he shall rise to shake terribly the Earth." and when the Lord himself shall descend from heaven in flaming fire, taking vengeance upon them who know not God, and obey not the Gospel!" Well then, let us with "meekness receive the engrafted word, which is able to save our souls," and acknowledge the authority of the one Lord, by taking his word alone, as the man of our counsel, and obeying all his divine precepts!

Art. 5. "There is one faith,"—Where shall we go to find it? To the Westminster Book! The Methodists say not there, *our* faith is not contained in that Book. Well, shall *we* go to the Methodist Discipline?

The Baptists say, we cannot go there; the faith of God's elect is not to he *found in that little book*. And were we to other *in* their turn, every human creed and confession of faith, from the "Solemn League and Covenant of the Kirk of Scotland," down to the fourteen articles of faith, of the "White Lick Association," we should find none but the party adopting it, willing to call it the *one faith:* and we do not believe that a denomination can be found, a majority of whose members would be willing to say, that the creed or confession of faith adopted by the party contained the faith of the Gospel as perfectly, as it can be found in the New Testament.

We would then, just propose God's holy book, as the only one in the world, which contains the *one faith,* in all its divine perfection. Our opinions and notions, with the many *essential doctrines,* found in the various confessions of faith of the day, whether true or false, constitute no part of the faith of the Gospel. The one faith, comprehends the whole Remedial system, as developed in the word of God. To God's divine Book then let us go; if we would become acquainted with the one faith: and there we shall find *truth* without any mixture of error. We think all *christians* will agree to this.

Art. 6. "One Baptism."—We think that all are bound to admit that the Baptism enjoined in the great commission. Matt. 28th, 19; Mark 16: 16, is the one baptism spoken of above. All the Commentators, Creeds and Confessions of faith, so far as we know, understand it to be *water* baptism. John Wesley in his Notes on the New Testament, calls it "One outward baptism." Dr. J. McNight in his note on the passage

"5—Ye all serve one Lord; have one and the same objects of faith; and have professed that faith by one form of baptism."

We therefore take the ground that the one baptism, which the Lord commanded his Apostles to administer to believers among all nations, is *water* baptism. This position we could abundantly sustain; but supposing we shall generally agree to it, I forbear any further argument or proof upon this part of the subject.

What is the *mode, or action of* this one baptism? We answer, unhesitatingly, *Immersion,* or *dipping.* To prove this, we shall quote some authority. *Baptidzo,* is the word in the original Greek, from which have *Baptize* in the common version of the New Testament: it follows then, that the word *Baptize,* can have no meaning which the original term does not possess. Let us then briefly enquire, what is the primary meaning of the Greek Word *Baptidzo!* Greenfield in his Lexicon, says, 'Baptidzo,—to immerse, immerge, submerge. sink," &c. He does not give *sprinkle* or *pour,* as any meaning of the word. But it is sometimes said, that *Bapto,* which is the root, does not signify to immerse, &c: well, let us see—Greenfield says: "Bapto,—to dip, plunge, to dye." From this it is plain that the primary meaning of both the root, *Bapto,* and the derivative, *Baptidzo,* is *to immerse, or dip.* John Calvin in his "Institutes," says, "The very word *baptize,* however, signifies to immerse; and it is certain that immersion was the practice of the ancient church," "Institutes," book 4th, vol. 3rd, chap. 15th, page 343. Mr. Wesley says that "Immersion was the ancient manner of baptizing." The great Luther says the same in substance. The Methodist Discipline makes it the duty of the Ministers of that church, to give to every adult candidate, his, or her, choice between *sprinkling, pouring,* and *Immersion.* (See Disciple published Conference office, New York, 1836, page 109.) Then it follows that the Methodist church holds *Immersion* to be equally good and valid, with *sprinkling* and *pouring:* so that if every member in it was to follow the blessed Saviour down into the water, and be *immersed,* it would be no violation of "the doctrines and discipline of the M.E. Church." The Presbyterians also admit the validity of Immersion, and they have been known to practice it. The Cumberland Presbyterian Church also believes in Immersion, and if we have been correctly informed, a majority of her Ministers in the Western country, have been "buried with the Lord in baptism." They also practice sprinkling and pouring, whenever it is the choice of the applicant.

From all the above facts and testimony; with much more of the same kind, which might be adduced, with all that is written in the New Testament upon the subject, we feel authorized to draw the condition, that *Immersion* is acknowledged by all Christians to be good and valid baptism; while *sprinkling* and *pouring* are not acknowledged by all, perhaps not by a majority, to be valid baptism. Then we could not all unite upon either sprinkling or pouring, as many of us, perhaps a majority, believe them to be mere human traditions; but we can unite upon Immersion, as we *all* agree to its validity.

As to the Subject, and design of baptism, we have only room to say, that all parties agree, that a penitent believer is a proper subject; and that by baptism we are initiated into the church, where we enjoy privileges and blessings, which cannot be enjoyed out of the church! Baptism then, administered to a penitent believer, changes his relation; as Peter said, Acts 2: 38, "Repent and be baptized every one of you in the name of Jesus Christ, for the remission of sins and you shall receive the gift of the Holy Ghost." Ananias said to Saul of Tarsus, "Arise and be baptized and wash away thy sins, calling on the name of the Lord."

"According to his own mercy he saved us, by the washing of regeneration and renewing of the Holy Ghost." Titus 3: 5. We might quote scripture to almost any extent, upon this subject, but we forbear. We ask our friends to give up that which is doubtful, and cannot be found in the word of God, and meet us upon the word of God alone, believing and doing, what the Lord has enjoined. We promise to do the same; then we shall have union. On this art, we do think, that we can all agree.

Art. 7. "One God and Father of all, who is above all, through all, and in you all."—This crowns the whole matter. We all have one Father, even God. Then we are all brethren, and of course should not be divided off into sects and parties! But notwithstanding we acknowledge that God is our common Father, we act unworthy of that paternity, whenever we become divided contrary to the express authority of our Father.

God's authority is supreme over his house, or family, and he does not ask any of his children to assist him in making laws for their government; and he must be a very rebellious child who would presume to do so. God is *through* all his children. His love is shed abroad in every Christian's heart, and thus he is through them all, binding them all together in a bundle of love.—Love is the golden chain, that binds all the happy spirits together, in heaven and on earth. Paul calls love or charity, 'the bond of perfectness." We ask then, how is it possible for division to obtain between two individuals, who have the love of God in their hearts?

But God is in all Christians.—By his Holy Spirit he dwells in the one Body or church, and in every member of it. Paul says, "Know you not that your bodies are the temples for the Holy Ghost to dwell in?" Again, "If you have not the Spirit of Christ you are none of his." From this, we are prepared to say, that no two individuals can be found, who have the love of God in their hearts, the Holy Spirit dwelling in them, enjoying the one hope, and having the one Faith, and Baptism, and acknowledging the one Lord: we say, two such individuals cannot be found, hating one another: but on the contrary, they will love one another with pure hearts fervently.

We have now briefly examined the 7 items of this *summary*, not for the purpose of *differing* with our religious friends, but for the purpose of *agreeing*, if possible. We hope that we shall not be understood, as proposing to take the above summary out of the Book, for the purpose of making another confession of faith! We wish to keep it in the Bible, just where inspiration has placed it: nothing short of the *Bible, the whole Bible, and nothing but the Bible, do* we propose as a confession of faith. We advocate no union of *sects;* we believe such a union would be a curse, rather than a blessing. The union we contend for, is a union of all the lovers of the Lord, upon the *one foundation;* not a union in opinions and doctrines; but a union in heart, in faith, in spirit, in love, in obedience to all the will of God. In short, the union for which Jesus prayed.

J. M. M., Ed.

UNIVERSALISM—NO. 6.

Universalism denies a future judgment-day. It shall therefore be our object in the present number, to prove that the judgment day *is yet future*. If we succeed in this matter, Universalism must fall to the ground, for this *assumption,* is one of the pillars upon which the whole theory seems to be built.

In reference to the judgment-day we understand Universalists to teach, that it commenced at the destruction of Jerusalem and the Jewish Temple, and has continued ever since—that it simply means the *Gospel-day;* and that the judgments and punishments are all temporal, that is, all suffered in this life. There is perhaps no text in the Bible which proves more clearly, a future judgment, than the one recorded Heb. 9: 27 and 28th: "And as it is appointed unto men once to die, but after this the judgment; so Christ was once offered to bear the sins of many; and unto them that look for him shall he appear, the second time, without sin unto salvation." It will perhaps be amusing to the reader, to see how Universalists attempt to get round the plain and obvious meaning of this passage. Well, we will gratify his curiosity.— Mr. Whittemore, after laboring at some length to show, that the appointment to die, was not for *all* men, but for a particular *class of* men.—The Jewish high Priests, he says, "After this the judgment."—That is, after the figurative death of the high priest came the judgment. Hence we read of Aaron, the first high priest, "and thou shalt put on the breast-plate of *judgment,* the Urim and the Thummim; and they shall be upon Aaron's heart, when he goeth in before the Lord; and Aaron shall bear the judgment of the children of Israel upon his heart before the Lord continually." This judgment came after the figurative death of the high priest; and he, it is said, "As it is appointed unto men (*the men,* it should be translated,) once to die. and after this the judgment, so Christ was once offered," &c. Plain guide to Universalism,—pp 202, 203. And with Mr. W. agrees every Universalist of note, whose writings or preaching, has come under my observation.

There are several points in Mr. Whittemore's interpretation of this text, that we will examine: 1s—He says, the *men* referred to, who *were appointed to die,* were the Jewish high priests under the law: 2d,—He says, "it should, be transacted, *The men.* "(Mr. Rogers in his pro and con of Univ.—p. 211, commenting on this text, says, "truth is that Paul, (or whoever is the author of this epistle) is speaking of a particular class of men, and not of men in general; this is confirmed by the Greek reading of the text, "And as it is appointed unto *the* men (*Tois anthropois*) once to die," &c.: 3—that the judgment spoken of in the text, has reference to the judgment of the children of Israel, which Aaron the high priest, bore upon his heart continually before the Lord.

Now, we shall notice these items, in the order we have set them down. And first, of the men, to whom it is appointed once to die. Universalism says, as we have seen, that all men are not here intended, but a particular class of men, namely "the Jewish high priests! To reduce this to an absurdity, let us read the next verse, with this interpretation, supplying "Jewish high priests," where *men* occurs, or the pronoun *they,* which stands for the noun *men.* "And as it is appointed unto the *Jewish high priests* once to die, but after this the judgment, so Christ was once offered to hear the sins of many, and unto *the Jewish high priests* that, look for him, shall he appear, the second time without sin unto salvation." According to the system then, Christ appeared without sin unto salvation, to none, but that portion of the Jewish high priests, who were looking for him! there is an end then to the Christian's hope of seeing the Lord: for if the system be true, none will see him, but those Jewish high priests, who were looking for him! But we have another objection to this interpretation. If the high priest died *figuratively,* when he made atonement for himself and the errors of the people, as Messrs. Whittemore and Rogers affirm: then it will follow according to the system, that it was appointed unto them to die every year! for the high priest had to make his offering every year. Paul says, of those offerings, "they were offered year by year continually," and that there was a remembrance again made of sins every year, in those sacrifices, Heb. 10, The passage under consideration, then, to suit Universalism, ought to read, "And as it is appointed unto the Jewish high priests to die every year figuratively," &c. But Paul says, "it is appointed to men once to die," not yearly!! Who does not see the absurdity! But Universalists contend, that as there is an article before the noun *men*, in the original Greek, that the meaning is thereby restricted to a particular class of men, and cannot refer to all mankind, Let us allow this criticism for a moment, and we shall see what becomes of the strongest passages upon which Universalism relies for support.

Take the celebrated text, Luke 2: 10, "Behold, I bring you good tidings of great joy, which shall be to all people," This text is often quoted with an air of peculiar triumph, by Universalists, to prove the unconditional salvation of all men. But we tell them, according to their own showing, it does not mean all *mankind,* but a particular class, perhaps the *Jewish high priests;* for in the original Greek, the article comes before he noun people—(*To Lao.*) the people!

Again, the promise made to Abraham is perhaps, more relied on than any other text of scripture, to prove the final holiness and happiness of all mankind. But we tell them according to their own criticism, it falls entirely short of the mark. Let us see: Paul quotes the promise thus; "And the scripture, foreseeing that God would justify *the* heathen (*ta ethna*) through faith, preached before the Gospel to Abraham, saying, in thee shall all nations (*ta ethna, the* nations) be blessed;" then according to the criticism, the blessing of Abraham was not to come upon all nations, but on a *"particular class."* Peter quotes the promise again, Acts 3: 25; "And in thy seed shall all *the* kindreds of the earth be blessed." The article is here used, it cannot mean all kindreds, therefore, but a *particular class!*

We now invite the attention of the reader to the 15th chap, of 1 Cor. It is confidently maintained by Universalists, *great* and *small,* that the Resurrection of the dead spoken of in this chapter, includes all mankind who have died. Now let us apply the above rule to several passages in this chap., where the resurrection is spoken of, and see what will become of Universalism! "But some man will say, how are the dead (*hoi nekroi*) raised up? and with what body do they come?" 35th verse. Again, verse 42nd, "So also is the resurrection of the dead:" (*Toon nekroon.*) According to the system then, the resurrection of all the dead is not meant in the above passages, but a *particular class;* for the *article* stands before the noun *dead,* as it does before the noun men, in the text under consideration.

Universalism has then to take choice, between the two horns of the dilemma: it must either surrender the declaration made by the Angel to the shepherds in the field—the promise made to Abraham, and all its arguments drawn from the resurrection of the dead, in 1 Cor.; or, it must admit that the death of all mankind is embraced in the expression, "And as it is appointed unto men ounce to die, but after this the judgment:" Heb. 9: 27, either of which would be ruinous to Universalism!

Having seen the weakness of the first two points, which Universalism makes on this text, we are now prepared to examine the third and last, which is, if possible, more absurd than either of the former. The system affirms that the "Judgment after death." spoken of in this text, "refers to the Judgment of the children of Israel, which Aaron the high priest bore before the Lord, upon his heart continually."— Now this is so perfectly ridiculous, that it really seems unnecessary to expose it, but we will give it a passing remark. We then say, that instead of dying *once,* which is affirmed in the text, we have seen that the high priest figuratively died *often, yearly,* and the judgment of the children of Israel, which he bore upon his heart, was borne *before* as well as *after* his figurative death; for he had to bear it *"continually."* Beside, this interpretation throws the whole passage into obscurity. The gospel is designed for the poor and illiterate; but if Universalism be true, the poor and unlearned, can know nothing about it, until they are instructed by some of the more highly favored ones!

We ask, what ordinary man, or woman, reading this text, would ever dream that the Jewish high priest was signified by *men*—that the appointment to die, meant the sacrifice offered by the high priest —that the appointment to die *once,* signified to die *yearly*—and that the word "Judgment," which was inscribed on Aaron's breastplate, and which he wore upon his heart continually before the Lord, was the *"Judgment?"* said to take place after death!! Indeed, according to Universalism, the Bible is the most unmeaning book in the world!!

But we promised in the out set, to prove that the judgment is yet future: and we now proceed to redeem our pledge. Our first proof text is the one now under consideration, to wit: "And as it is appointed unto men once to die, but after this the judgment," &c. The plain obvious meaning of which is: that it is appointed for all men to die once: that is, a temporal death: and that after this, (this death,) the judgment is appointed, where all will have to appear, "before the judgment seat of Christ." We shall now quote a number of scriptures without much comment as all can see the force of them. Rom. 2: 12 and 16. "For as many as have sinned without the law, shall also perish without the law; and as many as have sinned in the law shall be judged by the law: (16) In the day when God shall judge the secrets of men by Jesus Christ, according to my Gospel." Paul speaks of the judgment day as yet future, which was wrong, according to universalism. Acts 11: 30 and 31. "And the times of this ignorance God winked at; but now commandeth all men every where to repent, because he hath appointed a day in which he will judge the world in righteousness by that man whom he hath ordained: whereof he hath given assurance unto all men, in that he hath raised him from the dead." In Matt. 12: 41, Jesus connects the resurrection and the judgment: "The men of Nineveh shall rise up in judgment with this generation and shall condemn it: because they repented at the preaching of Jonas; and behold a greater than Jonas is here." Universalists themselves admit, that the resurrection is yet future; and this text proves that the judgment will succeed the resurrection, and of course the system is false. The *last day,* is a form of expression, which always refers to the resurrection. Take an example or two; "John 11: 24. "Martha said unto him, I know that he shall rise again in the resurrection at the last day." Again Jesus says, the judgment will take place, at the last day, or the resurrection: John 12: 48. "He that rejecteth me and receiveth not my words, hath one that judgeth him: the word that I have spoken, the same shall judge him in the last day." 2 Pet. 2:9. "The Lord knoweth how to deliver the godly out of temptation, and to reserve the unjust unto the day of judgment to be punished." The language here shows that Peter thought the judgment day was still future, but Universalism says, or seems to say, that it was all a mistake, the judgment day is the gospel day, and of course was then going on when Peter wrote!

Jude 6: "And the Angels which kept not their first estate, but left their own habitation, he hath reserved in everlasting chains under darkness unto the judgment of the Great day." Again, 2 Cor. 5: 10. "For we must appear before the judgment seat of Christ; that every one may receive the things done in his body, according to that he hath done, whether it be good or bad.'

Acts 24: 25. "And as he reasoned of righteousness temperance and judgment to come, Felix trembled, and answered, "Go thy way for this time: when I have a convenient season, I will call for thee." Paul here reasoned of a judgment to come; not of one which had already come! but if Universalism be true the judgment day had *already come,* and of course Paul's reasoning was fallacious! Who can believe it!

But we need not multiply quotations, though we have brought forward but a moiety of what we could produce upon this subject. We think however that enough has been said and proved, to satisfy the most incredulous that Universalism is wrong upon this radical point. And here we rest the matter for another moon. If our next we shall show that Universalism is wrong about the second coming of Christ which is the Christian's hope.

J. M. M., Ed.

JUSTIFICATION—NO. 3.
[THE CONCLUSION.]

This will bring us to notice, 1st, the moving cause of our justification, The love of God, see John 3: 16, "For God so loved the world that he gave his only begotten son, that whosoever believeth on him should not perish, but have everlasting life." Rom. 5: 8, "But God commanded his love towards us, in that while we were yet sinners, Christ died for us." Here then, the very source that sinners least could look for help, is the only one from whence it comes. The love of

God moves him to seek and to save that which was lost. A plan is to be devised for man's recovery, and this is done by the wisdom of God. "For after that in the *wisdom* of God, the world by wisdom knew not God, it pleased God by the foolishness of preaching to save them that believe."

The wisdom of God then, being engaged in devising a plan by which he could be just, and the justifier of him that believeth in Jesus, we may safely rely upon it without fear, or doubt, for it is the work of *Infinite Wisdom*. Well, man had become the enemy of God, by wicked works, and must be reconciled; had become defiled with sin, and must be cleansed. He had become helpless, without strength, and must be afforded help, and strength. And who dues the Almighty elect of all the intelligences in the Universe, to stoop to man's relief? His only begotten son; who is the brightness of his Father's glory, and the express image of his person. Him that had a glory with the Father before the world was. He it is, upon whom help is laid—He it is, that is mighty; unto him the Father of all communicates *his will* upon this all-important subject. The Father speaks. What must be done my father? The Father replies, you, my beloved son, are rich, but must become poor; that sinners through your poverty may be rich. Here you enjoy the songs of Angels—but must exchange them for reproaches, and become a man of sorrows and acquainted with grief. Here you dwell in glory, but you must exchange this habitation for stable, and a manger; you must pass by the ranks of Angels, and take upon you the seed of Abraham, the form of a servant, and become obedient to death, even the death of the cross—a death the most ignominious; in order to save sinners Who are our enemies; to save them from death, your life must be given as their ransom; your blood must be shed to reconcile them to me and my government; that they may receive strength whereby they may recover themselves from the snare of the Devil, who are led captive by him at his will; and be justified through the blood of the cross; that they may be acknowledged by me as my sons and daughters.

To do thy will, O God, is my delight; therefore, to save sinners! cheerfully lay aside my antecedent glory, give up riches; and quit the songs of Angels, Willingly do I go to earth, the habitation of a fallen race, I will endure the *cross,* despise the shame to save sinners. To bring them into a state of justification with the Holy Father, I'll give my life a ransom, shed my blood for the remission of their sins—and consent to be buried, that I may rise again from the dead for their justification. Thy will be done.

The Angel Gabriel seems to catch the inspiration of the subject, and at the bidding of his Maker, wings his way *to* a city of Galilee called Nazareth. There he appears to Mary, a virgin espoused to a man whose name is Joseph, of the house of David: and accosts her thus: "Blessed art thou among women. Fear not Mary, thou hast found favor with God. Behold thou shalt conceive, and bring forth a son, and shall call his name JESUS. He shall be great, and shall be called the son of the highest: and the Lord God shall give unto him the throne of his father David: and he shall reign over the house of Jacob forever: and of his Kingdom there shall be no end."

At the time appointed of the Father, Mary brought forth her first born. No sooner is Messiah born than the Angels appear anxious to wing their way to earth to tell the news to man. 'Midst all the throng one quits his company and appears to humble Shepherds, and says, "fear not: for behold, I bring you glad tidings of great joy which shall be *to all people;* for unto you this day is born in the city of David a Saviour which is Christ the Lord. And suddenly there was with the Angel a multitude of the heavenly host praising God, and saying, Glory to God in the highest, on earth peace, and good will toward man."

Jesus, at the age of thirty, appears at the Jordan where the Harbinger, John, is baptizing. The son of God demands the sacred rite, but John (conscious of his own inferiority) forbade him, saying, I have need to be baptized of thee and comest thou to me? Jesus said, suffer it to be so now, for thus it becometh us to fulfill all righteousness. Then John suffered him. "And Jesus when he was baptized, went up straightway out of the water: and lo, the heavens were opened unto him, and he saw the spirit of God descending like a dove, and lighting upon him; and lo, a voice from heaven, saying, this is my beloved son, in whom I am well pleased." Acknowledged from the skies by his Father and his God, in the presence of the assembled multitude, he leaves for the wilderness, to be tempted of the Devil forty days and nights This finished, he begins teaching the doctrine of the Kingdom, and by signs an miracles which he wrought, gave demonstrable proofs of his Messiahship. His lips are ever teeming with grace and truth; his hands are ever stretched forth to heal the afflicted and soothe the sorrowful. Finally, when his work of teaching was finished, he is delivered into the hands of sinners; brought before the counsel—thence before Pilate, who declares him guiltless. Notwithstanding Pilate's conviction of his innocence, the voices of the multitude and chief priests prevailed, and he is delivered to them to be crucified,

They drive him to the solemn spot, bearing his own cross, to which he is nailed, and reared between the heavens and the earth. His persecutors bow their knees in mockery, and tantalize him in the very agonies of death, saying, he saved others, now let him save himself. If thou be the son of God come down from the cross. But no, for this end was he born, and for this purpose he came into the world, "Thus it is written, and thus it behooved Christ to suffer." From the third until the ninth hour, he endures the cross, despises the shame, when he cries with a loud voice: it is finished, all things are now accomplished, that the scriptures might be fulfilled. My blood is shed for the remission of sins—to procure the justification of the transgressors.

He then says, Father into thy hands I commend my spirit, and thus expires: "Behold what manner of love the Father hath bestowed upon us, that we might be called the sons of God." He is taken from the cross to Joseph's tomb, wherein he is laid until the third. The promised morn rolls round, when, by the Eternal Spirit, he is brought back from the dead. He arose for our justification. And after a short stay with his Disciples, in order to give them ample evidence of his identity as the same Jesus who suffered on the cross, and furnishing them with instruction preparatory to the execution of the great Commission he was about to give them. He meets, them at the place appointed, and says, all power is, given unto me in heaven and earth, therefore, go ye into all the world and preach the gospel to every creature; he that believeth and is baptized *shall* be saved, and he that believeth not shall be damned. (Mark 16: 16.) And when he had spoken these things, while they (the Disciples) beheld, he was taken up, and a cloud received him out of their sight. He is received into heaven—exalted at the right hand of God, to grant repentance, and the remission of sins, The great plan of justification is now laid, and God can be just and the justifier of him that believeth in Jesus. However, the Apostles were not yet qualified to fill their mission, and for this reason, they were required to tarry at Jerusalem until they should be endued with power from on high, until, they should receive the promise of the Father—the Holy Spirit to guide them *into all truth.*

Nov. 1843.

TYCHICUS.

N. B. In our next we shall notice the endowment of the Apostles, and how they acted under their new commission. T.

DEBATE.

The "Teacher," of the 18th inst., says, "Bro. Manford has made arrangements for another discussion. Rev. T. J. Edmondson (Campbellite) is his opponent. The debate will come off in Franklin, Johnson county, Indiana, on the 18th, 19th, and 20th, of January next."

Will the Editors of the "Teacher" inform us in their next, *when* Bro. Edmondson *turned* "Campbellite?" He was no *Campbellite* when we saw him last. The Editors of the Teacher have published to the world as a *fact,* that Bro. Edmondson is a *Campbellite;* of course, they will have no objection to give us the testimony; the name of the place where the "wonderful affair" took place, and also the name of the man by whom he was converted. EDITOR.

"PRESSLY'S LECTURES" REVIEWED—NO. 2.

In our former No. we reviewed the Dr.'s first lecture, and found very little to condemn, and much to commend. We now come to his second Lecture, which commences on the 21st page, and is devoted to *"the proper subjects of baptism."* In this lecture the Dr. sets out by remarking 1st, that "All those who make a credible profession of their faith in Christ, are to be regarded by the church as having a right to baptism." Again, on 23d p., "We do not call for proof that adults are to be taught, and that they are to give evidence that they are believers, before they can be admitted to baptism. All this the scriptures clearly teach, and we must firmly believe."

On this part of the lecture then, we have no dispute with the learned Dr. He next complains of unfairness among the Baptists, for laboring to prove, what he says no one denies, to wit: believers' baptism, and then inferring from premises which he says all admit to be solid, that the infants of believers have no right to baptism. The Dr. says, "Between the premises and the conclusion there is an impassable gulf. The conclusion embraces a class of persons not included in the premises." But we might ask, if infants are not embraced in any of the many passages of scripture, which speak of baptism, how will the Dr. prove their right to the ordinance? We think he must rely wholly upon inference, unsatisfactory and inconclusive! but we shall see. "But will any one," says the Dr. "maintain that the declaration of the Lord, "he that believeth and is baptized shall be saved," authorizes the conclusion that none except such as are capable of believing are proper subjects of baptism, and that, therefore, infants are excluded? I reply," says the Dr., "that such a conclusion is not legitimate; and should we adopt this principle of reasoning, it would lead to consequences of the most revolting character." The Dr. then proceeds to apply the rule, "Our Lord further declares," says he, "He that believeth not shall be damned." Apply this mode of reasoning which we are examining, to this declaration. Infants are not capable of believing; therefore all infants shall be damned." Now in the above criticism, the Dr.'s remarks are calculated to mislead: he treats the matter as though the Baptists believed that *salvation* and *baptism* were the same thing, or at least, that none could be saved in heaven but these who are capable of baptisms. This is very unfair; as we know of none, unless Dr. P. himself be one, who understands the salvation spoken of in the text, to refer to the *eternal* salvation in heaven: but on the contrary we believe and teach, that the salvation here spoken of, which the Lord connects with faith and baptism, is pardon of sins, and reception into the church of God, together with all the privileges, blessings and immunities of citizenship. With this view of the matter, all can see how short of the mark the Dr.'s argument falls. Infants, though incapable of faith or baptism, may nevertheless be saved in heaven, no doubt they will be, is a doctrine we most firmly believe.

But while on the subject of the great Commission, we beg leave to make another remark by the way. Every commission under which mortals act, is necessarily limited, for it implies a superior, from whom the authority to act is derived.. Well, a limited commission restricts the person commissioned in all his acts; and he is not authorized to do any thing officially, but what his commission clearly specifies. The great commission then, which is the law of baptism, authorized the Apostles to go into all the world:" this then, was their field of labor; "And preach the gospel to every creature." This teaches them exactly to whom they were to preach-: and we might ask, does the commission authorize them to baptize every creature! The answer is, "He that believeth and is baptized shall be saved?" &c. This commission then authorizes the baptism of none but believers, and if the disciples, while professing to act under it, had baptized any but believers, whether infants or adults, they would have transcended the limits of their authority. Indeed the command to baptize believers (Matt. 28: 19—Mark 16: 16,) as positively forbids the baptism *of* others, as the command. (Num. 6.) Bring the tribe of Levi near, and present them before Aaron the priest, that they may minister to him," prohibits every other tribe from exercising that sacred office.

But we need pursue this matter no farther here, for the learned Dr. admits himself, that infants are not included in the commission, any more than they are in the command of Paul, (2 Thess., 3: 10,) "If any will not work, neither shall he eat." Speaking of the declaration of the Lord, "He that believeth and is baptized shall be saved," and some other passages, the Dr. remarks, page 25, "They say nothing whatever in relation to infants. And, therefore, from other parts of the oracles of truth, which relate to the case of infants, we must learn what is the will of God respecting them."

Now we wish the reader to bear in mind, that Dr. P. claims no support for infant baptism, from the great commission, which is the law of baptism; he says that "*nothing whatever respecting infants is said in it:*" and farther, he says, that. *he admits* that Mark 16: 16, and Acts 2: 28, *afford no evidence of the right of infant* baptism! We are happy to find the Dr. so candid; it speaks well for the goodness of his heart. But Dr. P. says that the right of infant baptism must be sustained from other portions of the Oracles. Well, so we think, if it is sustained at all.

On page 26, the Dr. remarks: "The point at issue is simply this: have the infants of believers a right to Christian baptism?" In support of the affirmative of this question, the Dr. abandons the New Testament, for the time being, and goes to Moses! he affirms that "the infants of believers were, under the former dispensation, constituted members of the visible church of God." Well, suppose we admit it, what then? Baptism is an ordinance of the New Testament, not the Old, instituted by Jesus Christ, not Moses, nor Abraham! This all the creeds and confessions of faith affirm, and we suppose Dr. P. will very readily admit. Why then should the Dr. go to the Old Testament to prove any thing in reference to an institution, which all acknowledge, is not so much as once mentioned in it? We regard this as virtually giving up the question in debate, But the Dr. assumes that the church under the former, or law dispensation, and the church under the gospel dispensation, are one and the same church. Now this is all *assumption,* and permit us to say, that it is contrary to the facts in the case. The old Covenant with the church established under it came to an end, when Christ the Lord, came into the world, and set up his own glorious kingdom. For proof, we shall here introduce the prophet Daniel 2: 4-1; "And in the days of these kings shall the God of heaven set up a kingdom which shall never be destroyed." Now Daniel lived and died a member of the Jewish church, and yet he speaks of the kingdom as still *future,* an establishment *yet to be* set up. How can this be reconciled with Dr. P.'s theory of the identity of the Jewish and Christian churches! Again, in the 6th chap, of Matt. Jesus taught his Disciples to pray, saying, "Our Father who art in heaven, hallowed be thy name! Thy Kingdom come!" &c. How inconsistent to pray for that to come, which had already come, and was set up in the days of Abraham! and yet this is the case, if Dr. P. is correct! But the argument in favor of the identity of the churches, derives all its strength from the *supposed* identity of the *Old* and the *New* Covenants. Let us then interrogate Paul! upon this subject. Paul will you please tell us what you know about the Covenants? Paul answers, Heb. 8: 6—9) and 13, "But now hath he obtained a more excellent ministry, by how much also he is the Mediator of a better covenant, which was established upon better promises. For if that first Covenant had been faultless, then should no place have been sought for the second. For finding fault with them, be saith, Behold, the days cometh saith the Lord, when I will make a new covenant with the house of Israel, and with the house of Judah: Not according to the covenant that I made with their Fathers, in the day when I took them by the hand to lead them out of the land of Egypt." In our next we shall examine the Dr's assumption, more thoroughly.   J. M. M., Ed.

MILLERISM AND SECOND ADVENT—NO. 10.

WITHOUT tendering any apology for our long silence, we will proceed as proposed in our last, to the further consideration of the doctrine of our friend Miller and the Alarmist. But that the readers of the Christian Record may understand our object in writing these numbers, it is proper to state, that we did not commence Writing for the purpose of giving our own opinions upon the subject of scripture prophecy-; but to show the absurdities, contradictions, and inconsistencies in their expositions—to show from their own documents and the scriptures, that they know not what they have said, nor whereof they have affirmed. If we cannot teach men what is truth upon the subject of scripture prophecy, let us endeavor to show them what is error; for when we show or convince a man of what is error, we have done a great deal for him, and he is then prepared to shun the evils attendant upon the practice of that error, and stimulated to search for, and receive the truth.

We will now proceed to make a few more quotations from the visions of our friend Miller. On page 34th, speaking of John's *Sea,* death and hell, he says, "By the *sea,* death and hell, I understand the sea, grave and place of punishment. Render, "I understand" Mr. Miller here to say, that he understands John in a literal sense. Now, let us hear him again, when and where a literal understanding of the term *sea* will not jingle with his theory. On page 221. he quotes Rev. 18 and 3d, "and the second angel poured out his vial upon the *sea,* and. it became as the blood of a dead man." Let us now hear his prophetic interpretation of the term *sea.* "The *sea,* in prophetic language, is. the centre of some great nation or society of man, as in a restless and turbulent state." "This vial was then poured out in *France,* the principal Kingdom of the Roman ten horns, in the year A. D. 1572, at the massacre of the Huguenots on St. Bartholomew's eve." Reader, how do you now understand Mr. Miller? A question is now to be decided. In what sense did John in the Rev., first use the term *sea.?* Did he afterwards, use it in a different sense? We take the negative.

Now, for our edification, let us read a few texts from Rev. in accordance with Mr. Miller's "prophetic" interpretation, of the term, *sea.* Rev. 5th, and 13th, "and every creature which is in heaven, and on the earth, and under the earth, and such as are in the sea," (that is, such as are in the centre of France,) "and all they that are in them, heard I, saying," &c. Again, Rev. 8: 8, "and the second angel sounded, and as if were a great mountain was cast into the *sea.*" (that is, into the centre of France,) "and the third part of the *sea,*" (i. e. the third part of the centre of France,) "became blood." 9th verse, "and the third part of the creatures which were in the *sea,*" the centre of France,) "an had life died; and the third part of the ships," (that were in this sea.—i. e. the centre of France,), "were destroyed." Again, 10: 2, "and he had in his hand a little book open; and he set his right foot upon the sea," (i. e. upon the centre of France.) The reader, can proceed to read the 5th, 6th and 8th verses. Again, 12th and 12th, "Woe to the inhabitants of the earth and of the *sea,*" (i. e. the inhabitants of the centre of France,); "for the devil is come down unto you having great wrath." Did the devil come down into France on St. Bartholomew's eve? Once more, and we will leave the reader to gain further edification by further reading. Thirteenth, and 1st, "and I stood upon the sand of the *sea,*" (i. e. upon or near the centre of France,) "and I saw a beast coming up out of the *sea,*" (i. e. out of the centre of France.),

Now let us return to Mr. Miller's text as considered in our last, and further examine the doctrines he has set forth. Rev. 13: 18, "Here is wisdom," &c. In the first verse John says, "and I stood upon the sand of the and saw a beast rise, up out of the *sea,* having seven heads and ten horns," &c. In the above text, did not the objects, which were represented to John's vision, have the appearance of the literal *sea,* and a literal beast? We answer in the affirmative. Were not those objects as different, one from the other, as is a literal lake of water, from a literal horse? We answer they were.

Then the beast, and the sea out of which it arose, were not the identical self-same object; but were as different and distinct objects, one from the other as literal lakes and horses.

Mr. Miller has told us, that Paganism was the first beast—the beast that John saw come up out of the sea. Just here we will inform the reader, that when Mr. Miller speaks of Paganism, he always means *Rome* Pagan, or Pagan *Rome*. Then if Paganism was the beast that John saw arise out of the sea, it was some thing different from the sea out of which it arose; for the beast was one thing, and the sea was another. What then was the sea? "The centre of France." This is a fair conclusion, from Mr. Miller's premises. But here is another of his absurdities. He positively makes Paganism, both *sea* and *beast*. We are yet considering the doctrines of his 5th Lect.

In the 14th verse John says, "and I beheld another beast coming up out of the earth." Then, according to Mr. Miller, the church was John's earth, for Mr. Miller has said that Rome Papal or Popery, was the second beast. Did not Popery arise out of the church? In fact, Mr. Miller says the two beasts, described in the 13th chap. of Rev. were not two, but one and the identical self-same beast; and that John saw him in his Pagan and Papal forms. Now let us figure out the result of this position. When John saw him emerge from the *sea* as described in the first verse, he had *seven heads and ten horns*. But when he saw him resurrected from the earth, as described in the 11th verse, he had but *two horns* like a lamb; and we cannot reasonably infer that he had any but *one head*. We would take it us a favor of Mr. Miller if he would inform us by what process of mystical metaphysics the transmutation was made, from the Pagan to the Papal beast. It appears that during his sojourn in the earth he lost six of his *heads* and *eight of* his *horns*.

But now let us turn directly to Revelations and make a few quotations. Rev. 1: 1, "The Revelation of Jesus Christ, which God gave unto him to show unto his servants things which *must* shortly come to pass." 4: 1, "After this I looked, and, behold a door was opened in heaven, and the first voice which I heard, was as it were of a trumpet talking with me, which said come up hither, and I will show thee things which *must* be *hereafter.*" The reader will observe the reading of the above texts, they speak of things which must shortly come to pass; and of things which *must* be *hereafter.*

A revelation is the communication of knowledge to a person, concerning things of which he is perfectly ignorant. The reader will remember that Mr. Miller has said that Paganism took its rise 158 years before Christ; of course it had been in existence and full power, for at least 200 years before John saw his visions. Did not John know all about it —how could it be a revelation to him? How could the angel, with any degree of propriety, say 'I will show thee *things* which *must* be *hereafter*. The things which the angel said *must* be *hereafter,* had no existence at that time; and of course, Paganism was not the beast that John saw came up out of the *sea*. Again: Does not John say, "a door was opened in heaven." Then all the things which he saw and heard, were seen and heard in heaven. Now, was Paganism or the "centre of France" in heaven?

But let us return again to those beasts and horns, for we have not done with them. We are now about to notice particularly the first, the one that come up out of the sea. Then let us hear Mr. Miller first. We are yet in his 5th Lect. "By this beast," says Mr. Miller, "I understand the same as Daniel's fourth kingdom, the *Roman* government," Now reader, turn to Daniel, 7th chap., and read from the 7th verse, and see what Daniel says about the fourth beast or kingdom. Daniel's fourth beast or kingdom, had but one head, and 11 horns, the 11th plucked up three of the original ten, he then had but eight. Now, if Pagan Rome was Daniel's 4th beast or kingdom, how does it come to pass, that when John saw him emerge *from* the *sea,* that he had *seven* heads and *ten* horns? Mr. Miller quotes Rev. 17:3, to prove that the beast there described, was the same as John's *sea* monster, and Daniel's fourth beast. Mr. Miller says, the personage described in Daniel 11th chap, and 31st verse, is the same as Daniel's 4th beast, and John's sea beast. Now turn to Daniel, 8th chap. 11th verse, and see the identical self-same personage described, admitted to be the same by both our prophets. Now the difficulty. This last described personage was a *Greek,* and not a *Roman* horn. More in our next, JOHN McCORKLE.

WE commend to the attention of the brethren every where, the following interesting Report, from the "Southern District" meeting of the churches, written by that distinguished old servant of God, Eld, John Wright, in his own peculiar loving style. EDITOR,

REPORT of the annual Meeting of the Churches of God. in what is called the "Southern District," at Hill Creek, Washington County, Indiana, including the 1st Lord's day in September, 1843.

DEAR BRO. MATHES—Permit us, through the "Christian Record," to inform our dear brethren and sisters every where, that we met in our annual meeting, on Friday before the first Lord's day in Sept, last, being our 8th annual meeting, at Mill Creek, Washington county, Indiana. Twenty nine churches represented themselves by letters and Messengers, or Messenger. Total No. in those churches about 2,000.

DEAR BRETHREN—It would have done your souls good to have heard all those beloved brethren speaking the same things, all taught of God, all willing to live together, on the one foundation. Never have so many of the churches come up before by letter, their messengers filled with love and zeal for the good cause. New churches came up desiring to be known and received into christian union with all the beloved people of God. Our old Fathers and tender Mothers were refreshed again— the younger much encouraged; all expressing a desire to obey the gospel of God's Son, and Jesus Christ to be Lord over them all. The church here has done much in the last 8 years to sustain the good cause, and Vernon church has assisted like men and women of the Lord —old Blue River church has also had some faithful brethren who assisted much in feeding the hungry, and giving drink to the thirsty. All those dear brethren, with their labours of love, will not soon be forgotten.—We had but one foreign proclaimer, our excellent and beloved brother Henry Mavity. Our number of additions was 29, notwithstanding the churches have increased in coming up every year, and the assembly still larger, it was thought best in christian counsel, to remove the Annual Meeting into another section of country, for the advancement of the Redeemer's Kingdom. Therefore, we have agreed to meet next year with the respectable and beloved church of Christ, at Driftwood, Jackson county, on the state road 2 miles North of DePauw's old mills; where we hope to meet again with all the churches, by letter or Messengers, on Friday, 12 o'clock, before the first Lord's day in September, 1844.

Beloved brethren of the South, all come up with your letters written short and plain, heart cheering; speaking the same things: and now, dear and beloved brethren in the churches, North, East, and West, we having moved the yearly meeting North for your convenience, we shall expect to meet you also, by letters and Messengers. It is heart cheering to think of meeting our strange and beloved brethren from every quarter; all taught of God, and great shall be the peace of God's children, in the church of God, in Christ Jesus. Here we meet the rich and the poor, the aged and the youth, the widow and the orphan, all with equal rights, and together worship God our Maker, through Jesus Christ our Lord. May the great God of heaven bless our dear brethren every where, and enable them to come up to our next Annual Meeting.

We have many strong and beloved men in the Lord, whose hearts are pure, whose hands are clean, and some of them are yet strangers to us. You mighty men of God, will you also come up to the help of the Lord, and with us spend your time and talents in the service of the Lord, in sounding forth the Word of Life, the old ancient gospel *of* Christ, for the comforting of God's people, and for the conversion of the world.

We also have the pleasure of informing you that we have again received a corresponding letter and Messengers from the Annual Meeting of churches, in Clark county. They met with the old and beloved church of Christ at Silver creek, which is called the Silver Creek District, on Friday before the 4th Lord's day in August. Their letter came with good tidings to us, abounding with peace, love, joy, and fellowship in the churches. Their total number is about 1800. At their meeting 19 valuable souls were added to the army of the faithful.

Another corresponding letter and Messengers were received by us, from the South-western District of churches, Crawford county—they lament in their letter, that they had for a few years, ceased to correspond with us by letter, but now rejoiced having the opportunity— also rejoiced with them, there being many precious souls in that District.

We shall long to hear from those districts again. Therefore, come up again, beloved brethren, with your corresponding letters and Messengers, to our next Annual Meeting, or any other District on "Columbia's free and happy soil,"

Now, in conclusion, as the wheel of time is moving us all forward to the Great Morning of Eternity, may God our Heavenly Father, who is over us all, and blessed forever more, prepare us for usefulness, for living, for death, for the Resurrection, and for the general and glorious meeting of all the saints of God, and with the good of all ages be permitted to meet around the throne of God, there to praise God and the Lamb, forever and ever. Amen.

JOHN WRIGHT, SEN'R., in behalf of the Meeting.

THE INQUISITION IN AMERICA.

Sufficient testimony has appeared to confirm the fact, that at a National Convention, recently invoked in the "Republic of the Equator," (Central America, for the purpose of supplying certain supposed deficiencies in the Constitution, the powers of the old "Inquisition" are given to the Romish Bishops of the Republic! Reader, attend: The following is one of the provisions of the New Constitution. "Article 6th.—The religion of the Republic is Roman Catholic Apostolic, with *the exclusion of every other public worship.* The political authorities are obliged to protect it, and make it respected in the use of patronage."

Now if this is not the *Bloody Monster,* who has, under the influence of the Jesuits, in past ages cursed Portugal and Spain; and caused the blood of the best of mankind to how; what is it? But we will prove that Catholics themselves, so understand it? The Roman Catholic Bishop of Quito, in his pastoral address, thus speaks of the above '6th. article:" "Yes, beloved diocesans, (says he,) they are pleased to explain the aforesaid article, by giving us to know, that far from protecting toleration, which we justly feared, it confirms and strengthens the law which authorizes the Prelates to have cognizance of causes of faith, as did the extinguished tribunal of the Inquisition, with this restriction only, that they shall not in this present molest foreigners in their private belief while they do not propagate their errors."

The language of the Bishop cannot be misunderstood: "He feared that toleration would have been protected! But he now rejoices, that according to the laws of the Republic, the Prelates have *cognizance of matters of faith, equal to that of the Inquisition,* as it formerly existed! So the Roman Bishop of Quito understands it. Foreigners are in this case not to be molested in their *private* belief! No, not while they keep it private: but let a Protestant go to the Republic, and speak of his faith, so that it becomes known, and he would find himself among the "*Racks and Fires*" of the 'Bloody Inquisition." Protestants if they reside there can hold no meetings of worship. And no Protestant, of course will be allowed to preach, within the Republic of Panama!

Let Roman Catholics in these United States prate as much as they please about liberty, *toleration,* and, the *rights of conscience:* it is all a *hoax.* It is all a cry of "Peace, Peace," when there is no peace! Here is an example of Roman Catholic Liberty, carried out to perfection. Only give this *Hoary headed, scarlet colored Beast,* the power, and it is precisely the same that it was in the Darkest ages of Popery,

Let the Americans look well to their "civil and Religious Liberty." The Papal power seems, at present to be under the influence of some new exciting cause. The Woman that sits upon the blood-red beast, seems to be riding forth to trample down the liberties of the Nations of the earth; and we cannot suppose that she is indifferent to her interests in the Mississippi Valley. The Established church of England is now heaving with the *leaven* of Popery, under the name of "Puseyism." Of the 12,000 Episcopal Clergymen in England and Wales, 9,000 are said to be "Puseyites!" Romanism is already exulting in the prospect of soon regaining England. The troubles in Ireland, has Romanism at the foundation. O'Connoll is an inveterate Roman Catholic! Romanism, under the garb of Puseyism, is gaining friends, and advocates among the Episcopal Clergy of the United States! We would therefore say to the people of the United States, be awake, and ready for the content! J. M. M.. ED

Mr. MANFORD,, of the *Teacher,* is very anxious to know the "name of the Universalist Preacher, who was so *used* up by the Dutch." He also wishes us to inform him, "In what village the wonderful affair took place? the name of the venerable German," etc.

We were not a little surprised, to find such a request, coming from such a man!! Look again at the "Illustrative anecdote," and you will see that we gave our authority for it: the article is duly, credited to the *Xenia Reformer.* If the Editor of the *Teacher* wishes to know the names of the parties, their place of residence, etc., he can be enlightened, we suppose, by applying to the *Reformer,.* The name of the "venerable German" may be "Danie Winder," for any thing we know, (the Editor of the Reformer,) as we are informed that he is quite a *venerable Dutchman.*

J. M. M., Ed.

AGENTS: FOR THE CHRISTIAN RECORD.

All the public teachers of the true gospel in the State, who are friendly to the work, are requested to act as Agents: and all others who see the abbreviation, "Agt." written upon their Nos., are requested to act as Agents for the Record. EDITOR.

FOR THE "CHRISTIAN RECORD."
A WORD TO THE BRETHREN.

Although a stranger to most of you, I feel a very lively interest in your welfare, and the success of our beloved Master's cause; and although I am not in the habit of writing, I feel disposed to say a word to you, through the pages of the 'Christian Record;' for the purpose of encouraging, you to trust in the Lord, and conform in all things to his divine will.

The Lord our God has made us, and given us all things which we enjoy: he has given us understanding that we might know his will, and search after his wisdom. Then brethren let us remember, that 'the testimonies of the Lord are pure, enlightening the eyes;' that the 'Law of God is perfect, converting the soul;' again, David says, 'The entrance of thy word giveth light, it giveth understanding to the simple.' Then let us search the Holy Bible, for 'that wisdom which comes down from above, that our feet may be guided in the way everlasting. His word is settled in the Heavens, and his faithfulness is unto all generations. He has established the earth, and it abideth: by his understanding he has spread abroad the Heavens, and they remain. By his power he has laid the foundations of the earth: he binds up the waters as with a garment, weighs the mountains in scales, and the hills in a balance, and takes up the Isles as a very little thing: he holds the winds in his fists, and before him all nations are as nothing and less than nothing! How sweet are his words! 'sweeter than honey or the honey comb.' 'His word is a light to our paths and a lamp to our feet;" but the way of the disobedient is darkness before him. Solomon says, "The light of the righteous rejoiceth; but the lamp of the wicked shall go out:" again, 'the wicked are driven away in their wickedness; but the righteous have hope in their death.'

Brethren, if we ever expect to be *crowned*, we must strive lawfully. God must be obeyed, or we have no promise of heaven and glory at the end. Let us then patiently seek for glory, honor and immortality, that at last eternal-life may be given to us.

My dear young Christian friends; we are so constituted, that we are apt to drink into the spirit of those with whom we associate: we ought therefore to be very particular in the choice, of our companions. If we associate with the vicious, vain and giddy part of community, no matter how strong our resolutions maybe, we may by degrees, be brought into their unholy spirit and practices! Let us then beware! But we should choose our companions among them who fear God and keep his commandments, in order that our spirits, temper and dispositions may gradually assimilate to theirs, and we grow in grace as we grow in years. Let the word of God, be continually the man of your council, and endeavor when in company with the wise and good, to improve by their wisdom.

Beloved brethren, the Lord has called us to the honor of being his children, let us then live worthy of our high relationship! Paul says, 'Because you are sons, God has sent forth the spirit of his son into your hearts crying Abba Father." Let us therefore make it the great business of our lives, to *learn* what the Lord would have us to do, and then *practice it*. It is only in this way, that we can acquit ourselves like men of God: that we can be strong for the Lord and the power of his might.' And then by proving with all prayer, and supplication in the spirit for all saints,' and for every thing that God our Father has promised us, we shall be enabled to tread down the powers of darkness; fight the good fight of faith,—conquer all our spiritual enemies, overcome the world by faith— lay hold of the crown, through the blood of the Lamb, and 'enter in through the gates into the city of the New Jerusalem,' to bask forever in the ocean of God's eternal love. 'Amen.'
W. H. WATSON.
November, 1843.

NEWS FROM THE CHURCHES.

Indianapolis, Nov. 28, 1843.

Dear brother Mathes:—A few Lord's days ago, at New Friendship, some 7 miles south of town, 8 of our Baptist brethren came off from the "Little Buch Creek Baptist church," and united with us, and the prospects are good for several more. We also immersed 4, at the above named place about the beginning of Autumn. Within the last four weeks, there have been 7 additions to the church at this place, by immersion, and I think we shall see some more before long. Your brother in Christ.,
L. H. JAMESON.

Owen County, Indiana, Dec. 6th, 1843.

My dear brother J. M. Mathes:—I have just returned home from a meeting of some days 4 miles west of Martinsville, Ind, Our beloved brother Wm. Baker, co-operated with me: On Saturday the 2d inst , we organized a church of 29 members upon the "one foundation." At the close of our meeting on Lord's day, we had the pleasure of hearing several persons make the good *confession*. and 5 willing converts were "buried with the Lord in baptism." 3 others confessed the Lord at night, and two others united with the church. On Monday morning the church met for the purpose of setting apart the officers, and we delivered a short discourse, after which another confession was obtained. We then repaired to the water, where we immersed the 4 who last confessed our Lord and Master. One of those whom we immersed was from the Lutherans. O that all the Lutherans would examine these matters without prejudice! I feel confident if they would, they would certainly come to the conclusion, that they ought to "go and do likewise." Since my last to you, I have had the pleasure of immersing in the great name of the Lord Messiah, 42 willing converts. Truth is mighty and will prevail over the vain traditions of men. 'Amen.'
JOHN BROWN.

Martinsburg, Ind., 1843.

My dear bro. Mathes:—The church of Christ at Driftwood, Jackson county, Ind., numbers near 150 members: at her annual meeting including the third Lord's day in September last, there were 12 valuable additions by immersion, and the church is in a very healthy condition.

The church of God at Little York, Washington county, Indiana, at her annual meeting, including the fourth Lord's day in September last, obtained 8 additions from the world, 1 from the Baptists, 1 restored, and 2 from the Methodists, making in all 12 Additions; the church is in good order: and during the last year has had more than one hundred additions.

My dear brother, I must now return home from my field of labor, and fill a private station: to console an old and tender companion, and only daughter. My only son at home, and youngest, named John Wright, jr. departed this life on the 19th of November, inst. He died a Christian and is gone to the land of the blessed; aged 19 years, one month and nine days.

Farewell.
JOHN WRIGHT.

Carlisle, Ind., December, 1843.

Beloved brother Mathes: In 1840 I delivered 105 discourses on the great subject of Christianity. and immersed 37 of my fellow beings, and gained from other churches who had been immersed 10, in all 47.

In 1841, I delivered 121 discourses, immersed 105, and gained 21 from other churches, who had been immersed, making in all 126.

In 1842, I preached 153 set discourses, immersed 147, and gained from others who had been immersed 24, in all 171.

In 1843, I delivered 194 discourses, immersed 210, and gained from others 48, in all 258, making an addition to the church of God during 4 years ending with the present month, December, (December, 1843,) of 602.

Your brother in the Lord.

JOSEPH W. WOLFE.

Morgan County, In., December, 1843.

Brother Mathes: For the first time in my life I have taken up my pen to give the result of my labors. Well, I would just inform you, and the brethren, that I have just finished my two last years' labor in the cause of Christ, which was principally confined to the counties of Morgan, Monroe and Brown, which resulted as follows: in the year 1842 I immersed 75. In the year 1843, I witnessed the reception into the church of 48. Besides my own labors, I was aided by other proclaiming brethren. During the same time, many were reclaimed who had gone astray, and three churches were organized which are truly in a very prosperous condition. I am your brother in hope of a blessed immortality beyond the grave.

WILLIAM BAKER.

*- We can still furnish back Numbers to new subscribers. Brethren, will you try to increase the number of our readers? If you are pleased with the work, and think it profitable, recommend it to your neighbors, and friends, and send us the names of all good paying subscribers you can. If any No. of the Record fails to reach the subscriber, he has only to notify us through his Postmaster, and it will be supplied.

EDITOR.

"THE GLORIOUS APPEARING OF THE LORD."

We design in our next No. to give some of our reasons for rejecting Mr. Millers theory upon this subject. EDITOR.

Elder M. R. Trimble will meet the friends in Spencer, God willing, on Friday night before the 4th Lord's day in February, to continue over Lord's day.

OBITUARY.

DIED at his residence, in Fayetteville, Lawrence county, Indiana, on the 12th of January our much-esteemed brother HAWES ARMSTRONG. He died of Consumption. He has been much afflicted for some years past, and his last illness was very distressing—he bore it however, with Christian fortitude. He has for many years been a member of the Christian Church, and now he sleeps in Jesus. He has left an interesting family, and a beloved companion. to mourn their loss. — "But we sorrow not as those who have no hope.

J. M. M.

THE CHRISTIAN RECORD.

VOL. I.]   BLOOMINGTON, IND., JANUARY, 1844.   [No. VII.

CHRISTIAN UNION—NO. 7.

IN the present paper, *we* are disposed to recapitulate, and draw our arguments on this topic to a close for the present. In the six numbers under this head, we have stated and proved the following points, viz: 1st: We set out by quoting the prayer of Jesus, John 17: *21,* in which we ascertained, that the Union for which the Lord prayed, was not a union of *sects;* but a union of his disciples in the truth, and on *the one* foundation—the union of heaven; for he says, "As thou Father art in me and I in thee." We stated, and proved, that persons become *one* in the present day, just as they did in the days of the Apostles, which was by *"obeying the truth.'* 3. We stated and proved, that all denominations *desired* union. This we proved by the concessions, and prayers of all parties. They all pray for union, and then reject the answer of their petitions. 4: We stated and proved, that all Christians could never unite, according to the prayer of Jesus, upon any Creed, or confession of faith that has been manufactured since the grand apostasy. 5: We stated that human creeds, &c., were unnecessary—this we proved by the acknowledgements of all parties. We also proved, that they stand opposed to Christian Union, the prayer of the Divine Jesus, the conversion of the world to Jesus Christ, and that they have in them the essence of rebellion against God's moral government. In the 6th place we stated, that the word of God *alone,* without any human creed superadded, was a sufficient rule of faith and practice. This we proved by the word of God itself, and also by the concessions of all parties—for they all say, "the word of God is the only infallible rule of faith and practice." 7: We stated and proved, that each disciple of Christ was a *Branch,* of the true vine; and that the popular notion, that all the self-styled. "Evangelical sects," are branches of the true church, is a cunningly devised fable. 8: Concerning party names, we proved by the acknowledgements of all parties, that they are *non-essential:* but we went further and proved that they stand opposed to Christian Union, and the world's salvation, and therefore ought to at once discarded by all the friends of the Redeemer. We also proved that the primitive church was addressed by the Apostles, not as Methodists, Baptists, Presbyterians of the Old or the New school, Lutherans, Quakers or Campbellites: but they were addressed as "the church of God," "The church of the living God," "The Saints and faithful in Christ Jesus," Disciples," "Christians," &c. From all which, we drew the conclusion, that the church of God in the present day should wear no names, as a congregation, or as individuals but those scriptural appellations.

9: We proposed as a summary of the gospel, seven Articles of faith, found Eph, 4: 1—6, viz: "one *body, one spirit, one hope, one God, one faith, one baptism, one God and Father of all."* We did not propose to take these seven articles out of the Bible, for the purpose of making another confession of faith; but we offered them as a heaven-inspired summary of Gospel truth, far more convenient, comprehensive, and certain, than any human creed or confession of faith ever made.

We hope now, that we are distinctly understood upon all those great matters, which we have discussed in these numbers. We have been actuated by no selfish motives in presenting these matters for the reflection of our friends. We never have, nor do we now expect that all denominations will consent to lay their creeds and confessions of faith, and their party names aside, and unite upon the *one foundation,* according to the prayer of Jesus. There is at present, too much denominational pride; too much glorying in men, and too much sectarian prejudice and ambition, and too little humility to authorize the found hope. We believe that nothing will convince the sectarian world, *as a whole,* of its error, but the "glorious appearing of the great God, and our Saviour Jesus Christ," Yet, we do expect, that many individuals among the different sectarian parties, will lend a listening ear; become convinced of their errors, yield to the force of truth, obey the Gospel, and come into union with the whole family of God.

But while we indulge this fond expectation, we cannot shut our eyes against the fact, which is every day becoming more apparent, to wit, that SECTARIANISM IS becoming more unfair and violent in its opposition to the *ancient gospel* than formerly, and we should not be at all surprised if it should yet fill up the picture drawn by inspiration of Mystery Babylon, at the time of her downfall, Rev. 16: 2, "The hold of every foul spirit, and a cage of every unclean and hateful bird." We would therefore at this time, reiterate the heavenly warning, Rev. 18: 4, "Come out of her, my people, that ye be not partakers of her sins, and that ye receive not of her plagues."

But we have no compromise to make with any party under heaven, Dearly as we love union, and ardently as we desire to see a more general union effected, we would not give up one particle of "the faith once delivered to the saints," if by doing so, we could bring about a general union of all Protestant christendom. Because such union would be dishonoring to God; a serious injury to the cause of Christ, and perhaps, a curse to the world!

We do not expect, nor desire a union with our Paido-baptist friends, *as such;* yet, we rejoice to see them, one by one, renouncing *human* creeds, and taking the word of God *alone,* as the rule of their lives! To our Baptist friends, we sustain a very different relation—they agree with us in the main—the one Lord, one faith, and one Baptism. We both believe that baptism is an ordinance of the New Testament, ordained by Jesus Christ for the solemn admission of the party baptized into the visible church, or *one body of Christ*. We both agree that remission of sins is, in some sense, connected with baptism. *We* both believe and teach, that the *mode* or *action* of baptism; is *Immersion,* and that *sprinkling* and *pouring* are not baptism in any proper sense of the word. We both believe, that none are proper subjects of the ordinance but those who "believe with the heart unto righteousness, and confess with the mouth unto salvation." We need not go on to point out all the matters in which we agree: we have said there is a general agreement. But that we also differ in some things of vast importance, is too manifest to all to be denied. For instance, in the use of creeds and confessions of faith; *rule of decorum,* telling of Christian experience before baptism; the use of the "mourning bench," and "anxious seat," at protracted meetings, &c., &c.

Now, we propose to our Baptist brethren, to unite with them upon the word of God alone—with this distinct understanding, that each party will give up whatever it holds in *name,* faith and practice; which cannot he found in the word of God: and that the will believe and practice whatever is taught, and commanded in God's sacred volume. Such an agreement would bring us together at once; and we can see no good, reason why we should not unite. What say you to it brethren? Many noble spirits among you, are anxious for such a union to be brought about: let the Preachers only sanction it; and the work is done! We would then say to our Preaching brethren among the Baptists, remember what an amount of good you have it its your power to accomplish, by encouraging the spirit of union among your brethren: and the vast amount of spiritual wickedness you may commit in those high places where you stand, by opposing such a union; and keeping the Lambs of the flock of Christ separate. Remember too, that for all our actions, we shall have to give an account at the judgment seat of Christ. In conclusion, we commend you to God and to the word of his grace! May our minds and hearts be directed into all truth, that we may all come in the unity of the faith, and the knowledge of the Son of God, to the measure of the stature of the fullness of Christ; that we may have fellowship one with another, while we remain in the world; and that finally when the storms of life shall have blown over, and Jesus shall have come to raise the dead, and crown the righteous, we may enjoy his everlasting benediction—"well done!"

"Where the saints of all ages in harmony meet, "There Saviour and brethren transported to greet;"While the anthems of praises unceasingly roll, "And the smile of the Lord is the feast of the soul."
"Amen."

J. M. M., Ed.

UNIVERSALISM—NO. 7.

ACCORDING to our promise, we are now to show that Universalism is wrong about the "second coming of Christ." Universalism teaches that Christ came the second time, at the destruction of Jerusalem! If any of the special pleaders of the system should deny this, and call it *misrepresentation,* we are prepared to prove it, beyond the possibility of a reasonable doubt. Universalist preachers and writers, from the *least* to the *greatest,* so far as we are able to understand them, teach that Christ came to destroy the city and temple of Jerusalem, and "scatter the power of the holy people;" and that, all those scriptures which speak of his "coming in the clouds of heaven with power and great glory;" "In the glory of his Father with the holy angels;" of his "Judging, and rewarding every man according to his works;" of his "sending his angels with a great sound of a trumpet, to gather the elect together from one end of heaven to the other;" we say, that Universalists teach that these passages, and all parallel ones, referred to Christ's coming to destroy the wicked Jews; and that the matters and things embraced in these, and all such prophecies, had their accomplishment about Forty years after the crucifixion of Messiah, when the vengeance of heaven overtook the rebellious Jews; when Jerusalem fell, by the victorious arms of the Roman Legions, under Titus and Vespasian!

We understand them to teach also, that Christ's coming was "not *real, nor actual but allegorical!!" We* shall now take the negative, of these unscriptural *assumptions,* and proceed briefly to discuss them. The reader will now please turn to 24th and 25th chapters of Matt., and read them. In the 3rd verse of the 24th chapter the reader will find the questions propounded by the disciples to the Lord, as he sat upon the Mount of Olives. 1st: "When shall these things be?" 2nd: "What shall be the sign of thy coming?" 3rd: "And of the end of the world?" The answer to their first question is given from the 4th to the 26th verse inclusive, in which the terrible Judgments, about to burst in all their fury, upon the devoted City and Nation, are clearly foretold. In the 27th v. the Saviour takes up their second question, and before proceeding directly to answer it, he tells them *how* his coming would be: he says, "For as the lightning cometh out of the east, and shineth even unto the west; so also shall the coming of the Son of man be." He then proceeds at once to answer their second question, which was "what shall be the sign of thy coming?" 29th v. he says, "Immediately after the tribulation of those days shall the Sun be darkened and the Moon shall not give her light, and the Stars shall fall from heaven, and the powers of the heavens shall be shaken. These signs were to be the harbingers of his coming. When did these wonders appear? Why if Universalism be true, they must have appeared before Jerusalem fell; for they tell us that Christ came to destroy it. Well, the *signs* of his coming were to *precede* his coming, and he must have come, according to our friends, before Jerusalem was destroyed, for they tell us that the circumstances *ensuent,* upon his coming was "the demolition of the temple and city of Jerusalem:" according to the system then, these *signs* must have all appeared some time before that awful event. But Jesus, as though he had anticipated our friends, says, "Immediately *after* the tribulation of those days." Now reader, which will you believe, Christ, or Universalist Preachers?

But Jesus proceeds with the question; 30th v. "And then shall appear the sign of the Son of man in heaven; and then shall all the tribes of the earth mourn, and they shall see the Son of man coming in the clouds of heaven, with power and great glory. And he shall send his angels, with a great sound of a trumpet; an they shall gather together his elect from the four winds, from one end of heaven to the other."

Now will our friends pretend that *all tribes of the earth mourned,* at the destruction of Jerusalem!! They are bound to say so, or give up the point. And yet we know that only a small part of mankind were in any way effected by the downfall of the "Beloved City." The ten tribes of Israel were not made to mourn on that occasion; for they had long before that time, been carried, away into captivity, and had never returned. The Romans did not *mourn,* but they *rejoiced* greatly at the success of their arms. Well then, it turns out that only a remnant of the "twelve tribes of Israel," *mourned on* that occasion, and as *all tribes of the earth,* were to *mourn,* when Christ came, it follows with the clearness of demonstration, that the coming of Christ here spoken of, did not take place at the destruction of Jerusalem, and of course that Universalists are mistaken.

But Jesus said, as we have seen, that "they (all tribes of the earth) shall see the Son of man coming in the clouds of heaven." Did all tribes of the earth see him coming at the destruction of Jerusalem? They did not, Universalists themselves being judges, for they tell us, that his coming "was not *real,* nor actual, but *allegorical."* Well, the conclusion is inevitable then, that he did not come at that time, as spoken of above, and that Universalists teach that which is untrue in itself, and at war with the facts of the case. In a parallel passage, Matt. 16: 29, Jesus says, For the Son of man shall come in the glory of his Father with his angels; and then he shall reward every man according to his works." Who were the angels, with whom the Son of man was to come; and who were to be sent with a great sound of a trumpet, to gather his elect together? Mr. Whittemore, one of the most popular authors among the Universalists, answers: "Here it is certainly meant," says he, "that the Roman armies were the Messengers [angels] which God sent to destroy his rebellious people the Jews." "Plain guide to Universalism," page 122.

Now this is so absurd, that it would seem needless to spend time in noticing it! How ridiculous to talk about the idolatrous Roman soldiers, being "Holy Angels." We would just us soon believe that Titus, the Roman general, was the Son of man spoken of in the text, as that the Roman soldiers are the angels with whom he came. Indeed it seems to us, that it would follow as a matter of course: for it is said that "the Son of man shall come with *his* angels.— Well, Titus came with *his* soldiers, and destroyed the city, and if these soldiers were the angels spoken of, Titus must have been the Son of man!! But we need not pursue this *assumption* any further; all can see its absurdity. But these angels were to go "with a great sound of a trumpet, and gather *his* (the Son of man's) elect together, from one end of heaven to the other." Was there any such *universal* gathering of God's elect, at the destruction of Jerusalem, as is here spoken *of!* We answer positively, *there was not!* The Jews, who are sometimes called the *elect,* were not gathered together; but they were scattered to the four winds, like chaff before the wind! The christians, who are God's *elect* in a peculiar sense, were not gathered together; but those of them who were in the city al the commencement of the siege, having effected their escape, went into distant places of security, and were also scattered among all nations. We see then, that Universalism is wrong—*it must be wrong,* for it contradicts the Bible!

The matter is again described Matt. 25: 31—46. In the 32d verse it is said, "And before him shall be gathered all nations; and he shall separate them one from another, as a shepherd divideth his sheep from the goats," &c. Were *all nations* gathered before Christ at the destruction of Jerusalem? They evidently were not. Only a small part of mankind were present on that occasion.— Well then, we can come to no other conclusion but that the Son of man, did not "come in all his glory with his holy angels," at that time, and of course that Universalism is a delusion!

Once more: did he *reward every* man according to his works at the destruction of Jerusalem? Universalists say he did. This we deny and call for the proof. Every man was not there to be rewarded! But we might ask the friends of this doctrine, *in what did the reward consist?* But it is absurd in the extreme. In our next we shall examine other scriptures which speak of Christ's coming; and prove positively, that his coming was to be *actual,* and *real,* and that it did not take place at the destruction of Jerusalem, as Universalists affirm

J. M. M., ED.

The fourth No. of "Tychicus" was not received until the fifth was in type. This will explain the appearance of both in this number.

JUSTIFICATION—NO. 4.

IN our last No. we gave a short view of the moral condition of the world—what God, in his great love, had done for the redemption of the transgressor, through the gift of his well beloved Son—what the Son of God endured for sinners; that he died, was buried, and arose again from the dead; commissioned his witnesses, the Apostles, and was exalted at the right hand of God to grant repentance and remission of sins. But before he was parted from the Apostles, he charged them to tarry at Jerusalem until they should be endued with power from on high. Obedient to their Lord, they repaired to Jerusalem and in an upper room, where, with the women, and Mary, the mother of Jesus and his brethren, they continued with one accord, waiting at the appointed place to receive the promise of the Father which they had heard of Jesus, "that they shall be baptized with the Holy Ghost not many days hence," which should enable them to reconciled all things whatsoever Jesus had commanded them, to teach, and to confirm their teaching by signs and miracles.

The Appointed day arrived, and lo! a sound from heaven, as of a rushing mighty wind, came and it filled all the house where they were sitting, and they were all filled with the Holy Ghost, and began to speak with other tongues as the spirit gave them utterance. Being thus endued with power from on high, the chosen Apostles were amply qualified for the solemn duties assigned them by their Lord and Master; and which we, find pointed out by the Evangelists as follows, to wit: Matthew 28: 18 —20, "And Jesus came and spake unto them, [the Apostles,] saying, All power is given unto me in heaven and in earth. Go ye therefore and teach all nations, baptizing them *into* the name of the Father, and of the Son, and of the Holy Spirit; teaching them [the baptized] to observe all things whatsoever I have commanded you: and lo, I am with you always, even unto the end of the world."

Mark 16: 15, 16, "And he said unto them, go ye into all the world and preach the gospel to every creature: he that believeth and is baptized, *shall be saved;* but he that believeth *shall be damned,* Luke 24; 46, 4.7, records the commission in these words. "And be said unto them, Thus, it *is* written, and thus it behooved Christ to suffer, and to rise from the dead the third day: and that repentance. and remission of sins should he preached in his name among all nations, beginning at Jerusalem. And ye are witnesses of these things. John 20: 21—23. "Then said Jesus to them again, Peace be unto you as my Father hath sent me, even so send I you. And when he had said this, he breathed on them, and saith unto them, Receive ye the Holy Spirit. Whose soever sins ye remit, they are remitted unto them, and whosesoever sins ye retain, they are retained."

We have been thus particular to lay before the reader, in one view, the grand commission of the Son of God to his ambassadors, for the purpose of having all the things mentioned in it laid clearly before his mind. For it should be observed, that, although Matthew, Mark, Luke and John record the Commission in different words, yet their record is substantially the same, and must be taken altogether.

We shall therefore notice the capital items mentioned in the commission, by each of the Evangelists, Matthew speaks of the authority with which the Saviour was invested, in consequence of which the Apostles were authorized to go and teach all nations, and baptize the taught into the name of the Father, Son, and Holy Spirit—teaching the baptized to observe all things whatsoever he had commanded them; and that he would be with the Apostles always, Mark shows the extent of the commission, what was to be preached, the conditions of salvation; and the fearful consequences that would follow the unbeliever—he shall be damned. Luke shows, that Christ had suffered, died, and arose from the dead—that repentance and remission of sins should be preached in the *name* of *Jesus*—among all nations—BEGINNING at Jerusalem. John shows, that as God, the Father had sent his Son, so the Son had sent the Apostles with plenary power to remit and retain sins.

From all the premises submitted, what do we find to be the Lord's plan of justification? The following is clearly shown. 1: God loved the world, and gave His only Son to save them. The Son of God came into the world to suffer and die the just for the unjust to bring them to God. He died for our sins, was buried, and arose again, was exalted at God's right hand to grant repentance and remission of sins, 2: The Apostles were to teach all nations. 3; The nations were to believe. 4: They were to repent. 5: They are to be baptized in the name of Jesus, Then, 6th, the promise is the remission of sins, in order to the reception of the Holy Spirit. 7: And the baptized believers should be taught to observe all things which Jesus had commanded. 8: And that Jerusalem should be the *beginning* place.

The plan thus made known—the witnesses of Jesus awaiting the appointed time. It arrives, 't is pentecost, a Jewish festival, which brings together at the beginning place thousands: Devout men out of every nation under heaven. A sound from heaven as of a rushing mighty wind is heard, and by it thousands of perishing sinners are drawn together where were assembled the Apostles of the Lamb— the newly commissioned ambassadors of Jesus Christ.

This, probably, to these holy men of God was the most solemn day they had ever witnessed. They look over the vast assemblage, and reflect: These are the persons for whom Christ died, but they are in their sins, they have crucified the Messiah, and are on the road to hell. Jesus has ascended upon high, and authorized us to preach repentance and remission of sins in his name, to make known to these perishing creatures the terms of forgiveness. What a solemn responsibility! But here is the right place to begin, and the place to begin right. Then for the first time after the new covenant had been sealed by the blood of Jesus, the Apostles stand up to make known to blood-bought sinners the terms of reconciliation, the great plan of justification though the name of Jesus.

Now remember, dear reader, that he that hears these heaven-taught Apostles, hears Jesus, and him that sent him; and that he that rejects what they teach, rejects the Lord Jesus, and God who sent him. See then that you refuse not him that speaketh, (See Hebrews 12: 25.) Peter, the man-with-the-keys, stands up with the eleven, (other Apostles,) and explains to the confused, and astonished multitude that which they saw and heard, that it was not the effect of wine as they supposed, but of the Spirit which God had sent according to his promise by Joel the Prophet. He then preaches to them Jesus and him crucified, and that they did it, but that God had raised him from, the dead, according to the prophecy of David, of which they (the Apostles) were witnesses; that he was exalted at the right hand of the Majesty of heaven; that he had received of the Father the promise of the Spirit; that he had shed it forth and was that which they then saw and heard; and that God had made that same Jesus, whom they had crucified, both Lord and Christ. How plain the facts presented. How well the proofs are applied to the facts; how powerful the effect. Thousands believe—are pierced in their hearts, until in the anguish of their souls they cry out *men and brethren what shall we do?* Acts 2nd chapter,

Peter, and the eleven, (conscious of the importance of their position.) are now for the first time, after they were commissioned and endued with power from on high, to make known to the listening, inquiring multitude, the terms of remission of sins. Whatsoever they now bind on the inquirers as conditions of forgiveness is to be bound, or ratified in heaven. Here is the beginning place, and as they begin, so must they continue in Judea. Samaria, and the uttermost parts of the earth—to all nations. Do the Apostles hesitate? No: They speak, and that too by divine authority. The answer is, Repent and be baptized everyone of you in the *name* of Jesus Christ for the remission of sins, and you shall receive the gift of the Holy Spirit—and by way of encouragement to them, Peter adds, that "the promise is to you, and to your children, and to *all* that are afar off—as many as the Lord our God shall call. And with many Other words did he testify and exhort, saying save yourselves from this untoward generation." Then they that gladly received the word obeyed— and realized the promise, because they praised God—an evidence of joy, a fruit of the Spirit, We here have a plain question to ask all the candid. Were those inquirers pardoned, or justified, when they asked the Apostles what they should do? We answer no; because Peter commanded them to do two things—to repent and be baptized, that they might receive remission of sins, and the gift of the Holy Spirit. But we must defer further to prosecute our subject until our next. TYCHICUS.

ORTHODOX PREACHER.

Tint 1st No. of the 2nd vol. of this excellent periodical is on our table. In his *preface,* brother Crihfield complains of the multiplicity of periodicals; and after making some very pointed remarks, as to the *motives of* his brethren, which he seems unwilling *directly* to impugn, he says: "I mean to say, if I may express the whole in other words, that as some have been known to commence and to continue preaching merely from the love of fame or money, others may edit and print from the same motives. God only knows the true state of the case." Will our *good* bro, read 1 Cor. 13th chap., where, among other things, it is said, "Charity, or love, *thinketh,* no evil." On 4th page our brother says, "I would rejoice if a thousand more preachers and writers, good men and true, would spring up and wield the sword of the spirit mightily."— Well, why does our brother complain of the present number of papers which have sprung up among us if he wishes to have a thousand more! We are at a loss to understand him!

But bro. C. thinks that the people, and especially the *Preachers*. have become very selfish. He thinks they sometimes meet at "protracted meetings," for the purpose of preaching *races!* That such may sometimes be the case, we will not deny; but we have no idea that there are among us many such *little spirits*. We speak only at present for our preaching brethren of Indiana; We believe that there is no man of talents among them, who goes to *protracted meetings,* under the influence of such God-dishonoring and *pitiful* feelings!

But on 5th page, the Editor says of the Preachers, "Time was when our preaching brethren generally interested themselves in circulating and spreading periodicals; but very few of them now do so." And he supposes that the reason why they do not, is because "they have become more selfish than formerly." We beg leave to say, that the preaching brethren of Indiana form an exception to the above rule. Many of them exerted themselves in extending the Circulation of the Christian Record, for which we now tender to them our grateful acknowledgements.

On 6th page bro. C. predicts, that all the periodicals now *starting,* or *aiming* to start, will not be sustained. He seeing to think, and perhaps, he is correct, that many of them will starve to death, for want of "the bread which comes from the people." The papers in Indiana, for instance," says our Orthodox brother, "will obstruct those in Illinois, and the contrary. Those in Kentucky will impede those of Tennessee, &c. Now there is *not one* State in this Union that will support a paper. The farther South you go, the worse and more unfavorable is the atmosphere necessary to the lungs of a periodical. Kentucky, herself, supposed to contain more churches and *more* disciples than any of the States, has never yet given one thousand patrons to and paper published in it—perhaps not out of it."

These statements of bro. A. C. gives us very sanguine hopes of succeeding. He thinks, and he has a right to know, that Kentucky had never given one thousand patrons to any paper published in it, and thinks the same is true of any other State. We take great pleasure in informing our Orthodox brother, that the Christian Record has already more than one thousand readers in Indiana *alone,* besides some hundreds are read in the adjoining States, and the number is daily increasing. But still, nothing of the kind would make us more unhappy, than to think that our humble efforts to promote the Master's cause in the Great West, should prove an injury to the papers of Illinois, Ohio, or Kentucky. Brother A. C. disclaims wishing to have a censorship established over the presses of the reformation, and adds, "There seems no way of doing but just to let things alone, that they may find their own level. Yes, that is the only chance brother Crihfield; the public will eventually decide upon the fate of every periodical.
"So MUST IT BE."

But on the 8th page, our Orthodox brother says: "But, under present circumstances, among others who are candidates *for* public favor, we file our name on the list of 'periodicals to be continued.'" Our beloved brother will not complain, we presume, if we file our humble name by the side of his own, as a candidate for *continuance*. But we would distinctly say with our brother, "if our paper should be among the number *not needed,*" let it quietly into oblivion and join the great number who have gone before; as we have *no* desire to continue a day longer than we can be useful.

Further notice of this *preface* would be tedious, we will therefore conclude our notice by saying, the Orthodox Preacher is a valuable paper: about the size of the Christian Record, at the same prices. It is ably conducted by our excellent and devoted brother, A. Crihfield, who is, and has been a faithful public servant: we will cheerfully forward subscriptions to the Orthodox Preacher

J. M. M., Ed.

JUSTIFICATION—NO. 5.

In our last No. we left the reader with the result of the first gospel discourse before him, which was delivered in Jerusalem, the beginning place. The next discourse delivered by the Apostles, was at the gate called Beautiful, where a notable miracle had been performed in curing a lame man. It greatly excited the wonder of the multitude, and drew them together, and Peter preached to them Jesus and him crucified, buried, and raised from the dead. The prophets were referred to, in proof of all he had said to them. The Apostle then addressed them thus: "Repent ye therefore and be converted, that your sins may be blotted out, when the times of refreshing shall come from the presence of the Lord." Acts 3: 10 "Howbeit many of them which *heard* the *word* b elieved and the number of the men was about five thousand." Here we see the order of the commission followed as is the first discourse. That is, Jesus was preached as the Saviour, then 2d: The people believed. 3: They are commanded to repent. 4: To be converted.

5: The blotting out of their sins was promised. 6: The times of refreshing from the presence of the Lord, which was the gift of the spirit, Observe that the word *converted*, stands in the same place in the order, of this discourse, that baptism does in the first on Pentecost, and that they had to be converted that their sins might be blotted out. Then, according to Peter, conversion takes place before forgiveness, and is not the same thing with remission of sins, as many suppose.

The witnesses were to preach repentance and remission of sins in the name of Jesus in Jerusalem, Judea, Samaria, and to the uttermost parts of the earth—to all nations. (See Acts 1: 8.)

Persecution against the church at Jerusalem, scattered the disciples abroad throughout the regions of Judea and Samaria, And Philip went down to the city of Samaria and preached Christ to them; the people with one accord gave heed to those things which Philip spake, hearing and seeing the miracles which he did—and when they believed Philip, preaching the things concerning the kingdom of God, and the name of Jesus Christ, they were baptized both men and women:" (and if it was right, why not infants too?) The next discourse recorded, was delivered to an individual of distinction under the Queen of Ethiopia. He had been up to Jerusalem to worship, and was returning home in his chariot, reading the prophecy of Isaiah, when Philip was directed by an angel of the Lord to go down towards the south. He was obedient; and when became near the Eunuch, the spirit said to Philip, Go near and join thyself to the chariot. He ran near and heard him read, and asked him this important question. "Understandest thou what thou readest?" "How can I except some man should guide me?" was the answer; and he desired Philip to take a seat with him, which he did, and took the same scripture which the Eunuch had been reading, and preached unto him Jesus; and as they went on their way they came to a certain water, and the Eunuch said. Here is water, what doth hinder me to be baptized, and Philip said, if thou believest with all thy heart thou mayest. And he answered and said, I believe that Jesus Christ is the Son of God. The chariot was stopped—they descend into the water and Philip baptized him. And when they were come up out of the water, the spirit of the Lord caught away Philip—and the Eunuch went on his way rejoicing." Acts 8: 27—39.

Saul of Tarsus, the bitter persecutor of the Disciples, was on his way to Damascus with letters of authority from the chief priests to bind all who followed Christ, and bring them to Jerusalem to have them punished: when suddenly a light from heaven shone round about him, "He fell to the earth, and heard a voice saying to him, Saul, why persecutest thou me and be said, who art thou Lord? and the Lord said, I am Jesus whom thou persecutest—and he, said, Lord what wilt thou have me to do? and the Lord said, arise and go into Damascus; and there it shall be told thee. Ananias, a devout man, came to Saul, when he had arrived in Damascus, and informed him that God had chosen him: that he might know his will—see Jesus, hear the voice of his month and be his witness of all things which he had seen and heard, and said now why tarriest thou? arise and be baptized and wash away thy sins, calling on the name of the Lord. Ananias told Saul to do two things, be baptized, and to call on the name of the Lord. Trembling penitent, if you have, like Saul, been praying Lord what wilt thou have me to do? fear not to obey the directions of the devout Ananias, for he taught aright the enquiring Saul, and no doubt be realized the forgiveness of his sins. God is no respecter of persons.

The Gentiles are next to be visited with the glad tidings. Peter was directed to go down to Caesarea, and by a vision was convinced that it was his duty. Having been sent for by Cornelius, he no sooner arrives at his house, and hears his statement of all the circumstances of his being sent for, and that Cornelius and his friends were there present before God to hear all things that were commanded Peter of God, then he declares, "Of a truth I perceive that God is no respecter of persons; but in every nation, he that feareth him and worketh righteousness, is accepted with him." He then preaches Christ crucified, buried and arisen from the dead, ordained of God to be the Judge of the quick and dead; and that to him gave all the prophets witness that through his *name* whosoever believeth in him shall receive remission of sins. And while he was yet speaking, the Holy Spirit fell on all them that heard the word. It did not fall *in* them, nor upon any who did not hear the word! Why they were enabled to speak in different languages —languages they never knew before. (See Acts. 10th chap.) Then said Peter, "Can any man forbid water that these should not be baptized, which have received the Holy Ghost as well as we? And he commanded them to be baptized in the *name* of the Lord, for it was through his *name* that whosoever believed on him was to receive remission of sins—see verse 43. Stop, says one, Cornelius and his household were devout; they had nothing to be saved from—no sins to be forgiven. Do not be too fast. Acts 11: 14, Cornelius told Peter that an angel had directed him to send for him (Peter) who should tell him words whereby he and all his house (family) should be SAVED; and to be baptized was part of those words.

We shall next see how the great Apostle of the Gentiles acted, after the Jews had opposed themselves to his preaching, and he had turned to the Gentiles. He entered into the house of a man named Justus, and Crispus, the chief ruler of the synagogue believed on the Lord; and many of the Corinthians, hearing, believed, and were baptized. Acts 18:6, 7, 8. See also the 16th chap. of Acts for the cases of Lydia, and the Philippian jailor. They heard the word, believed, and were baptized.

In all the foregoing specimens of the Apostles' preaching what a similarity. True, they do not, in every case, record every particular item, as contained in the great Commission, but as far as they do, we see the same divine order—they do not preach another gospel. But they first teach the people to believe, repent, be baptized; and assure them that they shall receive remission of sins, and the Holy Spirit.

Thus, you see how God's called, commissioned, and qualified preachers anciently acted; how the people then acted under their preaching; and what they did to be justified from their sins, while the precious blood of their Divine Redeemer was yet warm at the foot of the cross. All this teaching was done too, under the special direction of the Holy Spirit. To resist it, was to resist the Holy Ghost. In all the Apostles teaching to sinners or mourners, we have no account of altars, anxious seats, mourners' benches, *et cetera*. No sneering at Christ's institutions for remission. These holy men of God had too much of his fear before their eyes, to act in that manner. Query—If the Lord's called ministers thus anciently taught sinners how to be saved, are those his called ministers who do not teach sinners to now? And if God's preachers then, under all the holy influences which surrounded them, taught sinners to believe, repent, and be baptized in order to the remission of their past sins, who dare now tell sinners that they can be saved without attending to each and all of them?

In all the cases we have noticed; indeed, of all the instances recorded after the Lord Jesus was glorified, none are said to be justified until they had heard the word, believed, repented, and been baptized.— Therefore faith and obedience are inseparably connected with our justification.

In our next we shall consider objections that are urged against the above views—until then, reader adieu.

TYCHICUS.

"PRESSLY'S LECTURES" REVIEWED—NO. 3.

We closed our last number by quoting Heb. 8: 6—9, which the reader will please turn back and examine in its connection, together with Jeremiah 31: 31, from which the quotation is made. Now let us examine the 13th v. of the 8th chap. of Hebrews. Here the Apostle adds, "By saying, a new covenant he hath made the first old. Now that which decayeth and waxeth old, is ready to vanish away."

Now in this text, is proof positive, that the Old and New covenants are not the same; but very different arrangements; for the Apostle speaks of the *first* as *old,* and ready to *vanish away;* while he declares that the *second* or new covenant is established upon better promises: and this, in the estimation of the Apostle, constitutes a better covenant. We must therefore regard the Dr.'s *assumption* of the *Identity of the churches,* growing out of the *supposed identity* of the old and the new covenants, without any foundation, either in common sense, or the word of God, and of course affording no proof whatever of the right of Infant Baptism. *Assuming* that the old, and new covenants, are the same, and that the church under the former covenant, and the church established by Christ and his Apostles under the second, or new covenant are one and the same church, the Dr. remarks, 27th p.: "Baptism it will be admitted, is now the appointed sign of connection with the visible church, and consequently, to this sign the infants of believers have a "right."

That Baptism is now the appointment of God, through which, individuals become members of the church of the living God, under the gospel, will not be denied, for the Apostles so teach us. But *we* are not prepared to admit the Dr's consequence, that is, "that Infants of believers have a right to it." The conclusion is not found in the premises! But on page 28th, Dr. P. quotes the promise made to Abraham, Gen. 17: 7, "I will establish my covenant between me and thee, and thy seed after thee, in their generations, for an everlasting covenant, to be a God unto thee, and thy seed after thee." He then adds, "Here is a covenant established between God on the one part, and Abraham and his seed on the other. The seed of Abraham, here spoken of, are not so particularly his natural descendants, as true believers in every age, whether they be Jews or Gentiles."

We wish the reader to bear in mind, Dr. Pressly's interpretation of the term "seed," in the promise above quoted: he says it means *"true believers in every age."* Well, we might now ask the Dr. if he thinks that *"infants"* are *true believers?* We know that the Dr. will admit that they cannot be! We would then ask, how are they made parties in the covenant! since, according to the Dr.'s own showing, "God is one party in the covenant, and Abraham and all *true believers* in every age, are the other party to it!!" This admission cuts the throat of the Dr.'s whole argument, drawn from the promise made to Abraham, and shows that he makes the *conclusion* embrace a class of persons, not alluded to in the premises.

From the 28th to the 31st p. the Dr. labors very hard to prove, what we suppose no one ever denied, to wit, "That Infants of believers were by divine appointment constituted members of the Jewish church."— But we would go farther, and say, not only the "Infants of believers," but the Infants of unbelievers too, were members of that church; for faith, in parent or child, was no condition of membership, in that ecclesiastical establishment. Examine the law of circumcision, and you will find my remarks true. Well then, if baptism came in the room of circumcision, as Dr. P. contends, then it would follow, that females have no right to baptism; and that the male Infants of infidels, Jews, Mahometans, and Pagans, as well as those of Christians, have a right *divine* to baptism. Thus we see that the *conclusion,* which legitimately flows from the premises, is one that Dr. P. would reject. The premises therefore, *assumed* by the Dr. proves too much for his theory; and therefore proves nothing!

On 31st p. the Dr. says: "He who at first appointed circumcision to be the sign of his covenant with his people and their seed, has abolished that rite, and has ordained baptism in its stead." Now we deny this assertion, and call for the proof! When did the Lord ordain baptism in stead of circumcision! If he has done surely some one of the inspired writers have said so! But the Dr. produces no proof; he only *infers,* that it must be so, because circumcision was abolished, and baptism was ordained by Jesus Christ. But this is very unsatisfactory, for upon the same principle of reason, we could prove, that Baptism came in the room of Jewish sacrifices! Let us see.—"He who ordained" the offering of bloody sacrifices at first, has abolished *that,* and ordained baptism: therefore baptism came in the room and stead of the Jewish sacrifices'. But again, a covenant cannot be changed in any thing, without the consent of both the covenanting parties. And Dr. Pressly says, that "God was one of the parties in this covenant, and Abraham and his seed (that is all true believers) were the other party." Now, as Abraham was dead some hundreds of years before baptism was instituted, he could not consent to the change. The conclusion therefore, to which we must come, is, that no such change was made.

On 38th p. Dr. P. attempts to present some points of coincidence between circumcision and baptism: he says, "1: They are alike divinely appointed *initiatory* rites of the church of God." Not quite so fast Dr., you are *begging the question*. Before you can, with any propriety, make such an argument, you must prove positively, that the *old* and the *New* covenants, are one and the same covenant!—that the Jewish and Christian churches, are one and the same church! and this we know you never can do! The phrase "Church of God," is a form of expression which is never applied to the Jewish church, so far as we know; but invariably to the church established by Jesus Christ and his Apostles, and circumcision never was an *initiatory* rite, into the church of God, and indeed the infants of Jews, were not *initiated* by circumcision into the Jewish church. They were born into the Jewish church by a natural birth; and after they had been in it eight days, they (the males) were circumcised, not to *bring* them into the church, but because they *were* in it already!! We are therefore prepared to say, that circumcision was not, properly speaking, an *initiatory* rite at all! But it was a token, bound upon the necks of those who were already *initiated* into the Jewish church! We have no doubt but this view of the subject may seem very strange to many. But we would just say, strange as it may seem to those who have been in the habit of taking every thing for granted which they find in the "good old confession of faith;" we are nevertheless prepared to prove it, whenever it is called in question, by Dr. Pressly.

On 43d p. the Dr. admits that circumcision and baptism differ in some respects, but he concludes that this difference does not prove, that baptism did not come in the room of circumcision. According to the Dr.'s own logic then, their *agreement* in some things, proves nothing in favor of his favorite position! Their *disagreement* proves as much *against* the Dr. as *their agreement* does *for* him; nay, *more,* for the difference is much greater, than the agreement, as we may hereafter show; but for the present, one or two points will be sufficient. 1: None but males were circumcised; but *females* as well as males, were baptized by the Apostles. 2: Circumcision was administered to infants at eight days old, consequently without faith? but baptism was not confined to any particular age, and was invariably connected with faith in the subject.

Circumcision was not property *initiatory* but was designed for those who were already *initiated*. But Baptism is *initiatory,* and is the divinely appointed means, through which the believing penitent puts on Christ, and enters into the church of God.

We leave the reader to examine those points of difference, between circumcision and baptism, and others which his own reflections and reading, will readily supply, and proceed to notice another matter. On 44th p. the Dr. undertakes to prove that baptism is Christian circumcision, and quotes as proof Col. 2: 10—12. "Ye are complete in him, who is the head of all principality and power; in whom also ye are circumcised with the circumcision made without hands, in putting off the body *of* the sins of the flesh, by the circumcision of Christ. Buried with him in baptism, wherein also ye are risen with him, through the faith of the operation of God, who hath raised him from the dead." This the Dr. relies, on very much to prove that baptism is Christian circumcision. But unfortunately, the text proves too much for the Dr.— The circumcision of Christ, here spoken of, is said by the Apostle, to be made without hands; but baptism, is always performed by hands, therefore, baptism is not the circumcision of Christ. But if this text be allowed to prove that baptism is Christian circumcision, still it would not prove "Infant Sprinkling;" for it speaks of being *"buried* with Christ in baptism." Again, "the body of the sins of the flesh" is said to be put off by the "circumcision of Christ." Now, if Dr. P. is correct, and this means *baptism,* then it follows, that the "body of sins," is put off by Baptism *alone;* for according to the Dr., infants are proper subjects of it, without faith, or any other condition! Surely here is "Campbellism," with a witness! But here *we* must take our leave of Dr. Pressly, and his second Lecture for the present. In our next we shall examine his third Lecture.

J. M. M., Ed.

THE GLORIOUS APPEARING OF THE LORD.
LETTER TO ELDER JOSEPH FASSETT.

My dear Brother in the Lord: It is known to you, and the brethren generally, that, I have not adopted Mr. Miller's theory of the "Advent nigh," and many are anxious to see some of my reasons for rejecting it. When I conversed with you last upon this subject, we agreed very well, but since that time, I am informed that your mind has undergone an entire change upon this important subject; and that you have fully committed yourself to Mr. Miller's theory of the "glorious appearing of the Lord," in 1843! I for one, feel anxious to see some of the evidence which preponderated in your mind; and I know that a multitude of brethren and friends, in this part of the State, are anxious to hear from you.

I have therefore concluded to state my reasons for rejecting this theory, in a series of letters, addressed to you, hoping that you will examine them, and point out to me and the readers of the Christian Record, my mistakes, or, misunderstanding of the theory. I assure you, my dear brother, that, I have no interest in sustaining a single objection to the doctrine. God forbid, that I should "cry peace and safety, when sudden destruction is at the door." I should be an unfaithful watchman were I to do so, and of course, would be turned out of the stewardship when the Master comes.

I have been a constant reader, of the "Signs of the Times," for the last six months or more: and I have been edified by the independent essays of its gifted Editors; but still I have felt no conviction of the truth of the system, as a *whole.* Indeed; when such men as Litch, Bliss, and Himes, fail to make out a case, it is strong; *presumptive* evidence, that the point cannot be reached, I have witnessed too, with sincere regret that many misrepresentations, and downright *slanders,* which have been circulated throughout the length and breadth of the land against the "Second Advent" brethren; and that too, by those who *profess* to be Christians! But the Judge of all the earth will do right.

When I commenced publishing the Christian Record, it was my intention to discuss the "fundamental principles," upon which the "Second Advent" cause is based; and accordingly, I commenced laying the foundation for such an investigation; but other matters crowding upon me, occupied my attention, until the year "1843," was so nearly exhausted, that I felt disposed to be quiet, until this prophetic period had passed by. I supposed too, that after '43 had run out, these good brethren would reconsider the whole premises, and perhaps come to different conclusions. But finding the advocates of the doctrine, determined to contend for it, even after the time is out, I have now determined to recommence the investigation.

In the "Signs," which is Elder Miller's principal organ, the 5 following propositions are given, as the "fundamental principles upon which the second advent cause is based:"

"Fundamental Principles on which the Second Advent cause is based.
I. The word of God teaches that this earth is to be regenerated, in the restitution of all things, restored to its Eden state; as it came from the hand of its Maker before the fall, and is to be the eternal abode of the righteous in their resurrection state.

II. The only Millennium found in the word of God, is the eternal state of the righteous in the new earth wherein dwelleth righteousness.

III. The only restoration of Israel yet future, is the restoration of the saints to the new earth, when the Lord my God shall come, and all his saints with him.

IV. The signs which were to precede the coining of our Saviour, have all been given; and the prophecies have all been fulfilled but those which relate to the coming of Christ, the end of this world, and the restitution of all things. And,

V. There are none of the prophetic periods, as we understand them, that extend beyond the [Jewish] year 1843.

The above we shall ever maintain as the immutable truths of the word of God; and therefore, till our Lord come we shall ever look for his return as the next event in historical prophecy."

The first part of the first proposition, or principle, I am willing to admit; but the latter part needs proof. The 2d proposition, I object to, because it has not been proven, and because I am sure it never can be. In the 20th chap., of Rev. we are told of a "thousand-years," that the Martyrs, and perhaps the righteous dead generally, will live and reign with Christ on the earth, and we are also told in the same chap., that the "thousand years shall be finished." I find myself unable to believe that "the *eternal* state of the righteous," will come to an end; and that Satan will then be loosed from his long confinement, and go up on the Earth, and again deceive the people!

The 3rd prop., or principle, I object to because I believe it contradicts the Bible! Now, brother Fassett, it does seem to me, that nothing is more clearly taught in the word of God, in both Testaments, than a literal return, of the literal seed of Abraham to their own land. I admit that the terms "Israel," and "Jew," are sometimes used *figuratively,* to represent God's people and church under the Gospel; but to suppose that this is *always* its meaning, because it is sometimes used in that sense; in a connection too, which shows them to be used figuratively, is very absurd! I understand the 39th and 40th chapters of the Prophecy of Ezekiel, to contain promises of the literal restoration of the tribes of Israel, yet future. The 10th and 11th chaps. of Romans, contain, it seems to me, satisfactory proof of the final restoration of Israel, after they have borne their shame, among the brethren. And permit me to say, that this is one serious objection I have to the "Advent Cause," as taught by Mr. Miller, Peter says., "And he shall send Jesus Christ, which before was preached unto you: whom the heavens must receive (rather retain) until the times of restitution of all things, which God hath spoken by the mouth of all his holy prophets since the world began."

I find myself, therefore unable to believe, that the "Glorious appearing of the Lord," will take place in the (Jewish) year 1843; because the twelve tribes of Israel are yet far from their ancient home—the prophets speak of their return; and Peter informs us that "the heavens will retain him until the restitution of all things spoken by all the holy prophets since the world began."

The 4th prop. needs proof. Let me see the proof brother Fassett, and I am willing to believe it; but until I see the testimony I must be excused.

The 5th prop., from the manner in which it is qualified may be true; they say, *as we understand them.* But I am not at all convinced that bro. Miller's Chronology is correct; but on this point I have no room to enlarge in this paper. I have many other objections to the theory, but will bring forward no more of them at present; and will say in conclusion, that if these difficulties can be removed, I will unite with you in proclaiming the "Advent nigh."

Hoping to hear from you in time for the 8th No. of the Record, I subscribe myself yours, in hope of the "Glorious appearing of the great God and our Saviour Jesus Christ."

JAMES M. MATHES.

◄———————►

TO CORRESPONDENTS.

WE have on file a number of communications, some of which will be published as soon an we can get room; the writers therefore will exercise a little patience. But we have on file some articles, which cannot appear in the Record, as they are at least 50 years behind the times! Some articles are so badly written, that our compositor can with much difficulty decipher them. Writers for the press, should always write a plain hand. Others assault Murry's Grammar, with such fury, that they have to be "laid on the table," or "indefinitely postponed!"

Other communications do not appear in our paper, just because we never receive them! Brethren O'Kane, Houshour, and Jameson, will therefore excuse us for not publishing their articles, on this ground.— How long, brethren, shall we have this apology!

One individual has become offended at us for not publishing his articles, and has sent them to the little "Teacher," at Terre Haute, accompanied with a very abusive letter, containing the *precious fruits of* HIS *spirit.* Well, we have no objection, and as the Editors of the Teacher have already done themselves the honor to publish his abusive letter, and something *purporting to be* his first letter to us, we would say to all, who cannot get their articles published in the "Christian Record," just send them to the "Teacher," as we suppose such commodities will find a very ready market at Terre Haute, especially if they should be *spaced* a little.

But to our brethren generally, we would say, write, and send us your communications, *free of cost,* and if your first effort is not successful, don't be discouraged; sharpen your pen and *try it again.* But we can assure all, that we have some *mental independence,* and shall therefore, without partiality, select from among the communications on file, or which may hereafter be received, such articles as are, in our judgment, best adapted to the genius of our paper; and in taking this independent course, we hope to give no offence "to Jew or Gentile, or the Church of God." J. M. M., ED.

Rev. J. D. PAXTON'S LETTER, in the "Protestant and Herald," shall appear in our next.

FRANKLIN DEBATE.

WE had the pleasure of attending the discussion, at Franklin, Johnson county, Ind., on the 18th, 19th, and 20th days of January, between Mr. E. MANFORD, one of the Editors of the "Teacher," the gentleman with whom we debated, at Greencastle last May; and Brother THOMAS J. EDMONDSON, Evangelist of the Church of God at Columbus, Ind.— Two propositions were discussed, which were as follows: "1—Does the New Testament teach the doctrine of the endless punishment of the wicked?" Edmondson aff.; Manford neg. "2—Does the New Testament teach the final holiness and happiness of all mankind!" Manford aff.; Edmondson neg.

As bro. Edmondson was a young man, and altogether inexperienced in public debating, many of his friends at first felt some misgivings, as to his ability, to sustain the cause of truth, against one of its most wily and eloquent opposers. A good many fears were also manifested, by the two principal churches at Franklin;—the Baptists and Presbyterians—as they each held meetings during the debate. But the debate had no sooner commenced, than all the brethren and friends present, became sanguine of success, as they saw that the cause had nothing to fear in the hands of bro. T. J. Edmondson. He took hold of *Modern* Universalism with a giant's grip; exposed its vain philosophy, and with great power, showed "*the nakedness of the land*," to the conviction of many. We do not speak unadvisedly; we know that those who heard the debate will bear us out. Mr. Manford did the very best that he could no doubt, to sustain his theory, but we think his failure must have been manifest to all.

On Saturday night after the debate closed, Mr. M. and some 16 others met in a school house in town, and constituted a "Universalist Society," composed, as we were informed, of 9 members, to which some additions were afterwards made; how many we know not. But we are sure, no Universalists were made during the debate, and some who were expected to have united with them failed to do so.

We delivered three discourses while we remained in Franklin, to very attentive audiences, and had the pleasure of Immersing a very intelligent lady, who was a member of the Presbyterian church in that place. We were much pleased with our visit to Franklin, and we have determined to visit this place again, in the Spring, at which time, we hope to continue a week or more, if we can get a house to preach in.

Will our Baptist brethren permit us to occupy their commodious house?

We would here suggest to our brethren throughout Johnson county, the propriety of building a good meeting house in Franklin, the county seat, during the present season. Brethren, you are very able to do it we know: why then hesitate. You must see the propriety, and even the necessity, of a house there. Let the Elders in each congregation then, at their next meeting, bring this matter before them, and ascertain at once, what each brother will do for the Lord, in building him a house in Franklin, and then appoint some time to meet in Franklin, to bring all the "free-will offerings" together, and make what further arrangements are necessary to the erection of the building. On one occasion it is recorded of the Children of Israel, that "they had to be restrained," because they were too liberal! We will lay but one restraint upon our brethren of Johnson, and that is, be sure no one of you gives too much, as all, no doubt, with to have the honor of giving something. We intend to do something ourself; but if the brethren please, we will do it in labor, after the house is erected.

J. M. M., Ed.

FOR THE CHRISTIAN RECORD.

CHRISTIAN OBLIGATIONS—NO. 4

BROTHER MATHES: Having, for some time delayed my Nos. on Christian Obligations, I again resume my pen, for the purpose of saying a few things on this important topic.

Having been sailing on the boisterous sea of controversy, on which the waves of "UNIVERSAL SALVATION" rolled high and murmured loud, blown by the vociferous winds of a dark and lowering cloud, big with the *threatening* thunders of devastation and ruin to *those little* ships, that would presume to sail from the coast of time into the ocean of eternity, in order to get a right to the harbour of eternal repose, I am now in the harbour of safety, having survived the storm, enjoying the peaceful reflection, that a ship that is well girded with *truth,* need fear no ill from such tempestuous storms as these.

> But if these winds WERE *sent* by God,
> To dash our bark anon
> Upon the craggy racks of time,
> Then we would float along its stream,
> Borne on breezes from above,
> Until again we sail, on high
> In oceans of eternal love.

But laying all figures aside, I will introduce a few of the many passages of Scripture that might be brought forward to show the necessity of perseverance, in order to gain the prize which lies at the end of the race. When Paul was brought before Nero the second time, a short time before his execution, he writes a second letter to Timothy, in which he says, "I have fought a good fight, I have finished my course, I have kept the faith; henceforth there is laid up for me a crown of righteousness, which the Lord, the righteous Judge, will give me in that day: and not to me only, but to all them also that love his appearing." How did Paul know there was a crown laid up for him? Because he had fought the fight, &c., but not for him only, but for all them who love his appearing. Readers do you love the appearing of the Lord, the righteous Judge? If you do, this furnishes presumptive evidence, *at least,* that there is a crown laid up for you; but if you do not love his appearing, be assured he will not say to you, "Well done good and faithful servant." Our blessed Lord, while he was on the earth, said to his disciples, "Lay not up for yourselves treasures upon earth, but lay up for yourselves treasures in heaven." Here we are plainly taught, that earth is the place to lay up for ourselves, treasures in heaven. O! my dear brethren, are we sowing the seed in time; the fruit of which will be gathered into the granary of eternity. "He that soweth to the flesh shall of the flesh reap corruption; but he that soweth to the spirit shall of the spirit reap life everlasting."

The Saviour once said: "Where the treasure is there will the heart be also." This passage teaches us, that if our treasure is in this world, we will care more about this world than we do about preparing for another and a better; but if our treasure is in heaven, then we can say in the language of David, "As the heart panteth after the water brook, so panteth my soul after thee O God:" and then when the Saviour comes again, "these vile bodies of ours shall be fashioned like unto his glorious body."

"This glorious hope revives Our courage by the way, while each in expectation lives, and longs to see the day."

I will now proceed to speak of Christian Obligations. In the general character of a Christian; and 2: In the positive commands he is bound to observe. The general character of a Christian may be expressed in the following language of the Apostle Paul: "Finally, brethren, whatsoever things are true, whatsoever things are honest, whatsoever things *are* just, whatsoever, things are pure, whatsoever things are lovely, whatsoever things are of good report, if *there be* any virtue, and if there be any praise, think on these things." Phil. 3. The Apostle's language, in this place, is worthy of repetition; "THINK ON THESE THINGS." Again: "Do justly, love mercy, and walk humbly before the Lord." Once more: "Do unto all men as ye would that they should do to you." A want of conformity to these moral precepts, is the cause of a great amount of infidelity in the world. The moralist, instead of looking at the true evidences of Christianity, looks at the conduct of the luke-warm, or ungodly professor, and concludes that the character of such is proof that the Bible is not adapted to the nature and wants of man, and consequently he is opposed to Christianity. He concludes, there is more divinity in human nature than there is in the authenticity of the Bible, and, therefore he attributes the good qualities which some Christians possess, more to the organization of their nature, than to the influence of the Bible, and hence he sets up, in opposition to what he calls Christianity, some of its own moral precepts. Others set the moralist in opposition to the ungodly professor: not for the purpose of imitating him, but for an excuse to indulge in immorality and crime.

The Lord once said of a certain church, "So then, because thou art lukewarm, and neither cold nor hot, I will spew thee out of my mouth." How loathsome a professor must be, in the eyes of a just, and holy God! O what an awful account is registered against such professed Christians in the book of God's remembrance, which will be opened before their eyes at the. judgment seat of Christ, "where every one shall receive the things *done* in *his* body, according to that he hath done, whether good or bad." Reader, are you prepared for that awful day, when "our Lord Jesus, that great Shepherd of the sheep," shall separate the righteous from among the wicked, as a shepherd divideth *his* sheep from the goats?

It is not enough for us to know what the theory of Christianity is, in order to be the subjects of its moral precepts, but it must be written on "fleshly tables of the heart, with the spirit of the living God." A certain individual once asked the Saviour, saying, Master, which is the greatest commandment in the law: the Saviour answered, "Thou shalt love the Lord, thy God with all thy heart, and with all thy soul, and with all thy mind, and that which is like it: Thou shalt love thy neighbour as thyself: upon these two commandments hang all the law and the Prophets." It would be just as easy to build a house without a foundation, as it would be to rear a temple fit for the dwelling-place of Jehovah, by his holy spirit, out of materials that do not possess, the two radical principles, "on which hang all the Law and the Prophets." Paul says: "The temple of God is holy, which temple ye are." Again. "Without holiness no man shall see the Lord." "Now if any man have not the spirit of Christ he is none of his." This is plain language, and cannot be misunderstood. If we have the spirit of Christ, its fruits will be seen in our lives, which are "Love, joy, peace, long-suffering, gentleness, goodness, faith, meekness, and temperance, against such there is no law." "The spirit itself beareth witness with our spirit that we are the children of God; and if children, then heirs; heirs of God and joint heirs with Christ; if so be that we suffer with *him,* that we may also be glorified together." Here I drop the subject until another No.

T. J. EDMONDSON.

STAR IN THE WEST.

WHERE is the "*Star in the West?*" As a citizen of the *West* we did expect that the *Star* would occasionally appear in our horizon! But in this we have been mistaken; and we would ask, why is it, that friend J. A. Gurley will not send us the Star in the West? Have we sinned so much against the spirit and genius of modern Universalism, that he has turned us out of the *Universal* church, and doomed us to darkness for ever and ever, by refusing to let the *Star shine upon us!* Or is he afraid to let his Star come to Bloomington! For six months past we have sent the Christian Record to "The Star in the West," and as he has so far refused to reciprocate, we have come to the conclusion, that friend Gurley believes "prudence to be the best part of valor;" and therefore has determined to keep the Star out of our way! Well, we admire his *courage,* and would advise him not to send it to us, if he don't want to have it *used up!* EDITOR.

APPOINTMENTS.

The church of Christ at Bloomington has determined to hold a meeting, commencing on Friday night before the 1st Lord's day in March, to continue over Lord's day. We expect to attend, the Lord willing.

We expect also, the Lord willing, to hold a meeting at the School House, some 4 miles North of Martinsville, near bro. Major's, on Saturday, at 11 o'clock, A. M., before the 5th Lord's day in March, and on the next day, (5th Lord's day,) in Martinsville.

Also, the Church of God, at Union Meeting House, near Elder A. Kern's, 7 miles South-west of Bedford, have resolved to hold a protracted meeting, commencing on Friday night before the 4th Lord's day in May, to continue several days. I (and some other brother, whose name will be announced, so soon as we ascertain who) expect, the Lord willing, to attend with the brethren at that time.

J. M. M., ED.

NEWS FROM THE CHURCHES.

Manhattan, Ind., Jan. 1st, 1844.

My dear brother Mathes: You will no doubt be pleased to hear of the success of the cause you have so zealously advocated, for the last eight or ten years. I will therefore state, that some 12 months ago, we commenced holding society meetings in this place, and about Christmas we were visited by our beloved brethren Swinford and Snoddy, at which time arrangements were made to secure their labors once a month, during the ensuing spring and summer. Other brethren have labored with us occasionally; and the result has been, some 40 or 50 persons have been added to the Lord at this place. Last evening closed a two days' meeting, during which eight additions were made to the congregation. The laborer on the occasion was our beloved brother A. P. Law of Terre Haute, who is an efficient proclaimer. The Lord be praised.

We now have a comfortable meeting house, and most respectfully do we solicit our beloved brother Mathes to visit us. Do come bro Mathes! In hopes of realizing your society in a blessed immortality, I subscribe myself your bro. in the Lord,   AMBROSE D. HAMRICK.

*-- We hope to visit the brethren at Manhattan, some time during the spring.
ED.

Brother John Harrod of Vienna, writes under date of Jan. 2, 1844, that he "is preaching four times a week, and that the good cause is gaining ground in his part of the State." He also wishes the preaching brethren to visit them.

Eld. J. B. New of Greensburg, per brother W. Mounts of Columbus, informs us, under date of Jan. 9, 1844, that within the last year he has baptized about 200 persons, and obtained about 65 from the sects ED.

Bruceville, Ind., January 1st, 1844.

Brother Mathes: Last week brothers Fields and Noyes held a 'protracted meeting,' at Edwardsport, the result of which was, 25 additions, 5 or 6 of them were from the Baptists. Saturday last, they commenced a meeting at Maria Creek; one had made the good confession yesterday at 12 o'clock. The Lord prosper their labors! Next Saturday they are to commence

operations at this place, at which time and place, we should be delighted to see you, or some of the brethren who labor in word and teaching. May the good Lord prosper you in your labors of love.
W. BRUCE.

Near Stilesville, Ind., Jan. 4th, 1844.

My Dear Son: I will inform you, that our beloved brethren M. Combs and A. P. Law, were with us in Stilesville, on the second Lord's day in last month.—They presented the Gospel of God, in a very impressive and powerful manner. They are truly "workmen that need not be ashamed." On Lord's day night, two persons confessed with their mouths the Lord Jesus, and to my inexpressible joy, my son, your brother William H. Mathes, was the first who came forward. Being fully impressed with the great importance of their duty, they wished to go forward immediately in baptism, and accordingly were baptized "the same hour of the night." Love and peace do you. Farewell
JEREMIAH MATHIS..

Our beloved brother T. J. Edmondson of Columbus, informs us, that within a few weeks past, he has immersed some 16 persons, mostly in the 'Haw Patch;' and that the prospects *there,* and in Columbus, and vicinity, are good, for the cause of God. May heaven prosper brother Edmondson and the brethren about Columbus, in building up the Redeemer's Kingdom.

Our beloved brethren M. R. Trimble of Bruceville, and Elijah Goodwin of Mount Vernon, visited us at Bloomington recently; brother Trimble was with us for several days, including the 5th Lord's day in Oct.; and brother Goodwin came on before brother Trimble left, and remained with us over Lord's day, (1st in December.)

These servants of the Lord, and of the people, presented the great truths of the gospel, with much clearness and force, and we feel authorized to say, that they gave general satisfaction, and the stubborn prejudice which sectarian zeal had excited against us, was, we think, in some degree softened. The church was much refreshed, and the brethren and sisters encouraged to press "towards the mark, for the prize of the high calling of God." May these devoted servants of God, long live to plead the cause of him who was born in a Manger, but now sits on the throne of the Universe! During the stay of these brethren, some 16 additions were made to the church, 12 of them by baptism.

We visited Harrodsburg, on Saturday before the 1st Lord's day in December, and continued the meeting till over Lord's day, and the result was two very intelligent persons, Dr. Beetly and his companion, obeyed the Lord in baptism. In the bounds of the same congregation, at bro. Kutche's, we met with the brethren again on the 4th Lord's day in December, and two others were immersed. Praised be the name of the Lord. ED.

OBITUARY.

Madison, Ind., January 7th. '44.

Elder J. M. Mathes': My mother died in the State of Michigan, on the 11th Sept, last: aged about 84, having been a professor of Religion from her 18th year. She was a member of the Regular Baptist church. Thus, has departed EUNICE BENEDICT, who lived in a state of widowhood, from Aug. 5th, 1791, to the day of her death.

I am yours in Christian affection,
H. T. N. BENEDICT.

How often do speakers and writers destroy the force and beauty of their performances, by the too frequent use of *adjectives*.

THE CHRISTIAN RECORD.

VOL. I.] BLOOMINGTON, IND., FEBRUARY, 1844. [No. VIII.

UNIVERSALISM—NO. 8.

IN the present number we are to prove, that the second coming of Christ will be *real* and *actual,* an not *allegorical,* as Universalists affirm. We are also to show by scripture testimony, that Christ did not come the "second time" at the destruction of Jerusalem.

The first text we shall introduce, is the declaration of the angels to the disciples at the ascension of Christ, recorded Acts 1: 11."Ye men of Galilee, why stand ye gazing up into heaven? this same Jesus which is taken up from you into heaven, shall so come in like manner as ye have seen him go into heaven." Universalists will hardly say, that his ascension was not *actual* nor *real:* indeed, to deny this, would be virtually to "deny that Jesus Christ came in the flesh," and John says, that such are "Antichrist!" But we suppose that our friends will admit that Jesus Christ did come, in the flesh; and that he ascended to heaven in the same glorified body, in which he rose from the dead—and of course that his ascension was *actual, real,* and *visible,* Well, the angels tell us, that he will come again "in *like manner,*" Our friends then are bound to admit that his second coming was to be *real, actual* and *personal,* or contradict the Messengers of heaven!

With the above declaration of the angels, agrees the Prophet Zechariah, 14: 3, 4. "Then shall the Lord go forth, and fight against those nations, as when he fought in the day of battle. And his feet shall stand in that day upon the Mount of Olives, which is before Jerusalem on the east," &c. From the Mount of Olives Jesus ascended to heaven while the disciples stood anxiously gazing up into heaven after him. The Prophet says, "his feet shall stand in that day upon the Mount of Olives. The very place where his feet last stood, before he ascended. Nothing can be plainer, than that his second coming will be just as *real* and *personal,* as was his first. Again, Rev. 1: 7, "Behold, he Cometh with clouds; and every eye shall see him, and they also which pierced him: and all kindreds of the earth shall wail because of him. Even so. Amen." Now this text sustains both our propositions; for in the first place, it declares that he will come with *clouds,* just as he *ascended,* and as the Prophet Daniel saw him coining, and that "every eye should see" him when he come. Will our friends affirm that every eye saw him coming in the clouds of heaven at the destruction of Jerusalem? They cannot admit it, for they say, his coming was *allegorical,* and not actual, nor *real.* How absurd! But in the second place, the text declares, that "all kindreds of the earth shall wail because of him." How could all kindreds of the earth *wail* because of him, at the downfall of the city of David, since there were comparatively very few of them present, or at all effected by that dreadful event? But if all kindreds of the earth had been present at that time, none of them would have seen him, for Universalists themselves say, that his coming was *allegorical,* and not *real,* and of course invisible! Again, the Prophet Zech. 12: 10, says, "And I will pour upon the house of David, and upon the inhabitants of Jerusalem; the spirit of grace and supplication and they shall look upon me whom they have pierced," &c. But we would ask, how could they *look* upon him, if, as our friends say, his coming was not *real!!*

But the Apostle Paul seems to have fully refuted our friends; speaking of the glorious appearing of the Lord, 1 Thess., 4: 16, he says; "For the Lord himself shall descend from heaven with a shout," &c.

We now call the attention of the reader to a passage which completely refutes the Universalian notion about the second coming of Christ: "And to you, who are troubled, rest with us, when the Lord Jesus shall be revealed from heaven with his mighty angels, in flaming fire taking vengeance on them that know not God, and that obey not the gospel of our Lord Jesus Christ; who shall be punished with everlasting destruction from the presence of the Lord, and from the glory of his power." 2 Thess. 1: 7—9, This text is so clear, that we shall make no comments upon it at present. In the 2nd chap. of 2 Thess. Paul settles the question forever: hear him: "Now we beseech you brethren by the coming of our Lord Jesus Christ, and by our gathering together unto him, that ye be not soon shaken in mind, neither by spirit, nor by word, nor by letter, as from us, as that the day of Christ is at hand. Let no man deceive you by any means: for that day shall not come, except there come a falling away first, and that man of sin be revealed the Son of Perdition." It would seem, that these brethren had come to the conclusion, that the Lord would come during their lifetime, or in a very short period. Paul having heard of their mistake, writes his second letter for the purpose of correcting them. He informs them that a great falling away, or apostasy from the true faith and practice of Christianity must take place, before the Lord would come. Now no such "falling away" took place before, nor at the destruction of Jerusalem; therefore, the coming of Christ to punish the wicked and reward the righteous, did not take place then. But Paul further says, that the "man of sin" must be revealed, before the Lord would come. Universalists will hardly say, that this personage called "the man of sin, the son of perdition," was revealed in the Temple of God, showing himself off as a God, previous to the destruction of Jerusalem. All Protestant Christendom, so far as we know, agree that the Apostle is here describing Papal Rome. And that the Bishop of Rome did not assume *infallibility,* or universal authority, until some five hundred years after the fall of Jerusalem, is known to all. Paul further informs us, that the Lord will *consume* this man of sin, by the "spirit of his mouth," [the Bible,] and "*destroy* him by the brightness of his *coming*" Well, as he is not yet destroyed, we conclude with confidence, that the Lord has *not yet come:* but if he came at the destruction of the city of Jerusalem, as Universalists say, then Paul was mistaken! Reader, which will you believe, Paul, or Universalists? You cannot believe both, for they contradict each other!

But the friends of the system will say, "the Lord promised to come again, in that generation in which he lived;" for he says, "Verily, I say unto you, this generation shall not pass away, till all be fulfilled." Luke 21: 32, and parallel passages. To dispose of this apparent difficulty, it is only necessary to look for a moment, at the meaning of the word *generation.* The Greek term, here rendered *generation,* is Genea, the primary meaning of which, according to Greenfield and other standard Lexicographers, is "A family;" it also means a *race,* a *tribe,* an *age,* a generation, including upon an average about 30 years. Take the first meaning of this word then, and all is clear. Let us try it.— Our Lord is here addressing the Jews, and after having told them of the utter desolation of their city and temple, and their dispersion among all nations; his coming in the clouds of heaven, and the circumstances which would be connected with his glorious advent, he declares to them, "This *genea* (family, or race) shall not pass away, till all be fulfilled." As much as if he had said, "This very people, the Jews, notwithstanding all their calamities, shall not pass away, or cease to be a distinct people, until all these things of which I have told you shall come to pass." How beautifully this prediction of our Lord corresponds with the facts. The *family,* or generation of Israel, though scattered and peeled, and trodden down by all the nations of the earth; are still a distinct *family,* or generation, a standing memento of the faithfulness of God. So Dr. Adam Clark understands this passage, and with him agree many learned Commentators.

But Universalists seem to think, that the word always means a *lifetime,* or a period of about 30 years! Let us try a few passages, and see how it will do. 1 Peter 2: 9, "But ye are a chosen *generation,* a royal priesthood." Who were a chosen generation? Surely no one will contend that Peter meant none but those Christians who were then living! Peter certainly had the whole Christian family in his eye. from the beginning of the gospel, down to the end of the dispensation. Just substitute the term *family, for generation,* and you have the *idea.*

Take another example, Matt. 1: 1, "The Book of the generation of Jesus Christ the Son of David, the son of Abraham." According to Universalists, this would mean simply the "Book of the lifetime of Jesus Christ." But take the primary meaning of the word generation, which is *family,* and you have the true interpretation: for Matthew immediately goes on to give the history of the family lineage of the Saviour—the history of his fleshly descent. But we have said enough upon this point; as we suppose all can see the force of our criticism.

J. M. M., ED.

THE CHRISTIAN (UNIVERSALIST) TEACHER.

SEVERAL articles have recently appeared in this paper, which we design briefly to notice,

1: In the 8th No. one of its Editors, Mr. E. Manford, after complaining of our severity, says, "Does he owe us a grudge on account of the result of a debate we once had with him? We can assign no other reason. Though fairly vanquished, he still seems dissatisfied, because, perhaps, his vanquisher was a 'boy.'" We disclaim the idea of holding a *grudge* against our young friend. Malice has no place in our bosom. We believe in the doctrine of pardon! We never had but one debate with Mr. M , and the result of that was just what we desired. But who says we were vanquished? Why the "boy," who claims to have been our glorious vanquisher!! O shame! And could he get no one else to say it for him! We believe that he is the only person who heard the debate, that has ever made such a declaration! Well, we have but one apology for him, and that is, *he is a 'boy;'* we hope therefore, that our readers will not judge him harshly; and perhaps when he has more experience he will learn to be more modest.

2: In our 5th No. we quoted from another Universalist paper, in which the Editor, Jonathan Kidwell, charges friend Manford of acknowledging, at a certain meeting of Universalists at Perrysville, Ind., that he did not believe all the Pentateuch. Our friend M. says the charge is false! Well, be it so: we have affirmed nothing upon this point; let Mr. M., and his elder brother Jonathan settle the matter between themselves.

3: In the same paper, our pugnacious little friend proposes to meet us again in debate, if we *desire it.* If Mr. M. vanquished us so completely at Greencastle last May, why does he seek another interview of the same character with us! It is not common, for a conqueror to challenge his unfortunate antagonist, who has fallen under his powerful arm, to another contest! But perhaps he takes the liberty to do so because he is a 'boy.'

But we would most distinctly say, that we have no *desire* to debate with any *man* or *boy*. It is only when we think the cause of truth requires it, that we are willing to "break a lance over the steel cap" of any son of the apostasy. And we are sure such a debate is not needed in this community. But we would further remark, that last summer and autumn, we had a correspondence with Mr. B. F. Foster, a Universalist Preacher, who seemed to be very anxious to debate with us.— We then stated distinctly, that if the Universalist church in Terre Haute would endorse for him, and jointly with us make arrangements for the publication of the debate, so that there might be an end to the matter, we would consent to meet him in Terre Haute, and discuss the points of difference between us. We also stated, that if Mr. F.'s brethren preferred another as the champion of their cause, we would have no objection, as we wished the system to have its ablest advocate. We agreed also, to stand aside, if our brethren should prefer another to advocate their cause in such a discussion. This proposition is yet undisposed of. We cannot therefore pay any further attention to friend Manford's challenge.

4: Mr. Manford's attempt at proving that we believe in "going to glory by water," is not even good sophistry. We think he had better try again: perhaps he can do better.

5: An article under the head of 'Unfairness of the Christian Record,' appeared in the 9th No. of the Teacher, in which we have some *of* the fruits of Mr. Manford's spirit! He says that most we have written and published on the subject of Universalism, is *misrepresentation!* Assertions are very cheap articles! But why does he not *come to the rescue,* and show that we have misquoted Ballou, Rogers, Whittemore, and others, from whose writings we have quoted largely! We have not submitted a single proposition in our numbers on Universalism, but what we have fully sustained by the testimony of its principal advocates. If the reader has any doubts upon this point, let him turn back and examine for himself. But he says that "all Universalists believe in the Divinity of Christ." We would simply ask, if this be so, what does Hosea Ballou mean by saying, "we shall contend that the Mediator is a *created, dependent* being!"

But the gentleman's wrath waxes very hot against us for saying, that some Universalists were "opposed to public prayer," and says, "Well, how does the mighty Editor of the Record prove that all the Universalists in the East, West, North and South are opposed to public prayer? Here is the knock-down proof: In a *tale*. written by a Universalist, an old ignorant man, who is said to have lived some where among the Allegheny mountains, is represented as saying public prayer is wrong." Now we would remark, that we never said that all Universalists were opposed to public prayer: the gentleman himself has been heard to pray in our town. But we said that it was a difficult question, to be satisfactorily answered, as some had been known to pray publicly, while others opposed it. But the way our friend attempts to get out of it, is truly laughable. He says, "Suppose he should write a *tale,* in which was a character who professed to be a Reformer, that should condemn baptism; would that be proof that the Campbellites are all opposed to baptism. Agreeable to Mr. M.'s logic it would." To which we answer, if we should write a *tale* for the purpose of showing the influence of the Gospel of Christ upon "individual and social life;" we would select no characters, which would not show that influence to the best possible advantage. And if in such a *tale,* we should introduce a character, professing to be under that influence, and put into his mouth language, which would "condemn baptism," all would understand, that we did not believe in the utility of baptism, and that we wished it to be so understood. Well, the *tale,* from which we quoted, was written by Mr. Geo. Rogers, a prominent Universalist Preacher and writer, and forms a part of his celebrated book entitled "The Pro and Con." Mr. Rogers informs us in the outset, that he writes this *tale,* for the purpose of "showing the influence of certain religious doctrines upon individual and social life." The characters are of course fictitious, chosen by Mr. R. to the very best advantage. And the "Old Squire," whose language was quoted, as condemning public prayer, so far from being "an old ignorant man, living some where among the Allegheny Mountains," is a being of Mr. Rogers' own creation, and is a personification of Universalism in the "Pennsylvania Valley;" and if he was ignorant, it was because his maker, Mr. Rogers, was ignorant.

One of three things is therefore true; Mr. R. was ignorant of what Universalists believed and practiced, on the subject of public prayer, or it was his object to deceive us; or Mr. R. himself, and the Universalists in the "Pennsylvania Valley," do not believe in, nor practice public prayer! Mr. Rogers has traveled very extensively, if we are correctly informed, and of course cannot be ignorant of what Universalists teach upon that subject; we cannot suppose that he aimed to deceive. The only conclusion to which we can come, which is rational, is, that he made his "Old Squire" tell the truth!

6: In the 10th No. of the Teacher, is a letter, written by Mr. Manford, from Franklin, to his brother Editors, concerning the debate, and certain other matters, which we beg leave briefly to notice. In this letter the gentleman gives a history of his travels, from Terre Haute to Franklin. Gosport was the first point he mentions, and here, he says, he preached to "a large congregation," collected too by an hour's notice! We pause not a moment to inquire into this matter. From Gosport, our friend says, he proceeded to Martinsville, where is a Universalist church, he says, "in a prosperous condition!" Of the prosperity of this little society, we have nothing to say at present, as we know not what are the gentleman's views of prosperity! But here, Mr. M. says that he gave notice on Monday night, that "on the subsequent evening he would deliver a discourse concerning the Lake of fire, mentioned in Revelations;" and he adds, "The next day the Reformers and Presbyterians, to prevent the people from hearing my sermon, gave notice that there would be meetings on the evening of that day, at their respective places of worship. They were defeated, however, if I was correctly informed; for I was told more attended my meeting than did both of the others." Now we pronounce the greater part of the above sheer "misrepresentation." If Mr. M. suffered himself to be thus imposed upon, by what *he was told,* be deserves to be pitied.— But if he has willfully perverted the truth, his conduct is highly reprehensible.

In the next paragraph, he informs his readers, that we were the individual who held the opposition meeting! We pronounce it false! we held no opposition meeting. Indeed, if his effort that evening, was not superior to one we heard him make on the "Lake of fire," in Franklin, we should be pleased to have the whole community to hear him; not that we would wish *every* man to give him $5 00 for proving that there is no *future* punishment, that would make him too rich; but because it would be its own refutation.

But what are the facts in regard to this opposition meeting? On Lord's day previous, we gave the appointment to a brother, and requested him to give notice to the people of Martinsville, that we would preach in that place on Tuesday evening, not knowing that Mr. M. would be within fifty miles of the place! Accordingly, we rode from home to Martinsville on that day, and when we arrived in town, the horns were already sounding at several places, and we saw the courthouse lighted up. We inquired if that was the place where we were to hold forth, and were told that Mr. M. was to preach there. This was the first notice we had of his being in town! And yet he gravely tells his readers, that we held an opposition meeting! Let the people judge between us! But friend M. says, that our effort was not successful, as he had more to hear him, than *attended both the others!* We have only to say, that the house in which we met was *full,* and we were told by a gentleman of respectability, who attended Mr. M.'s meeting, that he and a very small audience, and that he complained of it at the time, saying, that he "believed the people were preached to death," or something like it. But enough of this. Speaking of our efforts at Franklin, he says, "The Reformers made a strong effort to gather a church." Now we made no such effort. We could have gathered a church in Franklin if we had chosen; we preached the Gospel and tried to get persons to obey it, and we design, *Deo Volente,* to gather a congregation in Franklin. What we have said of the debate in another paper, will supersede the necessity of any further remarks upon this article. J. M. M., ED.

VALE OF PEACE, NEAR SPENCER, IND.
February, 1844.

Beloved Brother Mathes: I have taken pains to collect some statistical information in this (Owen) county, concerning the religious body of people who reject all *human,* creeds, confessions of faith, and disciplines, and have taken the word of God *alone* as their only rule of faith and practice, and have discarded all party and sectarian names given by erring men; and take and wear the name by which the ancient followers of Christ were called by their Lord and each other; and who contend for, and are willing to unite with all God's people upon the above principles. I will give the number of churches, of the members in each, with the name of the place where planted, and some of the names of brethren near the preaching places.

No. of Churches.	Members.	Names of members living near each church.
Union Meeting House,	185	Zachariah Dowden, D. Goss.
Bethel, Jefferson Township,	156	F. Hauser, J. F. Conrad.
Lower Raccoon, Franklin tp.	30	M. Coley and J. Carpenter.
Bethlehem, near Millgrove,	53	Widow Hartsock.
Spencer, (county seat,)	68	T. C. Johnson, T. R. S. Howe
Wm. Boyles', Jefferson tp.	56	Eld. O. Winters.
James Wallace's, Morgan tp.	15	
Liberty, Lafayette township,	27	Jacob Hicks.
New Concord, Clay township,	55	W. Reeves, Thos. Pirtle.
Antioch, Franklin "	70	Sam'l. Scott, Willis Wood.
Mill Creek, Jackson "	18	Michael Rader.
West Liberty, Grhyson "	55	Patrick Sullivan.

At Eld. John Brown's, in Harrison township, a church was planted which now numbers 95; but as their house of worship is in Morgan county, I will not include it in this. Then leaving out the church at bro. Brown's, there are twelve separate Christian congregations, whose total No. is 788.

It is very desirable that in each county in the State, some brother or brethren would gather information as above, so that our numerical strength in this State can be known, for the encouragement of the friends of the good cause.

Some of the above congregations meet every Lord's day for public worship—others do not, which is to be regretted, because anciently they that feared the Lord met often together, (not once a month,) and the Lord looked upon and heard them, and said they shall be mine in that day when I come to make up my jewels. Now, beloved brethren, if you would be the Lord's in that great day, forsake not the assembling of yourselves together, but exhort one another and so much the more as you see that day approaching. T. C. JOHNSON.

We hope that our beloved brethren will send us the result of their labors in the Master's good cause. It is a matter in which all feel deeply interested. And we would call the attention of the brethren throughout the State, to our beloved and zealous bro. T. C. Johnson's Report, of the statistics of Owen County. Our beloved bro. has been at some pains, to draw up a statistical report of all the churches, and members in Owen County, for the information and encouragement of the brethren. We would suggest the propriety of some active brother in every County in the State, preparing a similar report. Such statistical reports cannot fail to be interesting. What say you brethren? It will cost you but little labor. We will most cheerfully publish such reports, and then at the close of the present vol. of the Record, we would be able to arrange a statistical table, showing to our brethren every where, the strength of the cause in Indiana. Brethren will you try?

J. M. M., Ed.

A DISCOURSE ON ROMANS 1: 16.

"I am not ashamed of the Gospel of Christ, for it is the power of God unto salvation, to every one that believeth, to the Jew first, and also to the Greek."

From the above declaration, many have supposed, that all that is necessary on the part of the unregenerate, in order to their acceptance with God, or their induction into the kingdom and patience of Jesus Christ his Son, is the genuine belief of the gospel facts; or faith (alone) in Christ Jesus—as sayeth a certain little book, to which me might refer. That such is erroneous doctrine; and not the doctrine of Christ, we design briefly to show, as we think the text clearly proves. We shall therefore proceed by asking a question: Can the possession of power to obtain and object, ever be considered the object itself—we think not. Let us try this position, whether it be correct. That God our heavenly Father, possesses power to save all mankind, will, we think, be doubted by no one who believes in the divine authenticity of the Bible. Then if our position is false, Universalism must be true; for if all who possess power to become saved persons, viz. those who, with all the heart, believe the gospel facts, are considered as in possession of the salvation spoken of in the text, from the more consideration of their possessing power to attain it. Then it follows upon the same principle, that all mankind will be unconditionally saved—for God possesses power to save all.

But who, in possession of his reasoning faculties, with God's revealed will before his mind, can suppose for a single moment, that the Great Sovereign of the Universe, will exercise that power in the salvation of the liar, the whoremonger, and the cut-throat, when the Bible every where affirms the contrary. It appears then, gentle reader, that it would manifest folly on our part, to suppose that we are in a state of salvation, from the fact of our having possessed power to obtain it. But to illustrate still farther: the time is fast approaching when the Presidential chair will be vacant; provision must be made by the people of these United States, to fill that vacancy. An individual is nominated as a candidate to fill the vacancy, in a public convention called for the purpose, by the almost unanimous voice of the people, as expressed through their Representatives: in short, the fact is demonstrated to all, that the election of the nominee depends solely upon his own discretion: if he consents to the nomination his election is sure. Then reader, you see that the nominee possesses power to become Chief Magistrate—do you not? But can you now satisfy yourself that he is in the Presidential chair—we think not; for, say you, he must first consent to the nomination, and then an election must be held, in accordance with the law in the case; after which the votes must be counted, that the result may show to all, the right of the nominee to the office of President—and to consummate the whole matter, he must be duly sworn, and then exercise the office of Chief Magistrate.

Now reader, can you make the application; if you cannot, we will lend you a helping hand.

You have seen in the case of the nominee, that it was not merely his consent to the nomination, nor his faith in the people, though each had its influence, that promoted him to the high and respectable office of President; but his obedience to the institutions of his country. So reader, we say in the case of the sinner. It is not his faith exclusively, nor his repentance, though both are essential, to the salvation spoken of in the text: but it is that obedience which his faith teaches, or as Paul says, "Obedience to the faith," Romans 1: 5, and 16 and 26. Thus as in the case of the nominee, we would have that individual sinner to do, who having heard the gospel of our salvation, is induced to believe with the heart unto righteousness, thus possessing the power of God unto salvation. Yes, like the nominee, would we have him exercise himself under the influence of that power which he now possesses, to become a saved person; and thus obtain the salvation promised, by obeying from the heart that form of doctrine delivered by the holy Apostles; in doing which he may embrace the promise—the remission of sins. For says Paul, Romans 6: 17, "But God be thanked, that you were the servants of sin, but you have obeyed from the heart that form of doctrine delivered you;" and in the following verse he adds, "Being then made free from sin ye became the servants of righteousness." Verse 22d hear him: "But now being made free from sin, and having become servants to God, you have your fruit unto holiness; and the end everlasting life." Here then is not only a freedom from sin obtained on condition of obedience to the faith: but the promise of everlasting life on condition, that we bring forth fruit unto holiness. Mark it well, fellow professor of the religion of Jesus—ponder well the language of inspiration, as quoted in the verses above. Observe the Apostle does not say, that the character addressed, had been made free from sin by believing from the heart, that form of doctrine; but by obeying it. Neither does he say to the Hebrew brethren, that "Christ having been made perfect through suffering, has become the author of eternal salvation, to all them that believe him," but to them that obey him. Nor does Peter, the man with the keys, say to those who had been induced to the obedience of faith, "seeing you have purified your souls in believing the truth," but, in obeying it.

From the above quotations, combined with many others; which we might adduce, we are constrained to acknowledge, what the text teaches, and in the language of the text, to affirm, that "the Gospel is the power of God unto salvation to every one that believes." And just here we would say to the inquiring world, if you desire to know where God's power is, by which you are to be saved, it is in the Gospel. And reader, if you desire an interest in the salvation of which we have been speaking, seek first to possess the power; which you are to obtain by waiting on God's ministers, by hearing the word of truth, the gospel of your salvation—for you are assured that "faith comes by hearing, and hearing by the word of God," Romans 10th chap. But again, John 20th chap., "Many other signs truly did Jesus; in the presence of his Disciples which are not written in this Book, but these are written, that you might believe that Jesus is the Christ, and that believing, you might have life through his name." Having through this means; placed yourself in possession of the power of God to become a saved person. Then like the noble hearted of primitive times, go forward in humble obedience to the commands of Christ; having in your heart unfeigned faith in the promises of Christ, through the Gospel, and having repented of all your sins, be baptized in the name of the Father, Son, and Holy Spirit; for in thus doing the Apostle Paul affirms that we get into Christ, (Gal. 3d chap.) and getting into him, brings us to the heavenly promise, that "in thy seed shall all the families of the earth be blessed." Here then you may rejoice in God forevermore; the blessing of faithful Abraham has now come upon you; your sins are all blotted out; times of refreshing have now come from the presence of the Lord, you are now filled with the Holy Spirit, as an earnest of the heavenly inheritance, by which you are enabled to cry Abba Father. Then, gentle reader, and not until then, will you have demonstrated to your soul's content, that the "Gospel is the power of God unto the salvation of everyone that believes."

J. G. CAMPBELL.

EXTRACT FROM A DISCOURSE BY A. G. COMINGS.

Crucified and Buried with Christ.

In becoming Christians, men are represented as being crucified and buried with Christ. "The old man," which I can understand only as signifying a life of subjection to the desires of the flesh, is declared to be "put off." The body of sin is said to be destroyed, that henceforth we should not serve sin.

Those who are buried with Christ in baptism are represented as being raised therefrom to walk in newness of life, or a new life.

A religious profession, without a moral salvation, as common as it may be thought to be, is but an empty show, at best.

Men who are not morally saved, may make good *sectarians,* but as to a *Christian* influence, their lives are worse than a blank. As well might we look for fertility on an ice island, as fruitfulness in the life of such professors. The root that produces evil must be taken away, which cannot be, without a settled and firm expectation of an abundant reward in heaven.

Three points of influence.

While I have spoken of the power of the hope set before man, I am conscious that there are three points of influence operating in the production of a state of moral deliverance. These three are, the hope of reward, the fear of punishment, and the sympathy of Christ's sufferings.

The first of these is to encourage men, the second is to deter men from sin, and the sympathy of Christ's sufferings is to affect the heart with tenderness.

Neither hope nor fear is really calculated to produce humility. The story of Calvary melts the stubbornness of the human heart. It is Christ set forth, as crucified among men, which claims gratitude and creates tenderness of affection.

The story of murders and robberies arouse the coarsest and most violent feelings of nature to action and exercise. But scenes of suffering innocence and self-sacrificing goodness excite the tenderest sympathies and feelings of which man is possessed.

Those teachers who bring only the promises of the gospel before the minds of men, excite them to a happy confidence, the extreme of which is presumption. Those who dwell most on the threatenings of God's word, produce a gloomy austerity, in the minds of their hearers, the extreme of which is desponding timidity. Those who dwell on the sufferings of the Savior, produce a weeping but irresolute spirit, the extreme of which is effeminacy. All these must have a proper degree of notice by religious teachers, or that which is desirable and necessary to constitute a moral change need not be expected. *Confidence, prudence,* and *sympathy,* are the natural results of the full reception of the truths of the gospel. A Christian confides in God, is prudent in his decisions, and lends his sympathetic care and assistance to his suffering fellow men. His confidence lays hold upon God, his prudence upon himself, and his benevolence upon his fellow beings,

The peculiar moral characteristics of various works, which have passed under the name of reform, at different times, have grown out of the peculiar manner of urging these points, namely, the promises, the threatenings, and the sympathetic benevolence of Christ.

During the last century, a religious system began to be advocated in England, and was soon after introduced into America, which made continual use, in preaching, of the threats of scripture, and the sympathies of Christ. The consequence was, that the most nervous and the most sympathetic portions of society were drawn together, and, as might have been expected, it became a proverb in comparison, as zealous as a *Methodist.*

At the same time, the divine promises were not studied; but the hopes of the Christian were supposed to depend on a peculiar and certain degree *of feeling,* which was regarded as the only ground of hope. The fears and the sympathies of the people were aroused, and so exciting was the progress of religious affairs, that, to use an expression deriving its force and meaning from facts.

"Those who went to scoff, returned to pray."

When a reason was asked of any one, why he expected eternal life, it was not answered, "Because God has promised eternal life to all that obey Christ;" but an answer was given perfectly natural in its relation to the system advocated, "Because I *feel* the assurance *within me.*"

That system of things has failed to take the place of Christianity; and even now, out of the multitude of Methodists, who all claim a present witness of God's acceptance and fellowship, a host of belligerent parties have arisen, who are in no acceptance or fellowship with one another. I am fearfully constrained to regard any such system as wanting in its elements of reform, while men under its influence are so far from being morally saved, as to be breaking into numerous contending parties.

Soon after the commencement of the present century, another plea of reform began to be urged, forcing its way (in New England, especially,) by presenting and urging the sympathies of Christ, Preachers preached through floods of tears, and the hardest hearted rebels felt the general sympathy, and wept. A tender spirit moved, a voice of melting love was heard, and it seemed as if all heaven wept in pity for the lost. I feel sometimes sad to think a spirit so desirable might not have been associated with life, and enabled to continue. When brethren met, they wept for joy; at parting they wept for sorrow; and when I hear them tell of former times, I weep. I am not destitute of sympathy; and when I hear men tell of joys decayed, I would weep in pity.

But that state of things bordered too much of effeminacy, lovely as it was, to live in our rough world. Few, indeed, of the numerous churches formed under the progress of a great excitement, (but about thirty years ago,) have now even a trace of their former existence to be seen.

In this course of things, it was thought that weeping affection constituted both the soul and substance of religion. Though with a degree of truth it might be regarded as near to the former, yet, from the latter it was more distant.

Had the motives of fear and hope been set forth, as connected with the practical conditions of the gospel, it is perfectly sure to me that the authority of God's word and the duties enjoined therein, would have been attended to with a greater degree of reverence, and the work done would not have so soon become as water spilt upon the ground. But, as it was, some apostatized and others turned to shameful scenes of wickedness, too gross to be mentioned.

It ought to admonish all reformers to remember that in the mention of Calvary, hell or heaven, there is no fictitious idea.

Within a few years past, another kind of religious reformers, exciting revivalists, have been introduced; numbering their thousands of rapidly marshaled converts. The peculiarity of these new reformers is not that they labour to show to the understanding of the people the grounds and conditions of hope; nor yet do they exhibit and set forth the suffering sympathy of the Son of God: but by the most impressive and startling anecdotes, and by an appeal to the threatenings of eternal damnation, they labor to wake a slumbering world to flee from the wrath to come upon the sinner.

There is little of the weeping spirit of tenderness in the progress of their efforts; but an easy inclination to the more austere feelings which sometimes accompany self-righteousness and bigotry. The generous spirit which is cherished and encouraged by hope, with the impartial and universal affection for man which was exhibited on Calvary, and not their charms add strength to the progress of their efforts.

The result of their labor is—a multitude of converts.

To produce a proper and Christian state of things, all the bearings of truth are necessary.—Confidence in the divine promises, reverence for the laws of God, and impartial benevolence, depend on a true exhibition of the Christian system.

Let us all consider and realize that the conversion of the world depends on the character and conduct of professed Christians; and their character and conduct is suspended on the question of moral salvation. Those who profess Christianity but do not copy the Saviour's life, are not morally saved.

That Christian, who can see that among his brethren which is opposed to the laws of Christ, and not speak against it, can look upon *sin* with at least some little allowance. *God* makes *no* allowance.

"PRESSLY'S LECTURES" REVIEWED—NO. 4.

We are, in this number, to commence the examination of some of the prominent features of Dr. Pressly's third Lecture.

On 47th page, 2d par., he remarks: "It is therefore altogether unreasonable to demand positive and express proof from the New Testament, to show that the children of believers are connected with the church of Christ; or which amounts to the same thing, that they have a right to baptism." Now is not this passing strange! Dr. Pressly admits that "Baptism is an ordinance of the New Testament ordained by Jesus Christ;" and he *affirms* that the infants of believers have a right to it! Now every one *ought* to know, and the Dr. does know, that the burden of proof rests upon the affirmant. But when we demand positive proof, from the New Testament, *precept or example,* he cries out, "O! it is unreasonable to demand such a thing of us!" "You who take the negative must prove that they have not the right!" Though the Dr. does not use precisely the language above, yet it is substantially what he does say upon this point! But reader, you must not suppose that because the Dr. makes this remark, he can produce no such "positive proof from the New Testament," or that he is unwilling to undertake the work: very far from it; he takes up the Testament immediately, and as an honest man, who is not afraid to have his sentiments investigated, goes to work, and brings forward his "positive proof." Now we shall with all humility examine the Dr.'s *positive proof,* and if we find that it does not partake of the nature of the proposition, which we are perfectly sure will be the case, then we shall conclude with confidence, that the doctrine of "Infant Baptism," is not taught in the New Testament; and no one pretends that it is taught in the Old Testament.

"1—My first argument, in support of the right of Infant baptism," says the Dr., "is founded upon the doctrine of the New Testament, which maintains that believers in Christ are the seed of Abraham." Now, we most cheerfully admit, that believers in Christ are the "seed of Abraham, and heirs according to the promise:" but we ask what has this to do with infant baptism? The premises are good, but the Dr. draws from them an unwarrantable conclusion. Are infants believers in Christ?—if they are not, they are not embraced in the Dr.'s premises! But to prove this clearly, let us hear Paul on the subject: "For ye are all the children of God by faith in Christ Jesus. For as many of you as have been baptized into Christ, have put on Christ. There is neither Jew nor Greek; there is neither bond nor free, there is neither male nor female: for ye are all one in Christ Jesus. And if ye be Christ's, then are ye Abraham's seed, and heirs according to the promise." Gal. 8: 26—29.

Now every one must see, that none are here said to be the "seed of Abraham," but those who become so, by "faith in Christ Jesus," and consequently, that it does not touch the case of infants! Let us now attend to the Dr.'s second argument in favor of the "right of infant baptism." "2—That the children of believers are proper subjects of baptism, appears from the declaration of our Lord to those parents who brought their offspring to him to receive his blessing: "Suffer little children and forbid them not to come unto me, for of such is the kingdom of heaven.'" Matt. 19: 14. We affirm, that this part of the Dr.'s *positive proof*, does not partake of the nature of the proposition! It is not said, that these parents brought their little children to Jesus for the purpose of having them baptized: neither does the text affirm, that they were baptized! In short, it says nothing whatever about baptism. A *blessing* was what they sought, and a *blessing* was what Jesus conferred upon them, not baptism. Or, does Dr. Pressly believe that no blessing is centered, out of baptism? If this is his view of the subject, he is more heterodox than even a "Campbellite;" for if we have been correctly informed, they do not believe that God's blessings are confined to *water*. But we suppose the Dr. believes no such thing: and hence the inconsistency of his bringing forward this text to prove "infant baptism." But Dr. P. lays some stress upon the phrase "of such is the kingdom of heaven." He regards this phrase as referring to the "visible church." Well suppose we admit it—what then; it would not follow, that infants are members of the *visible church!* Mark well, Jesus does not say of *these,* or of *infants,* is the kingdom of heaven; but "of such," that is, of persons resembling little children in disposition, innocence, et cetera. In accordance with this view of the matter, Jesus, in order to show who was greatest in the kingdom of heaven, placed a little child in the midst of them, and said, "Verily, I say unto you except ye be converted, and become as little children, ye shall not enter into the kingdom of heaven," Matt. 18: 3.

The next text quoted by Dr. P. in support of infant baptism, is Acts 2: 38, 39: "Then Peter said, unto them, Repent and be baptized, every one of you, in the name of Jesus Christ, for the remission of sins, and you shall receive the gift of the Holy Ghost; For the promise is unto you and to your children, and to all that are afar off, even as many as the Lord our God shall call." Now we would ask, what has this to do with infants! We answer, just nothing at all! and we shall prove it by Dr. Pressly himself. On 25th page, after speaking of the application of certain passages of scripture, the Dr. remarks: "The plan and obvious truth is, that neither the declaration of our Lord nor that of the Apostle, has any reference to the case of infants, and consequently, determines nothing in relation to them. Such expressions as these, "He that believeth and is baptized;" "Repent and be baptized;" it is admitted, do not afford any evidence of the right of infant baptism." Out of Dr. Pressly's own mouth then, we condemn his argument. O consistency, thou art a jewel! But perhaps the reader is ready to ask, does not the text speak of *children?* We answer yes, but children are not necessarily *infants*. The promise was unto the Jews whom Peter addressed on that occasion, and to their descendants, or children in all time coming; and also to those who were afar off, the Gentiles; but there is not a word said about infants in the passage, and therefore it fails infinitely short of the proposition!

Having made a lengthy, and very ingenuous argument, predicated upon the promise made to Abraham, the good Dr. comes in the 3rd place, to speak of the *practice* of the heaven-inspired Apostles. Now notwithstanding the Dr. has utterly failed, as we think, to prove the right of infant baptism, by any *positive* testimony: yet if he can now produce one clear case, in which the Apostles practiced it, we shall submit! for we believe the Apostles fully understood their commission, and would not have practiced infant baptism, if it had not been the divine arrangement. But the question is, *did* they practice it? Dr. Pressly affirms, and agrees to prove it; let us hear him. On 59th page he says: "This conclusion is drawn from the fact, that when the Apostles baptized the head of a family, his household also were baptized." To this we reply, that we have no evidence that this was *always,* or even *generally* the case. So far from it, only about *four* households were baptized, out of the many thousands who were converted to Christianity, in the apostolic age, so far as we have any account! The households of Stephanas, Lydia, the Jailor, and Cornelius the centurion, were baptized. Speaking of these, the learned Dr. remarks: "Now my brother should say to me, "produce your positive proof that there were children in any of these households," I would say with all kind feeling, "I will cheerfully comply with your demand, as soon as you have brought forward positive proof, that any one person of these families believed, except the head."

Now from this declaration, it is evident, that the Dr. believes we have just as much evidence to prove the faith of others beside the heads of those families, as he has to prove that there were infants among them. He believes that we have no testimony, therefore he *admits that he has none!* Well, this looks to us very much like giving up the argument based upon *household* baptism! Let it be understood then, that we accept the Dr.'s challenge. We shall now attempt to prove the faith of some others in these families, beside their heads; and if we succeed, the Dr. will stand pledged before the world, to *prove positively,* that there were some infants baptized, in those households—let the reader mark it well!

We shall briefly examine these household baptisms, in the order we have them narrated to us by the sacred historian. 1—The household of Cornelius the Gentile. This affair is recorded Acts 10th chap. When Peter came to the house of Cornelius, he demanded of him his reason for sending for him, to which Cornelius, among other things, answered, (v. 33) "Now therefore are we all here present before God, to hear all things that are commanded thee of God." Now every one must see, that Cornelius had his household *all* present, to hear the words from Peter's mouth. Will any man in his sober senses, suppose that infants are capable of *hearing* the word, in the scriptural sense of the word! No, every member of the family were capable of *hearing* the word, and were all present, for that very purpose. Again, (verse 44,) "While Peter yet spake these words, the Holy Ghost fell on all them that heard the word." Who will affirm, that little unconscious babes, were baptized with the Holy Ghost! But to put this matter out of dispute, we are told (48th v.) "For they heard them speak with tongues, and magnify God." Who spake with tongues? Why the *household of* Cornelius, or all the Gentiles present. Does our friend. Dr. P. believe that infants spake with other tongues, and magnified God on that occasion! We suppose he does not. "Then Peter answered and said, (47th v.,) can any man forbid water, that these should not be baptized, who have received the Holy Ghost as well as we?" (48) "And he commanded them to be baptized in the name of the Lord." Now it is admitted on all hands, that the whole household were baptized, under this command of Peter. The question to be settled then is, who were baptized, infants, or adults? or both? We answer from the evidence of the case, none were baptized, but those who "were present to hear the words" of Peter, who, when they heard, were baptized with the Holy Ghost, spake with tongues and magnified God. And as infants are incapable of doing these things, therefore we deny, that there were any infants among the baptized. Will Dr. Pressly affirm, that persons may "speak with tongues, and magnify God," without faith or knowledge. He must say so, or yield the point! But we affirm, that no one ever spake with tongues and magnified God without faith; as all who were baptized on that occasion did so: therefore, every member of this household, had faith, as well as Cornelius the head. But the question is settled forever by Peter himself; Acts 11: 17; hear him: "Forasmuch then as God gave them the like gift as he did unto us, who *believed* on the Lord Jesus Christ, what was I, that I could withstand God?" Now in the above text, Peter to convince his Jewish brethren, that he Had acted properly, in admitting the Gentiles at the house of Cornelius to baptism, informs them that God put no difference between them. Their gifts were the same, and their faith also—Peter could no longer resist, and no objection to their baptism being offered by the five Jewish brethren who accompanied him from Joppa, he commanded them to be baptized.

As we have now proved, as we thing, beyond the possibility of a rational doubt, that every member of this household had faith before baptism, as well as Cornelius the head, we hold Dr. Pressly bound by his own pledge, to prove by *positive testimony*, that there *were infants* in *this household?* But we presume the good Dr. will never attempt it.

In our next we shall examine the other household baptisms, spoken *of* in the New Testament. And in doing so, we expect to prove satisfactorily, that every member of them had faith before baptism, and consequently, that there were no infants among them.

J. M. M., E<small>D</small>.

MR. J. D. PAXTON'S LETTER.

A<small>T</small> the request of Mr. H<small>ILL</small>, Editor of the *Protestant and Herald,* we here insert the letter of J. D. Paxton, in reference to the "Baptism of the three thousand on the day of Pentecost." We are perfectly willing to let our readers see *both sides* of the question. And we the more cheerfully comply with this request, since the Editor of the "Protestant and Herald" has had the goodness to let his readers see our remarks upon this subject, in the 5th No. of the Christian Record, which the leader will please read again.

And as brother Hill did not reply to our remarks himself, but employed a third person, J. D. Paxton, to do it for him, we will re-publish the remarks of our fellow-laborer, brother R. F. F<small>URGUSON</small>, Editor of the "Christian Journal," upon this said letter. Bro. Furguson has so completely disposed of the statements of Mr. Paxton, that it will supersede the necessity of any remarks of our own. Another remark, and we shall let Mr. Paxton speak for himself: and-that is, that Mr. P.'s letter does not touch the main points embraced in our remarks—it has reference only to one of the *minor points.*

J. M. M., E<small>D</small>.

MULBERRY, JANUARY, 19, 1844.

R<small>EV</small>. W. W. H<small>ILL</small>:

D<small>EAR</small> S<small>IR</small>:—Your letter containing several questions has just come to hand, and without delay I will answer and give my reasons— 1. "Was the Pentecostal the rainy season of the year?" Most assuredly not; but near the middle of the dry season. The word Pentecost is of Greek origin, and signifies the fiftieth day; and is used in the New Testament to designate what in the Old Testament is called the Feast of Weeks—so called from its taking place seven weeks after they began their harvests, and offered the sheaf of first ripe grain. See Deut. 23: 10—17, and Deut. 16:9—16. At the end of these seven weeks, on the fiftieth day, all Israel were to appear before God, and a special offering was to be made.—Deut. 16: 16. This is the Pentecost of the New Testament. It took place then fifty days after they began their harvest. Now it is known that their harvests in Palestine began about the 25th of April. In 1838, I passed with my family from Beirut to Jerusalem, which I reached on the 25th of April. The people were beginning their harvests on the plain of Sharon—a few fields were cut, but the great mass of the harvest on the plains, and *all* on the hill country of Judea, was not fully ripe. Fifty days from the 25th of April will bring the middle of June, as the time of Pentecost.

Now it is well known to those who have made proper enquiries, that the winter and not the summer, is the rainy season in Palestine. The rains usually begin in November, but not with much severity until December. I have, however, known slight falls of rain in the latter part of October—December, January and February have the great rains. In March they moderate, and very little falls after the first of April. There is then no rain until the following November, when they again came on.

The full force of Samuel's declaration to Israel is seen from this: 'Is it not wheat harvest to-day? I will call upon God, and he shall send thunder and rain that ye may perceive your great wickedness," &c—1 Samuel 12: 17. It was made to rain and thunder in harvest time. It was a miracle to do so at *that time* in Palestine. The Pentecost took place at the *close* of harvest—near the middle of the dry season—farther still from the time of rain.

Again, you ask—"From your observations about Jerusalem, do you think it probable that there was water enough in the city to baptize, by immersion, such an immense crowd on the day of Pentecost?"

So far as the quantity of water, and facilities for using it, are concerned, the probabilities are, as it appeared to me, altogether against immersion being used—and for the following reasons:

There is no natural stream of water in the city, nor about the city, nor within five miles of the city, (*I believe I may safely say ten miles*) that, without special preparation, would afford a sufficient depth to immerse in. There is not a spring in the city. There is no constant spring near the city, that I know of, but the Siloam, which is a very small spring, and so situated as to afford no facilities for immersing. Its waters are soon absolved, and seldom run one hundred yards from the pool. The Kedron, or what is called the "brook Kedron," is a dry, deep valley, which has no water in it, except when rain water passes along it. The same is the case with the Gihon. At the head of the Gihon, about a mile from the city, there is a wall made across the hollow, forming a pool in which I have seen water. I think there is a small spring there during the rainy season. There is another wall across the Gihon, near the city, which appears to have been designed to hold water, and forms what is called the lower pool. The road to Bethlehem passes on this side wall as a bridge. I never saw any water in this pool.

I know of no *well* in the city, and but of *one* in the vicinity. That is the well of Nehemiah, at the junction of the Kedron with the Gihon, and in the lowest parts of that deep valley. It is a very deep well with some water in it. My impression is, that it must have been from fifty to seventy feet to the water, when I saw it; although it is said in very wet times to overflow.

I saw or heard of but one pool in the city that had water—the pool of Hezekiah. The sides were nearly, if not wholly, perpendicular, and from fifteen to twenty feet deep, with a narrow set of stone steps at one place. The pool is surrounded with houses, and its structure is such as to unfit it for immersing in it. There are excavations in the city called pools, but had no water. There is a small supply of water brought into the city through pipes for the use of the mosque of St. Omar, which stands where the Temple formerly stood. This water is brought from the pools of Solomon about nine miles off. The Koran requires the Moslems to wash their hands and feet before they go into the mosque to pray. This water is not for the common use of the people, but for the use of the worshippers at the mosque.

The water which supplies the city, is the rain-water collected during the rainy season from the tops of their houses, and preserved in cisterns, which are under their houses, or in their courts. The cisterns are holes dug in the earth, and made in the shape of large jugs, with narrow mouths, large swelling bodies, plastered within with lime mortar or water lime. They are made so deep as to keep the water cool, so large as to contain great supplies of water, and with narrow mouths, that they may be kept clean, secure, and the water not much exposed to the air. You might every whit as easily immerse people in our common wells, as in the eastern cisterns. The

Jewish notion of cleanliness, also, would forbid the immersion of persons in pools and streams, from which, at times, water might be taken for drinking or family use.

There are facts in the scripture which prove that there was but little water formerly about Jerusalem, and that their supplies were from cisterns.

We learn from 2 Mc. 32: 2—4, that in order to prevent the siege of Jerusalem by the Assyrians, Hezekiah and his people stopped up all the fountains of water without the city within the reach of the besieging army. How could Hezekiah stop, so as conceal for days, and weeks, and months, even a good spring that flowed off! much more a considerable stream, such as many seem to think the Kedron to be? A pool may easily be destroyed by letting the water off, or throwing it out. Many springs do not flow off, and may easily be filled up. Such are many of the fountains in the hill country of Palestine—as it is many Such we have in Kentucky—they do not flow twenty yards in a dry season. Had there been one good spring or brook within several miles *of* Jerusalem, that could not be hidden, stopped or covered, it would have been useless in Hezekiah to stop up the rest.

The fact stated that he stopped the brook that ran through the land, argues with the above remarks. It could not have been much of a stream, or he could not have concealed it from the Assyrians. This relates, we suppose, to the small rising of water at the upper pool of the Gihon, and is explained by what is said in verse 30 of the above chapter: "This same Hezekiah stopped the water course of the upper Gihon, and brought it straight down to the west side of the city of David."

There is yet the remains of an underground passage for the water from the upper pool, leading, as I think, to the pool of Hezekiah, within the city, that answers the above description. It can be seen at several places; a small hidden channel being prepared for the small spring the whole could be covered over and concealed.

Or it may possibly relate to the fountain of Siloam. There is now an underground passage for the water, under that part of Mount Moriah called Ophel, and coming out at the mouth of the valley of the Cheese mongers, which was anciently within the city. The water there passes through a small excavation called pool of Siloam, and when let off on the side of the hill, is soon absolved, seldom appearing, in the dry season, fifty yards from the pool, or passing much, if any, beyond where the ruins show that the walls of the city formerly stood.

These are the only two risings of water that I recollect near the city, and from both there are remains of channels leading the water under ground within the city—the fountain could easily be covered—the well of Nehemiah could easily be hid.

The account of this Assyrian invasion brings out another fact that bears on the case. In Rab-Shekeh's address to the Jews on that occasion, as recorded in 2 Kings 18: 31, he refers to their drinking "every man of his own cistern," in argument with the fact that cistern water was that in universal use in Jerusalem. As there are no springs nor wells within the city, had they not been supplied with cistern water, the people could not have stood the siege, for the two small springs I have referred to, (I think that at the head of Gihon dries up soon after the rains cease,) would be insufficient for the supply of such a city. Respectfully yours,   J. D. PAXTON.

From the Christian Journal.

HARD PRESSED.

THE Editor of the Protestant and Herald seems to be hard pressed for available arguments against the Bible doctrine of Immersion. In his paper of the 1st inst., he introduced a letter from the Rev. J. D. Paxton of Shelby country, Ky., to prove, that the three thousand, baptized on the day of Pentecost, could not have been immersed.

The Saviour once said, "If I bear witness of myself, my witness is not true." Mr. Hill seems to have forgotten this principle, when he appealed to his Paidobaptist brother to aid him in deciding the question of baptism in their own favor, Mr. Paxton being as deeply involved as himself. And, yet, Mr. Hill seems to think, that his readers are so easily gulled, as to regard this testimony of a man, in his own favor, valid and conclusive; and, that they will confide in the testimony of Mr. Paxton under circumstances, in which the Saviour affirms, that his own testimony would be unworthy of confidence. Nor do we impeach the honesty of Mr. Paxton in these remarks. It is perhaps impossible, in our present imperfect state, for any man to be an impartial and credible witness in his own favor. And it is surprising that the Editor of the Protestant and Herald should have overlooked this plain principle of common sense and common justice, and thereby have exposed his cause to well merited suspicion.

If a truth thus self-evident were susceptible of farther confirmation, it would be confirmed by the document, which has elicited these remarks. The reasoning in Mr. Paxton's letter is substantially this: Pentecost was not "at the rainy season of the year; but near the middle of the dry season. It took place fifty days after they began their harvest. Now it is known that the harvests in Palestine began about the 25th of April. Fifty days from the 25th of April will bring the middle of June, as the time of Pentecost." Again, he says: "The rains usually begin in November, but not with much severity until December. I have, however, known slight falls of rain in the latter part of October. December, January, and February have the great rains. In March they moderate, and very little falls after the 1st of April. There is no rain until the following November, when they again come on."

Now admitting this (for argument's sake) to be in every respect a correct statement of facts, does it justify the conclusion, that there was not, in or about Jerusalem, water enough to immerse three thousand on the day of Pentecost? We think not. And it seems to us, that a little reflection will bring every unbiased mind to the same conclusion. After a steady fall of rain from the 1st of November till the 1st of April, is it reasonable to conclude, that there would be such a scarcity of water by the middle of June? And, if so, what would be the condition of the country before the following November, no rain having fallen meanwhile? Must not vegetation perish, and animal life become extinct? Every person of sufficient observation and reflection must see, that after a continuous rain of five months, or upwards, the earth would be perfectly saturated with water, and all the, subterranean reservoirs, whence originate the springs and rivers, completely filled, so as to furnish an abundant supply at least for many weeks. Nor is this mere conjecture. For while the *"Reverend."* Mr. Paxton informs us, that there was such a scarcity of water about Jerusalem at Pentecost, or the close of the harvest, that it is exceedingly improbable that facilities could have been found for immersing—Jehovah, whose name alone is Holy and *Reverend*, positively affirms the opposite, and tells us, that there was such an abundance of water in Judea at this season, that, "Jordan overflowed all his banks *all the time of harvest."* Joshua 3: 15.

Even admitting, then, that Mr. Paxton's premises were true, his conclusions are evidently false, the Bible, as well as common sense, being judge.

But it would be as easy, as it is unnecessary, to show, that his premises are not wholly correct. The Jewish year, unlike ours, was not measured exactly by the revolution of the earth round the sun. Its months were so many revolutions of the moon round the earth; and the year itself was generally twelve of those revolutions. The first month began with the first moon, that came to the full after the vernal equinox. Hence, if the full moon immediately followed the equinox, the year would begin about the 7th of March; but if it immediately proceeded the equinox, the year would not begin until the 4th of April. The Jewish months being thus moveable, the feasts, which were regulated by those months, were moveable also. The Passover was always on the afternoon of the 14th day of the first month. It is generally admitted, that Christ was crucified on the 3d day of April, according to our method of computing time; and that Pentecost occurred on the 50th day from the Sunday, or first day of the week, immediately following that event. Now, if the Friday, on which Christ was crucified, happened to be the 3d of April, fifty days from the Sunday following that event will bring us, for Pentecost, to the 24th of May, and not to the middle of June, according to Mr. Paxton's calculation. This argument, however, as we have already seen, is wholly unnecessary. For, whether Pentecost came as early as the 24th of May, or not, still we have evidence, which, we presume, neither the Editor of the Protestant and Herald, nor Mr. Paxton will question, that there was water enough in Judea to cause the Jordan to "overflow all its banks all the time of harvest," or till the feast of Pentecost. Consequently, there could not have been an insuperable difficulty in the way of immersion. And when the Bible says that three thousand were *baptized, and when all, who have any* intelligence on the subject, not even excepting the opponents of the practice themselves, tell us, that the primary meaning of *baptize,* is, *immerse*—we are justified in believing, that the Bible tells the truth in the plain, obvious and primary meaning of the terms used, and the persons alluded to were actually *immersed*. If Mr. Hill can prove the contrary of this, it must be by better arguments than the aforesaid letter of Mr. Paxton, or any thing of a similar kind, that has ever fallen into our hands.

[PUBLISHED BY REQUEST.]
JERUSALEM.

By Jacob Wolfe, of Sullivan County, Indiana.

Jerusalem—O blessed place;
The happy pilgrim's home,
Where Angels bright and saints unite
Around God's dazzling throne.

The rolling seas are passed away,
And Heaven and Earth made new;
The Holy City new descends,
And joins the Church below.

Her walls are made of splendid stone,
Most glorious to behold;
Her gates are all of single pearls,
Her streets transparent gold.

Her Heav'nly domes need not the Sun,
Nor Moon's faint glim'ring ray;
No night will ever there be known,
But one eternal day.

God and the Lamb shall be its light,
Outshining e'en the Sun;
Such radiant splendors ne'er were seen
Since Heaven and earth begun.

Those Jasper walls the light reflect,
O'er all th' eternal hill.

And streets of gold unite their rays.
And make, it lighter still.

There God himself will wipe all tears
From every weeping eye;
Nor sickness, death, nor pain, or grief
Shall ever cause a sigh.

Then life's blest river shall proceed
Out from th' eternal throne;
There every thirsty soul may drink,
Whom Christ the Lord will own.

These, marshaled in the wedding dress,
 Fine linen, clear and white,
Shall, in the righteousness of saints.
Be their own Lord's delight.

There crowns of glory all shall wear,
And palms grace every hand;
They'll shout his praise no end to days,
In Salem's happy land

Their songs of praise will ever flow,
To Jesus Christ their King;
While at his feet their crowns they cast,
And hallelujahs sing.

Hail happy scenes! forever hail!
Let all your glories shine,
Upon our earth-born nature here,
And render it divine

Then with the spotless bride of Christ,
And angels from the skies,
We'll through the pearly gates go in,
To the new Paradise.

And when redeeming love we've sung,
Ten thousand years twice told,
New songs of praise we'll ever raise,
And strike our harps of gold.

DREADFUL CALAMITY AND LOSS OF LIFE ON BOARD THE PRINCETON.

Seven persons killed!! Among whom are The Hon. ABEL P. UPSHER, late Secretary of State; Gov. GILMER, late Secretary of the Navy; Com. KENNON, of the Navy; VIRGIL MAXEY, late Charge d'Affairs to Belgium, and Mr. GARDINER, proprietor Gardiner's Island, of New York.

About seven o'clock on Wednesday evening, intelligence reached Washington, that an appalling and heartrending accident occurred on board the Steamer Princeton, by the bursting of her large gun, by which Mr. Upsher, Secretary of State: Mr. Gilmer, Secretary of the Navy;

Com. McKennon, Chief of the Bureau of Construction and Repairs— Virgil Maxey, Esq., and Col. Gardiner of New York, were killed.

Senator Benton and Captain Stockton were severely, but it is said not dangerously injured; and others are mortally wounded.

NEWS FROM THE CHURCHES.

Vienna, Scott County, Ind., Feb. 20th, 1844.

Dear brother Mathes: The good work is yet going on in our county; we had five additions to the church in this place, on the 18th inst., and we think the prospect is good for many more.

Yours in the good hope, JOHN HARROD.

*--Brother HARROD will please accept our thanks for the new subscribers he has sent us, and for his efforts in behalf of the Christian Record: a few more such zealous, persevering agents, in the Eastern part of the State, would place the Record beyond the reach of contingencies, so far as patronage is concerned.—[ED.

Nashville, Ind., Feb. 10, 1844.

Dear brother Mathes: I will inform you and my brethren, that since the first of July last, I have been trying to the very best of my ability, and opportunity, to re-proclaim the gospel of the Kingdom; during which time, I have had the pleasure of seeing nineteen additions made to the good cause; ten of them by confession and immersion, and the other nine had been previously immersed. We are doing well at this place; the brethren are alive, and seem to be awake to the conversion of sinners.
D. D. WADDELL.

Eld. William Irwin of Johnson County, informed us a short time ago, that within the last twelve months, he had immersed some 75 persons on a profession of their faith in Christ.

Eld. M. R. Trimble was with us again in Bloomington, on the 4th Lord's day in January; at Richland on the 1st Lord's day in this month, (Feb.,) and at Clear Creek on the 2nd Lord's day in this month. The result of his labors at these points, was 7 immersions, and some other additions. —[ED.

Columbus, Ind., Feb. 22nd, 1844.

Dear brother Mathes:. Since I saw you at Martinsville, (23rd ult,) I have delivered 28 public discourses on the subject of Christianity, and witnessed the good confession of 6 persons. Yesterday I returned from Edinburgh, at which place I delivered 9 discourses, and two persons confessed their faith in Christ.

Your brother in Christ, T. J. EDMONDSON.

LEXINGTON DEBATE.

The debate between Rice and Campbell, will be ready for delivery in a very short time. The work will be put up in cloth binding; will contain some 800 pages, and will come to subscribers at $2 per single copy. Why do not our Pedobaptist friends subscribe for the work? They claim a splendid 'victory' for Mr. Rice, and certainly they would like to read the work! We wish to bring on a lot of them soon, but so far, with one or two exceptions, none have given us their names but those who are on Mr. C.'s side of the question! Why is this so? But we say to all who desire it, let us have your names.

THE CHRISTIAN RECORD.

VOL. I.] BLOOMINGTON, IND., MARCH, 1844. [No. IX.

"PRESSLY'S LECTURES" REVIEWED—NO. 5.

WE closed our last number, by proving that the entire household of Cornelius, had faith as well as Cornelius the head. In the present paper, we are to speak of the other household baptisms, spoken of in the New Testament; as Dr. Pressly seems to rely upon these, more than any other evidence he has to offer from the New Testament, to prove the "right of infant baptism."

We will now examine the case of the baptism of Lydia and her house, recorded Acts 16th chap. Before the good Dr. Pressly can bring this forward as *positive* evidence of infant baptism, he must prove *four* things, to wit: 1—That Lydia ever had a husband; 2—That she ever had children; 3—That she had brought her children with her from Thyatira to Philippi, a journey of some 200 miles mostly by sea, and 4—That her children were then infants. All this we say must be done, before Dr. Pressly's *positive* proof can be admitted! Now we unhesitatingly affirm, that the Dr. *cannot prove any one of the above circumstances*. Then what becomes of his positive proof? Indeed, the circumstances are all against the idea of there being infants in the house of Lydia! Let us see. That she was an unmarried woman, is most probable, from the manner in which she invited the Apostles to abide in her house. "If ye have judged me faithful to the Lord, come into MY *house.*"—From this language, it is evident that she was *sole proprietor,* and *head* of the house; and consequently, that she had no husband! But after Paul and Silas were released from prison, "they entered into the house of Lydia and comforted the *brethren.*" These *brethren* were most likely the members of Lydia's household. We therefore say, that no *probable,* much less *positive* evidence of infant baptism, can be adduced from the household of Lydia.

The third case of "household baptism" is recorded in the same chap. (Acts 16.) It is the case of the Philippian Jailor and his house, who were baptized the same hour of the night, in which they heard the word of the Lord, from the mouths of Paul and Silas. After the prison doors were miraculously opened, and the Jailor was prevented from committing suicide, by the voice of Paul, crying out of the prison, "Do thyself no harm for we are all here;" and after the Jailor had brought them out, (of the prison.) he said, "Sirs, what must I do to be saved?" (31st v.) "And they (Paul and Silas) said, Believe on the Lord Jesus Christ, and thou shalt be saved, and thy house." The plain and obvious meaning of which is, believe on the Lord Jesus Christ, and you shall be saved; and your house shall enjoy the same salvation, namely, by *faith in Christ*. But this is confirmed by the 32d verse; "And they spake unto him the word of the Lord, and to all that were in his house." The word was spoken to the jailor in order to *his faith;* and for the same purpose it was also spoken to *every member* of his household—"to all that were in his house." This proves that their faith was just as necessary in order to *their* salvation, as the *Jailor's faith* was in order to his. In the 33d v. we are informed that "he, and all his, were baptized straightway." So far, we are not told whether the Jailor or any member of his family *believed* or not! But in the 35th v. we are told all about it: "And when he (the Jailor) had brought them into his house;" that is, after the baptism, "he set meat before them, and rejoiced, believing in God with all his house." Now this puts *the faith, of* the entire household of the Jailor beyond the reach of cavil! Who believed in God! we might ask, in the present case. Answer—The Jailor believed in God, *with all his house*. Prepositions connect words and show the relation between them: and the preposition *with*, in this instance, connects the *Jailor* and his *house*, and shows that *their faith and rejoicing were precisely equal.*

Having now proved the faith not only of *one*, but of every member of the jailor's family, let Dr. Pressly proceed according to his *pledge*, to prove that there were actually infants in this household, and that they were baptized too! And before he can succeed in this, he must prove *positively* the *four* following particulars, to wit: 1—That the Jailor had a wife; 2—That he had children; 3—That these children were at that time infants, and incapable of faith, and 4—That infants are capable of hearing the word of the Lord, scripturally. If the Dr. thinks that he can prove any *one*, or all of the above particulars, in reference to the Jailor, we shall be pleased to see him try it.

The 4th and last case of household baptism, mentioned in the New Testament, is that of Stephanas, recorded 1 Cor. 1: 16. Paul after saying that of the members of the Corinthian church, he had baptized "Crispus and Gaius," adds, "And I baptized also the household of Stephanas: besides I know not whether I baptized any other." As nothing more is said in this place about this household, there might be some; room left for quibbling, were it not that Paul mentions the subject again, and puts it out of dispute: let us hear him—1 Cor. 16. 15, 16, "I beseech you, brethren, (ye know the *house* of Stephanas, that it is the first fruits of Achaia, and that they have addicted themselves to the ministry of the saints) that ye submit yourselves unto such, and to every one that helpeth with us, and laboreth." Who does the Apostle say, had "addicted themselves to the ministry?" Why, the *household of Stephanas*. Infants are not capable of addicting themselves "to the ministry:" therefore there were no infants in this household! But Paul exhorted the Church of God at Corinth, to submit themselves to *such*. But the church of God, is no where instructed, to submit herself to infants; therefore, there were no infants in this household! Again, the great commission (Mar. 16: 16,) authorized the baptism of none but believes; but Paul, one to whom the commission was given, and who was divinely inspired, baptized the household of Stephanas; therefore, they were *all believers*.

Now reader, we have examined, briefly, every case of household baptism, recorded in the New Testament; and as we think, fully proved, that there were none baptized in any of them without faith, and consequently, that there were no infants among them. We now ask you to look around you, and see how many households might be baptized in your own immediate neighborhood, and not an infant among them—but each member of the family upon *his*, or *her own* faith! We know you can find many such families: then ask yourself the question, were there no such families in the Apostolic age? You must answer, that it is quite probable, there were many such! Then examine all the evidence we have adduced in favor of our position, and we think you can come, to no other conclusion.

After Dr. Pressly has disposed of the household baptisms, spoken of above, he then introduces, and lays considerable stress upon "Proselyte baptism," which he says was practiced among the Jews before the coming of Christ. Now Dr. P. ought to know, and doubtless he does, for he admits it on page 65th, that proselyte baptism was not of divine appointment, but a *mere human tradition;* and therefore, has nothing to do with the question of infant baptism. The introduction of such testimony, argues the weakness of the cause, in whose support it is introduced!

On page 68th, the learned Dr. brings forward his fourth argument from the New Testament, in favor of infant baptism; it runs thus: "I argue, in the next place, from the declaration of the Apostle with regard, to those children, one of whose parents only is a believer; "Else were your children unclean, but now are they holy.'" 1 Cor. 7: 14. The Dr. admits, that the term *"holy"* does not in this case mean "moral purity of heart." He further says, "one of the most common acceptations of the term holy, in the sacred scriptures, is, separation to some sacred use, dedication to God." Now if we understand our learned author, he contends in another part of his book, that infants are dedicated to God in Baptism: and in this text, he understands the term 'holy,' to mean "dedicated to God." If the Dr. is correct in the definition of the term holy, then Paul would teach the Corinthians, that those children who had one believing parent, were *already dedicated to God, by the faith of that parent;* and of course, such children would stand in no need of baptism: for they already enjoy through the faith of the parent, all that our friend Dr. Pressly proposes to give them in baptism. Now we do think, that the most superficial observer can see that the Dr. is at war with himself, and consequently, must be in error upon this subject!

But perhaps the reader is ready to inquire, what does this text mean? We will let the learned Dr. McNight; who was a staunch orthodox Divine, of the Kirk of Scotland, answer. Dr. McNight, in his notes on the Epistles, speaking of this text, says, "The terms in the verse thus understood, affords a natural meaning; namely, that when infidels are married to Christians, if they had a strong affection for their christian spouses, they are thereby *sanctified* to them, they, are fitted to continue married to them; because their affection to the Christian, party will ensure to that party the faithful performance of every duty; and that if the marriages of infidels and Christians were to be dissolved, they would cast away their children as *unclean;* that is, losing their affection for them, they would expose them, after the barbarous customs of the Greeks, or at least neglect their education: But that by continuing their marriages, their children are *holy;* they are preserved as pledges of their mutual love, and educated with care." Dr. McNight, though a paido-baptist, has, in the main, given our views of this text: and we offer this as a complete refutation of Dr. Pressly's views upon the same text.

With this last text, Dr. P. closes his *positive proof,* from the New Testament, in favor of "infant baptism." We have briefly examined it all, and we think fully proven, that the Dr.'s *positive proof* is no proof at all. And now for the purpose of exciting attention to this point, we affirm, that neither Dr. Pressly, nor any other Paido-baptist scribe, *can prove, that infant baptism was practiced by the Apostle, or the first Christians!* One *fact* is worth a thousand *inferences;* we call for *positive proof* from the *New* Testament. If they baptized infants, surely the fact is some where recorded, and if so, our friends can produce it! If they cannot produce it, they ought to give up the *unscriptural* practice, which rests upon no other foundation, but *vague* and uncertain inferences drawn from Jewish customs, long since superseded by the "New and better covenant."

J. M. M., Ed.

JUSTIFICATION—NO. 6.

By referring to Nos. 3, 4, and 5, the reader will see that we have shown that the love of God was the moving cause; the wisdom of God the devising cause; the gift of God's Son, as the Saviour, and the shedding of his blood the procuring cause; the Holy Spirit, the efficient cause; and faith, repentance and baptism, the instrumental, or conditional cause of our justification. We shall now notice some objections that are urged against the foregoing:

I. The scriptures no where say that we are justified by baptism; but they do say we are justified by faith, therefore baptism has nothing to do with our justification, but faith is the only condition.

Ans—The scriptures no where say that we are justified by prayer, therefore, by parity of reasoning, prayer has nothing to do in our justification; but who would dare say that it has not! No believer in Jesus, surely. Further, we showed in our first No. that justification and the remission or forgiveness of sins, are substantially the same thing. And we have proved according to the commission given to the Apostles, (see Mark 16:16,) and their teaching under that commission, (Acts 2: 38,) that baptism is a condition of remission of sins, for Peter to the penitents, "Repent and be baptized every one of you in the name of Jesus Christ for the remission, of sins, and you shall (in the future tense) receive the gift of the Holy Ghost." Here you see that the proof partakes of the nature of our proposition, and must be admitted as conclusive. But (says the objector) the whole strength of the proof depends upon the preposition *for,* and it has more than twenty different meanings, and according to your understanding. does here mean *in order to,* but I contend that it here means because of, or on account of the remission of sins; and that we should be baptized because our sins are forgiven: not to receive remission.

"Well, the context or connection in which this word "for" stands, must determine the true meaning. Then let us try it with your definition, *because of:* Repent and be baptized *because of* the remission of sins. That is, we must repent for the same end that we are baptized; so that if we are to be baptized because our sins are remitted, we must repent because of the remission of our sins, an idea, the bare mention of which is sufficient to show its fallacy.

We shall quote some passages which go to show that our definition of this term is correct, that is, in order to. Matt. 27: 29, "For this is my blood of the New Testament, which is shed for (because of) many for (in order to) the remission of sins." No person-dare affirm that Jesus shed his blood because the sins of the people were remitted; but in order to their remission. Mark 1: 4, "John did baptize in the wilderness, and preach the baptism of repentance *for* the remission of tins." Again: Luke 3: 3, "And he (John) came in all the country about Jordan, preaching the baptism of repentance for the remission of sins." Acts 2: 38, "Repent and be baptized EVERY ONE of you in the *name* of Jesus Christ for the remission of sins." Matt. 27: 28, "For this is my blood of the New Testament, which is shed for many, for the remission of sins." The reader will see the similarity in the arrangement of the above sentences. Are we not safe in teaching that as certain as the blood of the Saviour was shed for, or in order to the remission of sins, that baptism was instituted by the Lord of all as a necessary condition in order to the remission of sins; that is, if the above testimonies are to be regarded? Most certainly. And may we not say in the language of Messiah, that if any one will not be convinced from the above testimonies, "neither would he be persuaded though one should arise from the dead."

II. The thief on the cross was pardoned, justified without baptism, therefore it is not a necessary condition.

Ans—That the thief had not been baptized before cannot be shown: but admit that he had not. The Master was then present in *propria persona,* and could grant forgiveness without that condition, as the thief was so situated that he could not obey that command. Moreover, the new covenant had not then been fully sealed and ratified, nor had the grand commission yet been given, which said he that believeth and is baptized shall be saved: that is, shall have forgiveness of sins. Hence the objection is invalid.

III. Simon, the sorcerer, was baptized, and he did not receive the pardon of his sins; therefore baptism is not for the remission of sins.

This objection at first view seems to be formidable; but it does appear to us, that one of three things must be certain: that is, that Simon received the remission of his sins when he obeyed the Lord in baptism, or that the promise of Jesus failed, or that Luke did not record the truth in relation to Simon's case. Now for the proof. Mark 16: 16, Jesus said "He that believeth and is baptized SHALL be saved;" that is, be forgiven. Luke says, Acts 8: 13, "Then Simon himself *believed;* and when her was baptized, he continued with Philip," &c. Now if Luke, when he wrote the Acts, did it under the guidance of the infallible spirit he recorded the truth, and he said Simon believed—and was baptized—and Jesus says "He that believeth and is baptized shall be saved," (pardoned.) Therefore, Simon received the remission of sins. But says an objector, the

Apostle told Simon afterwards that his heart was not right in the sight of God—that he was in the gall of bitterness and in the bond of iniquity. So that he was then in his sins, or Peter charged him wrongfully.

Reader attend! Peter does not say that Simon had not received the forgiveness of his sins; but on the contrary, charges him only with one sin, one thought, or act of wickedness, which was the thought that the gift of God could be purchased with money: that is, the power of conferring the Holy Spirit on others by laying on of hands. It was this privilege that he was told he had neither part nor lot in. It was a privilege peculiarly granted unto the Apostles. It was in reference to this *thought,* wicked thought, that he was commanded to repent of, and none other. See Acts, 8 chap. 14—24th verses inclusive. None will deny: but that persons may, after they are justified, commit sin—do wickedly—so did Simon. Please turn to Simon's case and read it attentively, and see whether you have not been mistaken in your former views of it.

IV. Justification, remission of sins, and being saved from past sins, are terms used to convey the same idea: and as the scriptures say we are justified by faith; that whosoever believeth in Jesus shall receive remission of sins: whosoever shall call on the name of the Lord shall be saved: therefore, we are justified without baptism.

Ans.—It is true, the scriptures say 'we are justified by faith:' Rom. 5: 1; and we are also said to be justified by his [God's] grace,' Rom. 3: 24; 'By the Blood of Christ,' Rom. 5: 9; 'In the name of the Lord Jesus and by the spirit of our God,' 1 Cor. 6: 11; 'By the faith of Christ,' Gal. 2: 16; 'and that we are justified by works,' James 2: 21, 24, 25. And as the phrase "shall be saved," is frequently used as equivalent to justification, or remission of sins. The scriptures also teach that we are 'saved by grace;' 'by faith;' 'by his [Christ's] life;' by 'calling on the name of the Lord,' 'with the mouth confession is made unto salvation,' 'he that believeth and is baptized shall be saved'— that we are saved 'by hope;' also, that 'even baptism doth now save us.' Shall we hence conclude that we are justified or saved from our past sins, by any one of the above causes alone? Certainly not. God has seen fit in his wisdom to reveal to us all the above means, or causes by, or through which he saves us from our sins; and he certainly has not revealed too much, nor was any further means necessary to be revealed to us or certainly they would have been revealed. Therefore we conclude that in order to our justification we must have faith in the blood of Christ, trust in his grace, and in the name of the Lord Jesus, by the renewing of the Holy Spirit. Submit to the faith, or gospel of Christ, by repentance, and calling on the name of the Lord, be baptized in his name, and we shall according to the promise receive remission of sins, send the gift of the Holy Spirit, and thus having peace with God through our Lord Jesus Christ, we should work out our own salvation with fear and trembling, for it is God who worketh in us both to will and to do of his own good pleasure; that is, that we should have our fruit unto holiness, and the end everlasting life.

MARCH, 1844. TYCHICUS.

CHRISTIAN OBLIGATIONS—NO. 5.

I CLOSED the last No. by showing what the fruits of the spirit are The Saviour says, "the tree is known by its fruit." "Men do not gather grapes of thorns, or figs of thistles." Now if we have the spirit of Christ, we will bear the fruits of the spirit. Not that we shall have an orthodox faith on the operation of the spirit, so called, for it is possible to have an orthodox theory on this subject, and at the same time bear the fruits of the flesh; in fact, the pride of orthodoxy, in this man-fearing, and man-pleasing age, is a fruit of the flesh. It is possible to have the head filled with theory, and untaught questions which gender strife, when the heart is far from God.

It is not only our duty to meet error, in logical argument, founded on the word of God, but we should show by our actions, that we are under the influence of that word, which is "quick and powerful and sharper than any two-edged sword." I have no doubt but that we have the best theory in the world, and it is our duty to show the difference between our system, and sectarian dogmas, creeds and confessions of faith. If we do not, then, we condemn ourselves in that which we allow. O! for a nearer approach to the purity and holiness of the ancient Christians, as well as an understanding of the golden rule by which they purified their lives:

"O for a closer walk with God,
A calm and heavenly frame,
A light to shine upon the road
That leads me to the Lamb."

It is not enough that we understand what the scriptures teach in reference to the influence of the spirit, for the Apostle says, "If we live in the spirit, let us also walk in the spirit. Let us not be desirous of vain glory, provoking one another, envying one another." Gal. 5: 25, An orthodox opinion with the fruits of the flesh is sometimes considered of more importance, than the faith of "God's elect," with the fruits of the spirit. Now, suppose that a child of God who walks in the spirit, is accused of being a heretic, then is a good opportunity to show the fruits of the spirit; to wit, long-suffering, gentleness, goodness, and meekness, and thus prove to the accuser by actions, as well as words, that he is mistaken. Paul says to the Colossians, "Do every thing that ye do, whether in word or deed, in the name of the Lord Jesus, giving thanks to God and the Father by him." Can we revile in the name of the Lord Jesus? Let Paul answer. "Consider him who endured such a contradiction of sinners against himself, lest ye he weary and faint in your mind;" "who when he was reviled, reviled not again, when he was persecuted, threatened not." Again: "Let the same mind be in you that was in Christ Jesus." But if when I am accused of denying the spirit of Christ, I manifest the fruits of the flesh by getting angry, and reviling in return, become a witness against myself, in proof of such a charge, and furnish my accuser with a weapon, without, which, all his attacks would be like casting arrows at the fixed stars, because they could never reach me. Here I will drop this part of the subject, by referring the reader to the 12th chap. of Romans, which contains more of the divine principles of the Gospel of Jesus Christ, than I could possibly express in the same number of words, without using the same language.

We will now commence at the memorable day of Pentecost, where the gospel was first preached after the Saviour rose from the dead. We frequently go to Pentecost for the purpose of seeing how the commission was carried out, in which it is said: " He that believeth and is baptized shall be saved." Matthew records the commission, "Go ye therefore and teach all nations, baptizing them in the name of the Father, and of the Son, and of the Holy Ghost; teaching them to observe all things whatsoever I have commanded you.".... The first half of the commission tells us how to be saved, and the last half teaches us what to do after we are saved. Peter explains the first half by preaching Jesus Christ and the resurrection, and telling those who were convinced, and cried out and said, "Men and brethren, what shall we do?" to "repent and be baptized every one of you in the name of Jesus Christ, for the remission of sins, and ye shall receive the gift of the Holy Ghost;" and "they that gladly received his word," and "were baptized," carried out the last half of the commission, by continuing steadfastly in the Apostles' doctrine and fellowship, and in breaking of bread, and in prayers. "They continued steadfast," that is, they were intently engaged in the observance of the precepts of the apostles. A part of these precepts were breaking of bread, fellowship, and prayers. Upon these, therefore, we will make some remarks. The breaking of bread, I believe, is understood by all to be the commemoration of the Lord's death. This was strictly attended to by the first Christians, which showed their unshaken faith in the Lord's death for the sins of the world. I believe it is generally admitted that the first Christians commemorated the Lord's death every first day of the week; but even many of those who thus believe, take but little pains to be at the Lord's house on every Lord's day, where the Lord himself has promised to be; and if they are not there, of course they cannot commemorate the Lord's death. Luke says, "And upon the first DAY of the week when the disciples met together to break bread," Acts 20: 7. This looks like they considered it their duty to break bread on the first day of the week, and for that purpose they met together. How many of them did not go, because they would take less trouble to show forth their faith in a crucified Saviour, than they would to gain a few cents of this world's goods, on any other day in the week, the sacred historian does not inform us. If our hearts are as much affected with the love of God, as they are with a desire for the goods of this world, we will take as much pains to meet at the Lord's house on the first day of the week, and break bread, as we do about our worldly affairs. We are too apt to think that the service of God is a matter that can be easily dispensed with, just to suit our own convenience. This shows that we do not believe that every man will be rewarded according to his works, as the Bible asserts; and that we have not given our hearts to God, as he commands us to do, but that we have given them to the god of this world. By meeting together and communicating the Lord's death, we show that we are his disciples, and bind ourselves by this solemn act, to abstain from sin. That the ancient Christians considered the sacrament a solemn pledge, that they would abstain from sin, may be proven from Pliny the younger, who was an enemy to Christianity. He says that "Christ was worshipped as a God among the Christians: that they would rather suffer death than blaspheme him: that they received a sacrament, and by it entered into a vow of abstaining from sin and wickedness, conforming to the advice of Paul; that they had private assemblies of worship, and used to sing together in hymns." This was written about the commencement of the second century. The same author speaks of the influence that these devoted Christians exerted, in the following language: "Many of every age, of every rank, and of both sexes were brought into danger. The contagion of this superstition had spread, not into cities merely, but also into villages, and fields. The temples were nearly desolate. The most sacred rites for some time were suspended. And scarcely any one was found to purchase victims for them." Plin. Epist., lib. 10, Epist. 97. This influence was not exerted by a MERE formal profession of Christianity; but by a strict adherence to its divine precepts. The professed Christian who does not live according to the import of this divine institution, "eateth and drinketh condemnation to himself." What a solemn, and what a pleasing thought it is to think of being permitted to commemorate the death of him by whom the worlds were made, in token of our heirship with him, "in whom are laid up all the treasures of wisdom and knowledge." Here we must drop the subject for another No.

T. J. EDMONDSON.

QUERY ANSWERED.

Brother Mathes: I would be pleased to see the subject of "feet washing," discussed in the Christian Record, as I think good would result from it. There is at this time a diversity of opinion among us upon this matter. Some suppose it to be a public institution, no less binding upon Christians than the Lord's supper: others suppose it to be connected with the Table of the Lord, and never to be separated from it: while others contend, that it has no necessary connection with the Lord's Supper, but is a private, or family institution, binding upon Christians, in every age of the new dispensation. Now brother Mathes, what is the truth upon this subject? Please answer through the Christian Record, and oblige your brother in the Lord,

JOHN ABRAMS.

ANSWER.

My dear brother: We are fully impressed with the importance of your question, and we perfectly agree with you, that *the truth* upon this subject, ought to be known. Well, among others, we have our views of the matter; which, in all humility, we will give you, and the brethren, and if any of our readers can throw more light upon the subject, we shall be glad to see it.

We do not believe that the ordinance of Feet Washing, has any necessary connection with the Lord's Supper, as it appears evident from all the evidence in the case, that Jesus washed his disciples' feet, and commanded them to do so, at least two days and nights before he instituted his own supper. Turn to the 13th chap, of John's testimony; and you will find that the washing was *before* the "feast of the Passover." The first verse commences, "Now before the feast of the passover," &c. You will learn in the connection also, that the Devil put it into the heart of Judas to betray his Lord, while they were at supper, from which Jesus arose, when he "poured water into a basin and began to wash his disciple's feet."

Turn now to the parallel passage in Mark, 14th chap., 1st verse: "After two days was the feast of the passover and of unleavened bread; and the chief Priests and the scribes sought how they might take him by craft, and put him to death. (2) But they said not on the feast-day, lest there be an uproar among the people. (3) And being in Bethany, in the house of Simon the leper, as he sat at meat, there came a woman having an alabaster-box of ointment of spikenard, very precious, and she brake the box, and poured it upon his head:" (10) "And Judas Iscariot, one of the twelve, went unto the chief Priests, to betray him unto him." Mark says, as we have seen above, that *two days before* the feast of the passover, Jesus was in Bethany, in the house of Simon the leper; that at that time the woman poured the precious ointment on his head; and that from that place Judas went to the chief Priests to betray him.

John 13th chap., says (30th v.) "He then having received the sop, went immediately out; and it was night." And this my brother you will observe, was after Jesus had washed their feet, and Judas' among the rest, and on the same night. Mark tells us, it was *before* the feast *two* days. Now you know, that the passover was killed the first day of the feast in the evening: and Jesus did not institute his own supper, until after the Paschal supper. See also, Matt. 26: 1—15. Here we are told that it was *two* days before the feast of the passover; that they were in Simon's house, in Bethany, and that Judas one of the twelve went from there to the chief priests for the purpose of betraying his master; and also, that the box of ointment was broken, and the contents poured on his head, on that occasion. So, then we see that the witnesses all agree: some of them tell some things which others of them omit, but there is no disagreement. For example, John tells of the "feet washing," and says nothing about the box of ointment: while Matthew and Mark relate the circumstance of the box of ointment, but say nothing about the "feet washing."

Now the general opinion among those who contend that "feet washing" should always be attended to, in connection with the Lord's supper, is, that Jesus washed his disciples' feet immediately after he had instituted his own supper, and therefore they conclude, it should always be so attended to; and we confess, if the premises were good, the conclusion would follow of course. But the premises are not true, as we have seen above. The Lord's Supper was instituted in an upper room in Jerusalem, the first day of the feast of the passover; but Jesus washed his disciples' feet *two-days* before that, not in Jerusalem, but in Bethany, in the house of Simon the leper: therefore, our good brethren are mistaken.

Neither do we believe, from a careful examination of the whole subject, that it was the design of Jesus to make it a public ordinance of Christian worship. In saying so, we are aware that we differ from many good and pious Christians: but this difference has nothing to do with our love and fellowship for each other.

There is no evidence that there were any but the disciples present, when Jesus washed their feet. Jesus did not command them to do it publicly; but to wash one another's feet, according to the example he had given them. It is not a commemorative institution therefore, it need not be done publicly.

But we do believe that Christians are all under obligation to wash one another's feet, according to the command, and example of their glorious head. And as Jesus washed the disciples' feet, before the old, or Jewish covenant was taken out of the way, and consequently before the New Covenant was ratified by the blood of Messiah; we will look into the apostolic teaching and practice, and ascertain if we can, how these heaven-taught Apostles, whose feet the Saviour washed, understood the matter, and how they practiced it, after the kingdom was set up.

The subject is only mentioned once, after the day of Pentecost, and that is found 1 Tim. 5: 10, and here the Apostle classes it with *good works*. Speaking of widows who were to be taken into the number, [of those who were to receive pecuniary aid from the church,] he says: "Well reported of, for good works; if she have brought up children, if she have lodged strangers, if she have washed the saints' feet, if she have relieved the afflicted, if she have diligently followed every good work." Now as this is the only place where the subject is mentioned by the Apostles; and as the duty is here spoken of as a good work, and not as a public ordinance, we have come to the conclusion, that it is binding upon every Christian, to "wash the saints' feet," whenever he can do it as a good work. No matter whether it is done publicly or privately; in the church, or at home in the family circle, so we do it with an eye to the command of the Lord, and show our love one for another.

Paul classes it with "bringing up children," "lodging strangers," "relieving the afflicted," &c. Now all can see the propriety of calling those acts of duty and benevolence, "good works," and we think upon a moment's reflection, you will see the propriety of the Apostle's classification. To give a disciple a drink of cold water, in the name of a disciple, is a good work, and shall not go unrewarded.

But who would say, that this must always be done publicly? We suppose that all will admit, that if we should see a disciple thirsting, no matter whether it were *public or private,* at home or abroad, we should perform the good work of giving him drink: and so, of "relieving the afflicted." Now bro. Abrams, we suppose you understand our views of this matter; examine the testimony prayerfully: "prove all things, hold fast that which is good."

Your brother in the good hope, J. M. MATHES.

BAPTIST POLICY IN ALABAMA.

BRETHREN EDITORS:—We have two Baptist papers in this State. The "Alabama Baptist" of this place, and the "Baptist Evangelist" of Huntsville. It seems that the editor of the latter periodical is becoming a little heterodox, and our Southern editor is castigating him for it. In the last number of the Alabama Baptist, Mr. Muse of Huntsville is declared to be a "Campbellite" and unworthy of the fellowship of all old "Regular Bible Baptists." I have never seen the Baptist Evangelist and cannot pronounce upon its merits, but judge it worthy of attention, from the fact that our Southern Baptist organ has sounded the tocsin.

The character of the heresy may be guessed at from the following items given in the strictures of our orthodox paper:

"ITEM 3. I have taught, that faith is a sentiment originated in the mind, by the force of testimony, and that this sentiment partakes of the nature of the testimony, whether it be human or divine, true or false."

"ITEM 6. I have taught, that the Holy Spirit operates upon the minds of men, alone through the words of truth."

"ITEM 7. I have taught, that the notion of an abstract spiritual operation is the sole inlet to all the fanaticism and superstition that now afflict humanity."

Upon this last item it is remarked, "Here is a flat denial of what has always been a most prominent item of Baptist belief. The notion of an abstract spiritual operation is held to, by the Baptists, as an important point, and that its rejection leads to the rejection of Christianity itself. Take away this and you take away the only hope which the Baptists have that another sinner will ever be converted to God."

"ITEM 8. I have taught, that the doctrine of the total depravity of human nature, is a libel upon the noblest works of God."

For these and similar sentiments, our Southern Alabama Baptists denounce Mr. Muse and say they only mean to strip off the sheepskin and show the wolf. But controversy on the merits of the points involved is positively declined. To show that be is *not a Baptist* is the avowed object; but the question whether he is right or wrong is not to be discussed. This will give you some idea of Baptist policy in South Alabama.—[*Christian Review*. A. G.

FOR THE "CHRISTIAN RECORD."

DEAR BROTHER MATHES: In the last No. of the "Christian Record" I see a letter, addressed to me in reference to the Second Advent of the Lord, with some of your reasons for not adopting Mr. Miller's theory of the "Advent nigh." You say: "When I conversed with you last upon the subject, we agreed very well, but since that time I am informed your mind has undergone an entire change upon this important subject; and that you have fully committed yourself to Mr. Miller's theory of the "glorious appearing of the Lord" in 1843." Now it is true, bro. Mathes, that when I last conversed with you upon this subject, I did not believe that the Lord would make his second appearing, by the close of the (Jewish) year 1843, as I now do; and if my understanding of the time the Lord would come, when I last conversed with you upon this subject, is what you mean by saying, "we agreed very well," and a change in my mind, in reference to the time, is what you mean by saying, "I am informed that your mind has undergone an entire change upon this important subject," then, you have been correctly informed; but if you understand that I have adopted Mr. Miller's theory in regard to all the events that are to take place in connection with the coming of the Lord, then, you are mistaken. I am not a little surprised that you should call upon me to defend the whole of Mr. Miller's theory upon this subject. You might as well call upon me to defend the "mourning bench system of getting religion," or prove that a person's sins are pardoned before he is baptized. In reference to the events that are to take place, when the Lord comes, my mind has not changed for several years. I do not consider that it is necessary for me to agree with Mr. Miller in the event, in order to agree with him in the time. I do not suppose that I disagree with you, in regard to the Millennium, and other events connected with the coming of the Lord, as much as I do with Mr. Miller; and if your disagreement with Mr. Miller in regard to the event, is a good reason for disbelieving the time, your agreement with me, in regard to the events, is a still better reason for believing the time as I do. You say you have been a constant reader of the "Signs of the Times" for the last six months and more, but still you have felt no conviction of the truth of the system "as a *whole.*" Very well, neither have I, as a *whole,* but that is no reason why I should reject the time. I have been a hearer of the doctrine of the Methodist church, for something near twenty-five years, but still I have felt no conviction of the truth of the system, as a whole, but this is no reason why I should not believe, with them, that Jesus Christ is the Son of God. The only objection that you have brought forward, that conflicts with my views respecting the advent nigh, is the literal return of the literal Jews, before the coming of the Lord. You refer to the 38th and 39th chapters of Ezekiel as proof that the literal Jews will return to the land of Canaan, before the Lord comes, I ask why not the 37th also, as the subject begins there, and continues to the end of Ezekiel. Now what are the events that are to take place, at that time? A few of them I will mention.

1st: David is to be their King forever; 24th and 25th verses. God's sanctuary will be in the midst of them, and his tabernacle with them; 27th and 28th verses. Now, if *literal* David is to be their King, there must be a resurrection before that time, as David has been dead a long time. If by David we are to understand Christ, then he must come at that time. Brother Mathes, I am compelled to put this whole matter in the thousand years of Christ's personal reign on earth; and I do not think that you, or any other person, can fix it short of that time, call them literal or spiritual Jews. The tree of life will be there, and the name of the city from that day shall be, The *Lord is* there. I have never seen a theory that comports with this prophecy, in my opinion, and therefore I believe none of them. The only passage that you have brought forward to prove that the Jews will return before the Lord comes, is Acts 3: 21, where Peter says, "The heavens must retain him until the times of the restitution of all things, spoken by the mouth of all the holy Prophets since the world began." It seems that this passage would prove too much, in the way you apply it; that is, that the restitution of all things must take place before the Lord comes. In this way we might prove that the Millennium and the restitution of the dead will *both* take place before the Lord comes, for these are a part of the "restitution of all things."

I will now give you some of my reasons for believing the Jews will not return before the Lord comes. The Saviour says, (Luke 21:24,) "And they shall fall by the edge of the sword, and shall be led away captive into all nations; and Jerusalem shall be trodden down of the Gentiles, until the times of the Gentiles be fulfilled." Rom. 11:25, "For I would not, brethren, that ye should be ignorant of this mystery, lest ye should be wise in your own conceit, that blindness, in part, is happened to Israel, until the fullness of the Gentiles be come in." 26th v., "And so all Israel shall be saved, as it is written. There shall come out of Sion the Deliverer, and shall turn away ungodliness from Jacob." Now these passages prove conclusively, to my mind, that there will be no more salvation for the Gentiles, after Jerusalem ceases to be trodden down by them: and I cannot believe that the Gospel will cease to be offered to the Gentiles until the Lord comes, and also that ungodliness will not be turned away from Jacob, until the "Deliverer comes out of Sion." So, you see, brother Mathes, that your objection turns out to be no objection, to the immediate coming of the Lord, according to my understanding of these matters; although I do not profess to understand every thing that is spoken in reference to the return of the Jews, whether *literal* or *spiritual:* neither do I understand the term Israel or Jew, always to refer to spiritual Israel, in the New Testament, and I do not know that any other person so understands it.

I will now give you some of my reasons for believing in the immediate appearing of the Lord. My first reason is found in the second chap. of Daniel. In this image which Nebuchadnezzar saw in his dream, we have the time given which was to elapse *from* Nebuchadnezzar to the setting up of God's everlasting Kingdom, unto the Son of man coming in the clouds of heaven, when all human governments are to be destroyed, and the saints take possession of the kingdom, and reign forever and ever. The ten toes of this image show that the 4th kingdom was to be divided into ten kingdoms, which took place between the years 356 and 483, A. D., which shows that we have been living in the toes 1360 years, which is proof to me that we are on the verge of the resurrection.

My second reason is found in Dan. 8th and 9th chapters, where we have the time given from the going forth of the commandment to restore and build Jerusalem, until the cleansing of the sanctuary, 2300 days. 70 weeks of which (490 days) were accomplished at the crucifixion of Christ. The remainder of the vision is 1810 days, which will terminate the present year, A. D. 1844. The cleansing of the sanctuary and the setting-up of God's everlasting kingdom are coetaneous events. A third reason is found in Dan. 12: 11, 12 and 13th verses; where 1335 days are given, commencing at the taking away of the daily, and setting up the abomination that maketh desolate, and reaching to the resurrection of Daniel. The taking, away of the daily or Paul's hindering cause, 2 Thess., 2 chap., 6th and 7th verses, and placing the abomination or the Papal power, took place in A. D. 508, as Gibbon satisfactorily proves. See Gib., vol. 4, p. 412, where his work is in 6 vols. At this- time, in 508, the Catholics for the first time waged a successful war against both the civil authority of the empire, and the church of the east, which were mostly Arians. The result of which was the slaughter of 65,000 heretics. The signing of an orthodox treaty by the dying emperor. Thus, they placed the abomination of desolation. 65,000 slaughtered at the commencement of the Son of Perdition, is a very fair specimen of what he has done since that time. Fifty million have licked the dust by this blasphemous power. How long was this desolating power to continue? The answer is, 1290 days. When did this- power fall, or lose its power to put the saints to death? Ans.—In A. D. 1798, the Pope lost his power to kill by law, as many witnesses attest. From 508 to 1798, is 1290 years. The facts in this case prove that Daniel's days stand for so many years: and permit me here to say, that the facts in the case are the only rule by which we can determine how our heavenly Father counts time. In this rule there can be no mistake. Forty-five years beyond 1798 complete Daniel's 1335 days, which will terminate some time in the present year, when Daniel and all the saints will stand in their lot; what day, week or month, I shall not say, as I have not the means of ascertaining, but I am looking for it continually. You will not hold me responsible, if you please, for any time except that which I have given. A few of the signs given in the New Testament, which were to precede the coming of our blessed Lord, will now be noticed.

The first I shall mention is found in Matthew 24: 29. Here we are informed that the "Sun shall be darkened, the Moon shall not give her light, the Stars shall fall from heaven." There are three signs given by the Saviour. Have they received their accomplishment! We verily believe they have. May 19, 1780, the sun arose clear in the morning, and by 10 o'clock, A. M. the farmers left their work in their fields, and retired to their dwellings—business within doors could not be attended to without the aid of lights. It continued so during the day—the night following was as unusually dark as the day. Notwithstanding the Moon fulled the day before, the darkness was as gross as ever it had been since the Almighty first gave birth to light.

Rev. Mr. Tenny of Exeter, N. H., in remarking upon the darkness, says, "I could not help conceiving at the time, that if every luminous body in the Universe had been struck out of existence, the darkness could not have been more complete. A sheet of white paper, held within a few inches of the eyes, was equally invisible with the blackest velvet." I have, myself, heard this strange occurrence related by many persons who saw it. The falling of stars.—It appears that the first shower of meteors of any magnitude, found on the pages of history, took place the 12th of November, 1779, and was witnessed 10,800 miles in length, and 7,000 in breadth; since that time several partial ones have been seen. Nov. 13th, 1833, and within the recollection of the present generation, the most magnificent and splendid scene, that ever occurred, took place. It could not be more truly described than it is in Rev. 6: 13, "And the stars of heaven fell unto the earth, as a fig tree casteth her untimely figs, when she is shaken of a mighty wind." If the above-mentioned signs have not been fulfilled, I cannot conceive how they can be, unless the very same scenes should be acted over again. But some will say that these meteors are not stars. Such persons I would ask: what kind of a star was that which went, and stood over the place where the Saviour was. Another sign I would mention, and that is to continue until the Master's return. It is found in 1 Thess. 5: 3, "For when they shall say peace and safety, then sudden destruction cometh, and they shall not escape." This cry is now being made. It is vociferated through the length and breadth of the land, and it is urged forward with a zeal worthy of a better cause. What is it? It is that which you, Mr. Editor, have been in contact with for several months. I will tell it. "The Lord came at the destruction of Jerusalem. The judgment is now in session. No future punishment. Give yourselves no uneasiness about a judgment to come. All will be holy and happy in the resurrection." This cry is of recent date. If this is not the cry of "peace and safety," bro. Mathes, please tell your patrons what that cry can be. I, for one, am looking for sudden destruction to come on the wicked.

I have complied with your request, in part, brother Mathes, by giving you, and through you, the readers of your valuable paper, a few, and only a few, of my reasons for believing that the coming of the Lord is nigh, even at the door. In giving these reasons, I have only sketched some of the out lines. To give all the reasons I have for believing what I have already written, would require more room in the "Record," than you could well spare. The testimony is such upon this subject, that it has produced the strongest conviction in my mind, that we stand upon the very thresh hold of a new order of things, which will take place at the coming of the Lord. The testimony relative to this matter I believe, no man can set aside. Nothing but a firm belief in the speedy advent of Christ, would have induced me to proclaim it to the public.

The events that are to take place in the Millennium, I say nothing about in my lectures. My greatest anxiety is to be ready to meet the Lord, and get as many more as I can. The events I am willing to leave with the Lord, believing that he will do right. I do not believe the whole of Mr. Miller's theory relative to the coming of the Lord, nor any other person's that I ever saw; and therefore do not feel myself responsible for any of them. The time when, has claimed my attention, for some two or three months. I regret, that inasmuch as you wish to correspond with me upon this important subject, that the correspondence did not commence sooner, as I should have had more time than I now have, to lay this matter before your readers. Time will soon tell whether I am right in my calculations; too soon for you and me to write much upon this subject, as I shall neither write nor lecture upon the time, after April next is past and gone, if I should live.

I think, brother Mathes, that you made a small mistake, by saying, "But finding the Advocates of the doctrine determined to contend for it, even after the time is out." The time given by Mr. Miller will not expire until the 21st of March, if I understand him. Why he fixed upon that time, I cannot tell, as I cannot see how 1810 full years, from the crucifixion of Christ, will expire at that time. From what testimony I have respecting that matter, I think that it would extend some distance into April; but as I said before, so say I now, again, I do not think the precise month can be known. I do not know that 490 full years were precisely fulfilled at the crucifixion of Christ, from the going forth of the commandment to restore and build Jerusalem. It may, for aught I know, have lacked some months. I do not know what month in the year the commandment was given, and of course cannot say, exactly, what time. I do not believe that it is absolutely necessary for a person to believe that the Lord will come soon, in order to be saved. But one thing I do believe, that it is absolutely necessary to do the will of God, in order to enter the kingdom of heaven. In order to do the will of God, we must do what the apostles of Jesus have taught, for in so doing we shall always be ready. Nothing else will secure admission there to those who have heard the Gospel. If we follow the commandments of men, we will knock in vain for admittance at that gate. My prayer to my heavenly Father is, that all the disciples of

Jesus may be able to say with the beloved John, Come Lord Jesus, come quickly. Amen and Amen.

Yours in hope of the first resurrection,

JOSEPH FASSETT.

N. B. You appear not satisfied with Mr. Miller's chronology. I have never examined it, but have examined the Bible to ascertain the age of the world; and here is the result. Point out the error if you see any.

	Years,	mo.	days.
From Adam to the flood,	1656		
From the flood to the 75th year of Abraham, to the Covenant,	368		
From the Covenant to the giving of the Law, (Paul,)	430		
From the Law to the death of Moses. -	40		
From the death of Moses to the first captivity, [Jos.]	38		
From the first captivity to Samuel,	450		
Bishop Usher gives from the death of: Eli to Saul,	46		
From the commencement of Saul's reign to the end of the captivity in Babylon, -	583	6	10
From the end of the captivity to the 20th year of Artaxerxes, [Rolin,]	85		
From the 20th of Artaxerxes to the crucifixion of Christ, A. D. 33,	490		
From A. D. 33 to A. D.. 1843, -	1810		
	5996	6	10

I do not believe that any living being can tell exactly how old the world is. J. F.

REMARKS ON THE ABOVE.

MY BELOVED BROTHER FASSETT: Your communication which was intended for the 8th No. of the Christian Record, came to hand too late for that, but with great pleasure, I now lay it before my readers, You tell me that you have not adopted Mr. Miller's theory of the "Advent nigh," as a *whole,* and seem to think strange that I should call upon you to *sustain* the whole of it! My object in this bro. F. was to give you an opportunity of defining your position, which you have now done. And permit me to say, that I hold you responsible for none of Elder Miller's vagaries.

But you say, "The only objection which you (I,) have brought forward that conflicts with my (your) views respecting the advent nigh, is the literal return of the literal Jews, before the coming of the Lord;" and on this subject you refer me to the 37th chap. of Ezekiel, in connection with the 38th & 39th chaps.—Well let us examine them.

In the 37th chap. we have the vision of "Dry bones;" and we are informed that these bones, which were exceeding dry, represented the whole house of Israel and Judah. 13th verse, "And ye shall know that I am the Lord, when I have opened your graves, O my people, and brought you up out of your graves.; (14) And shall put my spirit:" in you, and you shall live; and I shall place you in your own land:" &c. At the 16th v. we are told of the union of Israel and Judah, under the figure of the two sticks becoming *one* in the hand of the Prophet, and as no such union has ever yet taken place, we put it in the future. But at the 21st v. the. Prophet is told to explain the figure of the two sticks, thus: "And say unto them, thus saith the Lord God, Behold, I will take the children of Israel from among the heathen whither they be gone, and will gather them on every side, and bring them into their own land." In the 24th, 25th verses, we are informed, that after Israel and Judah have returned from among the heathen, and become united as one nation in their own land: "David my Servant shall be king over them." Now whether this text refers to Christ as the son of David according to the flesh, or whether David is to be raised from the dead, and be their prince forever, I consider entirely immaterial to the issue between us: as the whole connection shows, that Israel and Judah will be gathered, from among the heathen, into their own land, the ancient heritage of Jacob, *before* David will reign over them. And I most firmly believe that the first Resurrection will take place after the restoration of Israel, and at the glorious appearing of the Lord.

But to prove that *literal Israel and literal Judah,* will yet return to their own land, let us read the 25—29 verses of the 39th chap. "Thus, saith the Lord God, Now, will I bring again the captivity of Jacob, and have mercy on the whole house of Israel, and will be jealous for my holy name. ***** When I have brought them again from the people and gathered them out of their enemies' hands, and am sanctified in them, in the sight of many nations; then shall they know that I am the Lord their God, which caused them to be led into captivity among the heathen: but I have gathered them unto their own land, and have left none of them any more there. Neither will I hide my face any more from them; for I have poured out my spirit upon the house of Israel, saith the Lord God."

This most unquestionably refers to *literal Israel* and their *literal* restoration; for it was they who "went into captivity for their iniquity." But again, God by the mouth of the same Prophet says; "Therefore say, Thus saith the Lord God, I will even gather you from the people and assemble you out of the countries where you have been scattered, and I will give you the land of Israel," 11th chap. 17 v.

Now brother Fassett, if the foregoing prophetic declarations and promises, do not prove a literal return of the literal descendants of Abraham, I would ask you to tell us in what language such a promise could be given, that would not be liable to be misunderstood and misapplied? This prophetic people, though scattered abroad among all the nations of the earth, they yet remain a distinct race, a standing miracle in favor of the truth of prophecy; have no inheritance in any other land; and have always cherished a passionate desire to return to their own beloved Judea. Through their long and dreary captivity, they have kept themselves free from local attachments, ready at any moment to take up their line of march and return to their ancient homes! and recent developments render it very probable, that the time of their gathering together at Jerusalem, is not far distant.

As you do not insist upon the term *Israel* and Jew, always meaning the *spiritual* and not the *literal* children of Abraham, I shall let that pass for the present. We now come to Acts 3: 21, where Peter says, "Whom the heavens must receive until the times of the restitution of all things spoken by the mouth of the holy prophets since the world began." You seem to think brother Fassett, that this would prove too much for my own position, in the way I apply it. Well, let us see. By the mouth of the holy prophets God has promised that Israel and Judah, shall be gathered from all countries where they have been scattered, and again possess their own land. We therefore conclude with confidence that the text above quoted sustains our position showing clearly, that this promise must be accomplished, before or at the coming of the Lord.

You next introduce several passages from Rom. 11th chap. which you think disproves my views of the literal restoration of literal Israel.

Now I think you must admit brother Fassett, that the terms Israel and Gentiles, are here used in their literal signification. Well then we are here told of the blindness of Israel, of the salvation of the Gentiles, through their fall—of the fullness of the Gentiles, or the close of the ministry of reconciliation so far as the Gentiles are concerned.— Next comes the deliverer out of

Sion, and turns away ungodliness from Jacob, and the salvation of all Israel is declared. Now according to my understanding of this chap. it does not throw a single difficulty in my way. I believe when Israel shall have returned to their own land; The "times of the Gentiles" will then be over; at which time the Lord will come; the martyrs, and perhaps all the righteous dead, will then be raised, and Christ shall "reign over his ancients gloriously."

You next give us your reasons for believing in the immediate appearing of the Lord. You locate your first reason in Dan. 2nd chap. you say, "The ten toes of this image show that the 4th kingdom was to be divided into ten kingdoms, which took place between the years 356 & 483. A. D., which shows that we have been living in the toes, 1360 years, which is proof to me that we are on the verge of the resurrection." Now bro. F. I am not able to see the force, of your logic; as Daniel does not inform us how long these kingdoms, (toes of the image) shall stand. But suppose we admit that you are correct, and that "we are on the *verge* of the resurrection," this surely is not satisfactory proof that the second Advent will take place in April!

You locate your "second reason," in the 8 & 9th chaps. of Dan. On this testimony you remark: "Here we have the time given from *the* going forth of the commandment to restore and build Jerusalem unto the cleansing of the sanctuary 2300 days, 70 weeks of which (490 days) were accomplished at the crucifixion of Christ." "The remainder of the Vision," you remark, "is 1810 days, which will determinate the present year 1844."

I have but very little objection to this part of your essay, still I am not convinced that you are correct! The difficulty in my mind is this, "How do you know that the 70 weeks form a part of, and are to be cut off from the 2300 days?"

If I understand you, you teach that "the daily sacrifice" spoken of by Daniel, and Paul's "hindering cause," mean the same thing, namely Pagan authority; and that this was taken away in the year 508 A. D., and the "abomination of Desolation spoken of by Daniel, (papal power as you understand it) was then sent up." That the papal authority was established about A. D. 508, I admit; but I do not think brother Fassett, that you or any other man can prove that this was the "abomination" spoken of by Daniel; indeed I am sure that you are mistaken, as Jesus connects it with the destruction of Jerusalem, and gives it as a sign of its speedy downfall, Matt. 24: 15. "When ye therefore shall see the abomination of desolation spoken of by Daniel the prophet, stand in the holy place (whoso readeth let him understand:) Then let them which be in Judea flee into the mountains."— Now read Luke 21st chap, 20 v. which is a parallel text; "And when ye shall see Jerusalem compassed with armies, then know that the desolation thereof is nigh."

From all which it is plain, that the Roman Legions, who laid Jerusalem low in the dust, were the desolating abomination, spoken of by Daniel the prophet. As to what you say about the reign of the man of sin, we agree so well, that I shall pass it with a single remark—and that is this; If I knew certainly in what year the man of sin arose, I think I should know when to expect his ruin; but as the starting point is involved in so much uncertainty, I find myself unable to settle upon any particular year as the final consummation.

You next proceed to notice the signs which were to precede the coming of the Lord, You first introduce Matt. 24: 29. "The sun shall be darkened, the moon shall not give her light, and the stars shall fall from heaven." You then say that "you verily believe these signs have all received their accomplishment." In answer to the question, *Where?* you say, "The sun was darkened May 19, 1780:" It must be admitted that this was a very strange occurrence; but still it seems to me that it happened too long ago, to be considered one of the signs of the *immediate* coming of the Lord. You also mention the falling of stars at different periods, but particularly the splendid shower that fell Nov. 13th 1833. Now brother Fassett, I cannot consider this a fulfillment of the prediction found in your text; (Matt. 24: 29.) because the splendid scene to which you refer, was only a shower of meteors and not stars! But the text affirms that "the sun shall be darkened," this you understand *literally* and so do I. "And the moon shall not give her light." This you understand to be literal also, for you say it was accomplished on the night after the dark day. "And the stars shall fall from heaven," here you depart from your own rule of interpretation and suppose that the literal stars are not here meant, but meteors! Now bro. Fassett, as it is contrary to all correct rules of interpretation, to understand one part of a passage figuratively, and the other literally, I am compelled to make it all figurative or all literal—I cannot therefore believe that this sign has yet been given, that is if you are correct about the darkness of the Sun and Moon.

But you seem to anticipate my objection, and you answer it by asking me, "What kind of a star it was that went before the Eastern Magi, and stood over the place where the young child lay." I answer, the book does not inform me, "what *kind* of a star," it was, and therefore I do not know: but the Bible says *it was a star,* and I believe it.

You next quote 1 Thess. 5:3. "For when they shall say peace and safety, then sudden destruction cometh upon them, and they shall not escape." I am willing to allow the full force of your remarks upon this text. Indeed, this is much stronger evidence to my mind, that the day of the Lord's coming is at hand, than all you have said about the Sun, Moon and Stars. But still this is not satisfactory proof that the Lord will come in April.

You regret that our correspondence did not commence sooner, as you say that you "will neither write nor lecture on the *time,* after April next is past and gone, if you should live." This I regret too, and as you will perhaps only have time to respond to these remarks, within the time you have mentioned; and as Mr. Miller's time, if I understand him, expires about the 21st of this month, (March,) and the time you have mentioned expires next month, we have concluded to say but little, upon the prophetic periods, at present, as time will soon decide the question.

You think that I was mistaken, when I said that the adventists, "would contend for their theory even after the time is out." Well, brother Fassett, I now think that *you* will not: but I still think that Mr. Miller and his associates *will:* but we shall see. I have published your chronological table, without note or comment. We hope our readers will examine it carefully. And now in conclusion, my dear brother, I will briefly state what seems to me to be the principal points of difference between us.

1—You think the signs which were to precede the second coming of Christ, have all been given. I think in this you are mistaken.

2—You think that the prophetic periods will run out in April next, and the Lord come in the clouds of heaven, with power and great glory, sometimes between this and the last of April. In this I think you are mistaken, as I think I have clearly shown in these remarks, that the literal Jews must return to their own land, before the Lord comes: and as they have not yet returned, and as there is not time enough between this and the last of April, for Israel to return, we conclude with confidence, that you are mistaken. Now if it is your pleasure to correspond with me further upon this subject, I hope you will particularly notice these two points. I am looking for the glorious appearing of the Lord, not many years hence; and the gathering together of the Jews to Jerusalem, from all the countries where they have been scattered, would to my mind, be demonstration itself, that the fullness of the Gentiles was about come, and that the Lord would soon come in his glory, to reward every man according to his work. "Even so come Lord Jesus." Amen.

Yours in the glorious hope,

JAMES M. MATHES.

FOR THE CHRISTIAN RECORD.
ANNUAL MEETING.

THE annual meeting of the congregations in the State of Indiana, will take place in Indianapolis, on FRIDAY the 30th of August, 1844; to be held over the 1st Lord's day in September. Brethren from all parts of the State, are affectionately invited to attend; public teachers especially.

L. H. JAMESON,
Evangelist of the Church at Ind's.

☛ WE have just received a letter from Washington, Indiana, written by brethren E. DAVIS and G. A. WALLER, the contents of which shall receive due attention in our next.—[ED.

NEWS FROM THE CHURCHES.

Columbus, March 5l/t, 4844.

Brother Mathes: I am now in this place, on my way home, from Clifty, in this county, where we had the pleasure of immersing five persons on yesterday. I also obtained seven new subscribers for your paper, whose names you will find below.

I am your brother in the Lord, WILLIAM IRWIN.

☛ Brother Irwin will please accept our thanks. How many more of the brethren will go and do likewise."—[ED.

Indianapolis, March 1st, 1844.

Dear brother Mathes: On last night I spoke at the Bluffs, from 1 John 1: 1—3. Two noble souls were induced to make the good confession.

In hope of eternal life, I am your brother in Christ,

J. KANE.

Jennings County, Indiana, Feb. 26th, 1844.

Dear brother Mathes: I avail myself of the present opportunity of informing you and the brethren, of the progress of the good cause in this part of God's moral vineyard. The church of God at Coffee Creek in this county, numbers 170 members—we have had some accessions recently, through the labors of our beloved brother Jacob Wright eight by confession and baptism, and two from the Baptists.

Yours in the good hope, JAMES HOPKINS.

☛ Many thanks to brother Hopkins, for the new subscribers he sent us: he will please act as agent for the Christian Record, in Jennings County.—[ED.

Brother A. C. Thompson of Edenburg, writes under date of the 22nd inst., that our beloved brother M. B. Hopkins of Rush county, had just closed a meeting in that place, at which eight additions were made to the church: six by confession and baptism, and two who had been immersed.—[ED.

Spencer, Ind., March 4th. 1844.

Brother Mathes: Our meeting has closed. Brother Trimble was with us, and gave general satisfaction. During his stay, we had two additions by confession and baptism, and a time of refreshing among the brethren. As ever yours, T. C. JOHNSON.

Bartholomew County, Indiana, November 16th, 1848.

Dear brother Mathes: I will inform you and the brethren, that bro. Challen of Cincinnati, has been laboring in this county since I saw you at Columbus. He preached in conjunction with brother J. B. New. The result was twenty-five additions by immersion, and three from the Baptists, one of whom was my beloved wife.

Yours in hope of eternal life, J. BOGGS.

☛ [Brother Boggs' letter should have appeared last fall; but brother B. will excuse us, when we inform him that we never received it, till the 27th inst.—ED.]

☛ All those of our present subscribers who wish to discontinue at the close of the 1st vol., will notify us through our Agents, or Postmasters, by the 1st of May next; all those who do not, will be considered new subscribers for the second volume. We hope however, that none will withdraw.

☛ Our thanks are due to Dr. McGee, for his efforts in procuring subscribers for the Christian Record. Will our friends generally exert their influence to increase the number of our readers.

THE CHRISTIAN RECORD.

VOL. I.] BLOOMINGTON, IND., APRIL, 1844. [No. X

"PRESSLY'S LECTURES" REVIEWED—NO. 6.

In our last, we closed the investigation of the Dr.'s *positive,* New Testament proof of infant baptism. The good Dr.'s next effort, is, to prove by the "lights of history," that infant baptism was practiced in the ages immediately succeeding the Apostles. He first introduces Justin Martyr, and quotes the following from his Dialogue with Trypho the Jew: "We also, who by him have had access to God, have not received this carnal circumcision, but the spiritual circumcision which Enoch, and those like him, observed. And we have received it by baptism, by the mercy of God, because we were sinners; and it is allowed to all persons to receive it in the same manner."

Now we ask, what does this first witness say in favor of infant baptism? Why not one word! He talks all the time about another matter!! he says, "because we were sinners:" surely the Dr. will not say, that infants are sinners! But Dr. Pressly, aware that this most ancient father said nothing in favor of infant baptism, says: "My object in introducing this quotation, is to show that this most ancient father represents baptism as being to Christians what circumcision was to the church of God, of old." Well, does Justin Martyr so represent it? we answer no, he does not. He says, "We have received the spiritual circumcision, which Enoch, and those like him, observed." Will Dr. P. affirm, that Enoch, the seventh from Adam, observed the right of infant baptism? we suppose not! for such a supposition would be ruinous to the Dr.'s whole theory! It would place baptism, thousands of years before circumcision; so far then from baptism coming in the room of circumcision, it would be circumcision coming in the room of baptism! But Justin Martyr will not talk to suit the Dr.; he will not say that baptism is spiritual circumcision at all! Hear the witness again; he says, "And we received it (spiritual circumcision) by baptism, by the mercy of God." Spiritual circumcision then, is *one* thing, and the means by which it is produced is *another,* just as different as is an *effect,* from the causes which produce it. Baptism and the mercy of God, are mentioned by Justin Martyr as the instrumental, or concurring causes, through and by which, he and his brethren had received "the spiritual circumcision, such as Enoch, and those like him, observed." So, you see Dr. Pressly proves nothing in favor of his hypothesis, by this witness.

But our friend Dr. P., not satisfied with Justin Martyr, calls him up again, and quotes from his apology to the Roman Emperor, as follows: "There are many persons among us, both male and female, of sixty and seventy years of age, who, from childhood, were made disciples to Christ, who remain uncorrupted." Here is another total failure! The witness will not testify to *infant* baptism! Indeed, the Dr. seems very sensible of this, for when he comes to "sum up the evidence," page 73, he says, "It seems then, that this ancient father understood that *children* might be made disciples to Christ, and baptized in his name, according to the command of our

Lord and Saviour." Yes, that *children* might; not that *infants* might! Surely the Dr. need not be told, that *children* are not always *infants*. We could use the language of this most ancient father, in reference to ourself, and say, "from our *childhood* we were discipled to Christ;" not our *infancy*. John the Apostle says. "I write to you little children, because your sins are forgiven you, for his name's sake." John does not say, "I write to you little infants," &c.

The next witness which Dr. P. brings upon the stage, is the great Tertullian, who flourished from the year 194 till 216, and who is ranked among the writers of the third century. Now we admit that this father mentions "infant baptism:" but does he say that it was the practice of the Apostles, and of the whole church up to that period! very far from it! He opposes it, as something *novel and dangerous*. "It is true," says Tertullian, "our Lord says, Suffer little children and forbid them not to come unto me." To which he adds, "Then let them come when they are grown." So this famous witness so far from helping the Dr. *to establish* the "right of infant baptism," gives the whole weight of his testimony against the practice!!

The next witness which Dr. P. introduces, is the famous Origen, who flourished in the third century, and who was one of the greatest visionaries of those early times. This witness says, "The church had from the Apostles an order to give baptism to infants; for they to whom the divine mysteries were committed, knew that there is in all persons, the natural pollution of sin, which must be washed away by water and the spirit." If Origen is correct, and the Apostles did give such an order to the church, *where is it recorded?* It is mere assertion without the least shadow of evidence to support it! But this witness testifies also, that "the *natural pollution of sin, must be washed away by water* (baptism) *and the spirit,*" Does Dr. Pressly believe this? If he does, then he is obnoxious to the charge, constantly preferred against those, *invidiously* called "Campbellites." Now one of the plainest laws of evidence is, that when a man introduces a witness, to prove a point, he is bound to receive all the witness says on that subject; and if he reject a part he must reject the whole. Now, if Dr. P. will not receive Origen's testimony on the *design* of baptism, he is also bound to reject what he says about the *subject!* and if he receives the former, for the sake of saving the latter, he is then a heretic, according to the sentence of the "Evangelical sects," as they call themselves!

The next witness brought forward by the Dr., is Cyprian bishop of Carthage, who flourished in the third century, and who suffered Martyrdom in the year 258. The good Dr. makes no quotations from this father; but speaks in a general way, of his testimony in favor of infant baptism, and the celebrated council of 66, which was convocated in his time, which, among other important matters, settled the question, whether the baptism of infants should always be delayed till the eighth day, et cetera! Now we admit that this famous council did decide in favor of the baptism of new born babes; but what else did they decide? A certain bishop named Rogatian complained to this council, of the disobedience of one of his Deacons, and they decided, that "Deacons ought to recollect that the Lord Jesus himself elected Apostles, that is, bishops; but as to Deacons, they were instituted after the death of Jesus only by his Apostles. This Deacon ought therefore, to repent, and give the bishop full satisfaction; and if not, he ought to be excommunicated. If others encourage and imitate him, they ought to be treated in the same manner. Farewell, brother."

Another case which came before the council for their learned action, was the case of a certain "Christian man," or bishop it would seem, who had died leaving his "brother Geminius Faustinus, a preaching elder, executor of his will, and guardian of his children. This was a heinous crime in the eyes of the Fathers. For a man to presume to employ the Clergy in secular affairs, when God had appointed them as the tribe of Levi, to exercise themselves in divine things, and commanded all men to cultivate the earth and follow business, and to support the Lord's priests with the *tenth* of their labors, was a great crime and dangerous precedent. It was ordered that the dead man's name should be struck out of the diptychs: and that such as in future should imitate his example, and employ the Clergy to do any secular business, should be excommunicated." "Benedict's Robinson."

Such was Dr. Pressly's famous council of Carthage, which, with Cyprian at its head, in the year of our Lord 257, decided in favor of the baptism of new born babes! Now the amount of importance which should be attached to that decision, we leave our readers to judge for themselves.

Now we need not examine all the Dr.'s witnesses, as it is universally admitted, so far as we know, that some portions of the church practiced, infant baptism, (not Sprinkling nor pouring,) in the third, and succeeding centuries: but we affirm that it was an innovation upon "the faith once delivered to the saints;" and the practice of the Apostles.— Along with infant baptism, in the third century, was also introduced the unscriptural practice if having *sponsors,* to answer for infants, and afterward *god-fathers,* and *god-mothers:* this seems to have been designed to supply the place of faith in the subject; the necessity of which seems to have been universally felt.

But perhaps the curious reader is anxious to know something of the origin of infant baptism: to gratify him therefore we will give him an answer which we find already prepared to our hand; it is as follows, to wit: "Infant baptism very naturally grew out of the doctrines which obtained even among the most orthodox. To support and illustrate this, I have only to attend to the testimonies which are introduced from the fathers, to prove infant baptism. The proposition which is necessary to be established, may be stated as follows, viz: "*That it was the belief of the orthodox, that baptism washed away all the guilt of the subject, whether imputed, or contracted by actual transgression.*" This opinion constrained Tertullian to admit the baptism of infants, to use his own words, "in cases of urgent necessity," though he opposed the common and universal baptism of infants. These cases of urgent necessity were those which threatened the immediate death of the minor or infant; and, in order to wash away its guilt previous to death, Tertullian and others, his immediate successors, admitted them to baptism." * * * * "Origen the most famous of the Fathers, for the multiplicity and variety of his works, flourished from the year 215 to 252. His views of infant baptism, and of the use of baptism, may be seen in the following quotation:— "None is free from pollution, though his life be but the length of a day upon the earth, and it is for that reason *because, by the sacrament of baptism, the pollutions of our birth are taken away,* that infants are baptized." But perhaps we have said enough upon this point, for the present.— This closes the Dr.'s third lecture. In our next we shall commence our review of the 4th and last lecture, which is devoted to the "proper mode," or action of baptism. J. M. M., Ed.

INDIANA UNIVERSITY.

YES, reader, there is really such an institution as the Indiana University: it is located in the town of Bloomington, Monroe County, Indiana. We are thus particular, because to our own knowledge, many persons in the State know but little about the Institution, or its location. Indeed we have conversed with some persons not fifty miles from Bloomington, who seemed to be astonished to learn that there was a University here in successful operation. Almost any person in the State can tell you of the "Hanover College," under the patronage of the Old School Presbyterians; of the "Wabash College," at Crawfordsville, under the control of the New School party; of the "Indiana Asbury University," at Greencastle, under the patronage and control of the Episcopal Methodist Church; of the "Baptist Manual Labor Institute," at Franklin; while comparatively very few seem to know much about the State University at this place. It is true, many have heard, that there is an institution of learning here, but seem to know nothing of its character. Some speak of it as a "Seminary." Now whether this general ignorance has been produced by the negligence of the great mass of the people, in reading the public reports, which have been made concerning this institution, from time to time, and widely circulated; or whether it is owing to the zeal with which the agents of those denominational institutions, have discharged their duty in soliciting public favor for their respective institutions, while it was their interest, to say as little as possible about the State University; or whether it is to be attributed to the apathy of the friends of the University, We say whether any one, or all of these causes is to be charged with the result, we shall not now inquire, but simply proceed to speak for ourself.

The Indiana University is not a sectarian establishment; but is purely a State institution; entirely under the control of the State. The teachers of any particular denomination are forbidden by the charter, to be taught in the University. Its location is a good one, as Bloomington is situated on the high lands, between the two White Rivers, in a well-watered, rolling country. The health of this village, we suppose, is not surpassed by that of any other town in the Western country. It is near enough the center of the State, to make it convenient for students in every part of the State. It is not more than forty miles from Columbus, near which the Railroad now terminates; so that students from a distance, East, West, and South, could come by water to Madison, thence on the cars to Columbus; from which point they could be brought to Bloomington by stage.

The University was never, we believe, in a more prosperous condition than it is at present. The winter session has just closed, during which some 120 students were in attendance, as we are informed.

We were prevented, by other pressing engagements, from attending the examinations of the classes; but we understand that they were highly creditable to themselves, and their preceptors. We had the pleasure of attending on the evening of the 25th ult., a public exhibition of one of the societies in the University. Four young men delivered addresses on the occasion, to a large audience, to wit, 1: Mr. J. A. Millen; 2: Mr. W. S. McBride; 3: Mr. S. N. Martin; 4: Mr. W. E. Simpson. Popular Excitements, Spirit of Adventure, Independence of Mind, and Islamism, were the themes chosen by these young gentlemen. We do not wish to flatter them, but we must be permitted to say, that we were highly pleased with their performances: they certainly did honor to themselves and their teachers. We were particularly delighted with the many happy allusions which were made by the speakers, to the subject of revealed religion; each of them seemed to be under the influence of the true Protestant spirit, and each in his turn, hurled a thunderbolt at his Holiness of Rome, and bid defiance to his power. But enough of this.

The University has a faculty not surpassed, we suppose, by any west of the mountains. A. WYLIE, D. D., is President, and is, we believe, acknowledged to be one of the ablest men, and ripest scholars of the age. There is now a "Law Department," over which Judge D. McDONALD presides, which bids fair to become very popular. The government of the institution is mild, being conducted as far as possible upon parental principles.

Tuition fee is $8.50 pr. session, in any of the classes. There are two Sessions of five months each during the year; the first begins the 1st Monday in November, and ends the last Wednesday in March; the second begins the 1st Monday in May, and ends the last Wednesday in September. Boarding can be had very low, in good families, or at hoarding-houses, as the student may desire.

There is another fact that we wish to mention before we close this notice, and that is this: *Every County in the Slate is authorized to send two students to the Indiana University without paying any tuition fee!* If every county would avail itself of this privilege, the number of students would be greatly increased. We therefore say to our friends in every part of the State, apply to your county boards, and get certificates and come on, by the first Monday in May next; so that the number of students, the next session, may be double what it was last. Again, we say, look to your own interests, and COME ON! J. M. M., Ed.

INDIANAPOLIS, March 24th, 1844.

Brother Mathes: In the 7th No. of the "Record," I observed a letter, "from the Christian Journal;" written by Mr. Paxton, in which he undertakes to give certain reasons for believing "that immersion was not used on the day of Pentecost." If Mr. Paxton had not made a tour to the Holy Land, and written "Letters on Palestine," I might conclude to let him pass without further notice; but the simple fact that he is an *"oriental traveler,"* gives his reasons a weight in the estimation of the uninformed, that makes it necessary for some one to attend to them.

As soon as I read Mr. Paxton's letter, it occurred to me, that Professor Robinson of New York, arrived in Jerusalem but a few days before Mr. Paxton, and that things must therefore have presented about the same phase to the two travelers. I immediately referred to Robinson's "Biblical Researches in Palestine," and found several items in relation to the matter in hand, which, I think, will serve to remove any wrong impressions, that may have been made, by the aforesaid letter.

Before I introduce the extracts from Professor Robinson, it may be well to inform the reader, who he is. I find, after his name, on the title page of his "Researches," the following: "Professor of Biblical literature in the Union Theological Seminary, New York; Author of a Greek and English Lexicon of the New Testament," and I will add, Author of a Journal of Travels in Egypt, the peninsula of Sinai, Arabia Petraea, and Palestine, "in the year 1838, undertaken in reference to Biblical Geography." This last, is the work from which I purpose making some extracts.

The Professor says: "Jerusalem lies in the midst of a rocky limestone region, throughout which, fountains and wells are comparatively rare. In the city itself, little if any living water is known; and in its immediate vicinity are only the three small fountains along the lower part of the valley of Jehoshaphat. Yet with all these disadvantages of its position, the Holy City would appear always to have had a *full supply* of water, for its inhabitants, both in ancient and modern times,—in every age the truth of Strabo's brief description has been manifest, 'Jerusalem, a rocky well enclosed fortress, within, WELL WATERED, without, wholly dry.'" Bib. Res., vol. 1, page 479. *Always a full supply of water!* within, *well-watered!* The above remarks of the Professor are also corroborated by Tacitus, whose testimony I will here introduce, not so much for the purpose of showing what Jerusalem now is, as what it then was. He says: "A perennial spring supplied the place with water. Subterraneous caverns were scooped under the rock.— The rain water was saved in pools and cisterns. It was foreseen by the founders of the city, that the manners and institutions of the nation, so refulgent to the rest of mankind; would be productive of frequent wars; hence so many preparations against a siege." Wardle's Ed. p. 503. The Professor refers us to this very passage in a note on the 445th page of the above-named vol. of his researches: where he is speaking of the "large reservoirs or cisterns, which are said to exist under the surface of the Haram;" and about which Mr. Paxton says: "There is a SMALL SUPPLY [not a *full supply*] of water brought into this city through pipes for the use of the Mosque of St. Omar which stands where the temple formerly stood. This water is brought from the pools of Solomon about 9 miles off. The Koran requires the Moslems to wash their hands and feet before they go into the mosque to pray." The Professor says: "The Muslim worship, with its many ablutions, requires, [not a *small* supply, but] an *abundant* supply in or near the mosques, and the construction of cisterns was here almost a matter of course." See page 445. He assures us on the

480th page "that the *immense cisterns, now* and *anciently* existing within the area of the temple, supplied partly from rain water, and partly by the aqueduct, these of themselves, in case of a siege, would furnish a tolerable supply," of water, for the besieged. What becomes of Mr. Paxton's reasons, for believing that immersion was not used on the day of Pentecost? they vanish, when brought to the light of Prof. Robinson's researches. But I have a few more extracts. We shall leave the area of the temple now, and look around the private residences of the Holy City; and see if the JUG-like cisterns to which Mr. Paxton refers his reader, will afford a reason against immersion. The reader must be careful to observe, that the *small quantity* of water in the city, is Mr. Paxton's reason for concluding against immersion. But in the meantime, he informs his reader, that the cisterns are made in the shape of large JUGS. (!) and even if there was an abundance of water, it would be as inconvenient to immerse in these tanks, as it would be in our wells. So, when he finds water enough, he immediately hints that it is inaccessible.

The Professor says, page 480, "Almost every private house in Jerusalem, of any size, is understood to have at least one or more cisterns, excavated in the soft limestone rock on which the city is built. The house of Mr. Lennean in which we resided, had no less than four cisterns, and as these are but a specimen of the manner in which the better class of houses are supplied, I subjoin here the dimensions. No. 1, 15 ft. long, 8 ft. wide, 12 ft. deep: No. 2, 8 long, 4 ft. wide, 15 ft. deep: No. 3, 10 ft. long, 10 ft. wide, 15 ft. deep: No. 4, 30 ft. long, 30 ft. wide, 30 ft. deep." These are capacious jugs, truly. But hear the Prof, on the 481st page: "The Latin convent in particular is said to be amply furnished; and in seasons of drought is able to deal a sufficiency," of water, "for all the Christian inhabitants of the city." According to Scholz it has 28 of these cisterns: "Most of these cisterns have undoubtedly come down from ancient times, and their *immense extent* furnishes a full solution of the question as to the supply of water for the city."— And I add, in connexion with the pools without and within the city, furnish a full solution of all the difficulties that can be started by any aspersionist against immersion. And the Professor further observes, that "this trait is not peculiar to the Holy City, for the case is the same throughout all the hill country of Judea and Benjamin." Why did not Mr. Paxton notice these facts, and give them a place among his reasons, against the probable use of immersion on the day of Pentecost?

"The inhabitants collect water during the rainy season in tanks and cisterns in the cities, in the fields, and along the high roads, for the sustenance of themselves and of their flocks and herds, and for the comfort of the passing traveler." Page 481. Mr. Paxton says there is, that he knows of, but one well in the vicinity of the City—Mr. Robinson tells us there are three. The well of Nehemiah, the En-Rogel, of Scriptures, a well by the Damascus gate, and one just by the tomb of the Kings.

I shall in my next, give an account of the large open reservoirs for public use. They are all fully described by the Professor.

L. H. JAMESON.

From the Christian Journal.

BRO. FERGUSON: In accordance with the wishes of many of my brethren, I herewith forward you, for publication, a brief statement of the reasons which induced me, a few months ago, to leave the ranks of Paido-baptism, and embrace the Scriptural, and more rational doctrine of the baptism of believers "for the remission of sins."

It may not be amiss, to preface these reasons with some remarks on my early education and religious associations, together with a brief notice of some of the most important incidents in my history while connected with the Lutheran Church. This will the better prepare the reader to appreciate the motives which induced me to change my position on the subject of baptism; and serve, moreover, to correct a number of unauthorized reports, and reckless misrepresentations, which have been fabricated by the enemies of truth, and industriously circulated by the blinded devotees of Sectarianism.

Be it known, then, first of all, in the elegant style of Paido-Baptists, I was regularly born, baptized and raised a *Presbyterian*. I have no doubt, but my parents sincerely thought that they were discharging a solemn Christian duty, when they had me christened according to the forms and customs of the Presbyterian church; and for their well-meant efforts, and pious intentions, I entertain for them emotions of the most unbounded gratitude. I need not tell them, nor any one else, that the sincerity with which an act is performed, is no proof, that the act is a scriptural one. That they, and all my old friends, may speedily embrace 'the gospel of the grace of God,' in all its primitive simplicity, loveliness, and power, is my daily and most fervent prayer.

About 12 years ago, I voluntarily connected myself with the Lutheran Church, under the pastoral care of the Rev. J. Z. Senderling, on a profession of faith, and what I was then taught to regard, as proper evidences of conversion. So, you perceive, I commenced my career of apostatizing twelve years ago. And what was worse, my first step was the abandonment of the church of my Fathers, in which I drew my first breath, and received all my early religious impressions and education, and of which I was made a member, without my consent or knowledge, myriads of ages before the constitution of the mundane system, if the tenets of the old paternal church are to be accredited. I applied to the Lutheran church for admission, or rather, was invited by some of her zealous sons, to become one of her members. What disposition should she have made of my case? Judging from the spirit, tone and temper of one of her leading men, as displayed in an effervescent article on the subject of what he is pleased to call my 'apostasy from the Lutheran church,' and published in the Lutheran Observer, she should have frowned most indignantly on this proselyting conduct of some of her sons: She should have rebuked in tones, as solemn as the grave, this first indication of a vacillating disposition, on the part of a wayward youth. And to have given convincing, substantial proof of her 'holy abhorrence' of sectarian apostasy, she should have refused me admission to her communion most absolutely. But what did she do? Why, she flung wide her willing arms to embrace me and a few others at the same time. Nor was her pleasure any the less, because we were *apostates,* nor yet, because we preferred the Lutheran to the Methodist church; which, by the way, had as good a claim upon us as the former, and better, as far as our 'getting through' was concerned. And by way of comment on her 'holy abhorrence' of the unpardonable sin of sectarian, apostasy, her Pastor and leading members advised me to study for the Ministry! At length, yielding to their advice, I commenced a course of studies, in order to qualify myself for that office. Having spent about eight years in the prosecution of my Academical, Collegiate and Theological studies, during which time I received many unasked for, yet gratifying evidences of their confidence and esteem, I received according to the custom of the church, a letter of License from the President of the Maryland Synod, recommending me most cordially to the Lutheran community, and authorizing me to perform all ministerial acts, the same as an ordained minister. A similar letter was given me, by the Synod of the West, convened at Knightstown, Ind., Oct. 1842, and renewed by the same Synod, according to its custom, at its last meeting, held at Hopeful Church, Boon county, Ky., Oct. 1843, a few weeks only before my baptism. During my entire connection with the Lutheran Church, I was regarded and treated as worthy of the most implicit confidence of the brethren, so far as I knew. I say this not boastingly, but because an effort of late has been made, to create the impression, that I have always been regarded as a vacillating youth?

I preached under a Synodical License about one year and a half, and if my former friends are not satisfied with that labor as an offset to their favors and kindness, I now pledge myself to labor as much longer in any Lutheran congregation that may be selected, after my present engagements shall have been met; and if that is not enough, I will double the time.

The brethren, and the world generally, have already been informed of my baptism during the progress of the late debate at Lexington.

It should be remembered, however, that this did not take place, until several days after the first four propositions, embracing all that referred to baptism, had been disposed of.

It was the most deliberate, well advised, conscientious and solemn act of my life. One, the reminiscence of which is the sweetest, and the feelings produced by it, the most delightful, that I have ever experienced. True, my motives were then, and have since been, impugned, by persons, whose knowledge of me as so limited as to render any expression of opinion on the subject highly immodest on their part, not to say entirely unauthorized and reckless. I nevertheless rejoice in the sweet consciousness of having acted promptly and fearlessly, in the obedience to the highest sense of Christian propriety and responsibility, and the clearest convictions of duty.

Nor is this consolation at all abated, by the reflection, that after spending nearly three months in the most ardent and untiring search after some charge that might be preferred against my private character, to tarnish my name and destroy my usefulness—or rather, to destroy my influence among the old brotherhood, my enemies have been driven to the humiliating expedient of 'inferring' from their own fictitious premises, that my motives must have been sinister, and that I am, at all events, a little 'self-complaisant.' This appears to be the burthen of the article already referred to. Indeed, this is the common resort of all sectaries when placed in similar circumstances. Failing to find clear proof of what they would like to say, and not being able to adduce substantial evidence even, they dexterously fall back upon their well improved and almost magic powers of 'infering."

I have often been asked what my sentiments and feelings were, on my arrival at Lexington, before the debate commenced. To this inquiry I would reply, that I was not altogether a stranger to the subject at the time alluded to. I had read a great deal on the side of sprinkling and Paido-baptism, but not a dozen pages of any work on the opposite side—had not witnessed immersion more than 3 or 4 times. There was a time when it would have been difficult for me to admit the validity of immersion. For two or three years I had admitted its validity, but gave sprinkling and pouring the preference, on the ground of convenience. I could have sprinkled, poured, or immersed, with a good conscience on the day of the debate. I then stood in sentiment, where thousands of the various sects now stand, equally poised between what is sometimes called the 'three modes of baptism, as far as scriptural authority is concerned, but giving the preference to sprinkling and pouring; and if I was in advance of any of them in disposition to allow the applicant to choose his own mode, it must be attributable to my want of a gum-elastic conscience, which is so serviceable to them.

On the subject of Infant baptism, I never thought much before the winter of '42—3. At the meeting of the Synod of the West, (1842,) before alluded to, the subject of baptism was made the special business for a certain evening. It was then debated by every member of Synod in his turn. All seemed to be agreed in their opposition to immersion, but on the subject of Infant baptism, scarcely any two persons were agreed. One would require faith of the parents who offered the child; another would not be particular about the faith of the parents, provided their morals were good; another would overlook a little immorality if they were not entirely skeptical; a fourth would baptize the child if the parents were atheists; and a fifth said he would baptize a child if the Devil himself should offer it. If he had faith, that was sufficient. You may judge of my surprise, when, for the first time, I heard these matters thus treated, and ascertained that so many different views were held by the members of the same Synod, and such contradictory views too! I then resolved to examine the subject for myself. I did examine it some during the following year, but as my reading was all on one side, I could not, in my conscience, give up infant baptism. That I met with difficulties, I am frank to avow; but then, thought I, what subject has no difficulties? I could have sprinkled a child the day before the debate commenced, with a good conscience. All my early education and associations were placed in the scale with Paido-baptism, during the debate. I went there willing to ascertain the truth. I was a little prejudiced against Bro. Campbell, and more than a little against the Reformation. I listened with candor and attention. After the whole ground had been gone over, I was satisfied that nothing but immersion was Scriptural, and that Paido-baptism could not be defended from the Scriptures. I felt deeply interested in the whole matter. If Mr. Rice could have met all Bro. C.'s arguments satisfactorily to my mind, and have sustained his own propositions, he would have received my warmest thanks. He failed, however, in my estimation, completely failed in both. If I know my own heart, I have acted sincerely, candidly, conscientiously and intelligently. I have not the least unkind feeling for any person living. My old friends may persecute me, *if* they are disposed to, but I cannot retaliate. Christ is my pattern in that as well as every thing else.

I cannot cease to love my Lutheran friends still. They have my warmest thanks for all the favors they ever bestowed upon me. To do them good—to teach the Christian religion, both by precept and example, is my ardent purpose; I can throw my arms of charity and sympathy around them all, and beg them to, receive the truth in its simplicity. That we may be sanctified through the truth, and inherit eternal life, is the devout prayer of your brother, in the hope of a blissful immortality.
WM. R. McCHESNEY.
Louisville, Ky.

CHRISTIAN OBLIGATIONS—NO. 6.

IN our last we spoke of the importance of meeting together, for the purpose of commemorating the Lord's death. And as we cannot commemorate the Lord's death without meeting together, the importance of meeting together stands immediately connected with the grand design of the commemoration of one of the most important facts that ever transpired in the universe of God. With this view of the subject, shall we be indifferent about meeting together on the first day of the week, for the purpose of showing our faith in a crucified and risen Saviour? — which he has commanded us to do until he comes again. A willful neglect of any of the ordinances of the Lord's house is nothing less than to tread the new and everlasting covenant under our feet. The apostle says, "Having therefore, brethren, boldness to enter into the holiest by the blood of Jesus, by a new and living way which he hath consecrated for us, through the vail, that is to say, his flesh; and *having* a High Priest over the house of God; let us draw near with a true heart in full assurance of faith, having our hearts sprinkled from an evil conscience and our bodies washed with pure water. Let us hold fast the profession of our faith without wavering, (for he is faithful who hath promised,) and let us consider one another to provoke unto love, and to good works, not forsaking the assembling of ourselves together, as the manner of some is; but exhorting one another, and so much the more, as ye *see* the day approaching. For if we sin willfully after that we have received the knowledge of the truth, there remains no more sacrifice for sin, but a certain fearful looking for of judgment, and fiery indignation, which shall devour the adversaries." Who are those for whom there remains no more sacrifice for sin? Those who sin *willfully* after they have received the knowledge of the truth! and who are those who "sin willfully?" Evidently those who "neglect the assembling of themselves together." Now there is a material difference between neglecting to assemble ourselves together, and being hindered from so doing, if we do not hinder ourselves by willfully placing ourselves under circumstances that are calculated to hinder us. The TRUE disciple of Jesus Christ, on the altar of whose heart burns the fervency of pure devotion, when the first of the week rolls round, delights to take a respite from the busy cares of life, and hasten away to the house of God, and there, with kindred spirits, lisp the praise of him who died for us and rose again. He remembers that he is not his own, but that he is bought with the price of blood, even the blood of the Son of God, which flows through every vein of the New and everlasting covenant. Every commandment which the Lord has enjoined upon us by the mouths of his holy apostles, may be regarded as a vein of the body, which is his church, through which the benefits of that blood is conveyed which was so freely shed on Mount Calvary for the remission of our sins; and if we disregard the Lord's commandments, we shut up the avenue which gives to us the life-giving energy of the blood of Christ as a member of his body. The apostle John says, "If *we* say we have fellowship with him and walk in darkness, we lie and do not the truth." "But if we walk in the light, as he is in the light, we have fellowship, one with another, and the blood of his Son Jesus Christ cleanseth from all sin." 1 John 1: 6 & 7.

This plainly teaches us how the benefits of the blood of Christ are conveyed to us—by walking in the light,—and what else is it to walk in the light, but to obey the Lord's commandments? for they are the path-way from earth to heaven, that is made plain, by "the light of the knowledge of the glory of God, that shines in the face of Jesus Christ." This light is of advantage to us, individually, only, when we walk in it. Individuals sometimes conclude that the Lord's business can be conducted, on the first day of the week without them, and hence they conclude to stay at home. It is true, the worship of God might be conducted in an acceptable manner without my participation, but if without my participation, it will also be *without* any benefit to me. The Church is composed of individuals, members, and if I as a member of the body of Christ, fail to meet at the Lord's house on the first day of the week, I am just as guilty, as if the whole Church should fail to meet. It seems to me, that some Protestants, in order to be consistent, ought to adopt the sentiments of Costerus, a Jesuit, who says: "The Church loseth not the name Holy, as long as there is but one who is truly holy." If we believe that the sanctity of a few will secure the salvation of all whose names are enrolled on the church-book, or that the drinking of the wine by the "Priest," will benefit the laity, then, we might, with some degree of propriety, stay at home on the first day of the week, and excuse ourselves by saying, "The Lord will be acceptably worshipped without me." But when we hear the Apostle say, that "every man shall receive his own reward according to his own labor," it becomes indispensably necessary that we worship the Lord for ourselves, and then "shall we have rejoicing in ourselves and not in another." It is true, we cannot tell the hearts of men, and always know who worships God acceptably, but when a brother is in the habit of neglecting to assemble with the Lord's people on the first day, he gives sufficient evidence that he does not love the Lord with all his heart, and if so, what he does do is not acceptable with God, "for the Lord abhors the sacrifice where the heart is not found." Such professed Christians are like the Jews who "offered the blind and the lame in sacrifice;" and the Lord said to them, "is it not evil!" "You have robbed me in tithes and offerings;" and because they did not worship God according to his directions, he says of them, "I have no pleasure in you," saith the Lord of hosts, "neither will I accept an offering at your hand." If the Lord rejected the sacrifice of the Jews entirely, because they did not offer it according to the Law, will he not also reject the *sacrifice* of that Christian who attempts to accommodate the worship of God to his own convenience? He certainly will. The Saviour says: "Every branch in me that beareth not fruit he (the Father) taketh away;" and if every individual, who is a branch in the vine that does not bear fruit is taken away by the *Father,* he is not worthy of a standing in the Church, for if God has excluded him, of course, he does not design his name to be enrolled among the members of "the Church of the living God."

We will pursue the subject farther in our next.

T. J. EDMONDSON.

WASHINGTON, Ind., March 25th, 1844.

Dear Brother Mathes: It is due to you, as well as to ourselves, that you should know, that there is a report in circulation which is calculated to do you a serious injury as a proclaimer of the Gospel of our Lord and Saviour Jesus Christ.

A respectable member of the Baptist church of this place, says that whilst at Bedford last fall, he heard that Eld. J. M. Mathes raised a report injurious to the character of a Baptist preacher of the following character:—"That one Mr. Arnold, a Baptist preacher, had acted so imprudently, by running his congregation so deeply in debt to the merchants, that it came very near breaking up his congregation—you were called upon for your author; you gave his name; they then called on your author, who told them he never had any conversation with you on the subject. They called on you a second time for an author; you gave them a second name, and upon their conversing with him, he denied that he ever *heard* any thing about it. They called on you a third time, and demanded your author, but you turned your back to them and walked off." This is substantially what was related to us by our Baptist friend, who, we are informed, related the same last Lord's day evening, publicly, at a prayer meeting in the county, about two miles from this place. Very respectfully, your brethren in the Lord,

ENOCH DAVIS,   GEORGE A. WALLER.

P. S. Since this was written, we had another interview with our informant, who says that in addition to what you said of Mr. Arnold above, you said also that he defrauded a man in a horse or wagon trade, and the witnesses referred to, were in relation to this fraud, and not to running the congregation in debt—but so far as his conduct in running the congregation in debt is concerned, Mr. Arnold has procured a satisfactory settlement, by the procurement of certificates.

E. D.
G. A. W.

REPLY.

Dear Brethren Davis and Waller: You have laid me under particular obligations, by thus notifying me of the report, which your "baptist friend" has been circulating to my injury. I very much regret the necessity under which I am laid, from the publicity which this report seems to have attained, to publish your letter in the Christian Record, together with such remarks as seem to be necessary, in order to set your "baptist friend" right.

But believing it to be a duty, which I owe to the Church, to my family, and to myself as a man, a Christian, and as a public teacher of Christianity, to vindicate my character, I have concluded to make a plain statement of the facts in the case, which will correct the misstatements of your "friend." (!) But to the point.

It is *not true,* that I ever "raised a report" on Eld. B. B. Arnold, or any other man. But it is true, that some time in January or February, 1842, Mr. Jacob Piercy of Putnam county, told me, that it was reported in that section of the country, that the church (Baptist) at Belville, which had some time before employed Mr. Arnold to labor for them, had given him liberty to take up some goods upon her credit, indefinite as to amount; and also, that Mr. Arnold had *abused* that privilege. As to "breaking up his congregation," I never heard of it until *I* saw it in your letter! Well, Mr. Arnold left Belville, and removed to Stilesville, and labored awhile, if I am not mistaken, as a "home missionary." And it was publicly reported, through the country, that Mr. Arnold, some time after he settled in Stilesville, had taken the advantage of the necessities of a traveler, in a "wagon swap," in which it was said, that the traveler was worsted some 40, or 50 dollars.

I said nothing about it to any one that I recollect of, until May, 1842. When being in company with some two or three brethren, the conversation turned upon the operations of the Baptists, and among other names that of Mr. B. B. Arnold was introduced. These brethren were well acquainted with Mr. Arnold, by character at least, and made some enquiries concerning him; I told them that I had *heard* these reports, but knew nothing about their truth. But whether true or false, they were calculated to injure Mr. Arnold as a preacher. I said nothing more about the matter. But some time after, (July perhaps,) Mr. Arnold came into the neighborhood where these brethren lived, and held a meeting of some days. One of the brethren with whom I had the conversation, had told it to another, and so on till it was told Mr. Arnold. He denied the whole matter most positively, but he did me the justice, to tell his audience at the same time, "that he had known me from a boy, and that he *knew I would not manufacture a report.*" When I heard that Mr. Arnold denied the truth of the reports, I sent up to Belville, and Stilesville, to ascertain the truth of the matter: concerning the goods matter, I received no very definite information. As to the wagon swap, several certificates were forwarded me, which, to say the least of them, proved that there was such a report.

I availed myself of the opportunity of seeing Eld. Arnold, before the people of the same neighborhood, which occurred on Tuesday after the 4th Lord's day in August, 1842, if I recollect right, at the house of Mr. Wilson Coffey, near where the Baptists were then holding a protracted meeting. Several Baptist preachers, and quite a number of persons were present, and heard our conversation, which was public. I told Mr. Arnold, that I had come to see him and the friends there, that we might talk the matter over, and understand one another: that I did not know that there existed any difficulty between him and myself; but I was informed that some of his friends had at least intimated that I had had some agency in "raising the report," and I wished to exonerate myself from the charge. I told them that Mr. Piercy was my author for what I said about his taking up goods upon the credit of the church at Belville; and that I had certificates to prove the existence of the report concerning the wagon swap; I told them, that as to the facts I knew nothing about them myself, and that I did not appear as Mr. Arnold's prosecutor, as I considered that a matter for his brethren to attend to: but merely wished to set myself right before my baptist friends, by proving that I had no agency in getting up the reports, and that the reports existed.

Mr. Arnold did, then and there, publicly say, that he "never had charged me with having 'raised the report,' as he had no doubt but I had *heard* all that I had *said.*" But he *thought* I had done wrong in telling it, as he supposed I designed to injure him. I then proposed to Mr. Arnold, that the whole matter should be left to a disinterested committee of our fellow citizens, who should examine into the reports, and my conduct, and make a written report, which should be published in the "Banner and Pioneer," and the "Millennial Harbinger," as a final settlement of the whole difficulty. This proposition, however, was not accepted. Mr. Arnold then pledged himself to prove himself clear of what the report charged him, on the following Sunday evening; which give him time to send to Belville and Stilesville for certificates. He requested me to attend, but I told him that I could not, owing to a previous arrangement to attend the yearly meeting at Milcreek, Washington county. But said I, "it is not necessary that I should; you have exonerated me from the charge of having "raised the report:" this is all I am concerned about." I told him, that I was *willing,* nay, that I should rejoice, if he could prove himself clear to my satisfaction, I then stated, "if there was one person in the audience who thought I had exercised an agency in getting up the report, I would further prove my innocence;" but all remained silent; I then took it for granted, that all were satisfied, so far as that matter was concerned.

I am also informed, that at the time appointed, Mr. Arnold did read, or have read, a number of certificates, for the purpose of showing his brethren his innocence, and how far he succeeded, I know not; but I am informed by a Baptist friend, who now sits by me, and who was present at the time alluded to above, that Mr. Arnold satisfied his brethren, and one of the men to whom I had mentioned the matter, expressed himself satisfied. And so, the matter has rested ever since, and I will do Mr. Arnold the justice to say, that I do not *know* that he has said a hard word of me since.

But to return to your letter. It is not true, that *any man* to whom I referred, refused to bear me out, but it is true, that Mr. Piercy rode some twenty-five miles, unsolicited by me, to the ground of contention, a few days after, and publicly told the people that he was my author; he also left a certificate on the ground, stating that he had told me just what I had told these brethren. He also obtained a certificate from his author. This had reference to the goods. And as to the wagon trade, one of the certificates which Mr. Arnold produced himself, proved the existence of the report, long before I said any thing about it, for it bears date March 8, 1842, near six months before it was read in testimony at the time above mentioned: it proves therefore, that the report was *then* in circulation. But this whole story of my authors denying they ever told me any thing about it, and my *"turning my back on them and walking off,"* is a sheer fabrication! Your "baptist friend" has evidently suffered himself to be imposed upon by some unfortunate being, and as an honest man, who wishes to "do unto all men as he would have them do to him," he will go to the public prayer meeting again, and take back what he said.

A copy of this will be sent to the "Baptist friend," and also to Mr. Arnold, for his inspection; and I am sure he will acknowledge the truth of what I have said. If he does, he will remain silent; and if he denies what I have said, I will then prove it beyond the possibility of a doubt. Your brother in the glorious hope,

J. M. MATHES.

Harrison County, Ind., Feb. 4th, 1844.

Dear Brother Mathes: Do the Scriptures teach us to baptize in the name of the Father, Son, and Holy Ghost, as Matthew records it: or in the name of the Lord Jesus, as recorded in the Acts of Apostles? Please answer through the Christian Record.

Your brother in the Lord, SAUL W. OTT.

ANSWER.

Brother Ott—Your query is one of much importance, and the difficulties which it seems to present, have been felt by many. I suppose, my brother's question refers to the ceremony to be used at the time of administering the ordinance. Jesus says, "Baptizing them in (rather *into*) the name of the Father, an of the Son, and of the Holy Ghost." Matt. 28: 19. Luke records the baptism of the house of Cornelius thus: "And be commanded them to be baptized in the name of the Lord." Acts 10: 48. Again, speaking of the re-baptism of the twelve brethren at Ephesus, whom Paul found and instructed, Luke says, "And when they heard this, they were baptized in the name of the Lord Jesus." Acts 19: 5. Paul teaches the Colossian brethren thus: "And whatsoever ye do, in word or deed, do all in the name of the Lord Jesus, giving thanks to God and the Father by him." Col. 3: 17.

"In the name of the Lord Jesus," and "by the authority of the Lord Jesus," are two forms of expression which convey the very same idea. Well, as Jesus Christ is head over all things to the church, High Priest of the Temple of God, and Lord of all, whatever is done by his body, which is the church, must be done in his name, or which is the same thing, by his authority. Whatever he has authorized, can be done in his name, and nothing else can be done in his name. For example: he has authorized us in his word, to preach, to exhort, to pray, to sing, to meet together; to show his death till he come, to visit the sick, to feed the hungry, to take care of widows and orphans in their afflictions, to baptize believers, &c., &c. Well then, all these things can be done in his name. But he has not authorized us to make laws for the government of the church; therefore, we could not do this in his name. Neither has he authorized us to invite penitents to the "mourners' bench," to "get religion;" therefore we cannot do this in his name. Now as to the baptism of the centurion and his house, I would remark, that Peter issued the command, "in the name of the Lord," and their baptism was performed "in the name of the Lord." But I think there is no evidence, that this was the ceremony used in the act of baptism.

In the great commission, as recorded by Matt., the preposition in the original, is "*eis,*" the primary signification of which is "*into,*" and many learned Commentators have so rendered it. In our common version we have it rendered "in." In Acts 10: 48, the original preposition is "*en,*" and corresponds in meaning with our preposition "*in.*" And in Acts 19: 5, the preposition is the same as in the commission. These twelve brethren it seems, had been baptized into an acknowledgment of John's authority, but when they were more fully instructed into the nature and design of John's Mission, and that of Christ, they were baptized into an acknowledgement of the authority of the Lord Jesus.

From all of which, we have come to the following conclusion, viz: that every one who is baptized scripturally, is baptized *in the name* of the Lord Jesus, (i. e. by his authority,) and *"into the name* of the Father, and of the Son, and of the Holy Ghost." Thus acknowledging Jesus Christ as the Supreme Lawgiver, and head of the Church: into the name of the Father, as the fountain of all authority and power; into the name of the Son, as the only Saviour; and into the name of the Holy Ghost, as the sanctifier, and comforter of the children of God.

Yours in the blessed hope   J. M. M., Ed.

OWEN COUNTY, Ind., April, 1844.

Brother Mathes: As we contend that faith precedes repentance, in the Gospel scheme, and as there are many, no doubt honest in their views, who maintain that repentance is antecedent to faith, and for proof refer to Matthew, 21st chap., 32d v.; Mark 1st chap., 15th v.; Acts 20th chap., 21st v. Therefore, could you favor the readers of the Record with an essay on these passages, it might be instructive to many, and to none more than your humble servant.

J. G. STEVENSON.

ANSWER.

My dear brother Stevenson: The first text to which you refer me, is Matt. 21: 32, and reads as follows, to wit: "For John came unto you in the way of righteousness, and ye believed him not; but the publicans and the harlots believed him: and ye, when ye had seen it, repented not afterward, that ye might believe him." The word which is here translated *repent,* occurs but seldom in the original scriptures, and signifies *to change one's mind,* or *purpose, to concern one's self.* The same word occurs in the 29th V. of the same chap.—"He repented and went." That is, he *changed his purpose,* and went. Again, we have the same word in Heb. 7: 21, "The Lord sware and will not *repent:*" that is, will not *change his purpose.* Find the same word again, Matt. 27: 3. Here Judas is said to have "*repented himself,*" changed his mind, or purpose.

We will now return to your proof text, (32.) Jesus is here addressing a set of hard-hearted Jews, who had heard the preaching of John, and who yet remained unbelieving. They had purposed in their hearts and minds, that they would not believe on Christ, and therefore they shut out from their minds every ray of light, refused to examine the testimony, and attributed his miracles to the power of Beelzebub the prince of Devils. And when they saw Publicans and harlots receiving him, they did not then change their minds, that they might believe on him. While their minds were bolted and bared, by strong prejudice, and a fixed purpose to oppose him, truth could not find access to their minds—but if they had changed their minds, upon this subject, then the truth could have found access to their hearts and minds, and then they "might have believed." In fact, *we* very seldom use the term "repent," in the sense in which it is used in this text. We generally use it in the sense of sorrow for sin, and reformation of life.— Now in this sense, Repentance never can exist anterior to faith, but must, in the nature of things, grow out of, and follow after faith. This text therefore, proves nothing in favor of the dogma, in whose support it is sometimes introduced.

The next text you refer me to, is Mark 1: 15, "And saying, the time is fulfilled, the Kingdom of God is at hand, repent ye and believe the Gospel." This was what Jesus preached to the Jews, immediately after John was cast into prison. Repent, in this text, comes from a different word in the original, and by many good critics, is translated "Reform." The Jews had sinned against God, and become exceedingly wicked; but they are here called upon to reform their lives; that is, to cease their rebellion against the Most-High; that they might be prepared to receive Jesus as the long promised Messiah. Such language is never used in reference to the Gentiles, but always to those who believed in the true God.

The next and only, passage to which you refer, is found Acts 20: 21; "Testifying both to Jews and Greeks, repentance toward God, and faith toward our Lord Jesus Christ." The word from which we have repentance, in this example, is the same as in the text examined, and is equivalent in meaning to Reform. Now to my mind, it is very plain, that Paul is here speaking of these matters, *practically,* and not *philosophically.* And as reformation of life was manifest, or seen, before faith, and was itself the evidence of the existence of faith in the heart: and as the Apostle is speaking of faith and reformation, in their *practical* manifestations, he places reformation first, as we see it first. But this affords no evidence, that Gospel repentance must precede faith: indeed, the very idea is absurd in the extreme. The belief of the truth is that which produces *penitence:* a nd I cannot conceive how an unbelieving heart could be made penitent! sorry on account of sins, committed against the honor, government, and name of a being in whom the rebel has no faith! It is contrary to the nature of things, and therefore *absurd,* and of course false.

With much affection I am your brother in Christ,

J. M. MATHES, Ed.

MR. W. TERRELL'S PAMPHLET.

After a lapse of three months or more, since the publication of Mr. Terrell's communication in the Christian Record, and our 'Strictures' upon it, Mr. Terrell has come out in a pamphlet of some 16 pages. Mr. T. begins by saying, "I feel it to be due to *truth,* and to my own character as a man, and as a Christian, to publish the following correspondence, and thereby fully expose, the injustice done me by Elder James M. Mathes, in his "Notes on a tour to Vincennes and Washington," and in his "Strictures" on a communication of mine, published in the August and November Nos. of the Christian Record, [a periodical, published at Bloomington, Ind.,] of which he is Editor."

Now it is not our design to write a *review* of this wonderful production, which its author has dignified with the imposing title "*Misrepresentations Corrected:* " we only design to notice some of its more prominent features, and take formal possession of an important concession or two, made by our friend.

And first of all, we would say, we find no fault with friend Terrell for publishing the correspondence between him and the Washington brethren; this he had a perfect right to do: but some of his comments and remarks, are calculated to mislead, and to them we object. Indeed, taking this pamphlet all in all, we *think* that Mr. Terrell was willing to make "a little capital, in a small way."

Mr. Terrell labors very hard to prove, that he did not agree to make good his statements, by the side of a Christian Preacher, on the 26th of July, (last.) On this point we just refer the reader to the two letters of the correspondence, published in the November No. of the Record. But what does Mr. T. prove by the remainder of the correspondence? Why he has proved what no one disputed, and what we conceded, in our 'Strictures,' namely, that some time previous to the 26th July, he wrote to brother Noyes and others, informing them, that it would not suit his convenience to attend to the discussion sooner than the 3rd of Oct. But we *thought* and still *think,* that Mr. Terrell ought to have stood up to the agreement in his first letter, and the very fact that he attempted to put off the time, is evidence of a disposition to decline it.

On 8th p. our friend quotes from our "Strictures," as follows: "The Methodist Discipline says, 9th Art., "That we are justified by faith only is a wholesome doctrine and very full of comfort." This doctrine of his own discipline was what our friend T. preached; well, this part of *his doctrine* had a bearing upon the Christian Church, for she maintains that *obedience,* as well as faith, is essential to our justification." Mr. Terrell, after attempting to gloss over the matter, and construe my language, remarks, "And I confidently expect Mr. Goodwin to shoulder the responsibility and come forward in the defense of his doctrine." Now the reader can see at once, that Mr. T. is not disposed to defend his own doctrine, as presented in his discourses in Washington: but he now "confidently expects that Mr. Goodwin will shoulder the responsibility, and come forward in the defense of his doctrine!" *Let the reader remember this!* Mr. Terrell confidently expects Mr. G. to come forward and affirm this item of his doctrine, to wit: *"That obedience as well as faith is essential to our justification."* But we shall see how this matter will terminate.

On 15th p. Mr. Terrell denies "the bitterness of spirit which I had ascribed to him." But we ask, how does this denial comport with the facts in the case? Take the following *precious fruits,* and ask your self, what sort of spirit they spring from? "Christian (Campbellite) church;" with which his pamphlet abounds. "Afflicted adherents of Campbellism," "Emptying of *meat troughs,*" "Aqueous regeneration," and many such expressions! But Mr. Terrell further says, "I love primitive Christianity; it is the Christianity for which I plead," &c. Well, as Mr. T. is known to be pleading for Methodism, in speeches of from two to four hours in length, throughout his neighborhood, we can understand him in no other way, in the above declaration, than that our good friend Terrell believes Methodism, as set forth in the "Methodist Discipline," is primitive Christianity! Does Mr. Terrell "confidently expect Mr. Goodwin to come forward," and take the negative of this proposition?

But again, he says, "Mr. Mathes swells with manifest exultation, upon the subject of the creed, and thinks I may soon discover that either the general Conference had told a falsehood in the title page of their "Doctrinal Tracts," or *that* book contains the doctrinal tracts of the M. E. Church." I can inform my friend Mathes that he had as well save his exclamation points; for I have long since made that discovery, and I suppose he has too; for if I am correctly informed, he is in the habit of using that book occasionally, and seeks to hold the M. E. Church *responsible* for her doctrinal tracts. And I will further inform the gentleman, that it is precisely in the same sense that I hold the current reformation responsible for her "Christian System," and contend that it is a public confession, or declaration of *her* sentiments. It is so, or the author of it has told a falsehood in its title page.

In the above paragraph, from the 15th and 16th pages of his pamphlet, Mr. Terrell concedes one or two important points, which we will now take possession of in due form. 1st: He admits "that *that* book (Doctrinal Tracts) contains the doctrine of the Methodist Episcopal Church, and that she is *responsible* for her "Doctrinal Tracts."'— 2nd: "That it is precisely in the same sense, that he holds the Christian Church responsible for *her* "Christian System."' 3d: As Mr. T., in the very next sentence, declares, that the said "Christian System," is a "public confession, or declaration of her sentiments," therefore he admits that the "Doctrinal Tracts" "is a public confession, or declaration of the sentiments" of the M. E. Church.

We return Mr. Terrell our sincere thanks, for these concessions, and shall hereafter use the "Doctrinal Tracts" as acknowledged authority in reference to the "sentiments" of the M. E. Church; and we hope, that we shall no more be accused of misrepresenting her when we "seek to hold her *responsible*," for her sentiments contained in her "Doctrinal Tracts." We shall shortly present our readers with some extracts from this book, that they may the better understand what are the *sentiments* of the M. E. Church upon *certain subjects*.

But is it true, that the Christian Church is *responsible* for the sentiments found in the book, to which Mr. T. refers, entitled "The Christian System," in the same sense that the M. E. Church is responsible for her "Doctrinal Tracts?" We answer, it is not true.— The whole power and authority of the M. E. Church is concentrated in her Bishops, who compose the General Conference, and who hold their sessions, we believe, every four years. Now this august body, representing the whole M. E. Church, in 1812, if we remember right, ordered these "Doctrinal Tracts," to be left out of the Discipline, and to be put up in a separate volume; which was done accordingly, and of course this book comes down to us, "By authority of the General Conference," bearing upon its face the *broadest, seal,* which the M. E. Church can possibly place upon it.

But it is vastly different with the book called the "Christian System," above alluded to. It was written and published by Mr. A. Campbell, as its title page clearly shows. It has never been endorsed for by any "Conference," of the Christian Church; not a single church in the "current Reformation," has ever acknowledged it to be *"her* Christian System." And we can now inform our friend Terrell, that the Christian church never *has,* nor *never will* acknowledge any book as *her* "Christian System," but the "word of God which lives and abides forever." Mr. Terrell need not be told that any man in this country, has a right to publish his views and sentiments upon any subject he chooses, he being *responsible* for it. Well, brother Campbell, in the exercise of this right, which is enjoyed by every American citizen, brought together the principal Extras of the Millennial Harbinger, wrote some new Essays, revised the whole, and at his own private expense, published it, not as a 'confession,' or declaration of the faith of the church, or of his own faith, but for the purpose of setting forth some of the most prominent items, which had been discussed, and maintained by himself and brethren, in a controversy of some twenty years. And we repeat, that *he alone is responsible for it.*— But when the *Church* publishes the book for the use of her members, *then,* and *not till then,* can she be held responsible for it. We have neither of the books before us, or we would publish the 'title page' of each, for the purpose of establishing our proposition, beyond the possibility of doubt; but when we have a convenient season we may do this.

Once more, Mr. Terrell says, "Mr. Mathes "exceedingly regrets that I have not *proven* that the course pursued by himself and Washington brethren toward me, was too unfair for those who arrogate to themselves, with so much complacency the appellation of 'christian.'"

Now the above is sheer misrepresentation! But Mr. T. repeats it! He says, "But shortly afterward (his proposition to publish the correspondence) Elder Mathes gave his distorted view of the matter, in his "Notes on a tour;" and yet Mr. Mathes *thinks* this is all *very fair!* and exceedingly regrets that I have not proven my charge. I wonder if *sincerity* has no blushes." Yes, "*sincerity* has blushes," and if our friend T. has in his heart that precious virtue, his cheek will be mantled over with blushes, whenever he reflects how much he has misrepresented his neighbor in the above quotations.

But that the leader may see how shamelessly Mr. Terrell has misrepresented us, we will here give the paragraph from our "Strictures," from which he pretends to quote:

"Again, Mr. T. says, that he "*thinks* our course too *unfair,* for those who arrogate to themselves with so much self-complacency, the appellation *"Christian."* If our course has been u nfair, we exceedingly regret it: but our friend has not proven it to be so."

Now we *think* that Mr. Terrell *himself,* has too much good sense, not to see that he has grossly misrepresented us. We do not 'regret' that Mr. T. failed to prove the charge of unfairness against us. Indeed, we should have 'regretted' very much if he had succeeded! But we said, "If our course has been unfair, we exceedingly regret it; but Mr. T. has not proven it to be so." Further comment is unnecessary. Let the public judge.

In conclusion, Mr. T. remarks, "I am only sorry that Mr. Mathes, in declining to publish the correspondence in the Record, places me under the necessity of publishing it through another medium, or else the antidote would not be as extensive as the poison." From this, the reader of the pamphlet would be led to suppose, that Mr. T. had sent a copy of the work to all the readers of the Record. Now we know not how many copies he has issued; but we *think* that not more than *one* in every hundred of the readers of the Record will ever see it. Indeed, We *think* it was designed for "Home Consumption," and perhaps to appear in some of the "Christian Advocates," East, West, North or South, where nothing that we might write in reference to it, would ever be admitted.

Again, we take our leave of this matter, and hope that it will never be necessary for us to notice it again. EDITOR.

PROSPECTUS

FOR THE SECOND VOLUME OF THE CHRISTIAN RECORD.

THE favor which the first volume of the CHRISTIAN RECORD has received from the brethren, and the Public generally, induces us to make arrangements for the publication of the second volume. Notwithstanding the many discouraging and unpropitious circumstances, with which we were surrounded, when we commenced our Editorial labors, such as severe affliction, both of ourself and family, living some 18 miles from the place of publication, lack of suitable materials for the work; and me might add, being disappointed for several months in obtaining a Printer, as we had expected: yet our brethren and friends, confiding in our integrity, if not our ability, came nobly to our aid, by sending us a handsome list of subscribers, in many instances accompanied with the cash, which enabled us to go on, and gradually improve the work. Indeed, we have succeeded far beyond our expectations; and we suppose that the Christian Record, at this time, has a circulation equal to any periodical of its age West of the Mountains. We have therefore determined to issue a second volume, commencing July 4th, 1844, which will be just one month after the close of the present volume.

The second volume of the Christian Record will be published at Bloomington, Monroe County, Indiana, Edited and Published by JAMES MADISON MATHES.— Twelve numbers will constitute the volume, each number will contain 21 large octavo pages, neatly stitched and covered, with a table of contents at the close of the volume; making at the close of the year a handsome volume of 288 pages, of convenient size for binding. It will be issued regularly the first of each month.

Our PLAN.—1: Christian Union. 2: The movements of the various ecclesiastical bodies, both in Europe and America, will be noticed and faithfully reported. 3: Original Essays, and independent expositions of the doctrine of Christ. 4: Reviews of such books, Essays, Sermons, and other publications, as may from time to time, fall under our observation, and especially those which, in our judgment, are calculated to mislead the public mind, and hinder the Gospel of Christ. 5: We shall occasionally draw the contrast between *Ancient* and *Modern* Christianity, and insist upon an immediate return to the doctrine and practice of the Apostles, and first Christians. 6: We shall contend for the word of God, as an all-sufficient rule of faith and manners, for all Christians. 7: A Miscellany, embracing Queries, News from the Churches, and other religious notices; Education, and whatever we may judge interesting to our readers.

OUR MEANS.—1: A very large and choice list of Exchanges, which enable us, at least once a month, to look over the whole map of Christendom, and to present our readers with the result of our observations. 2: Some experience which we have in writing, a general acquaintance which we have throughout the State; together with the facilities we enjoy, by having access to some of the best Libraries in the West. 3: We have made permanent arrangements with bro. C. G. BERRY, to do the work, who is a true and faithful brother; and as a workman, we suppose he is not surpassed by any in the Western country. We have now removed to the immediate neighborhood of Bloomington, and expect- to devote as much of our time to the interest of the work as may be necessity. 4: We expect to print the work on new type, bought expressly for the purpose.

TERMS.—The work will be sent to subscribers at $1 per volume, in *advance,* or on the reception of the first number; for $5 *in advance,* six copies will be sent; and for $12 *in advance,* fifteen copies will be sent. Every subscriber must begin with the volume, and none will be permitted to discontinue, except at the discretion of the Editor, until all arrearages are paid.

*--Remittances can always be made through Postmasters, as they are authorized by law to frank letters to Editors, containing the names of subscribers or money. Don't forget this.

Those who are subscribers to the present volume of the Christian Record, need not subscribe for the 2nd volume, as all will be considered subscribers for it, who fail to notify us of their desire to discontinue, before the commencement of the second volume.

☛ All letters to be addressed (postage *paid,* or *free*) to "J. M. Mathes, Bloomington, Monroe County, Indiana."

J. M. MATHES, Editor.

THE CHRISTIAN RECORD

VOL. I.] BLOOMINGTON, IND., MAY, 1844. [No. XI.

"PRESSLY'S LECTURES" REVIEWED—NO. 7.

WE now come to Dr. Pressly's fourth lecture, which commences on the 82d page of his book. This lecture is devoted to the "mode of baptism." This is a subject which has been so often discussed, that we fear the reader will feel but little interested in the matter. But still we think it an important subject; and shall endeavor to treat it in such a manner that all may feel its divine importance.

On 82d page the Dr., after speaking of the moral pollution of the soul, and its removal, says, "But, it is perfectly evident, that this important end cannot be effected by water, no matter what may be the mode of its application, or the quantity which may be used. It is not the water of baptism, but *the blood of Jesus Christ, which, cleanseth from all sins:* and of the purifying efficacy of this atoning blood, water, in the sacrament of baptism, is the significant emblem. There is, consequently, an evident impropriety in making the validity of baptism depend upon the quantity of the external sign which is used, or the particular manner in which the water is applied to the body."

Now our good friend Dr. P. seems to be laboring under a mistake.— We do not make the validity of baptism to depend upon the quantity of the external sign which is used, or the particular mode of its application"! but we do make the *validity* of baptism to depend upon the authority of God,—the law in the case. If God has commanded *dipping,* then the "quantity of the external sign" must at least be equal to the fulfillment of the command. Take an example from Lev. 14th chap, 15 and 16th verses, "And the priest shall take some of the log of oil, and pour it into the palm of his own left hand: And the priest shall *dip* his right finger in the oil that is in his left hand, and shall *sprinkle* of the oil with his finger seven times before the Lord." Now in this example we have the command, to *pour, dip,* and *sprinkle,* sometimes called, "*The three modes of baptism.*" Dr. Pressly need not be told that each of these terms comes from a different word in the original. Now we reason thus, that as the command to *pour,* could not De obeyed by therefore, the *mode,* or *action,* is essential to the thing done.

On 84th page the good Dr. compares the sacrament of the Lord's Supper, or "Eucharist," as he calls it, with the institution of baptism; he then remarks, "Does the participation of a morsel of bread, and a taste of wine, in the Eucharist, bear any greater resemblance to a feast, than the application of a little water to the face, does to the washing of the whole body in water? Why then is the validity of the one sacrament made to depend upon the mode of administration, while no such importance is attached to the mode, in the observation of the other? To these questions, no satisfactory answer can be given, consistently with the principles and practice of our brethren."

Here again the Dr. is reasoning from false premises. We place no importance in the *quantity* of water; all we want is just enough to fill the command, and as God has commanded *dipping,* or *immersing,* (for such is the meaning of the original,) therefore we must have water enough to perform an immersion, or "burial." Now the Dr. is mistaken in our views of the "Supper," as we attach the same importance to the mode of its administration, that we do to baptism. The *mode* of administration, is not the *quantity* of water in baptism, or the *quantity* of bread and wine, used in the Supper. The mode of receiving the Lord's Supper is by "eating bread and drinking wine." We therefore say, that the *mode,* which is "eating and drinking," is essential to the validity of this ordinance. But if the Dr. thinks not, then let him show us how this sacrament can be observed without 'eating or drinking!!' We should like to see him try.

The Dr. next takes up the word 'baptize,' and proceeds to examine its meaning: and we understand him to admit that the Classics all use the word *baptidzo,* in the sense of immersion; and this he says, 'is all which the scholar can claim.' But he then contends that the scripture usage is very different, and that the writers of the New Testament use the term in a very different sense. We are glad that the learned Dr. Pressly, of the Associate Reformed Church, has conceded this much.— It is what many paido-baptists have denied. But how does our author prove that the original word *baptidzo,* from which our translators have given us *baptize,* is used in the New Testament in a different sense, from that which he admits is its "classical meaning!" Let us see:— "Our appeal," says the learned Dr., "shall be, not to Greek Lexicons, nor to Pagan classics, but to the plain language of the New Testament:" page 87. But we ask, why not appeal to Greek Lexicons, which have been prepared by learned paido-baptists themselves, for the express purpose of showing us the "New Testament use of words!" The reason is obvious; they go against the Dr., and of course he will not appeal to them! But that the reader may see the strength of the 'immersion cause;' notwithstanding Dr. P. has conceded to us the Greek Lexicons, and the Classics, we will introduce some authority, as to the New Testament use of the Greek verb *baptidzo.* It is well known to the scholar, that Parkhurst, Robinson, Donegan, Greenfield, and many other eminent Paido-baptists, have, in their Lexicons, which in some instances, have been prepared with a direct reference to the New Testament, uniformly given *Immerse, dip,* etcetera, as the first, or *primary* meaning of this word. Take an example from Greenfield's Lexicon, which is bound in the same volume with the 'Polymicrian Testament,' for the purpose of explaining all the words found in the Greek Testament.

"Baptidzo—(the word translated *baptize)* to immerse, immerge, submerge, sink: in N. T. to wash, perform ablution, cleanse, Mar. 7: 4; Luke 11: 38. To immerse, baptize, administer the right of baptism, Mark 1: 4, and others." Now let us hear Greenfield, on *Bapto,* the root:

"Bapto—to dip, plunge, John 13: 26; Lu. 16: 24: to dye, Rev. 19:13." It is well known, that from *Baptidzo,* we have the nouns, Baptisms, Baptismos, and Baptistas. Let us now hear Greenfield tell what these words signify in the New Testament.

"Baptisma— What is immersed, hence, immersion, baptism, ordinance of baptism."

"Baptismos—immersion, baptism, Heb. 6: 2; a washing, ablution, Mark 7: 4, 8; Heb. 9: 10."

"Baptistas—one who baptizes, baptist, Matt. 3: 1; 11, 11, & 12."—

No wonder then, that Dr. Pressly will not appeal to the Greek Lexicons; because they have already decided against him. But we will now introduce Dr. McNight, a learned Divine of the Kirk of Scotland, and let him tell Dr. Pressly, in what sense he understands the term *Baptism* to be used in the New Testament. ["Buried together with him by baptism."] Christ's baptism was not the baptism of repentance; for he never committed any sin; but as was observed, Prelim. Ess. 1, at the beginning he submitted to be baptized, that is, to be buried under the water by John, and to be raised out of it again, as an emblem of his future death and resurrection. In like manner, the baptism of believers is emblematical of their own death, burial, and resurrection." McNight on the Epistles: Note on Rom. 6: 4.

But who shall decide, when Doctors disagree? We are willing to leave it to the great Geneva Reformer, John Calvin, who, it is well known, was a Paido-baptist; to this Dr. P. cannot object, with any degree of propriety.

"The very word *baptize,* however," says John Calvin, "signifies to *immerse;* and it is certain that immersion was the practice of the ancient church." Calvin's Institutes, Book 4, chap. 15, page 343.

As Paul said to the Athenians, so say we to Dr. Pressly, and our Paido-baptist friends: "As certain also of your own Poets have said." We might quote authority of this kind to almost any extent, but we forbear, 'in the mouth of two or three witnesses, every word shall be established."

We will now go with our author into the New Testament. He Says, "Let me direct your attention to examples of the use of the word baptism, in which it does not convey the idea of immersion." The first example which the Dr. brings forward, is the baptism of the disciples at Pentecost, and the house of Cornelius, with the Holy Ghost: and because the Holy Ghost was *poured out* upon them, the Dr. concludes that *pouring* is a scriptural mode of baptism. But let us see. Acts 2: 2, "And suddenly there a sound from heaven, as of a rushing mighty wind, and it filled the house where they were sitting. (3) And there appeared unto them cloven tongues, like as of fire, and it sat upon each of them." The Dr. admits that it was the spirit that was *poured* out; well then, it was the spirit that came from heaven, according to the promise, Joel 2d chap., and it was the spirit that filled the house where they were sitting. Then the matter seems to stand thus: God *poured* out his spirit, and he continued to *pour* until the 'whole house was filled, where they were sitting,' and consequently they were *overwhelmed, or* immersed in it. If the Dr. says that it was the sound that filled the house, we would ask him to tell us what it was that sat upon each of them, and gave them utterance? The same *it,* that came from heaven filled the house. Now we do not object to *pouring;* our difficulty is, that our friends *stop too soon;* but if they will continue *pouring* until the subject is completely 'buried with the Lord in baptism,' we shall no longer complain. Now we affirm, that the *pouring* was only a circumstance necessary to their baptism. The spirit was in heaven, and of course they could not be immersed in it until it was *poured out*.

The next example brought forward, in which our friend thinks there was no immersion, is the baptism of the children of Israel, "to Moses, in the cloud and in the sea." 1 Cor. 10: 1, 2. Here Paul says, 'They were baptized into Moses in the cloud, and in the sea.' Mark this well: the *cloud* and *sea* both were necessary to constitute their baptism. (See Gen. 14 & 15th chaps.) Now as this text is much relied on by the Dr., we shall examine it with some minuteness. We wish the reader to bear in mind, that an individual can be baptized or immersed in any thing, in which he can be overwhelmed, or enclosed, as in a grave.

Now in the history of this baptism, we are told that 'the children of Israel went into the midst of the sea upon dry ground, and the waters were a wall unto them on their right hand and on their left.' Gen. 14: 22. Again: 'And with the blast of thy nostrils the waters were gathered together: the floods stood upright as an heap, and the depths were congealed in the heart of the sea.' Song of Moses and the children of Israel Gen. 15: 8. Taking then what Paul says of this matter, together with the account given of it by Moses, and the following appears to be clearly sustained, viz; 1: the waters of the sea were congealed, and stood up as a wall upon their right hand, and upon their left. 2: The cloud covered them. And 3rd: They passed through on dry ground:— Now their position in the sea resembled a man in a grave: as they were completely enveloped 'in the cloud and in the sea.' Indeed, we regard this as an unequivocal case of immersion, not in water, for they passed over as by 'dry land;' not in spray from the sea, for its waters were congealed, and of course, affords no spray; not in rain from the cloud, for there is no evidence that *one drop of water touched* even their *faces,* but 'in the *cloud* and in the *sea.*'

But the Dr. asks, 'Will it be said that they were plunged in the sea?' We answer no, it is not necessary that we should say so, in order to make out our case fully.

The above are the only examples which our friend, the Dr. brings forward, in which he thinks the term *baptize* cannot *mean to immerse.*— We have examined them all, and as we think fully disposed of every difficulty which the Dr.'s reasoning seemed to have thrown in the way of immersion; and here we let the matter rest another month.

J. M. M., Ed.

'J. H. J.' of the Christian (Universalist) Teacher has commenced a review of our article No. 7, on Universalism. When he gets through, he may expect to hear from us.

FOR THE CHRISTIAN RECORD.

Columbus, April 21, 1844.

Beloved bro. Mathes: Toward the close of your reply to my communication upon the return of our blessed Lord, you say: "If it is your pleasure to correspond with me further upon this subject, I hope you will particularly notice these two points." I am at a loss to know what two points you have reference to, as you say, "in conclusion I will briefly state what seems to me to be the principal points of difference between us." You then give three points, if I understand you, about which we differ. "1st: The signs which were to precede the coming of the Lord. 2nd: The prophetic periods will run out in April next, and the Lord come in the clouds of heaven, with power and great glory, sometime between this and the last of April." *April!!* Bro. Mathes, where have I said the Lord would come in April next? and still, several times, you have represented me as saying so. This is not quite right. 3: The literal Jews must return to their own land before the Lord comes. Here appears to be three things about which we differ. And now bro. M. it is my pleasure to reply to your objections to my views respecting these important matters. And 1: The signs that were to precede the coming of the Lord; I mentioned but four, three of them you do not object to. The 4th: namely, the falling of the stars, you do object to. And what is your objection? It is this: when I spoke of the falling of the stars, you say that I departed from my own rule of interpretation, by supposing that the literal stars are not here meant. Now I suppose no such thing; because I called them meteors to prevent the reply that they were nothing but *meteors,* is no good reason why I should consider them figurative. The people generally call them stars. The *Bible* no where calls them meteors; and because I called them meteors, and not stars, I have departed from my own rule of interpretation.—

Now bro. M., I am not able to see the force of your logic. When I asked what kind of star that was, that directed the eastern Magi to the birth-place of the Saviour, you gravely reply, "I do not know, the Bible says it was a star, and I believe it." Very well, you do not believe that it was one of the planets, or one of the fixed stars, or any other star that is located in the heavens. You cannot believe that it was any of those stars, because the *book* does not say that it was, therefore it must have been a meteor and a star both, for the Bible says it was a star, not a *figurative,* but a literal star. If you will look into Greenfield's Greek lexicon, you will find the meaning of the word translated star, to be: Star, luminous body like a star, luminary. You say you are compelled to make it all figurative, or all literal. Very well; so am I. If we make it all figurative, it could produce no conviction on the mind that the coming of the Lord was at hand, therefore I believe they were to be literally fulfilled. The stars were to fall before the Lord come. If by the stars falling, we are to understand the heavenly bodies, that are fixed in their orbits, (if astronomy be true,) there will be no necessity for the Lord's coming to destroy the wicked, as that would effectually do it; and as you say you understand the darkening of the sun to be literal, and of course the falling of the stars, you are bound to admit that those stars are meteors, or say that the heavenly bodies will fall to the earth. What you have said on this item has not convinced me that I am wrong, therefore the next sign that I am looking for, is the sign of the Son of man in heaven.

The next item that I shall notice, in your reply, is prophetic time. The first reason given by me for believing the advent nigh, is found in Daniel 2d chap. I stated that we had been living in the toes of that image 1360, years, which is proof to me that we are on the verge of the resurrection, Here, you cannot see the force of my logic, "because Daniel does not inform us how long these kingdoms (toes of the image) shall stand. But suppose we admit that you are correct, and that 'we are on the verge of the resurrection,' this surely is not satisfactory proof that the second advent will take place in April!" APRIL!! bro. M. I will help you to understand the force of my logic. The 2d chap, of Daniel brings us down to the setting up of God's everlasting kingdom. The 8th, to the cleansing of the sanctuary. This vision I said would terminate (not in April, but) in the present year. Now if you will connect the 2d and 8th chapters, you can see the force of my logic. I also stated that 1816 years from the crucifixion of Christ would terminate sometime in April, and so I now say, if our A. D. has been kept correctly; but this is surely not saying that the 2360 days will expire at that time, as you will see at the close of my communication.— You ask, "how do you know that the 70 weeks form a part of, and are to be cut off from the 2300 days'" I answer that Daniel did not understand the vision that he had in the 8th chap., as you will see by reading the last verse of that chap. Gabriel appears to Daniel when he, Daniel, was praying, for the purpose of giving him skill and understandings he says to him, "understand the matter and consider the vision." Dan. 9: 29. What vision? Evidently the vision he had in the 8th chap., for he had none in the 9th. Gabriel tells Daniel what should transpire in 70 weeks; also, when the 70 weeks would commence.— Now if the 70 weeks are no part of the vision, Daniel got no information concerning the vision, by this visit of Gabriel, and Gabriel failed to do what he was sent to do. This is how I know the 70 weeks are a part of the 2300 days. When you were immediately on my third reason for believing the advent nigh, you appeared to be somewhat surprised at my applying the abomination of desolation spoken of in Daniel 12: 11, to the pagan power; for you exclaim, "Indeed I am sure that you are mistaken." Now bro. M., you are not a whit more sure that I am mistaken, than I am certain that you are wrong, when you apply the same abomination to the Roman army. Now for some of my reasons for believing that you are mistaken; but first, let us turn to Dan. 12th, and read, commencing at the 11th v. and continuing to the end of the chap.: "And from the time that the daily (sacrifice is in italics) shall be taken away and the abomination that maketh desolate set up, there shall be a thousand two hundred and ninety days. Blessed is he that waiteth and cometh to the thousand three hundred five and thirty days: but go thou thy way till the end be, for thou shalt rest and stand in thy lot at the end of the days." Daniel here speaks of the setting up of the power that never before existed; also, the time from the setting up of that power to his resurrection, or standing in his lot, which I consider synonymous. Now let me ask, is there no difference between setting up a power that never before existed, and a power removed from Rome to Jerusalem, which had been in existence for hundreds of years! Say Mr. Editor. Again: If the Roman army was the abomination spoken of in Dan. 12: 11, then Daniel's resurrection would have taken place about the year A. D. 1405, 439 years ago, if we count a day for a year. If we say those days mean literal days, it makes the matter worse. If we say a day here represents a thousand years, then it will carry us down the stream of time 1,333,000 years to the resurrection of Daniel!! Once more: Where was the abomination of desolation to stand? Ans.—In the holy place. See Matt. 24: 15. Was Jerusalem, at the time it was destroyed, a holy place? It will not do to say it was once the place of God's presence. The question is, was it so at the time it was destroyed? No indeed, the glory had departed almost forty years before the destruction of that devoted city. The Messiah told the Jews before his death, that they had made his father's house a den of thieves—he told them on leaving the city, their house was left unto them desolate. Where was holiness then? It was forever fled from the Jews, as *such,* After this, they murdered the Son of God—they killed the Prince of life.

Now bro. Mathes, if you cannot remove these objections to your views, and I think you cannot, you must see that you are mistaken.— What you say relative to the return of the Jews will now be attended to; but before I proceed, permit me to state the question which we are debating, fairly. The proposition is the following: Will the *literal* Jews return to the *literal* land of Judea before the Lord comes. Do not forget these words, BEFORE the Lord comes. You affirm and I deny. By attending strictly to the matter in debate, much time and labor may be saved, as you have seen, if you have read the recent debate, held in Lexington, Ky. But to proceed: In discussing this matter, you appear almost ready to give up your cause; so much of it, at least, as says before the Lord comes; and this is the point about which I am contending. Not whether the Jews will return, but whether they will return before the Lord comes. The reasons which make me think so are the following: 1—You do not speak with that assurance and certainty on this subject that you are wont to do on many others. 2—In closing your remarks on the 11th of Romans, you say, "I believe when Israel shall have returned to their own land (I will say nothing, at this time, about Canaan belonging to the literal Jews) the times of the Gentiles will then be over, at which time the Lord will come." Now bro. Mathes, what made you believe the Jews would ever return to Canaan? Surely not anything found in the 11th of Romans, for Paul says not one word about it. You have not said, in so many words, that the return would be before the Lord comes, but you insinuate it. Inasmuch as you have not ventured the assertion, I conclude that you are satisfied that there is no proof to sustain you in that chap., therefore we will admit it for the present, and hear your concluding remarks on the 3rd of Acts.— Here they are: "We therefore conclude with confidence that the text above quoted sustains our position, showing clearly that this promise (the return of the Jews) must be accomplished before, or at the coming of the Lord." Very well, bro. Mathes: *before* or *at,* does not mean BEFORE; does it? I do not consider that you have removed my objection, in the least, to your application of this passage. I did not understand you to bring forward this passage to prove that literal Israel will return, but if they do return that their return must be before the coming of the Lord. But conceding the point that they must return, I cannot see that this passage proves that they must return before the coming of the Lord. The point to be settled, according to your application, simply this: Is the return of the Jews the consummation of the "restitution of all things," or are there other prophecies to be fulfilled after the coming of the Lord? I need not say that the millennium and the resurrection of the dead, are a part of the "restitution of all things," and subjects of the "Holy Prophets;" therefore I conduce that my objection lies with all its force against your application of this passage.

I will now dismiss the 3d of Acts, and see what you have to say on the 39th chap, of Ezekiel, 25—29. Also, Ezekiel 11: 17. Here is the sum of the whole. "Now bro. Fassett, if the foregoing prophetic declarations and promises do not prove a literal return of the literal descendants of Abraham, I would ask you to tell us in what language such a promise could be given?" Well, now let me ask you a question: Does all that is here said prove to you that the Jews will return before the Lord comes? Surely not; and why? Because if it did, you would have said so; but as you did not, I am constrained to believe, with you, that the proof is not here. You introduce several passages found in the *37th* chap. of Ezekiel. In the 24th and 25th *verses* you say: "We are informed that after Israel and Judah have returned from among the heathen, and become united as one nation in their own land: "David my servant shall be king over them."' Now bro. M., this or the half of it, is not said in the 24th and 25th verses.— You infer that David will be their king after, and not before they shall have returned to Judea. You infer it I presume, because their return is mentioned before David is, in the order of narrative. But it is by no means certain, that that which stands first, in the order of narrative, took place first in the order of time; but all this is well enough, if you did not insinuate that the return will take place before the Lord comes. David here, I presume, means Christ, I think no one will call this in question. From all that is said in the previous part of this chap., I shall infer that the Lord will come before the Jews return to the Land of Canaan, and I will give my reasons for thinking so. But first, let ns ascertain from the Bible the situation of the Jews, at the present time, and how long they are to remain so. Rom. 11: 8 —10, "According as it is written, God hath given them the spirit of slumber; eyes that they should not see, and ears that they shall not hear unto this day. And David saith, Let their table be made a snare and a trap, and a stumbling block, and a recompense unto them. Let their eyes be darkened that they may not see and how down their back alway." (25) "Blindness is happened to Israel until the fullness of the Gentiles be come in." Also, Is. 6 chap., 9—13, "And he said, go and tell this people hear ye indeed, but understand not, and see ye indeed but perceive not. Make the heart of this people fat, and make their eyes heavy, and shut their ears; lest they see with their eyes and hear with their ears, and understand with their heart and convert and be healed. Then said I, Lord, how long; and he answered, until the cities be wasted, without inhabitant, and the houses without man, and the land be utterly desolate, and the Lord have removed man far away, and there be a great forsaking in the midst of the land." Read the 13th v. for yourself, and ponder it well. How long are the Jews to continue in this deplorable state? The answer is given in Romans 11th, 26, "There shall come out of Sion the Deliverer, and shall turn away ungodliness from Jacob" None but the Lord is able to accomplish this work, and he will not do it until he comes out of Sion—comes again. Ezekiel 37 chap., compares the situation that the Jews are in, at the present time, to graves, to dry bones; and a recovery from that state to a resurrection; and Paul has just told us when this resurrection shall take place In the 12th verse, 37th chap. we have the following: "Therefore prophecy and say unto them, thus saith the Lord God: Behold, O my people, I will open your graves, and cause you to come up out of your graves, and bring you into the land of Israel." Here is proof positive that they will not go to Canaan, till after their figurative resurrection, and the Lord have put his spirit within them. After they go to that land they are to remain there forever: See 25th verse. Now what have we proved? We have proved that the Jews are not to return to Canaan, till after their figurative resurrection: 2—this resurrection will not take place until the Deliverer comes out of Sion. Then, and not till then, will David reign over them forever. In closing the 37th chap, you say, "I most firmly believe that the first resurrection will take place after the restoration of Israel." Brother M. you have twice said that you believed what I think has not been proved. Now bro. M. to sum up your argument, it seems to me to be about as follows, to wit: that literal Israel, as they now are, (and they are the most blasphemous people in the world,) must return to literal Canaan, and immortal David must reign over them forever, before the Lord comes!! Let me say in conclusion that I am not convinced that you have proved your proposition, and it is not my opinion that you can; but I am perfectly willing that you should try it again. If it is the truth, I should like to know it—if it is in the Bible, I am sure you are able to show it; if it is not the truth, it is an error, and all errors are dangerous in Christianity; some are more dangerous than others. It is on this account that I have said anything on this subject. So long as we believe that the Jews will return to their once happy homes, we shall be looking for that event instead of the coming of the Master. Here lies the danger. I recollect what my thoughts ware 10 *years ago*, while the stars were falling—I thought, and I believe that I remarked that the Lord was not coming yet, for the Jews had not yet returned to Palestine. But I am now looking and waiting for his coming. I do hope that what we have said on this important subject, will be the means of stirring up the Disciples to watchfulness, and diligence in every Christian duty, that we may be found of him in peace, and be prepared to enter into the marriage supper of the Lamb; ready at all times to say with the beloved John, "Come Lord Jesus, come quickly.— Amen."

JOSEPH FASSETT.

Greenville, Ind., April 20th, 1844.

My Dear Brother: I take the liberty of writing to you, (though a stranger,) as a co-worker with you in the cause of primitive Christianity. to request the publication in your periodical (the Christian Record,) of the within document, from the pen of the venerable Father Campbell, on church Government and Order. I take pleasure also, in informing the holy brethren, through the agency of your useful paper, of the progress of the good cause in this part of the State.— I commenced my labors in Floyd county in January last, since which time about 60 have "become obedient to the faith;" which has stirred up the unmitigated hostility of the traditionized, and sectarianized parties; and of the *last* and most detestable of all heresies—*Mormonism.*

God speed you my brother in your labors of love; for I know that you breathe the pure air of Canaan, from the mild and benevolent spirit, manifested by you toward your brethren of the press, and to all men.

On last Monday, I received intelligence of the death of a beloved sister, which has filled my heart with pleasing grief, and mournful joy. *Sorrow* for her death; but joy that she died in the Lord. "Blessed be the name of the Lord!!"

Respectfully your brother in the one Lord,

J. P. MARSHALL, *Evan.*

The document referred to by brother Marshall is the following.— Most cheerfully we comply with the request of our beloved brother? to publish it in the Christian Record. We have on file a number of queries upon the subject of which Father Campbell treats; to which we expect to respond, so soon as we shall have time to write a few essays on the subject: but in the mean time we commend the following brief, but comprehensive essay, to the prayerful consideration of the brotherhood.—Ed.

BETHANY, VA., NOVEMBER 12, 1843.

Brother J. P. Marshall: At your request, and through your agency, I would address our beloved brethren in Texas upon the subjects you propose.

And first of all, dear brethren, I would observe, that in order to get rid of the corruptions of our holy religion, we have fallen back upon its divine directory and standard, the New Testament, in which we are divinely favored with the divinely authenticated record of the Gospel and laws of Christ, the belief and obedience of which constitute genuine Christianity; to it therefore, we directly look for instruction, in relation to every thing we ought to believe and do. Wherefore, with respect to the qualifications of Bishops, Deacons and Evangelists, we should strictly advert to all the places where these officers are mentioned. See Phil. 1:1; 1 Tim. 3: 1—7; Titus 1:6—9; 1 Tim. 5: 17—19; 1 Pe. 5: 1--4; Acts 20: 17—25. So much for the qualifications and duties of Bishops and Elders; which are two names for the same office, where ruling and teaching are implied, as is the case in the above quotations. They must be elderly persons, heads of families, to qualify them, and to evince their qualifications, for teaching and ruling the church of God. "For if a man know not how to teach and rule his own family, how shall he take care of the church of God." The duties also of the Christian people to their Bishops and Elders are expressly taught. See Gal. 6:6—9, with Heb. 13: 7—17, and 1 Tim. 5: 17—19. With respect to their ordination, see Acts 13:1—3, and 14: 21—23, with 1 Tim.4: 14. It appears from these quotations, that both Bishops and Evangelists were set apart; that is, ordained to their sacred office of teaching and ruling, by the imposition of hands, with fasting and prayer. And that even the Deacons who were neither to teach nor rule, but to assist the church in the performance of its special relative duties, were so ordained. See Acts 6:1—6. And must also be elderly men, heads of families, of the same moral and religious character with the Bishops. See 1 Tim. 3: 12. Neither the one nor the other, young inexperienced persons, novices or new converts; but such as had proved themselves competent and trustworthy characters. Wherefore, the Apostle charges Timothy to lay hands suddenly on no man, lest he should be a partaker of other men's sins, by committing a sacred trust to persons not duly qualified. See 1 Tim. 5: 22. As for the Evangelists Timothy and Titus, it appears that they were both young men when they were set apart to the evangelical office: that is, to the office of preaching and teaching, and of assisting the Apostle by his direction, in the management of the affairs of the churches. See Acts 16: 1—3, and Rom. 16:21; 1 Thess. 3:2; 1 Tim. 1—4. Also, 2 Cor. 7: 6, 7, with Titus 1: 1—5. Whence it appears that these persons, though comparatively young, were nevertheless specially qualified persons. With respect to the former, see 1 Tim. 4:12—16.

And from what the Apostle says of the latter, in the above quotations, he appears to have been another of the same description of character. Such therefore are worthy to be entrusted with the evangelical office.

Having in the above quotations, (all of which I must earnestly recommend to the serious consideration of our brethren,) a scriptural view of the qualifications and duties of Bishops, Deacons, and Evangelists, and of the respect and obedience with which they ought to be treated in due performance of their official duties; it yet remains to advert to the scriptural mode of their induction into their respective offices, which is also contained in the above quotations; namely, by fasting and prayer, with the imposition of hands upon the candidates. But the question is: who is to do this, and by what authority. The answer is obvious: that as the church was divinely constituted by the Apostles; it is therefore the church's duty to maintain her constitution by keeping up the apostolic order; for which purpose she is divinely furnished with an authentic record. The church, then, is to ordain her own officers, these having the prescribed qualifications are to be set apart by the imposition of hands, with fasting and prayer, by certain elderly persons chosen by the church for said purpose; for it is the church that confers the office by the election, and not the persons that lay their hands on the heads of the candidates; for they do this in the name of Christ, by the authority of the church, which requested them so to do; for they may not even belong to said church, but may have been invited to assist upon that occasion; for certainly, churches being all members of the one Body of Christ, are all bound to assist each other, according to the doctrine of the Apostles, whose peculiar office it was to teach the disciples (to observe all things,) that Christ commanded them for this purpose. See Matt. 28:20. So that to believe and obey the Gospel and laws of Christ constitutes the *real Christian*.

Next as to the connexion between Baptism and the remission of sins; see Mark 16: 15, 16, with Acts 2: 38,39, and chap.22: 16. In these quotations we have the divinely instituted connexion between baptism and the enjoyment of salvation, which consist in justification and sanctification; or in the remission of sins, and the gift of the Holy Spirit, by the former of which we are justified, and the latter we are sanctified, which constitute our present salvation from the guilt and practice of sin. And being thus freed from the guilt and practice of sin, we have our fruit unto holiness, and the end, everlasting life. But with respect to all this blissful enjoyment, baptism is only a divinely appointed means; for the blood of Christ is the procuring cause, and the spirit of Christ the efficient cause, and his word the instrumental cause.

Lastly with respect to occasional communion with unbaptized persons the scripture is silent: there was no such thing in the Apostles' days, therefore I can say nothing about it. When the scripture is silent, we ought to be so too. Upon the whole, if official characters be what they ought to be in principle and practice, according to the scriptures, and if the brethren for whom they labor treat them accordingly, all will be well. The church will be edified, and God glorified. The Lord respecteth the heart. Divine knowledge, faith, hope and love, constitute the Christian, and these are derived from a proper use of the word of God and prayer; therefore, blessed is the man whose delight is in the law of the Lord; who meditates therein day and night, Psalm 1: 1—3: who lays it up in his heart and in his soul; and who teaches it diligently to children; talking of it when he sits in his house, when he walks by the way, when he lies down, and when he rises up: for in so doing, his days, and the days of his children, shall be as the days of heaven upon earth. See Deuteronomy 11: 18—21. Thus, by making a proper use of the Bible, and the throne of grace, we are to enjoy a foretaste of heaven in a present evil world. Indeed, while here, the Bible is to us in God's stead; though we cannot see him; yet when we open the Bible, we can hear his voice; therefore, if we love his company, we will love the good Book.

Respected brother, be pleased to present these few desultory thoughts to our beloved brethren, with my sincere desires for their present and eternal salvation.

Yours most respectfully, THOMAS CAMPBELL.

CHRISTIAN OBLIGATIONS—NO. 7.

BROTHER MATHES: I do not expect to offer anything new on the subject now before me, as so many able pens have written upon it, and so many eloquent tongues, fired with the pure benevolence of the heart- purified by faith—have poured forth their melting strains upon the delighted ear of the devoted Christian. I repeat, after all these efforts on the part of the faithful servants of God, I do not expect to offer any thing new on this important subject, *Christian Character!* What is it? The most distinguished honor conferred upon mortal man, and the most-worthy aspect of that salvation which cost the life of him, by whom the Universe was made. I confess that in writing upon this subject, its weighty importance seems to press upon me, and I trust that in my endeavors to lay this subject before your readers, I shall by the attempt, be as much benefited as those for whom I write. But to return to the subject: I shall introduce a passage from the prophet Malachi, in order to say a few things more on the importance of meeting together.—

"When they that feared the Lord spake often one to another, and the Lord hearkened and heard *it;* and a book of remembrance was written before him for them that feared the Lord, and thought upon his name. And they shall be mine, saith the Lord of hosts, in that day when I make up my Jewels; and I will spare them, as a man spareth his own son that serveth him." Mal. 3: 16, 17. A book of remembrance is written before the Lord for those who fear him, and "exhort one another," when they "assemble themselves together." Brethren, do we exhort one another? or do we depend upon the *preacher* to exhort us all, and hence refuse to go to meeting except when he is to be there? If we will not meet with the Lord's people when the preacher is not there, the Lord will not meet with us when the preacher *is* there. If those who speak often one to another, are to be the Lord's jewels, when he comes; the converse is equally true, that those who do not speak often one to another, will not be the Lord's jewels in that day. There is no escape from this conclusion. I will now proceed to speak of the fellowship. The passage that speaks of 'fellowship,' in Acts 2d chap., is generally understood to have reference to the contribution. The term *fellowship* is sometimes used to represent the whole Gospel economy:— for instance, Paul says, "God *is* faithful, by whom ye were called unto the fellowship of his Son Jesus Christ our Lord." 1 Cor. 1: 9. This passage evidently has reference to our heirship with Christ, which depends upon our union with him here, according to the Gospel. Again, the Apostle John says: "If we say we have fellowship with him, and walk in darkness, we lie and do not the truth: but if we walk in the light, as he is in the light, we have fellowship one with another, and the blood of Jesus Christ his Son cleanseth us from all sin." 1 John 1: 6, 7. This fellowship is to be maintained by "walking in *the* light." If we do not walk in the light, we lose our partnership in this fellowship, and of course, have not a lawful right to that "inheritance, which is incorruptible, undefiled, and that fadeth not away." But the passage spoken of in Acts 2d, cannot have reference to the whole Gospel economy, because there are things spoken of in connexion with it, which form a part. "Breaking of bread and prayers" is a part of that fellowship, to which God has called us by the Gospel.

I will now introduce a few passages where the term *koinonia* (fellowship) occurs, to show that it is used in reference to the contribution. "But now I go unto Jerusalem to minister unto the saints. For it hath pleased them of Macedonia and Achaia to make a certain contribution (*koinonia*) for the poor saints which are at Jerusalem." Rom. 15: 26. "Moreover, brethren, we do you to wit of the grace of God bestowed on the churches of Macedonia; how that in a great trial of affection, the abundance of their joy, and their deep poverty abounded unto the riches of their liberality. For to their power, I bear record, yea, and beyond *their* power, *they were* willing of themselves; praying us with much entreaty, that we would receive the gift, and *take upon us* the fellowship (*koinonia*) of ministering to the saints." 2 Cor. 8: 1—4. Again, 9th chap., 12th and 13th verses. "For the administration of this service not only supplieth the wants of the saints, but is abundant also by many thanksgivings unto God, while by the experiment of this ministration they glorify God for your professed subjection unto the Gospel of Christ, and for *your* liberal distribution (*koinonia*) unto them, and unto all men. Again, Phil. 1: 3—5. "I thank my God upon every remembrance of you, always in every prayer of mine for you all making request with joy, for your fellowship (*koinonia*) in the Gospel from the first day until now." I might introduce other passages for the purpose of showing how the fellowship was attended to in primitive times, but as I suppose that matter is generally understood, I will defer it for the present. With all the premises before us, we are prepared to say that attention to "the fellowship" is an essential part of Christian character. We shall, probably, have something more to say on "the fellowship," when we come to speak of the duty of Christians to send the Gospel to the destitute. We will now proceed to speak of prayer.

"Prayer is the Christian's vital breath, The Christian's native air."

Prayer is indispensable to the life of the Christian. In fact, a prayerless Christian, to my mind, is an anomaly in the Universe of God. It is like attempting to identify the ideas of opaque and transparent qualities in a simple substance, or to conceive of two substances occupying the same space at the same time. Paul makes use of four words to represent what we generally express by the term prayer. "I exhort therefore, that first of all, supplications, prayers, intercessions, and giving of thanks be made for all men, for kings and *for* all that are in authority, that we may lead a quiet and a peaceable life in all godliness and honesty." 1 Tim, 2; 1, 2. At the 8th verse the Apostle says: "1 will therefore that men pray every where, lifting up holy hands, without wrath and doubting." To the Thessalonians the Apostle says. "Rejoice evermore, pray without ceasing. In every thing give thanks; for this is the will of God in Christ Jesus concerning you." 1 Thess. 5:16—18. These passages teach us plainly the duty of all Christians to pray, and that continually, or "without ceasing." Not that we should always be engaged in vocal prayer, for that could not be; but we should always possess a praying spirit, and consequently make a continual practice of praying. The individual who does not so do, does not possess the spirit of Christ, for he often prayed to his heavenly Father; and Paul says, "He that hath not the spirit of Christ is none of his." I leave the reader to make his own deduction from these premises. It is not my purpose to speak of the philosophy of prayer; but of its necessity and the blessings connected with it. It may be contended, by some, that if we possess the spirit of prayer, that will suffice without formal or vocal prayer. This argument might be brought with equal force against every commandment in the Gospel. Some people bring the same argument against obeying the first principles of the Gospel. "Oh!" say they, "God looks not at forms and outward ceremonies, but at the heart." "He abhors the sacrifice where the heart is not found." Thus, people argue, and hence conclude to omit "the sacrifice" altogether, or offer it on an altar that God has not erected, and thus the virtue of the sacrifice is lost, for "it is the altar that sanctifies the gift." I could not make use of such an argument against an institution of heaven, except it were as an opiate to a guilty conscience, which was too weak to bear the wholesome, and strengthening doctrine of Jesus Christ and his Apostles. We will continue the subject of prayer in our next.

T. J. EDMONDSON.

VALLONIA, Jackson County, Ind., April, 1844.

Dear Brother Mathes: In reading the 9th No. of the Christian Record, I find the subject of feet washing proposed for discussion, by brother Abrams, and your answer to the same. Now I agree with you both, in thinking that the truth on this subject ought to be known, for as he observes, there is a difference of opinion among us, and consequently a difference in action, *and no action at all.*

You say it is evident (clear of course) from all the evidence in the case, that Jesus washed his disciples' feet, and commanded them to do so, at least two days and nights before the Passover. This, if I understand you, you think is clearly proven from the following testimony. John 13 you say, in the connection *we* will learn, that the Devil put it into the heart of Judas to betray his Lord while they were at supper, from which (supper) Jesus arose when he poured water into a basin, and began to wash his disciples' feet. This conclusion you think is fairly supported, by Mark 14: 1; after two days was the feast of the passover and of unleavened bread, and the chief priests and scribes sought how they might take him, by craft and put him to death; (2) but not on the feast day, lest there be an uproar among the people; (3) And being in Bethany, in the house of Simon the leper, as he sat at meat, there came a woman having an alabaster box of ointment of spikenard, very precious; and she brake the box and poured it on his head. (10) And Judas Iscariot one of the twelve went unto the chief priests to betray him unto them. You seem to think that John 13: 30, fully confirms the matter. Judas having received the sop went immediately out and it was night, the same night he washed their feet. And if I understand you, you bring up Mark again to prove that this (night) was two days and nights before the passover, hence it stands clearly proven, that Jesus washed his disciples' feet at the Bethany supper. I am aware that this is the commonly received opinion. But permit me to say (with all deference to my superiors) that I have never been able to come to that conclusion? consequently, while it appears clear to your mind, that Jesus washed his disciples' feet two days and nights before the passover; it appears clear to my mind, that he washed them the same night he ate the passover with his disciples. And in order to be corrected in this matter, (if wrong,) I will briefly state my understanding of the agreement of the Evangelists on all those points that have any bearing on the time. And first, I understand Matt. 26: 1—13; Mark 14:1—9; and John 12: 1—8; refer to the same time and circumstances. And first John says, Then Jesus six days before the passover, came to Bethany, (2) *there* they made him a supper: but he does not say in whose house, or at what time the supper was made. Matthew says *when he was in Bethany*. Mark says *being in Bethany*. Neither Matthew nor Mark says anything about the time he came to Bethany, but they both tell whose house it was in, and that it was two days before the passover. Then in this we see no disagreement. Again, in reference to the ointment *they all speak,* Matthew describes the box that contained the ointment; speaks of its precious quality, and says she poured it on his head. Mark says she poured it on his head; says it was spikenard, very precious, and describes the box. John says nothing about the box; tells the woman's name, says she had a pound of ointment of spikenard, and she anointed his feet, wiping them with her hair. Now some might conclude there was a disagreement between the witnesses on this point. But I can see no particular disagreement on this point; because John says she anointed his feet, saying nothing about the head; and Matthew and Mark say she poured it on his head, saying nothing about the feet. Now if we must have a disagreement between these witnesses, we would make Matthew disagree with Jesus, according to his own testimony, for he testifies that she poured it on his head. And in verse 10, he says that Jesus in explaining the matter, says she poured it on his body.— But they all agree that it was preparatory to his burial, and they all agree that there was a murmuring arose about the waste of ointment. Therefore, we conclude they all have reference to the same time and circumstance. Again Matt. 26: 14; Mark 14: 10; Luke 22: 3; John 12: 4; all point Judas out as the one that should betray his Lord. It is true, Matthew and Mark speak more fully on this subject than John, for they tell of his covenant with the chief priests, and that from that time he sought opportunity to betray him unto them. Luke says in the absence of the multitude. Again, Matt. 26: 4; Mark 14: 1; Luke 22: 2; and John 12: 10; all speak of the consultation to put Jesus to death— although John does not name Jesus, but he says they consulted that they might put Lazarus *also* to death. This form of expression shows that some other person was the object of their consultation, who evidently was Jesus. Again, we learn (John 12: 12) that Jesus went to Jerusalem the next day after the Bethany supper. And now coming to the 13th ch. of John we learn that Jesus knew (or perceived) before the passover, that his hour was come, to depart out of this world unto the Father, and having loved his own which were in the world, he loved them unto the end, (or last.) And supper being ended (or while they were at supper) the Devil having now put (or already put) it into the heart of Judas to betray his Lord. This sentence is enclosed in parenthesis, and of course does not belong to the thread of the narrative. We conclude therefore that it was given as an explanation, and explains a matter, the action of which was complete in itself, previous to its introduction into the narrative. We think it points back to the previous design of Judas to betray his Lord, who was only waiting for a secret opportunity. John 13: 17, after Jesus had washed his disciples' feet, and explained the matter to them, he said if ye know *these* things happy are ye if ye do them. (I wonder what things.) Again, at 21st v. Jesus was troubled in spirit, and said one of you shall betray me. Then the inquiry arose, who it was should do this thing. And Jesus says it is he to whom I shall give a sop after I have dipped it; and when he had dipped it he gave it to Judas, and after the sop Satan entered into him; he then having received the sop went immediately out and it was night. Therefore, when he was gone out, Jesus began to speak to his disciples of his glorification, and told them he was going to leave them. Peter seemed to think he could go with him, for he was ready to lay down his life for his Lord's sake, upon which Jesus told him the cock should not crow till he had denied him thrice. Now it seems to me, that if this night was two days and nights before the passover, *this was a long suspension* of the crowing operation; for all the Evangelists inform us when Peter denied his Lord and the cock crowing connected therewith. But this difficulty disappears when we remember that John 13: 21 says that one of you shall betray me, and that Matthew, Mark and Luke all agree in testifying that this declaration, with the connexion following, took its rise at or after the eating of the passover. Again, John says it was after Judas had gone out that Jesus told Peter the cock should not crow till he had denied him. Matthew, Mark and Luke all agree in testifying that Jesus told Peter after the passover, and after the institution of his own supper, that he should deny him before the cock crowing. One thing more: John 13: 21; then said Jesus unto him, that thou doest do quickly, (28) Now no man at the table knew for what intent he said this unto him; (29) Some thought because Judas had the bag, that Jesus had told him to buy those things we have need of against the feast. Now this is taken by some as positive proof that Jesus washed his disciples' feet in Bethany. But I think this is fully answered in the following passages: and first, John 18: 28; here we learn that immediately after Peter's last denial the cock crew. Then they led Jesus unto the judgment hall; but they themselves went not *in*, lest they should be defiled, but that they might eat the passover. This shows plainly that these Jews had not yet eaten the passover. Again, John 19: 13, we learn that Pilate brought Jesus unto the judgment seat: (14) and it was the preparation of the passover, and of course the proper day for buying provisions and other necessaries. Again, 19: 31, we learn that Jesus was put to death on the preparation day.

From all of which we come to the following conclusion: That Jesus came to Bethany six days before the passover of the Jews—two days before the passover of the Jews they made Jesus a supper in Bethany—on the next day he went to Jerusalem, and that night ate the passover with his disciples—instituted his own supper—washed his disciples' feet—was betrayed—brought to judgment, and on the next day was put to death, being the preparation day among the Jews.— Now brother Mathes, if these four sacred historians can be made to harmonize better under any other view of the subject, we hope you will make it known to us, not in figures, but plainly.

Your brother in the hope of a glorious immortality,   JACOB WRIGHT.

COMMUNICATION.

Brother Mathes: Will you be so good as to permit us to speak through the Christian Record to all your readers.

Dear Brethren: It is with pleasure we inform you that we have been abundantly comforted and also edified through the Christian Record; through that medium, we have had several subjects of great importance discussed, and we think to great advantage in the good cause. The news from the churches has been interesting; many of our worthy brethren have been intensely engaged in fighting the good fight of faith. Hold on brethren, and move forward; we are much pleased to see our beloved brethren bearing the fruit of the spirit; speaking evil of no man; but as we have opportunity let us do good unto all men, especially unto the household of faith. After seeing the movement of the churches every where, through the past Nos., are we willing to see the Christian Record expire for the want of patronage! No! never, never! For encouragement to the Elders of the Church of God, and all our dear brethren every where, with the agents of the Christian Record, I inform you that for the first vol., I procured upwards of 20 subscribers, and sent them on by the travelling agent, bro. Smith. I also assisted at the annual meeting in procuring a number more. We now feel disposed to make another effort to increase the number of readers of the 2nd vol. of the Christian Record. Brethren, will you do likewise.

The subject introduced by bro. J. Abrams, to be discussed in the Christian Record, (that of washing the saints' feet,) we think to be a subject of importance, and has been much neglected, and in many of the churches has not been attended to, or practiced as yet, either in private or public. Some indeed have made light of the subject; but we hope the remarks which have been made by our beloved brother J. M. Mathes, will cause many to reflect on this subject. We are much pleased with the generous and Christian spirit by which he has written in answer to the query, and he has also invited any of his readers to throw light on the subject if they can: we would assist him if we could. Dear Brethren in the Lord, as Christians together interested in one common cause, let us examine again Matthew 26th chap., Mark 14th chap., Luke 22d chap., and also John from the 13th, including the 19th chap., until he (Christ) was crucified; there we have the testimony with all the circumstances connected. According to the testimony, are we prepared to show any other supper than that of John 13th and 2d Verses. Supper being ended, (4th v.,) he riseth from supper and washed the Disciples' feet. From the 12th v. to the 18th inclusive, we have the example and command of Jesus to the Disciples to wash one another's feet, and if ye know these things happy are ye if ye do them. But some may object and say, the supper that ended was that supper in Simon's house in Bethany. Will the circumstances agree there too? We think not. Did not the Lord replace himself again at the table? From the 18th to the 30th v. inclusive, the whole transaction is rehearsed and brought to view; here we have the table, the supper, Jesus and the cup; and after he had received the sop he went out and it was night. Thus, John's testimony and the other Evangelists agree; but John continues the subject into the 19th chap. and 14th v.; and it was still the preparation of the passover, and about the sixth hour. At the 16th v. they led him away bearing his cross, &c.—No talk of a table or supper, after the 13th chap. Some object to washing feet because it is not taught in the Acts of the Apostles; neither is the cup nor wine.— But all will go to Matthew 18th chap., for a law to deal with trespassers; others object and say it was not taught in the Epistolary addresses: neither was the qualification of Bishops and Deacons taught there, but by Paul to Timothy and Titus. Paul is all the Apostle that ever taught the bread and cup, or wine, connected, Paul also teaches Timothy, a young minister, how to act in the house of God, and that he should not receive into the poor and indigent number as a church charge, except well reported of for good works, and amongst the rest if she have washed the saints' feet. Tim. 5: 10, for we are his workmanship created in Christ Jesus unto good works, which God hath ordained, that we should walk in them. Eph. 2: 10.

Brethren, let us take the New Testament; there we have the will of God—let us believe and obey what he has commanded, and it will be a good work, and also the work of faith. Our blessed Lord taught nothing to be done in secret or private, except the giving of alms; they should not sound a trumpet. The washing of feet certainly was a lesson of humility. Jesus and the Disciples being together, charging them to wash one another's feet, Paul says if any man teach otherwise and consent not to the wholesome words, even the words of our Lord Jesus Christ, and to the doctrine which is necessary to godliness, he is proud knowing nothing, but doting about questions, &c. Tim. 6: 3, 4. We are to let our light shine before men—how will it shine in private? Brethren, where is the example, or command for it to be done in private; but the command is from the Great Head of the church, that it should be done.

In conclusion on this subject, the best we know and understand, is for the brethren to have a meeting appointed for the purpose of washing one another's feet; for where there is no appointment for that purpose it is neglected; and many that would wish to obey the Lord, will live and die without attending to their duty, for want of opportunity.

Dear and beloved brethren, we are requested to walk worthy of our vocation or calling, with all lowliness and meekness, with long suffering, forbearing one another in love, endeavoring to keep the unity of the spirit in the bond of peace. We sincerely wish to obey the truth that it may make us free. Yours in the bond of the Gospel of peace and love,

April 27th, 1844.　　　　　　　　　　　　　　　　　　　JOHN WRIGHT, Sen.

QUERIES ANSWERED.

QUERY 1st.: Please read Heb. 11: 13. ("These all died in faith, not having received the promises, but having seen them afar off, and were persuaded of them, and embraced them, and confessed that they were strangers and pilgrims on the earth.")

Who were those who died in faith, and what promises were those which they had not received?

QUERY 2nd: What promise is that spoken of in the 39th verse, same chap., which the ancient worthies had not received! Will brother Mathes answer the above queries in the Christian Record!

　　　　　　　　　　　　　　　　　　　　　　　　A. J. KANE.

ANSWER.

My dear brother Kane: We will most cheerfully throw what light we can, upon the several subjects about which you enquire.

Your first query must be divided into two. The first part is, "Who were those who died in faith! We answer, Abraham, Sarah, and perhaps Isaac and Jacob were included. We conclude that Noah, Enoch and Abel are not included, as the promises were not made to them; but the promises were made to Abraham: we therefore limit the expression to the Patriarch and Sarah his wife, and their immediate descendants.

The second part of your first query is, "What promises were those which they had not received!"

We suppose the figure of speech called *metonymy* is here used by the apostle, putting the *promises* for the *things promised*. Paul is evidently speaking of the two promises made to Abraham; one concerning the permanent settlement of his posterity in the Land of Canaan, and the other referring to Christ and the blessings of the New and better Covenant. See the context; also Gen. 12th, 17th and 22d chaps.

Well, as these promises were made to Abraham, it could not be said, literally, that "he died, not having *received* the promises;" but as Abraham, Sarah, Isaac and Jacob, to whom these promises were made, died without receiving the things promised, either as it respects the one or the other of these promises, we are compelled to understand *the things promised,* to be signified by *the promises.* We would then translate the sentence thus: "All these died in faith, not having received the things promised." (*Tas epangelias:* by metonymy, *the thing promised.*) The same form of expression occurs, Luke 24: 49, "And behold, I send the *promise* of my Father upon you." Here we have the same word, (*epangelia,*) which signifies a promise; but the Saviour evidently uses it here by metonymy, for the *thing promised. See* also Acts 1: 4. Here the disciples are commanded to "wait for the promise of the Father." Now they already had the *promise*, but they were to wait for *the thing promised.* But we need not multiply examples.

In answer to your second query, we would say, that we understand the same figure of speech to be used in the 39th v., which is used in the 13th; but as it is *promise,* in the singular, and not promises, as in the 13th v., the question may rise, what promise, or which one of the promises is here referred to? From a careful examination of the context, we have come to the conclusion, that the promise made to Abraham, concerning the heavenly country of which Canaan was but a feeble type, is the promise alluded to: and the ancient worthies had not yet received the heavenly inheritance, which was the thing promised.

What we have said on the 1st query will supersede the necessity of further remarks upon this. All of which is humbly submitted by

J. M. M., Ed.

QUESTION BY A BAPTIST FRIEND.

BLOOMINGTON, May 1st, 1844.

Mr. Editor: I see by your prospectus, that one object of your periodical, is to answer such queries, as may be presented for your consideration. Throughout your work you have uniformly inculcated that none but professed believers in Christ, are entitled to baptism, and that that baptism can only be performed by immersion. Permit me to offer for your serious, and candid consideration, the following query: What is the nature and design of the Lord's supper, and who are the persons or characters that should partake of it? Your attention is particularly invited to the latter part of the above query.

ANSWER.

MY Dear Sir: The Lord's Supper has the nature of a positive command, "Do this in remembrance of me," said the Divine Saviour.— Its design is clearly set forth by the Apostle Paul: "As often as you eat this bread, and drink this cup, you do show the Lord's death till he come." 1 Cor. 11: 26. From which it is plain, that Christians in this institution, openly publish to the world their faith in the death and coming of Christ, for it was only to be observed until Jesus should come again.

But you particularly ask, "who are the persons or characters that should partake of it?" To answer this part of your query satisfactorily, it will only be necessary for us to refer back to the time of its institution, and ascertain if we can, for whom it was instituted, and who were commanded to observe it; and who were forbidden to partake of it. "And as they were eating, Jesus took bread, and blessed it, and brake it, and gave it to the disciples, and said, take eat, this is my body." Matt. 26: 26. The other Evangelists all agree with Matthew, and fully sustain the proposition, that Jesus instituted the supper for his disciples *alone,* and they *alone* were commanded to observe it. About this proposition we suppose there can be no dispute. We next inquire, who were forbidden to partake of it? Paul tells us in I Cor. 11: 29: "For he that eateth and drinketh unworthily, eateth and drinketh damnation (condemnation) to himself, not discerning the Lord's body." Paul is evidently here addressing the church at Corinth, some of the members of which, it seems, were unworthy to partake of the supper of the Lord. The unworthy conduct charged upon them in the previous part of this chapter, had disqualified them. Who is to be the judge in such case? "Let a man examine himself and so let him eat." So decided Paul. It is only necessary now for us to determine what constitutes a disciple of Christ, or a member of his body, to know who should partake of the supper.

You say, "throughout your work you have uniformly inculcated, that none but professed believers in Christ are entitled to baptism and that that baptism can only be performed by immersion." Yes sir, you are correct. I have also invariably taught, that none are members of Christ's body, or church on earth, but baptized believers. Infants, and those who like them are incapable of faith and obedience, I have no doubt will be subjects of the future salvation, and of

God's everlasting kingdom, though they cannot be constitutionally members of the church on earth. You will understand me then to say, that the supper was instituted for the disciples of Christ; and that a disciple of Christ, is one who is learning of Christ, believing and obeying him from the heart. If any others have a right to the Lord's Table, I have yet to learn it. But to all Christians I would say with Paul, "Let a man examine himself and so let him eat of that bread and drink of that cup." ED.

AN ACROSTIC
BY ELIJAH GOODWIN.

C-onducted by thy Holy Word,
H-ave I my labors now begun;
R-esolved to publish for abroad,
I-mmortal Lord, what thou hast done,
S-inners from wrath and hell to save,
T-o dwell with thee around thy throne,
I-n heaven, beyond the gloomy grave;
A-ll NAMES and RULES I must discard,
N-ot taught us in God's Holy Word:

R-eligious news I will record,
E-steemed by all who love the Lord;
C-ontend with meekness for the truth,
O-n which the Church of God is built.
R-edeemer, now thy power impart;
D-irect my MIND, my PEN, my HEART.

RELIGIOUS NOTICE.

THE Churches of Christ of Monroe, Owen, and Green counties, are hereby notified that there will be a meeting held at Brother Nesbit's meeting house, on Richland creek, in Monroe county, on the 3rd Lord's day of June next, commencing Friday before at 3 o'clock, P. M.— All the churches in said counties that wish to co-operate in calling out and sustaining an Evangelist the coming year, will consult together and say what they will do, (and be sure and do what you say,) and go to said meeting prepared to act with charity and zeal in the cause.

MAY 6, 1844.   T. C. JOHNSON.

ELD. JOSEPH FASSETT'S COMMUNICATION.

OUR answer to this article was prepared, but is left out of this number in order to make room for those articles on "Feet Washing." It shall however, appear in our next.

When we answered brother Abrams' question in the 9th No. of our paper, we did not anticipate what seems to be the result among the brethren. We gave our own views of this matter; we could not consistently have done less; but it was not our intention to dogmatically propound those views, as a rule of action for our brethren. We then said, that "if any of our brethren could throw more light upon the subject, we should be glad to see it." Accordingly, several of our beloved brethren have spoken: and we do most devoutly hope, that our brethren every where, will examine this matter, calmly, and prayerfully; and when they speak or write, be sure that they have the Spirit of Christ. We rejoice to say, that the brethren who have written upon this subject, and whose essays appear in the present No. have manifested the Spirit of Christianity. But how could "Uncle John Wright," and brother Jacob Wright, do otherwise? To do otherwise, they must cease to be what they are, and what the brethren everywhere acknowledge them to be, humble disciples of Christ, who love the law of the Lord, and who wish to obey all his divine precepts.

We may perhaps, at some future time, review the testimony from which these beloved brethren have drawn their conclusions. But we would most distinctly say, that we do not expect to have any controversy upon this subject. Indeed, we think there is no room for controversy. The matter in dispute is not whether the "Washing of the Saints' feet" should be observed; this we have admitted and sustained; neither is it, whether the work should be done publicly, or privately; for we have said that it may be done, we think to divine acceptance, either publicly, or privately; but we have said, that as it is not a commemorative institution, therefore it is not necessarily a public ceremony.

The principal issue that the brethren have made with us, is *the time* of its institution. We have said, that in our humble opinion, from all the testimony in the case, Jesus washed his disciples' feet "two days before he instituted his own supper," and that the ceremony was performed in Bethany, in the house of Simon. The brethren from the same evidence it would seem, have come to the conclusion, that Jesus washed his disciples' feet the same night in which he was betrayed, and immediately after he had instituted his own supper.

That we may all come to a proper understanding of our Master's will, in all things, is our humble prayer. Amen. EDITOR.

ORANGE COUNTY, Indiana, April 27th, A. D. 1844,

Brother Mathes: According to your request I herein give you the statistics of the Churches of Orange County, Ind., that are founded upon the Bible alone as a rule of faith and practice.

1. Liberty, Elds. J, Hostetler, C. Hostetler, D. Lewis & W. Hardman, No.	119
2. Bluffspring, Elds. J. Hollowell, and H, Moon,	115
3. Caterscreek, Elds. Arch. Alien, and Simeon Porter,	78
4. Caincreek, Deacons T. Cox, J. Hubbs, and J. Williams,	60
5. Union, on Stampers creek, Eld. J. Mavity; Dea. M. Mavity, & J. Snider,	35
6. Log Creek, Eld. P. Shively; Dea. A Campbell, and G. Briner,	27
7. Sain's Creek,	16
Total,	450

living members in Orange County. There are some throughout the county who have been baptized, but not yet attached to any particular church; but it is not known how many.

J. MAVITY, E. C. C.

NEWS FROM THE CHURCHES.

SPRINGFIELD, Ill., April 18, 1844.

Dear Brother Mathes: This will inform you that I am well as common, and in fine spirits, just having returned from a meeting some 10 or 12 miles from the city, where four noble souls confessed the Lord. Be assured, the good cause is on the march in this section of country. Yours in hope of eternal life,

A. J. KANE.

On the 4th Lord's day in last month, (April,) we visited Stanford, in the western part of

Monroe county. Here we co-operated with our much-esteemed brethren Cox and Kern; we delivered two discourses to a very solemn, attentive, and large audience, and the result was some four additions to the church, two of them by confession and Baptism. And the prospect for many more additions, we think is very good in this region. On the first Lord's day and Saturday before, of this instant, we visited the Church of God at Martinsville: brethren Baker and Devoe held a meeting in the immediate vicinity, the appointments accidentally coming together: the result of our joint labors was, some 5 or 6 excellent additions to the congregation.—ED.

FLEMINGS, Shelby County, Ind., April 5th, 1844.

Brother Mathes: It has not been two years since brother New first preached in this neighborhood, at which time there was not more than 4 or 5, who were members of the church of Christ; but we now number more than 50 members. If you can come any time in the course of this spring, to visit us and preach for us, you will please let us know when you can come. Your brother in Christ,

W. H. FLEMING.

(I have in contemplation, a tour through the Eastern part of the State, some time during the season, if the health of my family will permit, at which time I hope to see brother Fleming.—ED.)

THE CHRISTIAN RECORD.

Vol. I.] BLOOMINGTON, IND., JUNE, 1844. [No. XII.

"PRESSLY'S LECTURES" REVIEWED—NO. 8.

Dr. PRESSLY next attempts to produce examples, where the word baptize is used, to convey the idea of *"washing,* without designing particularly the mode in which the cleansing element is applied." He first introduces Luke 11: 38; "But the Pharisee was surprised that he used no washing before dinner." He then adds, "One of the traditions, of the Pharisees required, that after mingling in society, they should wash their hands before they sat down to meat," &c. Now we remark that this example does not sustain the Dr.'s conclusion, since the almost universal manner of washing the hands is by dipping, or baptizing them in water. As another example of the same use of the word, the Dr. quotes, "For the Pharisees and all the Jews, except they wash their hands oft, eat not, holding the tradition of the Elders. And when they come from the market, except they wash, they eat not. And many other things there be, which they have received to hold, as the washing of cups, and pots, and brazen vessels." Mark 7: 3, 4.

Now what is the first idea that strikes our minds, upon hearing of the "washing of cups, pots, and brazen vessels?" Do we think of *sprinkling* or *pouring* a little water upon them? No indeed; we think of no other mode of washing them, but *plunging,* or *dipping* them in water. The example therefore is against the Dr.! Dr. P. next affirms that all the various rites of ceremonial purification, used by the Jews, some of which were performed by *sprinkling* the water of purification upon the person or thing cleansed," are all represented by the term washing or baptism." Now this we positively deny, and call for proof! After speaking of the *sprinkling* ceremonies under the Levitical Priesthood, the Dr. remarks, "And the Apostle referring to the Levitical purifications generally, represents them as divers baptisms." Again, we take the negative, and call for proof! Where does the Apostle so represent them? Will the Dr. inform us? Divers baptisms is only once used by the Apostle, and that is Heb. 9: 10. Now we are willing to leave it to Dr. McNight, a Presbyterian Divine, to say whether this text does not refer to immersions, and not to sprinklings. McNight translates the verse thus; "Only with meats and drinks, and divers (*Baptismois*) *immersions* and ordinances concerning the flesh, imposed until the time of reformation." McNight on the Epistles. We are perfectly satisfied! How do you feel about it brother Pressly?

But the good Dr. P. adds: "We have therefore the authority of the Apostle for saying the person on whom the water of baptism is sprinkled, is baptized in a scriptural manner." And we have the authority of Dr. James McNight, who is one of the tallest sons of Presbyterianism, for saying that Dr. Pressly is altogether mistaken! Paul has no reference to *sprinkling,* but to the many *immersions* used under the Levitical Priesthood!

On 93d p. our friend P. remarks, "And as the face is not only the more prominent part of the body, but that part which we ordinarily wash, it is therefore appropriate that in baptism, which is significant of spiritual washing, water should be applied to the face." Now this is the Dr.'s *opinion:* but we think he will admit, that he has no scriptural authority for it! Well then, what is it worth? Paul says, "Having your hearts (not faces) sprinkled from an evil conscience, and your bodies (not your faces) washed with pure water." Heb. 10:22. Now if we discard the old-fashioned way of having "our *bodies* washed with (literally *in*) pure water," and turn ourselves loose, to choose according to our own fancy, what *part* of the body shall be washed, (sprinkled or poured) how will it be decided who is right! Dr. Pressly thinks because his face is the most prominent part of his body, therefore he will have his *face* baptized! But here is another man equally honest and sincere, who reasons thus: as baptism has reference to purification by the blood of Christ; and as the blood of animals shed under the law, for ceremonial cleansing, had reference to the blood of Christ; and this blood was in certain cases, to be put upon the *tip* of the right ear, the *thumb* of the right hand, and the *great toe* of the right foot, (see Lev. 14 14,) therefore he chooses to have the water of baptism put upon his right ear, the thumb of his right hand, and the *great toe of* his right foot: and it is administered accordingly! Now we ask, is not his baptism just as good as Dr. Pressly's, which was performed upon his *face?* If not, why is it not? Now we feel confident that every argument that Dr. P. can use against the validity of such a baptism, would bear equally against his own! But if we just take Paul's old-fashioned way, and "have our *bodies* washed," then we have none of these difficulties.

The Dr.'s next effort is to direct the attention of his readers to "some examples, in which all the circumstances are unfavorable to the claims of immersion." The first case which he brings forward under this head, (94th p.,) is the baptism of the three thousand, recorded Acts 2d chap.: "Then they that gladly received the word were baptized, and the same day there were added unto them about three thousand." He thinks these could not have been immersed, 1st: Because the multitude had not assembled for that purpose, and of course were not prepared with suitable clothing. 2d: There was not time enough, he thinks, to immerse so many. 3d: The Dr. thinks that a sufficient quantity of water could not have been obtained within the city, for the immersion of so many.

We will now consider the Dr.'s unfavorable circumstances, and see what they amount to. As to the first, we admit that they had not come together for the purpose of being baptized; but this difficulty vanishes when it is remembered, that the whole multitude were "dwellers in Jerusalem" at the time. (See Acts 2: 5.) When immersed therefore they could immediately repair to their own homes without any inconvenience, as it was summer time, and change their clothes. As to the 2d difficulty, we think the Dr. is altogether mistaken. An article recently appeared in the Protestant and Herald, and was copied into the Christian Record, which was written upon this very subject. The writer of this article (a Presbyterian) allowed the disciples 8 hours to baptize about 3,000. This he thought a fair allowance of time, from all the circumstances of the case. Now suppose none were engaged in Baptizing but the twelve Apostles, they would have had nearly two minutes to each candidate! Now every one who has had any experience in immersing, knows very well that this would have been time enough:— but add to this, the fact that it is quite probable, the seventy preachers whom Jesus had some time before his death, sent before him into all parts of Palestine, also assisted in the immersions on this memorable day, and the Dr.'s unfavorable circumstance is converted into one of the most favorable character.

His third difficulty is the scarcity of water. Now this vanishes at once, when we remember that the city abounded with water for public use. There were some pools of living water, and there was also an abundant supply in cisterns, and large open reservoirs, scooped in the solid limestone on which the city was built; (for a description of which see L. H. Jameson's articles in the Christian Record, in which he makes copious extracts from "Prof. Robinson's Biblical Researches.")

But admitting that there was water enough in the city, the Dr. still objects, and says that the inhabitants of Jerusalem would not have suffered the Apostles to pollute their pools, &c., by immersing in them! We answer, those who were immersed on that day were all Jews, dwelling in the city at the time, and of course had a right to use the public watering places, with which the city was well supplied, and none had a right to hinder them. Add to this, the important fact, that the word baptize, (*baptidzo,*) according to all the Lexicographers in the land, primarily signifies *to immerse,* and the Dr. himself, we suppose, will not deny it, and the whole matter is plain, *the three thousand* baptized on the day of Pentecost, *were immersed.*

The next case which the Dr. brings forward, the circumstances of which, he thinks were unfavorable to immersion, is the case of the Philippian jailor and his house. After speaking at some length of all the circumstances of the case, he remarks: "He procured water to wash the bleeding backs of Paul and Silas, who had been unmercifully scourged, before they were committed to prison; and with a portion of this water, it would seem, that he was baptized, he and his straightway." Page 98. But does the scriptures say that the Jailor "took water to Paul and Silas in the prison, and washed their stripes, and with a portion of the same water that he and his were baptized straightway?"— O no! This is Dr. Pressly's opinion! Do the scriptures authorize such a conclusion? We think not. But let us see. Acts 15: 29. "Then he called for a light, and sprang in, and came trembling, and fell down before Paul and Silas; (30) And brought them out, and said, sirs, what must I do to be saved!" *Out of what,* were Paul and Silas brought? A friend of ours answers, *out of the inner prison!* Well, be it so; they were evidently brought out of the place of their confinement. (32) "And they spake unto him the word of the Lord, and to all that were in his house." They were evidently out of the prison now, and in the Jailor's house. (33) "And he *took* th em the same hour of the night, and washed their stripes, and was baptized he and all his, straightway." (34) "And when he had brought them into his house, be set meat before them, and rejoiced, believing in God with all his house."

Now there is not a word here about taking water into the prison to wash their stripes; but in the verses which we have quoted, it is plainly declared, 1: That "he [the Jailor] brought them out." 2: That they (Paul and Silas) "Spake the word of the Lord to him and to all that were in his house:" which proves that they were at that stage of the business, in the Jailor's house. 3: And that the Jailor *took them* (not the water!) the same hour of the night, and washed their stripes and received baptism. 4: And after the ordinance of baptism was attended to, "he *brought* them into his house," &c. He first *brought them out;* he then *took them* (not the *water*) and washed their stripes, and was baptized, and then he brought them into his house. Now the question is, where did he *take* them to, in order to wash their stripes, and to receive baptism? Will any man in his sober senses say, or even imagine, that he *took* them back to prison? The ceremony was not performed in the Jailor's house, for after it was over, "he *brought* them into his house."— Now the words *took* and *brought,* mean something. The original word, translated *brought,* in this passage is *"Anagagon,"* from *"anago,"* and signifies *to lead,* to bring from a lower to a higher place, to lead out, conduct, &c. The original word rendered *took* in this text, is *"Parala-bon,"* from *"paralambano,"* and signifies *to take,* receive to one's self, to take with one, &c., &c. Now it seems to us that the whole matter is plain, the Jailor conducted them out of prison to his own apartment; he then took them, that is, with him, he *assuming* the responsibility. Now we do not care where he took them; it is sufficient for us that he took them and washed their stripes and was baptized, which could only be performed by immersion, according to the primary signification of the word. But on the same page, (98th.) the Dr. says, "Consider the place. It was not by the side of a river, but within the walls of a prison."

Now we pronounce this mere *assertion,* for the sake of the hypothesis! There is no evidence that it was performed "in the walls of a prison;" but as we have seen, abundant evidence that it was not! As to the river, if it was not hard by the prison, it was at least in the immediate neighborhood, for on the Sabbath day previous, Paul and Silas "went out of the city to the river side, and spake to the women that resorted thither, and there, it is evident they immersed Lydia and her household.

The above cases of baptism, are all that the Dr. mentions, the circumstances of which he thinks are unfavorable to immersion. We have examined them carefully, and we think fairly, and we are perfectly willing that the reader shall decide for himself upon this matter, as well as upon every other. "To the law and the testimony, if they speak not according to this it is because there is no light in them."

J. M. M., ED.

☞ Will the Rev. Mr. Hill have the goodness to copy into the Protestant and Herald, bro. Jameson's communications, found, one in the present, and the other in the 9th No. of the Christian Record? Let your readers see both sides brother Hill, and we will do likewise. ED.

◄―――――►

FOR THE CHRISTIAN RECORD.

Brother Mathes: Since writing my last, I have examined with care, Mr. Hill's "Baptism of the three thousand," in connexion with your "remarks;" and I must be allowed to say that the Editor of the Protestant and Herald," does not exhibit a great amount of candor in the reasons he gives against immersion. He refers his readers to "Robinson's Calmet;" (the same Robinson, from whose Researches, I am making extracts;) to the article "GIHON." While he was referring, why did he not refer to the article "Bethesda!" See Calmet pp. 165—7. He would have discovered, that, if there had not been a *running stream* within one thousand leagues of the Holy City, there was altogether enough of water, for the "use of immersion on the day of Pentecost," in *this single pool.* It is said in Calmet to be 120 paces long, 40 broad, and 8 deep. In Robinson's Researches, he says it is 360 feet in length, 130 feet in breadth, and 75 feet in depth. And there is abundant reason for believing that this pool was in good repair and full of water in the time of our Saviour. See John v. 1—4. I will give the passage as paraphrased by Mr. Taylor, and given in Calmet. "*Now there is in Jerusalem over against the sheep (gate) a pool (or place for swimming,) named in Hebrew Bethesda, having five porches, (porticos, or walking places.)— In these lay a multitude of debilitated persons, blind, contracted, wasted, waiting for the moving of the water; for an angel according to the season, descended into the pool and troubled the water.*" Here is a pool for swimming; a public pool; and of immense dimensions, surrounded by a MULTITUDE of sick folks, waiting to dip themselves in its waters. Why call the attention of his reader to the, probably dry valley of the Kidron? Why assure us that immersion in running streams was impossible, when such streams were actually unnecessary. Where we immerse, we seek for pools, such as Bethesda, the pool of Hezekiah and the upper and lower Gihon, and not for little dry weather streams, like the Kidron, if we may believe all Mr. Hill's speculations about the waters of Jerusalem. But I must attend awhile to Mr. Paxton. The reader will please turn and read the last two paragraphs of my last letter, as introductory to what follows.

Mr. P. may say that Prof. Robinson says, that "these wells are either dry, or the water low and bad." I grant it. See p. 482. But why did not Mr. P. relate the facts in the case? I answer, it would not have been nearly so good a reason against "immersion being used on the day of Pentecost," to have told the readers of the Protestant and Herald, that there were three wells, instead of one. Mr. Hill had said that the people were *not immersed* on the day of Pentecost, and Mr. P. had to prove it; *if he could!* And he, no doubt, thought a *little reason* better than none. But let us have the truth, the whole truth, and nothing but the truth, in this matter, and we shall find it not difficult to make up a correct verdict.

Cisterns "exist not unfrequently along the ancient roads, which are now deserted." Thus, on the long-forgotten way from Jericho to Bethel, "Broken Cisterns," of high antiquity are found at regular intervals;

That Jerusalem was thus actually supplied of old with water is apparent also from *numerous remains* of ancient cisterns still existing in the tract North of the city, which was once enclosed within the walls."—See Res. p. 482. The condition of Judea, and Jerusalem in the times of the Saviour and the Apostles, warrants us in the assertion, that all these pools were in good condition—well filled, in those days. From the above statement of Mr. Robinson, we learn what kind of "a water" it was, to which Philip and the Eunuch came, and into which they went *down,* and out of which they came up, on the highway from Jerusalem to Gaza.

"The same causes which led the inhabitants of Judea to excavate cisterns, induced them also to build, IN and AROUND most of their cities, *large, open* reservoirs for more *public use.*" The Jewish notion of cleanliness, forbade the immersion of persons in pools and streams from which at times, water might be taken for drinking or family use, says Mr. P. We grant it, *in part,* and observe that it was their sense of cleanliness, that induced them to build *large open* reservoirs *for public use, for bathing, and swimming,* if you please. "Such tanks are found at Hebron, Bethel, Birch and Gibeon, and various other places; sometimes still in use; as at Hebron, but more commonly in ruins. They are built up mostly of massive stones; and are situated chiefly in valleys where the rains of winter could be easily conducted into them." They are all of high antiquity.

"With such reservoirs Jerusalem was *abundantly supplied,* to say nothing of the immense pools of Solomon," (to which Mr. P. alludes, and which he says are about nine miles from Jerusalem;) "beyond Bethlehem, which no doubt were constructed for the benefit of the Holy City." On the west side of the City, "are two *very large* reservoirs, one some distance below the other." The Prof, supposes these to be the UPPER and LOWER pools of the Old Testament. See Isa. vii. 3; xxii. 9; 2 Kings xviii. 17. Res. p. 483.

"*The Upper Pool.* This is commonly called by the Monks Gihon, and by the natives Birket el-Mamilla. It lies in the basin forming the head of the valley of Hinnom or Gihon, *about* 700 yards W. N. W. from the Yafa (Joppa) gate." Mr. P, speaking of this pool, says it is *about* a "mile from the city." I would hint by the way, that Mr. P. is in this, like he is in some other matters, *about one* thousand yards from the truth. You must remember kind reader, that it was an object, on the part of Mr. P., to get this pool as far as possible from the Holy City. Every yard, added something to the length, if not to the weight of the reason he had to offer against "immersion being used on the day of Pentecost." The Prof. says, "The sides," of this pool, "are built up with *hewn stones* laid in cement, with *steps* at the corners, by which to descend into it;" p. 484. Mr. P. says, "There is a wall made across the *hollow!* forming a pool." The first traveler brings before the mind a well-constructed cistern; its walls built of massive stones, laid in cement, with steps for going *down into it;* the other, (Mr. P.) tries to bring before the mind, a wall, thrown over a gully, making a place, for a pool as a matter of course, something like the watering ponds in Kentucky, with this exception however, that the Kentucky ponds are generally well filled with water, while this is dry. Nor does he say a word about the *steps.* Do you know the reason gentle reader? I can tell you. Mr. P. was trying to find a reason against "immersion being used on the day of Pentecost," for the edification of the Rev. Mr. Hill. And instead of mentioning the steps into it, he was in quest of a reason for keeping OUT of it, and one would judge from the description he gives OF it, that he was not AT it, by at least one thousand yards. The size of this pool, it will be seen, is altogether sufficient for the immersion of the three thousand on the day of Pentecost. And then the steps at the corners, were so convenient *for going down into the water,* to perform the Holy rite. If I might be allowed to indulge for a moment in fancy, I should see multitudes upon multitudes, on the high grounds around the upper pool; on the walls, I see the fishermen of Galilee, and their associates, taking the willing penitents by the hand, and descending into the water, immersing them "into the name of the Father, and of the Son, and of the Holy Spirit." Nothing is heard in that vast assembly, but the voice of the great Apostle, exhorting them to save themselves from that untoward generation." But I am asked, is the pool sufficiently large?— Prof. R. says, "The bottom is level; the length from East to West is 316 feet—breadth at the West end 200 feet—at the East end 218 feet— Depth at each end 18 ft." See p. 284. I answer, it is large enough; and if it were not a fact that there are several equally commodious, I should think my fancy had drawn the true picture. The Prof, says further: "We noticed no water course, or other visible means by which water is *now* brought into the reservoir; *but* it would seem to be filled in the rainy season by the waters which flow from the higher ground round about." He says, "Such is its present state of disrepair, that it probably never becomes full, and the small quantity of water which it retains at first soon runs off, and leaves it dry." See p. iv. He says of the same pool on the 352d p.: "The tank was now dry, but in the rainy season it becomes full, and its waters are then conducted by a small rude aqueduct or channel to the vicinity of the Yafa gate, and so to the pool of Hezekiah within the city."

The dimensions of the *lower pool,* are as follows: It is South West from the city; about 100 feet from South end 275 feet—depth at the North end 35 feet, including 9 feet of rubbish; at the South end 42 feet, including about 3 feet of rubbish." See p. 486. This pool is now in ruins; so is Christianity in Jerusalem. But that does not prove that both were not in good condition on the day of Pentecost. Here is a reservoir, built for public use, large enough to immerse 10,000 in, if so many had required it.

There are three pools within the city, two of which are of *large size.*

No. 1: The pool of Bethsheba. "Monro calls it an oblong pit, 20 feet deep, lined coarsely with small stones." See Note 2, p. 487. No. 2: "The pool of Hezekiah," in the western part of the city. "It's breadth at the North end is 144 ft. Its length on the E. side is 240 ft. "The depth is not great." p. 487, Mr. P. says it is from 15 to 20 feet deep. No. 7: The pool of Bethesda, described in the first part of this letter.

In the light of these facts, what becomes of Mr. P.'s reasons against "immersion being used on the day of Pentecost?" What becomes of Mr. Hill's assertion, that the Pentecostian converts, were baptized, "not by immersion?" It vanishes, like shadows before the sun. Where are the *scripture* facts, alluded to by Mr. P., "which prove that there was but little water formerly about Jerusalem?" He cannot show them. If water was so scarce in the days of Hezekiah, why should the king have put himself to the trouble of "stopping up all the *fountains* without the city, within the reach of the besieging army?"— Why, take counsel with his princes and his mighty men to stop the waters of the fountains which were without the city? Why, gather much people together, who stopped all the fountains, and the brook that *ran (not overflowed)* through the midst of the land, saying, 'why should the Assyrian come and find much water?'" If as Mr. P. tells us, there "was but *little* water formerly about Jerusalem?" I should be inclined to think, that the King put himself to a vast amount of trouble for nothing. The very passage to which Mr. P. refers us, instead of proving that there was "but little water about Jerusalem," PROVES— positively says, that there was *"much." So much,* that it required a vast amount of labor to put it into such condition, that Sennacherib could not get at, for the use of his army.

It must be remembered by the reader, that Jerusalem in the days of the Apostles was in very different condition, from what it is in now. It was then full of people, and the country around it was covered with a heavy population. Every thing was in order; "the cisterns were not in a state of utter dilapidation," as observed by travelers now. Hence, to conclude against immersion, from the present appearances of the Holy City, and its environs, is about as reasonable, as it would be, for some future traveler, while travelling thro' some portions of Ky. observing the ruins of villages, towns and cities, and occasionally, places, where the farmers had watering ponds; and all remote *from running streams,* to conclude that such a people as the Baptists never lived in Kentucky. But why all this effort to prove that there was but little water in Jerusalem? If the valley of Jehoshaphat had been *full* of water, from the summit of Mount Moriah, to the summit of the Mount of Olives; and the valley of Hinnom, from the top of Mount Zion to the summit of the Hill of evil Counsel, it would not prove that the people on the day of Pentecost were immersed, if they were sprinkled; and if there had not been a drop of water nearer than the Jordan, it would not prove that they wore sprinkled, if they were immersed. What strange conclusions men will draw, when a favorite dogma is to be sustained. How carefully they conceal the true issue. And in nothing is such maneuvering more manifest, than in the conduct of those who for *immersion* practice sprinkling. In, means, *with!* Into, means, AT! Out of, means From! Much water, meant MANY WATERS! And when driven from every refuge of falsehood, then Baptism (immersion) means to *sprinkle,* or *pour,* or *purify,* or, —any thing else, rather than what it does mean.

L. H. JAMESON.

STAR IN THE WEST.

☛ We should ere this have acknowledged the receipt of the "Star in the West." Its Editor, Mr. J. A. Gurley, says that he is not afraid of having it "used up:" and he thought we were regularly receiving the "Star," until our notice of its failure appeared in our paper. We inform friend Gurley, that this is entirely satisfactory to us, and we shall endeavor to profit all we can by "starlight." ED.

INDIANAPOLIS, May 15th, 1844.

Brother Mathes: We have had some pleasant meetings in our vicinity lately. I will give you an extract from my report at the meeting, held in this place on the 1st Lord's day in this month.

On the 4th Lord's day in Feb. last, at a meeting at Friendship, one made the good confession. On the 3rd Lord's day in March, at a meeting in the Waterloo neighborhood; two made the good confession. On the 4th Lord's day in March, at New Friendship, three were added—two from the Baptists, and one by immersion. On the 1st Lord's day in April, four made the good confession at Waterloo. On the 3rd Lord's day in April, six made the good confession at Augusta. On the 4th Lord's day, seven made the good confession at Broad Ripple. On the 1st Lord's day in May, three made the good confession in Indianapolis. So ends the 1st quarter.

On last Lord's day four made the good confession at Waterloo—in all 28, within the last quarter.

Brethren Smith, Hollingsworth, Frazier, Taffe, and myself, have been engaged in labouring.
I am as ever yours, L. H. JAMESON.

REMARKS ON BROTHER FASSETT'S LETTER.

MY DEAR BROTHER FASSETT: Your Epistle of the 21st, I have with much pleasure laid before my readers; and I design now to make a few remarks, which should have appeared in our last, but were necessarily crowded out.

You seem much astonished, that I should represent you as expecting the Lord to come in his glory, some time between the date of your first letter, and the last of April! You say, "April!! Bro. Mathes, where have I said the Lord would come in April next! and still several times, you have represented me as saying so. This is not quite right."

Well, bro. Fassett, I do assure you it was not my design to misrepresent you. But I am not alone in this understanding of your letter: every one with whom I have conversed on the subject, and who have read your essay understood you as I did. But did you not give us some ground for this conclusion? let us see. In your former letter, Christian Record, 207th page you say, I regret, that in as much as you wish to correspond with me upon this important subject, that the correspondence did not commence sooner, as I should have had more time than I now have, to lay this matter before your readers. Time will soon tell whether I am right in my calculations; too soon for you and me to write much upon this subject, as I shall neither write nor lecture upon the time, after April next is past and gone, if I should live."

Again, on same page you say, "The time given by Mr. Miller will not expire until the 21st of March, if I understand him. Why he fixed upon that time, I cannot tell, as I cannot see how 1810 full years, from the crucifixion of Christ will expire at that time. From what testimony I have respecting that matter, I think that it would extend some distance into April; but as I said before, so say I now again, I do not think the precise month can be known."

Now brother Fassett, from these, and many similar remarks found in your letter, I came to the conclusion, that you fully expected, that the Lord would come in his glory, before the last of April, which has just past. It is true, you did not think that the precise month could be known; and you would not, like an enthusiast, pledge the truth of the Bible for the correctness of your calculations, but still, from all the testimony in the case, you thought the Lord's coming would not be delayed beyond April."

But if I have erred in this matter, I know you will forgive me, when I tell you that I honestly understood you, as I represented you.

I am disappointed, to some extent, in the turn which this discussion is likely to take. I fully expected you to take the negative of the whole question, relative to the *literal return* of the *literal Jews*. I expected that you would agree with Mr. Miller and all the adventists, in denying a literal return of the Jews at any time, either *before* or *after* the coming of the Lord. But you have displayed some ingenuity in dodging what I conceive to be, the most important part of the question. You now say that the issue between us is simply, "will the Jews *literally* return to their own land, *before* the Lord comes?"

I shall then take it for granted that you admit that the literal Jews will return to their own land some time; and that you simply deny that their restoration will take place *before* the Lord comes. I will now proceed to give you a few of my reasons for believing, that Israel will be restored to their own land *before* the Lord comes.

The first passage to which I shall refer, may be found in the 38th chap, of Ezekiel—Here the Prophet, after declaring that Israel shall return and dwell safely in their own land, says that Gog and Magog, shall assemble all their forces, and come against the land of Israel, and cover the land as a cloud. From the 11th v. we learn that when Israel shall return, they will dwell safely, without walls, bars or gates. Then their enemies are to come upon them thinking to make an easy prey of them, and to lake a spoil, of goods and cattle, silver and gold, which the Jews bring with them from among the Nations where they have been scattered. The Lord then declares his fury against the enemies of his ancient people, and at the 19th v. he says, "For in my Jealousy, and in the fire of my wrath, have I spoken, surely in that day there shall be a great shaking in the land of Israel; (20) So that the fishes of the Sea, and the fowls of heaven, and the beasts of the fields, and creeping things that creep upon the earth, shall shake at my presence; and the Mountains shall be thrown down, and the steep places shall fall, and every wall shall fall to the ground." 22nd v. And I will plead against him with pestilence and with blood; and I will rain upon him, and upon his bands, and upon the many people that are with him, and overflowing rain, and great hail storms, fire and brimstone." Now it is evident that this *shaking* in the land of Israel, will be *after* the restoration of Israel, and at the coming of the Lord.

In the 39th chap, after speaking of the utter destruction of Gog and Magog, who shall come up in the last day against the people of Israel who have been brought back from the sword, from among the nations, the Lord declares, 21st v. "And I will set my glory among the heathens, and the heathen shall see my judgment that I have executed, and my hand that I have laid upon them. (22) So, the house of Israel shall know that I am the Lord their God from that day and forward." Now the order in which this matter is detailed is this: 1—The restoration of Israel from among the nations, with goods, cattle, silver and gold. 2—They shall dwell safely in their own land, which has long been desolate, without walls, bars or gates. 3—Under some distinguished leaders, called Gog, and Magog, an immense army are gathered together, and come against Israel to take a spoil. 4—the Lord appears to fight for his people, with hail, rain, fire and brimstone. 5—A great shaking takes place in the land on account of the *presence* of the Lord, so that all nature, animate and inanimate, feels the shock. 6—The great army of Gog and Magog are overthrown, with great slaughter, and the heathen see God's glory. 7— And the house of Israel, shall know, or acknowledge him to be the Lord, from that day and forward. Now brother Fassett read Matt. 23: 37—39. Here Jesus wept while he looked over the devoted city, and thought of the miseries that were coming upon its inhabitants, and he declares, "Ye shall not see me henceforth, till ye shall say, Blessed is he that cometh in the name of the Lord." They will never be converted by the simple proclamation of the gospel; but the *presence* of the Lord on the trying occasion described by the prophet will have the desired effect, and they shall then say "blessed is he that comes in the name of the Lord," and they shall acknowledge him from that day, and forward. I have much more to say upon this point, but must defer it for another time.

On the falling of the Stars, you are very diffuse. Will you permit Elder Miller to say a word to you about the darkness of the sun, and moon, and the falling of the Stars, and the shaking of the powers of heaven? I quote from memory, as I have not "Miller's Lectures" before me, but I am sure I shall do him no injustice. Elder Miller understands this whole matter to be figurative, and to have received its accomplishment in the French revolution! By the *Sun,* he understands Louis XIV, King of France, and by the *Moon,* he thinks his Queen was intended, and that the "Sun was darkened and the Moon turned to blood, when Louis was beheaded! The powers of heaven, he understands to mean the *political* institutions of France. The *Stars,* he thinks mean, the French Nobility. And the Stars falling from heaven, he understands to have reference to the fall of the French Nobility from their places in the political institutions of that ill-fated country!!! But why speak of Elder Miller, you have not adopted his views *as a whole,* and this is one of the parts which you have rejected.

Now bro. Fassett, I do not pretend to understand all about these matters, and I have weighed your arguments and testimony with candor, for I am deeply interested in knowing the whole truth; but still I am not convinced that you are correct. I understand you to couple Rev. 6:

12, 13, with Matt. 24: 29, as parallel passages. Now in Matt. we are informed that at the time that the Stars of heaven shall fall, the "powers of the heavens shall be shaken." Now from this it is plain that the whole matter was to be preternatural. The Stars, whatever they were, were to fall unto the earth in consequence of the preternatural *shaking* of the powers of the heavens. So, in Rev. 6: 12,13. Under the opening of the sixth seal, there was a great earthquake, and immediately follows the darkness of the Sun and Moon and the falling of the Stars, as a *result,*

Now bro. Fassett, was there any thing preternatural in the splendid shower of meteors, which fell in Nov. 1833? Was it not an *effect,* produced by a natural *cause?* Has not the like often happened? How then can it be considered a *Sign?* But again, was there a "great earthquake" at that time? were the powers of the heavens shaken then? If so, in what did the *shaking* consist? I know bro. Fassett, that you have too much good sense, not to see the difficulties that surround your interpretation of these passages. So, we let the matter pass for the present.

As to what you say about the 70 weeks of Daniel forming a part of the vision of 2300 days, I am only disposed to say at this time, that your argument is quite plausible, and for any thing that I know you are correct in this. Indeed, I am sure there is no negative testimony that will disprove it: and yet I am not fully satisfied that your position on this point is true.

We next notice the "Abomination of desolation spoken of by Daniel the Prophet." Dan. 12: 11. You still persist in maintaining your position, to wit, that "papal power" was that abomination! Now bro. F., I still feel confident that you are mistaken in your interpretation of this text. "And from the time that the daily sacrifice shall be taken away, and the abomination that maketh desolate set up, there shall be a thousand two hundred and ninety days." The question then is, to what *abomination* does the "man clothed in linen" refer? Why he most unequivocally refers back to the 26th v. of the 9th ch. where the overspreading abomination had been described before.— "And after three score and two weeks shall Messiah be cut off, but not for himself: and the people of the prince that shall come shall destroy the city and the sanctuary; and the end thereof shall be with a flood, and unto the end of the war desolations are determined."— See also 27th v.

Now can anything be plainer, than that the abomination of desolation was the Roman Army, who laid waste Jerusalem? But I must attend to your difficulties. 1: You ask, "Is there no difference between setting up a power that never before existed, and a power removed from Rome to Jerusalem?" I answer yes, there certainly would be a very marked difference. But what does this prove? The idolatrous Roman Army, though it existed at Rome, yet it had never been set up in Jerusalem, and in the sanctuary before. But where did you learn bro. Fassett, that this power had never before been in existence? Will you tell the readers of the Christian Record?

2: Your second difficulty is, that it deranges all your calculations upon the prophetic periods! You say, "If the Roman army was the abomination spoken of in Daniel 12: 11, then Daniel's resurrection would have taken place about the year A. D. 1405, 439 years ago, if we count a day for a year," &c. Now bro. F. I am willing to admit that as a general rule, a day stands for a year in prophetic time; but you will not say that this is always the case. Daniel was to "stand in his lot, at the end of the days." Now *if* these days meant years, as you think, (and you may be correct,) then Daniel stood in his lot some 439 years ago; that is, if the abomination of desolation referred to the Roman Army! Well suppose we admit it, what then? But if I prove that Jesus understood it to mean the Pagan Roman Army that laid the holy city in ruins, your theory must give way to facts! But your last, and I might add, *least* objection to my interpretation of this text, is this: you say, "Jerusalem was not a holy place at the time of its destruction." Now bro,. F. this turns out to be no objection at all!

It was once a holy place you admit; and you are compelled to admit all that is necessary in this argument; that the Jewish sanctuary is, in the Old Testament, generally called the "Holy Place." It is true, Jesus told the Pharisees that they had made it a den of thieves, and house of merchandize, but still, he claims it as "his Father's house." It was therefore holy, on account of him whose holy name had been recorded there.

I will now prove positively, if I am not greatly mistaken, that Jesus applies the abomination of desolation to the Roman army.— "When ye, therefore, shall see the abomination of desolation spoken of by Daniel the prophet, (whoso readeth, let him understand,) then let them which be in Judea flee into the mountains." Matt. 24: 15, 16. Now bro. Fassett, you must see, that Jesus here is speaking of the destruction of the City and Temple, for he is answering the first question of the disciples, "When shall these things be?" Turn to the parallel passage in Mark 13: 14, and we have the same words; and the abomination spoken of by Daniel is given, and is one of the signs of the speedy downfall of the place. Turn we now to Luke 21: 20, "*And* when ye shall see Jerusalem compassed with armies, then know that the desolation thereof is nigh." 21st v. "Then let them which are in Judea flee to the mountains," &c. Now you must admit, that this is a parallel passage, and if so, it settles the point. Historians inform us that the disciples of Christ who were in Jerusalem during the siege, so understood the matter, and that whenever the Roman Legions surrounded the city they escaped to the mountains for safety, and were preserved.

In conclusion, you represent me as holding the absurd notion, that "Immortal David will reign over Israel after their return, forever, *before* the Lord comes!!" Now my dear bro. where have I said so?

I leave you to reflect, whether this is "quite right."

Hoping that we may all come to know all revealed truth, and have willing hearts to obey it, that we may be prepared to meet the Lord when he shall return to be glorified in his saints, and admired by all who love him, I subscribe myself

Your brother in hope of the first Resurrection,   JAMES M. MATHES.

TO THE READER.

TIME, the material of which life is made, never stands still! Sleepless and untiring, it is continually stealing away our precious moments, and hurrying us to that bourn, from whence no traveler has ever returned! Time has brought us to the close of the first year of our editorial labors, and the first volume of the CHRISTIAN RECORD. We commenced the work under very unfavorable circumstances, but with honesty of purpose. Having at best, but a feeble constitution; and having it almost entirely prostrated, through the incessant toil and labor of eight years' public speaking; and being desirous of promoting the Master's cause in the "Great West," to the utmost of my ability, I commenced the publication of the Christian Record; intending to itinerate, when my health and strength would permit. And through the great mercy of God, I have been enabled to devote a considerable portion of the last year to the public ministry of the Word; and I now find that my general health is much improved.

I am not vain enough to suppose, that I have committed no errors in this work: indeed, I am very sensible of many defects. "To err is human." Most of the articles which have appeared from my own pen in the Christian Record, were written in the dispatch of ordinary letter writing, and therefore there is not that order and arrangement in them that I could wish. I have however, written for a plain, but intelligent and enterprising community, who I supposed would love truth for its own sake, rather than for the dress in which it appeared. It has been my aim to do justice to all, and so far as might be consistent with truth, to give satisfaction to all my readers and correspondents; but how far I have succeeded in this, the reader of course must judge for himself.

Some articles have been received for publication, which I have deferred, on account of their speculative character. The *"Annihilation of the wicked," "Soul sleeping,"* &c., are matters, about which, in my judgment, there ought to be no controversy among those who believe the Bible. Some two or three communications from beloved brethren, have been received, which refer to individual, and church difficulties. These articles, though well written, and of the right sort of spirit, we have not published, as we feared they would give offence, without healing the difficulties.

So far as I know, the Christian Record is at a good understanding with all its co-workers in the good cause. This friendly relation we hope ever to maintain, inviolate.

I have had some little controversy, and perhaps some of my readers may have thought that, on some occasions, I was *severe;* but I think all impartial readers will do me the justice to say, that I have always treated my opponents with kindness and respect.

It was our design to have closed our Review of "Pressly's Lectures" in the present No., but I found that I could not do him *justice,* without writing some two or three numbers more on his fourth Lecture; the subject will therefore be continued in the next volume.

To those Editors who have favored us with an exchange, we return our thanks. And to correspondents, we would return our grateful acknowledgements, and hope they will continue to write for the 2nd vol.

We now commend you to God and to the word of his grace!

J. M. MATHIS, Editor.

FOR THE CHRISTIAN RECORD.
Russellville, Ind., April 30th, 1844.

Beloved brother Mathes: I have not written to you a single time since you commenced the publication of the Christian Record. I have been waiting to see what would be the spirit and style of the work; and having examined it carefully thus far, I am well satisfied. The grand object of those who are contending for the "Bible alone," against the vain traditions of men, in my judgment, should be, to enforce practical piety. When this is done, good will be the result. To "contend for the faith once delivered to the Saints," does not consist in theorizing, or teaching first principles *alone;* but the whole Christian Religion, beginning with its *alpha,* and ending with its *omega.* It is true, we may occasionally meet with a vain talker, "whose mouth must be stopped;" but the power of the truth is sufficient for that.

I will inform you, that on the 5th day of March last, I commenced a public debate with Mr. B. F. Foster, a Universalist preacher, at Portland Mills, which lasted four days, two days on each proposition. The two following propositions were discussed, viz: '1—Do the Scriptures teach the unconditional holiness and happiness of all men, without punishment after death?' Mr. Foster affirmed, and I denied. '2—Is the second coming of Christ without sin unto salvation, as taught in the New Testament, yet future?' I affirmed, and Mr. F. denied. A large audience were in attendance. The debate throughout, was characterized by the very best of feelings; and I must say, I never witnessed more seriousness and interest in any discussion in my life. The different denominations in the neighborhood attended, and I think were well satisfied with the discussion.

The general expression, so far as I was able to learn, was, that I sustained myself honorably;

and I would say for my friend Mr. Foster, that he is a gentleman, and a man of talents.
Yours in the blessed hope of a glorious immortality,

J. M. HARRIS.

P. S. I expect to send you more subscribers soon. J. M. H.

QUERIES ANSWERED.

Fayetteville, Ind., May, 1844.

BROTHER MATHES: What is the meaning of the expression, "Born of God," 1 John 3: 9? Some understand it to embrace those who make a profession of religion at the present time; while others understand it to have reference to those who embraced Christianity, in the Apostolic age only. Now what is the truth upon this subject? Please answer through the Christian Record, and oblige your brother in the Lord.

OLIVER WISTMAN.

ANSWER.

Brother Wistman: Dr. James McNight translates this verse thus:— "Whosoever hath been begotten of God, doth not work sin; because his seed abideth in him: and he cannot sin, because he hath been begotten of God." The word from which our translators have in this verse given us 'Born,' is 'gegennamenos,' (from 'gennao,') which, when used in reference to the masculine gender, signifies to *beget, generate* in this sense, it is evidently used in this verse, and Dr. McNight has very correctly rendered it '*begotten;*' and with him agrees every critic of eminence. We therefore conclude, that the expression will embrace not only the Apostolic age, but all Christians in every age since. But the question may rise, "How is an individual begotten of God?" John answers this question in the 5th chap, and 1st v., "Whosoever believes that Jesus is the Christ, is begotten of God." From this it is plain, that an individual is begotten of God, through *faith* in Jesus Christ; and Paul declares that "Faith comes by hearing, and hearing by the word of God;" Rom. 10: 17. The word of God is then the living seed, by which God begets us according to his own will, and which, while it remains in us, prevents us from "working sin:" as Paul says to the Corinthians, "By which also ye are saved, if you keep in memory what I preached unto you, unless ye have believed in vain." EDITOR.

GENERAL ASSEMBLY OF THE PRESBYTERIAN CHURCH.

THIS august body is now in session, in the city of Louisville, Ky.— We see by the Protestant and Herald of the 23rd ult., that this body commenced its session on the 16th of May. The opening sermon was preached by Dr. Spring of New York, who was the Moderator of the last General Assembly. At the opening of the session, 77 Ruling Elders and 110 Bishops, 12 of whom are Doctors of Divinity, laid their commissions on the table, as Commissioners to the General Assembly. The election of Moderator resulted in the choice of Dr. JUNKIN, by a majority of 47 over Dr. WILSON. A report on *"church extension,"* which, it seems, was prepared by a committee, in obedience to an order of the last Assembly, was presented, and has produced considerable discussion.

It would seem, that the committee in this, has proposed to raise funds for the building of Presbyterian church houses, all over the Western country, even in places where the Presbyterians have no congregation, as the best means of promoting "church extension." Dr. Spring doubted the propriety of the measure; and if we are not mistaken, most of the

Commissioners from the old States are opposed to it; while Western members seem to regard it as one of the most important matters that will come before the house during the present session. Drs. Spring, Hoge, Rice, Hall, Cuyler, Taylor, Brown, Smith, Young, Remington, Potts and Plummer, and others, took part in the debate. "Dr. Brown followed (Dr. Cuyler) in opposition to the report; and was understood to say, that he could hardly conceive of a congregation demanding a house of worship, that might not be able to construct at least a small house. He concurred in the opinion that the project was too mercantile and secular in its character, wanting in spirituality, and partaking too much of the character of the operations of Rome and Austria."

Dr. Plummer supported the proposition, in a speech of some length; we can only give the closing paragraph of his speech, as a specimen:— "It had been objected," said Mr. P., "that we ought to get the congregations and then they would build the house; but be would assure them that those who put up martin boxes in a town or village, would get the martins. He then proceeded to urge the importance of this subject, and appealed to them to do something efficient in this matter."

Now it is not our purpose to make any comments at present. We design to keep our readers advised of the movements of this highly respectable ecclesiastical body; which we shall be enabled to do, through the kindness of the Protestant and Herald, which is one of our most punctual weekly exchanges. We will only add, that we think the proposition of the Committee to *extend the church,* by building meeting houses, &c., is very well adapted to the object; and we can see no reason why the eastern members should oppose it, unless indeed, they fear that too heavy a draft will be made upon their resources.

EDITOR.

BAPTIST EVANGELIST.

THIS is the name of a periodical published in Huntsville, Alabama, and Edited by brother W. H. Muse, a Regular Baptist Minister. It is a monthly publication; each No. contains 16 large octavo pages, stitched, and put up in printed covers; subscription $1 invariably in advance. This is a very interesting work, and we think, destined to do good in Northern Alabama. As its name imports, it is designed to be the bearer of "glad tidings" to the Baptist denomination; and we should be much pleased, if the "Baptist Evangelist" could obtain a general circulation in the West; not that we are prepared to endorse *every* thing that brother Muse has written; but we love his independence, and liberality, and we must be permitted to say, that with the general tone, and spirit of the work, we are highly pleased, and wish the Editor all success in spreading a knowledge of the truth. Subscriptions for the "Evangelist" received at this office, where the work may be seen.

Some Editor down South, it would seem, has accused brother Muse of being a "Campbellite," or at least *tinctured with Campbellism,* to which he answers in the March No. as follows, to wit: "The reader will be surprised no doubt, at this statement of the Editor, when he is informed that I first connected myself with a Baptist church in Bedford County, Tenn.—afterwards removed to Nashville, where I was a member of a Baptist church for near five years—was ordained to the ministry by a presbytery of the ablest ministers we have in the South West, under the direction of a baptist church in Nashville—am now the Pastor of a baptist church, which is a member of a baptist association." Again: "What must a minister do, in order to be a 'Bible Baptist?' Must he teach every thing that has been taught by baptists? If so, his religious creed would be something like Joseph's coat, 'of many colors;' but nothing like our Saviour's, 'without seam, woven from top throughout.' Or are they baptists who adhere to the 'baptist tenet?' (the Bible alone.) If I had used my paper," continues bro. Muse, "in calumniating that great and good man, Mr. A. Campbell, I have no doubt but that I could have propagated all the sentiments I have, without one word of censure from these Clergymen. I again say, I firmly believe that the arguments that will refute Mr. C. will subvert the whole baptist superstructure."

The following, from bro. Muse's paper, will perhaps be read with interest by our baptist brethren in Indiana: we commend it to their serious and prayerful attention. EDITOR.

From the Baptist Evangelist.

BAPTISM—A CENTURY AGO.

Brother Muse—

The following extracts are from an article, entitled "A Serious Reply to the Rev. John Wesley, by Gilbert Boyce, a Baptist." It was written about one hundred years ago, and shows what the "Baptist tenet" was then on this subject. Should such a piece be written and published now, it would be instantly called "Campbellism," and its author branded with the name "Campbellite," or accused of "sympathizing with Campbellites," &c. Here then is "Campbellism," full fifty years before Alexander Campbell was born! What was it then?

"Baptism is necessary to penitent believers to entitle them to the promise of forgiveness of sins, which is freely given to all such, through the redemption which they have in Christ, through his precious blood, accordingly St. Peter says to his new made converts at Jerusalem, 'Repent and be baptized, every one of you, in the name of Jesus Christ, for the remission of sins,' Acts 2: 38. It ought to be observed that remission of sins is not promised to repentance only, but to repentance and baptism. The Apostle seems to make baptism as necessary as repentance to entitle them to the promise—not to either of them singly and separately, but to both conjointly—There-fore, it appears plain that baptism is to be an inseparable companion with repentance, as faith is to be with them both, in order to receive the promise. If any man will be so venturous as to cast out baptism from the above text, and declare remission of sins to repentance only, I may by the same authority cast out repentance, and declare remission of sins to baptism only. But I will only add the case of Paul, which seems plainly to confirm the necessity of baptism to entitle penitent believers to the promise of forgiveness of sins. Acts 22: 16, Ananias understood the necessity of baptism to answer its designed end, or he would not have expressed himself in such terms. Now suppose the three thousand mentioned in Acts 2: 41, and Paul in the above text, had objected against, and refused to have been baptized, would they, think you, have been received as members of the church of Christ? would the Apostles and the rest of the brethren, the church, have admitted them into fellowship with them? Or would they, without such admission and baptism, have received remission of sins? If not then what I have said of the necessity of baptism under this head, is just and right. Therefore, if it was so in the Apostles' time? it must be the same, the very same, in our time and I appeal to you, sir, and to every serious knowing Christian, for a decision on this point."

"Wherein may we not this day expect to receive remission of sins and every spiritual blessing in the same way, or in using the same means as they were wont to do in the days of the Apostles? Why not? Do you know of any man who lived in the Apostles' days who received remission of sins, &c., before he believed, repented, and was baptized? or can you show me any promise that God has made that it should ever be so in any age of the world? If not, what reason have you to think it is so now?—Have a care that you are not led by an enthusiastic spirit."

The following, from the same "Reply," is equally as true and just;

"Upon the whole, I may safely; and without erring, conclude that, let a man pretend to what he will, 'tis certain he can never be led by the spirit of God who is not led by the word of God: for the word and the spirit are one, and agree in one; they speak the same thing: whosoever, therefore, opposes and contradicts the scriptures, opposes and contradicts the spirit—The spirit doth not say and unsay—hath not said one thing by the Apostles, and another by the Methodists, (Presbyterians, Baptists, or any other sect). No, no; he cannot be guilty of self-contradiction, therefore whoever are led by the scriptures are led by the spirit; for the scriptures are the divine breathings of the spirit of God.—And whatever secret whisperings any one may pretend to have as an over plus, if those whispers contain any thing in them which is contrary to the plain spoken words of the scriptures, they are not the whispers of God's spirit, but of the Devil. Every man therefore ought to be very careful how he entertains a whispering spirit.

PERIODICALS.

The following Periodicals in the United States, are professedly devoted to the interests of primitive Christianity:

MONTHLY.

Millennial Harbinger, Bethany, Va., Edited and Published by Eld. A. Campbell. Terms $2 per vol.

Christian Messenger, Jacksonville, Ill., Edited by Elds. B. W. Stone and D. P. Henderson, terms $1 pr. volume in advance.

Orthodox Preacher, Cincinnati, Ohio, Edited by Eld. A. Crihfield, terms $1 pr. vol. in advance.

Christian Review Nashville, Tenn., Edited by an Association of brethren, among whom are T. Fanning, Dr. J. R. Howard. W. D. Carns, James E. Mathews, and others, terms $1 pr. vol. in advance.

Bible Advocate, Paris, Tenn., Edited by Dr. J. R. Howard, terms per volume in advance.

Christian Teacher, Lexington, Ky., Edited by Eld Aylette Raises, terms 50 cents per volume in advance.

Evangelist, Pittsburgh, Pa., Edited by Eld. Walter Scott, terms $1 per volume in advance.

Reformer, New Paris, Ohio, Edited by Eld. D. Winder, terms 50 cents in advance.

Christian Light, City of New Orleans, Edited by G. W. H. Smith terms $1 per vol.

Christian Loyalist, Whitesville, Miss., Edited by Eld. Wm. Mathews terms $1 in advance.

Christian Record, Bloomington, Ind., Edited by J. M. Mathes, terms $1 per volume in advance.

SEMI-MONTHLY.

Genius of Christianity, Boston, Edited by Eld. A. G. Comings, terms in advance.

Gospel Herald, New Carlisle, Ohio, Edited by Eld. I. N. Walter, terms $1 per volume in advance.

Christian Intelligencer, Charlottesville, Va., Edited by Eld. James W. Goss, terms $2 per volume in advance.

WEEKLY.

Christian Journal, Harrodsburg, Ky., Edited by Eld. R. F. Ferguson, terms $2 per volume in advance.

Gospel Publisher, Harrisburg, Pa., Edited by Eld. George McCartney, terms $2 per volume in advance.

The "London Christian Messenger," is issued monthly, Edited by Eld. James Wallis. This work is got up in good style, an is truly a Messenger of glad tidings. The first and third numbers of the current volume have been received at this office, for which bro. Wallis will please accept our thanks. We should be pleased to receive the Messenger regularly, but the distance is so great, and some uncertainty in the mails, that we fear this is impossible. This work, if well sustained by the brotherhood, is destined to do much good in building up the Redeemer's

Kingdom, in the land of our Fathers; and as such, we bid. bro. Wallis God speed. EDITOR.

SCOTTITES.

The last seceders from the Methodist Episcopal Church, who have recently held at Utica their first general convention, are designated by this appellation in the Christian Advocate and Journal. This same journal states, that in their articles of religion adopted at their convention, "they have left out every thing which explicitly protests against the cardinal errors of the Church of Rome. With a very little modification of the article of justification—and perhaps without any modification of the language, but simply allowing a little explanation of it—a Papist could subscribe their creed, without mental reservation or equivocation. The Scottites, therefore, are not to be included among Protestant denominations.—South. Churchman.

CONGREGATIONAL SINGING.

An American travelling in Germany gives the following description of the manner in which singing is performed in the churches in Germany. It is to be deeply regretted that the little attention paid to music as a science by the majority in our congregations in this country, renders it impossible for such a practice to obtain here.

"As is the custom here and elsewhere in Germany, the hymn is announced by means of a small tablet containing the number of the hymn to be sung, which is so placed that every worshipper upon entering the church door can see it. The large organ sent forth its thrilling tones, and the vast congregation joined a solemn song. To an American there is something peculiar upon hearing such a congregation in this part of divine worship. In the first place, they sing much louder here than we do; and then, *every one sings*. All have their hymn-books.— Half grown boys and girls scarcely think of such a thing as going to church without their hymn-books. How different with us in this respect! The very sight of such a number—such a *large number* in singing the praises of God, of all classes, of every age and sex, called forth feelings which I cannot describe—but it made me earnestly wish also, that in this particular, our American churches might imitate those of Germany." [*Cross & Journal.*]

NEWS FROM THE CHURCHES.

On the 24th ult., in company with our beloved young brother John B. Cobb, we rode to "White River Union," 7 miles West of Bedford, on the evening of which day our protracted meeting commenced at that place. The meeting continued until Monday evening. It was truly a time of refreshing among the brethren and sisters. Many of the dear brethren and sisters from the neighboring congregations were in attendance; it was supposed that more than *three hundred* set down together and partook of the Lord's Supper, on Lord's day evening. The audience throughout was large, solemn and attentive, and I am sure that our labor was not in vain in the Lord! During the meeting some 15 additions were made to the church, 11, I believe, were immersed at the time; one made the good confession, who has yet to be immersed, and some 2 or 3 who had been baptized, and once members of the congregation, were restored. The cause of the Bible alone, has a very firm hold in this part of the State, and the church at this place, which is large, is exerting a good influence upon the whole community. Eld. A. Kern, the Bishop, is a very intelligent and efficient man, and we must be permitted to say for this congregation, that she acted with noble liberality, in sustaining the meeting. A gentleman too, who is a member of the Presbyterian church, heartily co-operated with the brethren, in bearing the expenses of the meeting, and some who are members of no church did the same. We received marks of kindness from the brethren, and from friends of other churches, and of no church, that we expect never to forget. EDITOR.

From the Millennial Harbinger.
Bedford, Ohio, December 20, 1843.

I have just closed my first year's evangelical labors, in which I have devoted my whole time. I have seen added to the saved over seven hundred—six hundred and twenty by baptism—during that time. May the Lord keep them safe to the day of his appearing!

J. P. ROBISON.

CONTENTS OF VOLUME I.

A
Agents for Christian Record, ...102
A word to the brethren, ...103
Answer to J. Abrams' query, ...152
Answer to S. W. Ott's query, ...177
Answer to J. G. Stevenson's query, ...178
Answer to T. C. Johnson's query by
    A. Wylie, D. D. 32
Answer to A. J. Kane's queries, ...199
Answer to a Baptist, ...200
Acrostic by Eld. E. Goodwin, ...201

B
Baptist Evangelist, ...217
Baptism—a century ago, ...218
Baptist Policy in Alabama, ...154
Baptism of the Three Thousand, ...72

C
Christian Union,   No. 1, ...4
    No. 2, ...18
    No. 3, ...34
    No. 4, ...51
    No. 5, ...67
    No. 6, ...87
    No. 7, ...106
Christian Obligations,   No. 1, ...10
    No. 2, ...27
    No. 3, ...59
    No. 4, ...121
    No. 5, ...150
    No. 6, ...173
    No. 7, ...193
Columbus Debate, ...16
Creed, ...21
Christian Teacher, ...31
Christian Messenger, ...58
Communication from W. Terrell, ...77
Christian Record, ...86
Christian (Universalist) Teacher, ...128
Communication from L. H. Jameson, ...169
" 207
Communication from Eld. T. Campbell,
    Order, ...191
Communication from Elder Jacob
    Wright, feet washing, ...195
Communication from John Wright, ...197

D
D. H. Stephens on Baptism, ...24
Disappearing of fixed stars, ...33
Difficulty among the Baptists, ...45
Discourse, by Eld. E. Goodwin, ...83
Debate, ...96
Dreadful calamity, ...144
Discourse, by J. G. Campbell, ...133

E
Expense of christening, ...32
Exposition of John 3: 5, ...38
Extract of a discourse, by A. G.
    Comings, ...134
Eld. W. R. McChesney's reasons for
    leaving the Lutherans, ...170
Eld. J. Fassett's communication, ...201
Extract of L. H. Jameson's Report, ...207

F
Fictitious Names, ...29
Franklin Debate, ...121

G
Greencastle Debate, ...7
Glorious appearing of the Lord, No. 1, ...8
Glorious appearing of the Lord, No. 2, ...42

H
How to make a good Preacher, ...22
Hard pressed, ...141

I J
Illustrative Anecdote, ...32
Inquisition in America, ...101

Indiana University, ...167
Israelite—new arrangement, ...58
James Scott, ...17
J. McCorkle, Second Advent, No. 9, ...11
"   "   No. 10, ...98
J. D. Paxton's Letter, ...134
Jerusalem, by Jacob Wolf, ...143
Justification, No. 1, ...29
"   No. 2, ...62
"   No. 3, ...85, 93
"   No. 4, ...110
"   No· 5, ...114
"   No. 6, ...148

L M

Letter from J. M. Harris, ...215
Lost River Association, ...55
Letter from Eld. E. Goodwin, ...64
Letter from Ed. to Eld. Fassett, ...118
Lexington Debate, ...145
Letter from Eld. J. Fassett to Ed 155
Letter from G. A. Waller and E.
    Davis to Editor, ...227
Letter from Eld. J. P. Marshall, ...191
Minutes of co-operation Meeting, ...64

N

Notes on a tour to Vincennes, ...25
News from the Churches, 17, 49, 66, 104, 124, 145, 163, 202, 220

O

Our Paper, ...8
Opinionism, by A. Raines, ...14
Old Paths, ...44
Orthodox Preacher, ...112
Obituary, ...31, 142, 166

P

Preface, ...3
Prospectus of Ch. Record, ...32
"   "   2nd vol. 50
Pressly's Lectures Reviewed, No. 1, ...75
"   "   "   No. 2, ...96
"   "   "   No. 3, ...116
"   "   "   No. 4, ...136
"   "   "   No. 5, ...146
"   "   "   No. 6, ...165
"   "   "   No. 7, ...184
"   "   "   No. 8, ...204
Prayer, ...47
Puseyism, ...46

Parental fault finding, ...60
Presbyterian Gen. Assembly, ...216
Periodicals, ...219

Q

Question by T. C. Johnson, ...31
Questions by Moses Hall, Jr., ...61
Query by S. W. Ott, ...177
"   J. G. Stevenson, ...178
"   J. Abrams, ...153
Question settled, ...58
Queries, and Reply, ...216
Queries by A. J. Kane: 199
"   a Baptist friend, ...200

R

Report of Annual meeting, ...100
Remarks on Eld, J. Fassett's Letter, ...211
Reply to the Letter from G. A. &
    Waller and E. Davis, ...175
Remarks on Eld. Joseph Fassett's
    2nd Letter, ...211
Religious Notice, ...201

S

Strictures upon W. Terrell's
    communication 79
Scottites, ...220
Singing, Congregational 220
State Annual Meeting 163
Star in the West:...................................123, 210
Statistical Report, (by T. C.
    Johnson, ...131
    do   do   by J, Mavity, ...202

T

To our Patrons, ...30
To Correspondents, ...120
To the Reader, ...214

V W

Universalist Expositor, ...48
Universalism, No. 1, ...6
"   No. 2, ...20
"   No. 3, ...36
"   No. 4, ...53
"   No. 5, ...69
"   No. 6, ...90
"   No. 7, ...108
"   No. 8, ...126
Wrath and Bitterness, ...74